Religion, Media and Culture

 KT-569-808

Religion, Media and Culture: A Reader brings together a selection of significant writings to explore the relationship between religion, media and the cultures of everyday life. It provides an overview of the main debates and developments in this growing field, focusing on four major themes:

- religion, spirituality and consumer culture
- media and the transformation of religion
- the sacred senses: visual, material and audio culture
- religion, and the ethics of media and culture.

This collection is an invaluable resource for students, academics and researchers wanting a deeper understanding of religion and contemporary culture.

Gordon Lynch is Michael Ramsey Professor of Modern Theology at the University of Kent, UK. His publications include *Understanding Theology and Popular Culture* (2005) and *Between Sacred and Profane: Researching Religion and Popular Culture* (2007).

Jolyon Mitchell is Professor of Communications, Arts and Religion and Director of the Centre for Theology and Public Issues at the University of Edinburgh, UK. His publications include *Mediating Religion: Conversations in Media, Religion and Culture* (2003), *Media Violence and Christian Ethics* (2007), and *The Religion and Film Reader* (2007).

Anna Strhan is a researcher based in the Department of Religious Studies, University of Kent, UK.

LEEDS TRINITY LIBRARY

301828 0

Religion, Media and Culture
A Reader

Editors: Gordon Lynch and Jolyon Mitchell

Executive Editor: Anna Strhan

Routledge
Taylor & Francis Group

LONDON AND NEW YORK

201.7 LYN

3018280

LIBRARY STOCK
LEEDS TRINITY
WITHDRAWN

First published in 2012
by Routledge
2 Park Square, Milton Park, Abingdon, Oxon OX14 4RN

Simultaneously published in the USA and Canada
by Routledge
711 Third Avenue, New York, NY 10017

Routledge is an imprint of the Taylor & Francis Group, an informa business

© 2012 Gordon Lynch and Jolyon Mitchell for selection and editorial matter;
individual contributors, their contributions

The right of the editors to be identified as the authors of the editorial
material, and of the authors for their individual chapters, has been asserted in
accordance with sections 77 and 78 of the Copyright, Designs and Patents Act
1988.

All rights reserved. No part of this book may be reprinted or reproduced or
utilised in any form or by any electronic, mechanical, or other means, now
known or hereafter invented, including photocopying and recording, or in any
information storage or retrieval system, without permission in writing from
the publishers.

Trademark notice: Product or corporate names may be trademarks or
registered trademarks, and are used only for identification and explanation
without intent to infringe.

British Library Cataloguing in Publication Data
A catalogue record for this book is available from the British Library

Library of Congress Cataloging in Publication Data
Religion, media, and culture : a reader / editors, Gordon Lynch and Jolyon
Mitchell.
    p. cm.
  Includes bibliographical references (p.) and index.
  1. Religion and culture. 2. Mass media–Religious aspects. I. Lynch,
Gordon, 1968- II. Mitchell, Jolyon P.
  BL65.C8R4535 2011
  201'.7–dc22
                2011006876

ISBN: 978-0-415-54954-7 (hbk)
ISBN: 978-0-415-54955-4 (pbk)
ISBN: 978-0-203-80565-7 (ebk)

Typeset in Sabon
by Taylor & Francis Books

LEEDS TRINITY UNIVERSITY

MIX
Paper from
responsible sources
FSC
www.fsc.org   FSC® C004839

Printed and bound in Great Britain by
CPI Antony Rowe, Chippenham, Wiltshire

Contents

List of contributors

Tom Beaudoin is Associate Professor of Theology in the Graduate School of Religion at Fordham University.

Marion Bowman is Head of the Department of Religious Studies at the Open University.

Jeremy Carrette is Professor of Religion and Culture in the Department of Religious Studies, University of Kent.

Nick Couldry is Professor of Media and Communications in the Department of Media and Communications, Goldsmiths College, London.

Nabil Echchaibi is Assistant Professor in the School of Journalism and Mass Communication at the University of Colorado, Boulder.

Monica M. Emerich is a Post-Doctoral Fellow at the Center for Media, Religion and Culture within the School of Journalism and Mass Communication at the University of Colorado, Boulder.

Marie Gillespie is Professor of Sociology in the Department of Sociology at the Open University.

Lee Gilmore is Lecturer in Religious Studies in the Department of Religious Studies, California State University, Northridge.

Elaine Graham is the Grosvenor Research Professor of Practical Theology in the Department of Theology and Religious Studies at the University of Chester.

David Herbert is Professor of Religious Studies in the Institute for Religion, Philosophy and History at the University of Agder.

Stewart Hoover is Professor of Media Studies and Director of the Center for Media, Religion and Culture in the School of Journalism and Mass Communication at the University of Colorado, Boulder.

Richard King is Professor of Religious Studies in the Department of Theology and Religious Studies, University of Glasgow.

Gordon Lynch is Michael Ramsey Professor of Modern Theology at the University of Kent.

Colleen McDannell is Professor of History in the Department of History at the University of Utah.

Birgit Meyer is Professor of Anthropology in the Department of Social and Cultural Anthropology at the Free University, Amsterdam.

Jolyon Mitchell is Professor of Communications, Arts and Religion and Director of the Centre for Theology and Public Issues at the University of Edinburgh.

David Morgan is Professor of Religion in the Department of Religion at Duke University.

Robert Orsi holds the Grace Craddock Nagle Chair in Catholic Studies in the Department of Religious Studies, Northwestern University.

Christopher Partridge is Professor in Religious Studies in the Department of Politics, Philosophy and Religion at the University of Lancaster.

Stephen Pattison is Professor of Religion, Ethics and Practice in the Department of Theology and Religion at the University of Birmingham.

Lynn Schofield Clark is Associate Professor and Director of the Estlow International Center for Journalism and New Media in the School of Mass Communication, University of Denver.

Anna Strhan is a researcher based in the Department of Religious Studies, University of Kent.

Pete Ward is Senior Lecturer in Youth Ministry and Theological Education in the Department of Education and Professional Studies, King's College, London

Diane Winston holds the Knight Chair in Media and Religion in the Annenberg School of Communication, University of Southern California.

Acknowledgements

The catalyst for this Reader on *Religion, Media and Culture* was a series of seminars on "Religion, the sacred and changing cultures of everyday life." These were held in different locations around the UK, including Oxford, Manchester and Windsor. Contributors to this Reader participated in at least one of these international seminars, which were largely chaired by Gordon Lynch. They were funded by the UK Arts and Humanities Research Council (AHRC). We are very grateful to the AHRC for their support of this research network, which helped to clarify many of the central issues explored in this volume.

We are grateful to the Centre for Religion and Society at Birkbeck, University of London, and the Centre for Theology and Public Issues at New College, the University of Edinburgh, for their support with this publication. As editors we are also extremely grateful to all the participants at these seminars for their insightful comments and lively presentations, which have contributed to the formation of this reader. Alongside the authors, we would also like to thank the following for their permission to include pre-published material in this book:

Routledge publishers for permission to include extracts from Jeremy Carrette and Richard King, *Selling Spirituality*; Stewart Hoover, *Religion in the Media Age*; Marie Gillespie, *Television, Ethnicity and Cultural Change*; and Nick Couldry, *Media Rituals*.

Cambridge University Press for permission to include extracts from Jolyon Mitchell, *Media Violence and Christian Ethics*, "reprinted with permission."

Fordham University Press for permission to include an extract from Birgit Meyer, "Religious sensations: why media, aesthetics and power matter in the study of contemporary religion," in Hent de Vries (ed.), *Religion: Beyond a Concept*.

Karen Kelly, on behalf of the Dia Art Foundation, for permission to include David Morgan's essay "Finding Fabiola."

Paternoster Press for permission to include an extract from Pete Ward, *Selling Worship*.

Princeton University Press for permission to include an extract from Robert Orsi, *Between Heaven and Earth*.

Yale University Press for permission to include an extract from Colleen McDannell, *Material Christianity*.

On a professional note we are grateful to Lesley Riddle, Amy Grant and Katherine Ong at Routledge for all their help and encouragement with producing this volume. Likewise, we very much appreciate the assistance provided by Cathy Hurren, Clare Mitchell, Ruth Jeavons, and copy-editor Lisa Williams.

On a personal note we are thankful to our forbearing families for providing the space for working on this collection, so a particular thank you to: Duna and Hani, Clare, Sebastian, Jasmine and Xanthe, and Martin.

Introduction

Gordon Lynch, Jolyon Mitchell and Anna Strhan

Over the past twenty years there has been an exponential growth in the academic literature on religion, media and culture (see Hoover 2006; Clark 2007a;
Morgan 2008a; Lynch 2010; Meyer *et al.* 2010 for summaries of this). In part,
this is a more recent expression of the trend which began in the 1950s and 1960s
for scholars to take the media and cultures of everyday life more seriously as a
focus of study—a process which spawned the new academic subject area of
cultural studies. But, in part, it also reflects a growing awareness within the
study of religion that it is increasingly difficult to think about religious phenomena in contemporary society without thinking about how these are implicated with various forms of media and cultural practice. Radically new forms
of digital religion—such as virtual sacred sites on Second Life—may still only
touch the lives of a small part of the world's population. But public media now
represent a significant source of public knowledge about religion, and a form of
public space within which religious organizations have to act as their own
advocates or defend themselves from public criticism.

Contemporary media and culture encourage the "deregulation" of religious
ideas and symbols, allowing them to circulate through society in ways that are
increasingly beyond the control of religious institutions. The nature of religious
institutions and networks is increasingly shaped in relation to the possibilities
of new media and new forms of cultural activity, which also allow for new
kinds of trans-national interaction. The persistence of religious sub-cultures in
increasingly secularized societies is made possible through the development of
niche media and cultural products organized around particular religious beliefs
and lifestyles. Indeed, the very practice of everyday religious life is usually
dependent on how this is mediated through different forms of media and cultural product. The study of religion, media and culture is therefore becoming
increasingly central to the study of contemporary religion more generally (see,
e.g., Hoover and Lundby 1997; Hoover and Clark 2002; Mitchell and Marriage
2003; Horsfield *et al.* 2004; Deacy and Arweck 2009).

The literature on religion, media and culture also shares common interests
and concerns with the closely related work that has developed during the same
period on "lived religion" (see, e.g., Orsi 1988; Hall 1997; Ammerman 2007;
McGuire 2008). Both bodies of work are interested in everyday social and

cultural practice, distinguishing themselves from approaches to the study of religion which focus on abstracted textual or doctrinal content, the practices and beliefs of religious elites, or broad macro-level generalizations about religion and society based on quantitative data on religious belief, identification and behavior. By contrast, researchers studying religion, media and culture and lived religion are often engaged in a common task of trying to understand how religious life worlds are lived out in the context of media-saturated, late capitalist societies.

Whilst initially emerging out of different networks of scholars,[1] work on religion, media and culture and lived religion has increasingly focused on the same ground. As work on media and culture has increasingly shifted its focus from textual analysis to the uses of media and culture, so work on lived religion has recognized the importance of media and cultural products in everyday religious life. Usually, though not exclusively, grounded in qualitative and ethnographic approaches, this growing body of research has proven highly valuable for understanding different ways in which media and culture shape the substance of religion in contemporary society, and it is difficult to see how many of the theoretical ideas explored in this book could have been developed without such rich qualitative studies. There is also, however, considerable potential for connecting work in this field with the analysis of quantitative data which might provide more context for, or means of evaluating, some of its claims.

The aim of this Reader is to bring together a selection of texts that provide an overview of some of the main debates and intellectual developments within this field, as well as some of the new areas of discussion that are beginning to open up. To do this, we have chosen some extracts from important work that has been previously published elsewhere as well as commissioning new material to complement this. We do not claim that the Reader exhausts all of the key texts in this field and hope that the references and bibliography will provide a useful resource for reading beyond what we have included here. There were many other texts and voices we would have liked to include, both from our seminars and beyond. Nevertheless, we imagine that this book will provide a useful orientation to this field not only for students coming to it for the first time, but for postgraduate researchers and established scholars who want to explore some of the key ideas within this field.

In choosing the content of this Reader, we have been conscious of the importance of not replicating valuable work that has already been done by other recent publications. There is, for example, an excellent range of resources in religion and film (see, e.g., Mitchell and Plate 2007; Johnston 2007; Lyden 2010), and we have therefore not sought to address that field specifically in this text. The same is becoming increasingly true in relation to religion and the internet (see, e.g., Dawson and Cowan 2004; Campbell 2010). We are also aware of or have drawn upon earlier studies on religion and popular culture (see, e.g., Forbes and Mahan 2000; Stout and Buddenbaum 2001), religion and consumer culture (see, e.g., Clark 2007b; Einstein 2008), and collections of essays on religion and media (see, e.g., De Vries and Weber 2001). We would also refer readers to David Morgan's (2010) valuable edited collection *Key Words in Religion, Media and Culture*, which provides an overview of key concepts in this field, and which can usefully be read as a companion volume to this Reader.

In the first decade of the twenty-first century there were a number of ground-breaking research studies that focused on particular media or on specific historical and geographical settings (e.g. Akhtar 2000; Hangen 2002; Rosenthal 2007; Sinha 2011). While we are aware how such studies shed valuable light on particular moments in time and history, in selecting material for this Reader we have tried to avoid focusing on specific types of media as isolated phenomena (e.g. film, the internet, television, etc.), except in cases where scholarly attention to them has been relatively underdeveloped (see, e.g., Partridge on popular music, Chapter 16). We have taken this approach partly because contemporary society is a poly-media environment, in which the distinctions that scholars sometimes make between different media are not necessarily made by people themselves in their everyday religious practices (e.g. someone listening to religious music on an MP3 player whilst surfing the internet for religious content). More generally, this move reflects our interest in thinking about how the complex array of contemporary media and cultural practices provide the conditions and resources through which people encounter and practice different forms of religious and spiritual life.

The central questions that this Reader seeks to address are therefore:

- In what ways are media and culture implicated in how forms of religion persist and change in modern societies?
- How do media and culture shape the context in which people engage with religion in contemporary society?
- How might we understand the role that media and culture play in the embodied, affective and aesthetic basis of religious and spiritual life?
- How might the study of religion, media and culture challenge assumptions about the nature of "authentic" religion, or the nature of religious life?
- In what ways are religious lives and practices shaped in relation to the limitations and possibilities offered by different kinds of media and cultural product?
- What normative or ethical issues arise in relation to the media and cultural structures that frame contemporary religion and the sacred?

To present some of the answers to these questions emerging from this field, we have structured the parts of the Reader around four central issues. The first is how we might understand, and think critically about, the relationship between religion, spirituality and consumer culture. As the chapters in Part I make clear, the separation between "pure" religion and commerce is a false one. Indeed religious institutions are often dependent on their economic activity, and commercial exchange forms an integral element of some religious practices. A significant question, then, is how different forms of religion and spirituality are performed in relation to the conditions of late capitalist consumer culture. Answering this question involves thinking about the different ways in which the logics and practices of the marketplace are assimilated into various forms of religion and spirituality. It also opens up more fundamental ideological debates as to whether capitalist consumer culture can provide resources for creative acts of identity politics and cultural resistance, or whether it should be regarded with much greater suspicion in terms of its tendency to shape social and cultural life according to its own logics and ends.

In Part II authors examine how the expansion of different forms of media, in terms of both their type and their reach into social life, shapes the conditions through which religion is encountered and performed in the modern world. Since the turn of the twentieth century there has been an unprecedented emergence of "electronic", "new" and "digital" media across the world (including film, radio, television, audio cassettes, super-8, VHS and digital cameras, CDs, the internet, MP3 players, mobile phones, and networked game consoles). With the advent of digital technologies there has also been an increasing inter-meshing of these media. There is an ever-increasing number of media devices with multiple functions, as well as media producers involved in broadcasting and selling their content across a range of different media platforms.

Caution is needed in evaluating the impact of this rapid communicative evolution. It is not too much to claim that some of these developments have had a significant transformative effect on social life. Think, for example, about the effects of now being able to "see" the news live on television or via a news site on the internet. We should also keep in mind, however, that some claims about the transformative effects of media are not entirely novel, with similar claims about the globalizing effects of the internet having been made previously about the invention of the telegraph, for example. In Part II, the authors examine how the complex media environments of modern society shape the ways in which religion is encountered and acted out. A range of related topics are analyzed, including the possibilities that these transformations reverse trends of secularization, re-work the nature of religious authority, create new, hybrid and transnational forms of religion, and shape the grounds on which religious groups are legitimized or not within a public imagination. This work goes beyond being struck by the novelty of mediated expressions of religion, to thinking analytically about how media may be implicated in shaping the form of religion in the contemporary world.

Part III moves on to consider the role of embodiment and the senses in the practice of religious life. One of the main intellectual developments of work within the field of religion, media, and culture has been a shift in focus from the content of abstracted religious texts or objects towards the role of media and objects in lived religious practice. Particularly important in this regard has been the growing literature on material and visual culture in relation to religion, for which the journal *Material Religion* has become an excellent resource (see also Morgan 2009; Meyer 2010). One of the implications of this shift is that much greater attention is now being paid to the emotional aesthetic and embodied significance of the use of media and culture. Rather than thinking of media or cultural products as communicating information at a primarily cognitive level, this work explores how religious media and culture shape experiences of the body. This leads on to consider how interconnected media can become an aesthetic and emotional medium for religious experience. Such work challenges the still common assumption that religion is concerned primarily with cognitive beliefs, or is an interior, sincere spiritual life that is in some sense removed from the habits and practices of the body and the senses (see also Riis and Woodhead 2010). Instead, it examines how religious life is always mediated—that is, how it is always dependent on particular media and culture that make the sacred real in people's embodied experience.

Finally, in Part IV the authors primarily focus on a still relatively underdeveloped area within the literature on religion, media, and culture: the normative critique of cultural products and practices. Both David Morgan and Robert Orsi have previously identified the dangers of normative projects in this field, in which the rush to normative judgment can overwhelm scholars' capacity to observe and analyze carefully the object of their study and even unhelpfully distort what they consider to be appropriate objects of study in the first place. Although the rush to judgment can indeed limit understanding, there are also inevitably normative issues raised by contemporary media and culture. These include their role in sustaining healthy democratic societies, respectful civil societies or the promotion of peace and social justice. The chapters in Part IV (as well as chapters in earlier parts of the Reader, such as those by Carrette and King, Chapter 6, and Pattison, Chapter 17) provide an alternative approach to the formation of quick normative judgments that fail to give a sufficiently nuanced account of the objects of their critique. Instead they encourage a critical reflexivity towards assumptions about media sources, the content of media texts, and particular forms of everyday culture that creates new possibilities for interpreting and acting in the world around us.

In the introductions to each of our four parts we begin with a concrete example, which opens a window onto diverse communicative worlds. These include an eclectic Hindu website (Part I), a radio program about an Islamic ceremonial sword (Part II), a replica of the Lourdes shrine in New York (Part III), and a complex journalistic ethical issue set in the midst of a Balkan war zone (Part IV). Observed together they illustrate how diverse media spaces and materials can become the meeting point for a range of different traditions. Given this complex reality it is not surprising that scholarship in this field is still very much a work in progress. For this and other reasons we expect the positions set out in this book to be developed, refined, and challenged much further in coming years. By drawing this material together, we hope to clarify some central ideas and areas of debate in a way that can encourage precisely this process, as well as drawing new scholars into what is becoming such a rich and important field.

Notes

1 Work on lived religion has been developed particularly by historians of religion influenced by the wider turn to social and cultural history during the latter half of the twentieth century, as well as North American sociologists of religion trying to carve out an alternative project within their discipline compared to large-scale quantitative studies and work influenced by rational-choice theory. The international research network on religion, media, and culture has tended to focus on cross-disciplinary research conferences that have developed since the early 1990s, involving scholars in media and cultural studies, theology and religious studies, sociology and visual/material culture studies.

Part I

Religion, spirituality and consumer culture

Introduction

The Virtual Pooja website is a religious service provider for the digital age. Framed by adverts for horoscopes, on-line dating services, and holidays to South Asia, its web-pages allow consumers from anywhere in the world to order pooja ceremonies that can be performed in Hindu temples across India. Drop-down search menus allow the site's users to search for specific temples according to deity, city, or district, and another section of the site offers a range of pooja that can be performed for specific purposes, including for relief from loans and debts, success in court cases, relief of sins committed in previous lives, or achieving excellence in one's studies. Pooja packages, organized around a particular devotional focus, are also offered, with a pooja package for the five elements (air, earth, fire, sky, water) currently retailing at $35. Payment is made on-line through credit or debit card, and on completion of the payment the service user receives confirmation that the ceremony has been conducted, with the prasadam later being mailed back to them. The Virtual Pooja site exemplifies the potential of the internet to create new kinds of trans-national religious interactions and, more specifically, new kinds of economic interaction between consumers from the global Hindu diaspora, the local temples conducting the pooja, and of course the mediating commercial structure of the website itself (see Helland 2007).

The Virtual Pooja website is one contemporary example of the enduring relationship between religion and practices of economic production and consumption. The idea that religion is (or should be) distinct from the realm of economics is itself a particularly modern notion, reflecting the separation of religion into the private sphere of individual belief and conscience, and economics into the public sphere of political economy (Carrette 2007; Fitzgerald 2007). As the opening chapter in this part by Marion Bowman (Chapter 1) demonstrates, there is a long history of religious acts of economic production and consumption, and religious institutions have often been dependent on their economic activity for their survival. We should therefore not be surprised to find, in the chapters in Part I, that different kinds of economic and cultural consumption play an integral role in the development and persistence of various kinds of religious and spiritual activity in contemporary society.

Whilst there is a long history of the inter-section of religion and economic activity, a number of changes took place during the twentieth century that have arguably created particular conditions within which religious consumer cultures now operate. These include the rapid growth in the proportion of household income spent on non-essential commodities in the post-war period in many developed societies (partly facilitated by the increasing availability of consumer credit), and the shift from Fordist systems of mass-production to new production technologies that allowed smaller product lines to be produced cost-effectively. The rise of new digital technologies (particularly the microchip) also meant that the design of many everyday objects no longer needed to be defined quite so rigidly by the components required to make the object work. Niche product lines and new opportunities for product design also supported the growing importance of the "brand," as a particular image or imagined lifestyle that could be marketed across a range of different product lines. The rise of the inter-net, and other new digital media, also transformed patterns of production and consumption.

Alongside the emergence of major global on-line retailers such as Amazon and iTunes, who re-defined their respective markets, digital products (including music, film, and audio clips) could now be produced far more cheaply and dis-tributed to niche global markets through specialist websites. All this, it should also be remembered, has taken place against the backdrop of a new phase of global capitalism in which capital flows rapidly across national borders, multi-national corporations become as economically powerful as nation-states, and the expansion of neo-liberalism opens up ever more societies (and areas of social life) to market forces. In this new context of economic production and consumption, religious groups now find themselves seeking to articulate their "brand," develop products that reflect their particular identity, ethos and aes-thetics, reap the possibilities of new technologies of production and distribu-tion, and negotiate the challenges of bringing their products into a wider marketplace of goods and services (see, e.g., Clark 2007b; Einstein 2008).

The chapters in Part I attempt to make sense of religious production and consumption in this new context, offering three broadly different perspectives. In the first two chapters, Marion Bowman (Chapter 1) and Pete Ward (Chapter 2) explore how the logics of the marketplace have been assimilated into two very different forms of contemporary religiosity: the alternative spiritual milieu for which Glastonbury has become such an important centre and Charismatic Evangelical worship in Britain. In both of these cases, practices of production and consumption are inseparable from religious and spiritual practice, becom-ing a structure through which acts of healing, meditation, work on the self, and worship are made possible. Both cases demonstrate the economic logics on which these different forms of religion are based. In Glastonbury, the clustering of so many alternative spiritual providers is beneficial by continuing to sustain the Glastonbury "brand," provides an incentive for visitors to make repeat visits to the town, and creates a network of economic relations in which spiri-tual service providers simultaneously act as consumers of each other's products.

In the case of Charismatic worship, the larger audience and greater range of possible revenue streams meant that this kind of worship was able to establish itself far more successfully as a part of the British Evangelical sub-culture than Evangelical popular music was able to.

In the next two chapters, the focus turns to religious and spiritual forms of consumer culture which are being intentionally developed in opposition to different aspects of late modern society. In his chapter on new forms of Islamic production and consumption, Nabil Echchaibi (Chapter 3) traces the rise of a cultural Islamism that seeks to take existing consumer and media products and re-work these in a way that is understood as being more consistent with Islamic commitments. By contrast, Monica Emerich (Chapter 4) provides an introduction to the growing industry of lifestyles of health and sustainability (LOHAS), which embrace various forms of slow living, organic produce, and commitment to principles of personal, social, and environmental sustainability. Whilst very different in the content and meanings of their products, these two different movements can also be seen as reflecting an attempt to construct a form of identity and lifestyle politics that challenges a dominant, mainstream "other." For Echchaibi's Islamic cultural producers and consumers, this "other" is a morally vacuous and spiritually bankrupt Western culture which threatens to over-run Islamic societies in a new era of cultural and economic globalization. For Emerich's participants in LOHAS culture, the "other" is the mainstream consumer culture that alienates people from the stuff of their everyday life and threatens ever-greater environmental destruction. Both movements, however, reflect a belief that economic production and consumption can be used to develop an alternative religious identity politics that resists that which is perceived as threatening in the contemporary world.

Although these earlier chapters often note some of the limitations of such religious and spiritual forms of consumer culture, the final two chapters turn to more explicitly critical approaches to thinking about religion and spirituality in the context of late capitalism. In her chapter on the Reverend Billy and the Burning Man festival, Lee Gilmore (Chapter 5) provides an account of particular kinds of cultural activity which seek to disrupt traditional patterns of consumption and the spread of corporate capitalism, as well as offering alternative models of economic and material consumption. Whilst providing an explicit critique of important elements of late capitalist society, Gilmore's account is also striking for the ways in which the ironic and playful appropriation of religious tradition (arguably itself a sign of late modern consumption; see also Clark, Chapter 10) run through these activities. Yet, even in the ironic re-appropriation of religion in an anti-capitalist spirit, some form of religious ethos appears to persist. In the final chapter, an extract from Jeremy Carrette and Richard King's book *Selling Spirituality* (Chapter 6), it is argued that much of what passes as "spirituality" in contemporary culture is a symptom of the colonization of religion by capitalism. Carrette and King locate this process in a longer cultural history of the privatization, and then commodification, of religion, and provide a typology of different ways in which religion and spirituality intersect with late capitalism, ranging from anti-capitalist critique, attempts to re-work consumer culture in particular ways, religions of prosperity and the use of religion and spirituality to perpetuate capitalist structures and processes. As their argument suggests, the study of contemporary religion needs not only to think about how religion is performed through consumer culture, but, in a more normative vein, to think critically about the implications of this in terms of wider questions of individual flourishing and social well-being.

1 Understanding Glastonbury as a site of consumption

Marion Bowman

Introduction

Commodification is one aspect of contemporary spirituality which frequently attracts critical attention and negative comment. "Spiritually shopping around" and the business of "selling spirituality" are often portrayed popularly as proofs of the essential superficiality, gullibility, and narcissism of the clients and the cynically capitalist, exploitative tendencies of the providers of such goods and services. Academic critiques of such phenomena display a range of attitudes and analyses, from a hermeneutic of suspicion to more sympathetic accounts (e.g. Lau 2000; Ezzy 2001; Possamai 2002, 2003: York 2004; Carrette and King 2005; Redden 2005).

My intention is to ground some aspects of the debate in a specific context which, while not typical, is indicative of broader trends. I aim also to foster further understanding of the role of material culture in the contemporary spiritual milieu, by presenting the ways in which those involved in such transactions perceive and narrate spiritual consumption.

In this chapter, some of the prevailing perceptions of commodification and marketization in the contemporary spiritual milieu, and phenomena related to them, are explored in the context of Glastonbury. Drawing upon both fieldwork data and the results of a small scale pilot survey on Glastonbury's spiritual economy conducted in 2007, Glastonbury is examined as an example of a specialized site of religious and spiritual consumption where (in common with other pilgrimage sites) commercial transactions can have sacralized meanings and value. The significance of this for the construction of religious identities and communities is explored, alongside the issue of whether countercultural spiritual practices have been co-opted by capitalism, or whether, conversely, spiritual entrepreneurs challenge, disrupt, or reappraise existing commercial and organizational practices.

Since the early 1990s I have been conducting research in Glastonbury within the broad framework of vernacular religion, that is, "an interdisciplinary approach to the study of the religious lives of individuals with special attention to the process of religious belief, the verbal, behavioral, and material expressions of religious belief, and the ultimate object of religious belief" (Primiano

1995: 44). In using the term vernacular religion in relation to the sorts of religiosity and ritual, concepts and consumerism to be found in Glastonbury, I am not referring to carefully crafted, internally coherent worldviews but instead to the possibly conflicting mixture of belief and praxis; institutional, cultural, and temporal conditioning; personal experience; interactions with the material and non-material world; and perceptions of efficacy that constitute "religion as it is lived: as humans encounter, understand, interpret and practice it" (ibid.). This vernacular religiosity is observable in traditional as well as newer forms of religious life and, in studying it, instead of "reify[ing] the authenticity of religious institutions as the exemplar of human religiosity" (ibid.: 39), attention is shifted to individual meanings, experiential impact, and expressive forms.

Locating Glastonbury

It is helpful to start by locating Glastonbury, for often when I say I am working on Glastonbury people assume I mean the Glastonbury Festival of Contemporary Performing Arts, which is actually held on Worthy Farm in the nearby village of Pilton. While Glastonbury Festival does cater for consumption of diverse kinds, including religion, in fact I am referring here to the small town of Glastonbury (population c.9000) situated in an area of drained marshland known as the Somerset Levels, in the south west of England. There has been settlement in the area since prehistoric times, and before the marshes were drained Glastonbury was in effect an island, accessible only by boat. The town contains a variety of striking natural features, including the Tor, a curiously contoured hill which can be seen for miles around, the chalybeate spring at Chalice Well, whose water stains red, and a thorn tree that flowers both in spring and in December. Physically at the center of the town are the ruins of Glastonbury Abbey.

Glastonbury's economy was negatively affected during the twentieth century by declining agricultural activity and most significantly by the shrinkage of the area's significant leather related industries from the 1970s, although there is still building and engineering, and light industry, including the manufacture of plastics, wetsuits, and digital model railway control systems, in addition to a weekly street market. The Glastonbury Carnival (part of the network of West Country Carnivals, derived from 5 November celebrations) attracts many visitors, and ventures such as the Frost Fayre in December (with Christmas carols, street stalls, and so on) are designed to boost interest in the town.

However, very obviously in relation to the High Street, and pervading the town, Glastonbury has developed a unique spiritual service industry on account of its distinctive religious and sacred status.

Glastonbury is one of the most popular and multivalent pilgrimage sites in the UK, exerting an attraction for a variety of spiritual seekers (and scholars) on account of the many myths that surround it and the myriad claims made for it (see, for example, Hexham 1983; Bowman 1993, 2005, 2008; Carley 1996; Prince and Riches 2000; Ivakhiv 2001). Some believe that Glastonbury was a

significant prehistoric center of Goddess worship, while others regard it primarily as a Druidic site where, it is claimed, there was a great European center
of learning. For numerous Christians, Glastonbury's status rests on it being the
"cradle of English Christianity," where Christianity took root in England,
allegedly brought there by Joseph of Arimathea. Even more significantly, many
believe that Jesus himself came to Glastonbury, and some are convinced that it
is to Glastonbury that Jesus will return at the time of the second coming (see
Bowman 2003–4). Glastonbury is regarded by some as an exemplary site of
Celtic Christianity, and it has been identified with the Isle of Avalon, the place
where, in Arthurian legend, King Arthur was taken for healing after his last
battle. Now perceived by many as the "heart chakra" of planet earth, Glastonbury is also regarded as a center of earth energies, a node where leylines converge and generate powerful forces for healing and personal transformation.
Many people on varied "spiritual paths" narrate how they feel "drawn" to
Glastonbury (Bowman 1993, 2008).

It is in response to this hugely varied interest in Glastonbury that a unique
spiritual service industry has arisen, which includes the Glastonbury Pilgrim
Reception Centre, "open to all people on all paths;" "alternative" bookshops;
spiritually oriented workshops, conferences, and courses; a huge variety of
healing; "psychic services" such as tarot reading and clairvoyance; bed and
breakfasts offering meditation and assorted therapies; and shops selling goods
intended to enhance and expand people's spiritual lifestyles and practices. All
that in turn generates more visitors, for part of Glastonbury's importance and
value to a variety of people is as a site of spiritual consumption. One important
reason for visiting Glastonbury is that it is, quite literally, a place for spiritually
shopping around.

Material culture, pilgrimage, and Glastonbury

To gain a more nuanced understanding of Glastonbury currently as a specialized site of religious and spiritual consumption, it is helpful to consider briefly
the role of material culture in religion and ways in which commercial transactions
can acquire sacralized meanings, particularly in relation to pilgrimage sites.

David Morgan contends that

> If culture is the full range of thoughts, feelings, objects, words, and practices
> that human beings use to construct and maintain the life-worlds in which
> they exist, material culture is any aspect of that world-making activity that
> happens in material form. That means things, but it also includes the feel-
> ings, values, fears, and obsessions that inform one's understanding and use
> of things.
>
> (Morgan 2008b: 228)

While anthropologists and ethnographers have paid considerable attention to
religious material culture, there has been a tendency to underplay its

importance in some spheres of religious studies. As McDannell comments, "Traditionally, scholars have understood the religious impulse as leading away from the material toward the spiritual" (1991: 371), under the influence of a rather Western, Protestant, intellectual, text-based – and text-biased – approach to the study of religion which tended to be suspicious or dismissive of visual and material expressions of religion.

Pilgrimage centers worldwide traditionally often have been and continue to be places rich in material culture, with distinctive economies developed to serve both residents and visitors. Places perceived as special or sacred are frequently sites of commercialism, with "religious" artifacts such as relics, medals, statues, pictures, offerings, and other aspects of material culture on sale, and where various forms of quasi-financial transactions with the divine might be transacted, such as the donation of money or ex-votos promised or given in thanks for answered prayers and healing.

Coleman and Elsner refer to the souvenirs that pilgrims take home as "containers of the sacred," asserting that

> Pilgrimage is as concerned with taking back some part of the charisma of a holy place as it is about actually going to the place. One of the most characteristic aspects of pilgrimage art in all the world religions is the proliferation of objects made available to pilgrims and brought home by them as reminders and even as tangible channels of connection with the sacred experience. In this way, the influence of the site can be retained in the domestic or mundane context to which a pilgrim has returned.
>
> (Coleman and Elsner 1995: 100)

They point out that the value of objects and gifts purchased at a shrine or religious center is not so much to do with monetary considerations but in their origins at a pilgrimage center. Furthermore, the "memorabilia of pilgrimage" also mark the pilgrim's identity as one who has made the journey. The meanings of and significance invested in such objects and transactions are therefore complex, leading McDannell to caution that "If we immediately assume that whenever money is exchanged religion is debased, then we will miss the subtle ways people create and maintain spiritual ideals through the exchange of goods and the construction of spaces" (1995: 6). Notwithstanding the distinctive conditions of contemporary capitalism, secularity/post-secularity, globalization, new media impact, and so on, some of the behavioral traits and rationales in relation to material culture and economic transactions observable in Glastonbury, though perhaps more varied and "exotic" than in the past, have long histories and numerous analogues within the vernacular traditions of many religions.

The development of Glastonbury's "spiritual economy"

While speculations about Glastonbury's prehistoric spiritual and pilgrimage status are plentiful, in terms of contextualizing the present spiritual service industry, Glastonbury Abbey is the logical place to start. By the Middle Ages, Glastonbury Abbey was a major Marian shrine, with its Lady Chapel allegedly built on the site of the original church, a pilgrimage site rich in relics and associations with numerous saints and royalty, and a center of learning boasting a magnificent library (see Carley 1996). The Abbey molded the physical landscape and by its presence, activities, and significance shaped and influenced the life of the town.

The ground plan of the town exemplifies the extent to which it literally grew up around the Abbey, the symbiotic relationship between business and religion. Arguably the monastery played a major part in developing market capitalism in Glastonbury, with the Abbey as a major land owner, wool trader, and provider of a range of pilgrim attractions to the town, such as relics, a reputedly miraculous image of Our Lady, and the body of King Arthur allegedly discovered by monks in the Abbey grounds in the twelfth century. (It is worth remembering that some of the claims made for and by Glastonbury Abbey, in terms of its antiquity, which relics it possessed, and so on, were contested even in the Middle Ages.) The town in response provided visitor goods and services, in addition to the regular domestic economy. However, the Abbey was brutally suppressed in 1539 at the time of the Reformation, passed into private hands, and fell into ruin. After that, Glastonbury's economy no longer primarily depended on or benefited from religious associations. There was a brief flurry of activity in the eighteenth century when Glastonbury aspired to become a spa town, with curative claims being made for the chalybeate waters of what is now known as Chalice Well at an outlet near the Abbey, but this was short lived. From the 1870s sheepskin processing became increasingly important to Glastonbury's fortunes, an industry that remained significant for a century.

The restoration of public access to the Abbey grounds following their purchase by a Trust in 1908 boosted Christian pilgrimage and tourism to Glastonbury (in relation to which a number of souvenirs were produced, mainly focused on the Glastonbury Thorn). As the twentieth century progressed, however, spiritual seekers, visionaries, and creative practitioners of various sorts found themselves drawn to Glastonbury, giving rise to a remarkable degree of religious speculation, experimentation, and artistic creativity, which involved people such as Frederick Bligh Bond, Alice Buckton, Rutland Boughton, Wellesley Tudor Pole, and Dione Fortune (see Benham 1993; Cutting 2004; Hopkinson-Ball 2007). A distinctive spiritual and creative subculture began to flourish. The decline in the local leather industry in the 1970s coincided with Glastonbury increasingly gaining a reputation (fueled by the media) as a center for "hippies," "New Age Travelers," and people seeking alternative lifestyles and spiritual experiences (see Hexham 1983). Pilgrimage to Glastonbury was once again gaining momentum, but the pilgrims being drawn to Glastonbury and the reasons they gave for feeling called there were rather different from conventional Christian expectations and explanations.

"The Glastonbury Experience"

While there was a strong countercultural, anti-materialist bias among many visitors and settlers in the 1970s, the seeds of some of Glastonbury's longest lasting "alternative" businesses and institutions were sown then, a prime example being the Glastonbury Experience. One impact of the town's declining manufacturing activity and loss of local employment was the availability of commercial and domestic property. In the late 1970s a Dutch couple, Willem and Helene Koppejan (Dutch Israelites drawn to Glastonbury in part on account of the legend of Jesus in Glastonbury), purchased a collection of buildings at the intersection of the High Street and the Market Place, including shopfronts and the areas behind, together forming a complex with shops both on the High Street and in a courtyard accessed through an arch off it, plus galleries and function rooms above (see Taylor 2010: 104–10). Functioning as a significant "alternative" enclave, over the following decades the Glastonbury Experience has accommodated arts and crafts shops, the town's first vegetarian restaurant, the Bridget Healing Centre, the Library of Avalon (a volunteer-based, spiritually focused library envisaged as the modern successor of the once great Abbey library), the Isle of Avalon Foundation (originally the University of Avalon, to continue the tradition of spiritual education some believe started in Glastonbury with a Druidic university but certainly present in relation to the Abbey), the Bridget Chapel (no longer functioning) and later the Goddess Temple, and shops such as the Goddess and the Green Man, Stone Age, Star Child, Pendragon, Venus, and Courtyard Books.

Barry Taylor, a spiritually inspired philanthropist and former businessman who felt "called" to Glastonbury in the mid-1980s, assisted the widowed Helene Koppejan to sort out the considerable financial difficulties the Glastonbury Experience had by then accrued. Thanks to Taylor's efforts and financial acumen, since 1998 the Glastonbury Experience has been owned by the Glastonbury Trust, a charity "that works with individuals, schools and community groups to promote emotional well-being, citizenship, environmental improvement and spiritual growth" (http:// www.glastonburytrust.co.uk/), supported by rental income from the properties.

The story of the Glastonbury Experience is emblematic of the varied levels of business skills, the mixture of spiritual inspirations and aspirations, services and commodities to be found in Glastonbury, and ways in which Glastonbury is (re)developing as a pilgrimage site with an economy related to spiritual activity there more broadly based and highly developed than ever before.

Glastonbury, the contemporary spiritual milieu, and the spiritual service industry

A variety of religiosity is found in Glastonbury, including different forms of Christianity, Buddhism, Sufism, Indian-derived praxis with diverse foci and forms, Goddess Spirituality, Druidry, Wicca, Celtic spiritualities, assorted

Paganisms, and an eclectic range of individually crafted belief and practice. Undoubtedly, one distinctive feature of contemporary Glastonbury's role as a pilgrimage center is the diversity of beliefs and praxis found in the town, with clusters of events, shops, goods, services, workshops, and even accommodation specifically associated with them.

Christians of all sorts still visit Glastonbury, attracted by the Anglican or Catholic Pilgrimage; by the Abbey ruins; by the Shrine of Our Lady of Glastonbury in the Roman Catholic church; to visit St. John's Church; and to attend talks and residential events at Abbey Church House (the Anglican diocesan retreat house). The Abbey shop and some churches provide the opportunity for the purchase of goods specifically connected with Glastonbury's Christian heritage. Those more interested in Buddhism and Indian-oriented or derived religiosity and praxis might stay at Shekinashram (with its daily morning arati, kirtan, and meditation) or the Arimathean Retreat (combining Satyamvidya Yoga with psychology and spiritual development); attend workshops relating to various schools of yoga; participate in events run by Triratna Buddhist Community (previously known as the Friends of the Western Buddhist Order); shop at Enlightenment or Natural Earthling for devotional objects and yoga requisites; sample Tibetan pulsing healing and so on. Pagans of different sorts might be attracted to Glastonbury for seasonal ceremonies and events; for workshops or longer-term training programs at the Isle of Avalon Foundation and elsewhere; to sample shamanic healing; to attend a Witches Market and to explore the growing number of shops catering for pagan lifestyles such as Magick Box, Lillith, Cat and Cauldron, and Ceilteach. Goddess devotees might come for the annual Goddess Conference; to visit the Goddess Temple for seasonal ceremonies, healing sessions, or to purchase candles, music CDs and other items there; to participate in long-term training as a Priestess or Priest of Avalon; and to shop at the Goddess and the Green Man.

While some townspeople and non-religiously motivated tourists may simply be aware of a mass of "alternative" shops, events, and services, then, a variety of interconnected markets are being addressed. For pilgrims and visitors coming with specific foci, Glastonbury can provide specialist services, confirming or inspirational experiences, and goods which might function as "containers of the sacred" that can act as a link with the place on returning home. On numerous occasions, whether buying a candle from the Goddess Temple, mementos from the stall at the Roman Catholic Pilgrimage, or a crystal from Stone Age (clearly sourced far from Glastonbury), people have described their purchases as "special" because "they come from Glastonbury." Purchasers sometimes further enhance the Glastonbury connection by bathing a crystal in Chalice Well water, or touching a candle to a flame at an event then extinguishing it in preparation for travel. Participants in both the Anglican Pilgrimage and the Goddess Conference, for example, have described coming to Glastonbury as their "annual fix," giving them a sense of community and sustaining them at home in places where they lack like-minded others. While there are clusters of consumption, there is obviously crossover between them. I have accompanied Anglican pilgrimage participants exploring "alternative" shops such as Yin Yang, for instance, while people of many persuasions (dowsers, Sufis, Arthurian enthusiasts, Goddess devotees, British Israelites) visit the Abbey. Meanwhile, restaurants, cafes, the fish and chip shop, the bakery, the pharmacy, the Post Office, bed and breakfast establishments, banks, supermarkets, and charity shops all benefit from the range and quantity of visitors to the town.

While shops and businesses generally strive to be financially viable, there are sometimes other considerations in play, for having a shopfront in Glastonbury can be and has been seen as a way of staking a claim there. When Sheikh Nazim, the leader of the Sufi Naqshbandi-Haqqaniyya, visited Glastonbury in 1999 and declared it "the spiritual heart of England" he urged his followers to establish a presence there; this has been achieved through the Healing Hearts Charity Shop, which also functions as an informal center for dispensing booklets by Sheikh Nazim and information about his teachings. The coming and going of shops, the recent growth in the number of pagan-oriented shops, the preponderance of bookshops over crystal shops, the failure or success of certain shops or ventures might not simply reflect the entrepreneurial skills of the owners but can also be a marker of trends. Movement *within* Glastonbury is also a common phenomenon. When the Goddess and the Green Man moved from the Glastonbury Experience onto the High Street, this was regarded as significant progress in terms of the growing popular acceptability of the beliefs represented.

It should also be noted that not just what is being consumed but methods of consumption have altered in relation to Glastonbury, whether delivering a petition to the Roman Catholic Shrine of Our Lady of Glastonbury online, experiencing Glastonbury initially or even solely through virtual pilgrimage sites, or receiving goods from Glastonbury through the websites of shops based there. One result from a survey I conducted of Glastonbury businesses was that 74 percent of the businesses trading online considered it important to their customers that they are Glastonbury based.

In addition, the nature of religious consumption has changed and developed in relation to emergent patterns and trends in contemporary religiosity; as Ezzy points out, "the market is not a neutral influence on contemporary religious practices" (2001: 43). While the spiritual economy and certain sectors of the regular economy may appear to be focused primarily on pilgrims and visitors, Glastonbury residents and entrepreneurs are central to any understanding of Glastonbury's latest incarnation as a pilgrimage center. The development of non-aligned or de-institutionalized spirituality, the movement away from membership of institutions to the importance of networks, and the formation of new forms of community are all observable and significant there. The "autonomization" of spiritualities from religions, as Hanegraaff (1999) puts it, is obvious in the integrative spirituality of those who exercise a degree of choice in relation to ideas, beliefs, practices, and goods and services derived from and influenced by a wide variety of religious, historic, indigenous, and esoteric traditions in order to produce what are valued by participants as highly personalized forms of religiosity.

The ideas and principles operational among many engaged in Glastonbury's spiritual economy as both consumers and producers can be encapsulated by Possamai's description of "perennism," a "syncretic spirituality"

1 that interprets the world as monistic (the cosmos is perceived as having deeply inter-related elements; it recognises a single ultimate principle, being, or force underlying all reality, and rejects the notion of dualism; e.g. of mind/body);

2 whose actors are attempting to develop a human potential ethic (actors work on themselves for personal growth); and

3 whose actors are seeking spiritual knowledge (the way to develop oneself is through the pursuit of knowledge, be it the knowledge of the universe or of the self, the two being inter-related).

(Possamai 2003: 33)

While discussion of spiritual consumption frequently centers on what Possamai describes as the "hermeneutically deficient term" New Age (2002: 199), perennism encompasses a variety of worldviews, including the Aquarian and (neo-) Pagan. Perennists, according to Possamai, "construct their sense of self, their subjective myth, through consuming religions/spiritualities, indigenous culture, history and popular culture" (Possamai 2002: 210). The shared assumption of many visitors to and residents of Glastonbury is that spiritual seeking is an ongoing project, requiring constant exploration and experimentation. As Sutcliffe says of contemporary spiritual seekership, "multiple seeking proceeds multi-directionally and synchronically: an array of spiritual resources are exploited more or less simultaneously. Ideas, methods and techniques are decontextualised and reconstituted in new settings and adventurous juxtapositions" (Sutcliffe 2003: 204). Part of the attraction to Glastonbury (whether one-off, regular, or permanent) is that such resources and juxtapositions can be encountered there.

Hanegraaff characterizes the "New Ager" as the "ideal consumer," claiming that

the fact that every New Ager continually creates and re-creates his or her own private system of symbolic meaning and values means that spiritual suppliers on the New Age market enjoy maximum opportunities for presenting him or her with ever-new commodities.

(Hanegraaff 2007: 48)

It is worth noting, however, that frequently suppliers are themselves consumers. Despite some critiques, it is not necessarily the case that they are exploitatively or impassively providing goods to and services for unknown clients. In Glastonbury, there is an observable extent to which many spiritual entrepreneurs are sourcing and developing goods, events, and products for themselves and for each other, and doing so with a purpose. As Redden remarks,

While the instrumental aspect of market relations means that there is no bar to some of those purveying New Age products from seeking profit as an end in itself, a case could be made that much New Age commerce is value-driven.

(Redden 2005: 244)

Redden's insights on the nature of this commercial activity are particularly relevant to the Glastonbury context, arising from his studies of Body, Mind, Spirit Fairs where "products are presented side-by-side and the activities of many otherwise independent actors are interwoven" (Redden 2005: 237). He refers to the fairs as "intermediary spaces" on account of "their function of catalysing networked relationships between diverse actors (both providers and participants) through presentation of multiple options for belief and practice" (ibid.: 237), and notes that "Value-relativism, rather than simply being a hall-mark of New Age teaching, is an operating principle of New Age markets in knowledge and practice" (ibid.: 242). Arguably Glastonbury itself is such an "intermediary space," and while there are undoubtedly strongly held, exclusivist beliefs among some religious groups and individuals who visit and live in Glastonbury, on a day-to-day basis value-relativism is the *modus operandi*.

There are pilgrims and other visitors to Glastonbury who feel drawn to the place (often repeatedly and regularly), but who are nevertheless content to return home from it. Some, however, feel that they must stay. Among those who feel "called" to Glastonbury are members of the Glaston Group, responsible for bringing to fruition the idea of the Pilgrim Reception Centre. In its booklet *Glastonbury: A Pilgrim's Perspective*, the Glaston Group describes itself thus:

We are an eclectic and evolving group, with a diverse range of beliefs and interests. We too were drawn here, as pilgrims in search of truth and the sacred. Whilst some pilgrims come and go and return again, we put down our roots and stayed.

(Glaston Group 2005: 13)

Such people see Glastonbury's future primarily as a pilgrimage center, with their role being to draw people to the town and to support them materially, therapeutically, and spiritually while there. While some look with regret to the loss of the prosperity and employment brought by the tanneries and the leather industry, there are those who regard the period from the Reformation to the twentieth century as anomalous, a time when the town became temporarily distracted from its true function as a sacred center. For such people, Glaston-bury's restoration as a specialized site of religious and spiritual seeking, instruction, healing, experience, and consumption has only just begun.

Conclusion

By understanding how Glastonbury functions as a site of religious experience, spiritual seeking and consumption, we can usefully pursue a number of questions concerning the construction of religious identities and communities, and the ways in which "buying and selling spirituality" are perceived and narrated by those involved in such transactions. Dismissing spiritual entrepreneurs as exploitative charlatans, and their clients as deluded fools, simply is not an acceptable *modus operandi* for getting to grips with a significant economic and business phenomenon which potentially disrupts and challenges existing organizational and commercial theories and practices.

In this chapter, the importance of recognizing continuity as well as change in religious and spiritual consumption has been stressed, for commercial transactions have had sacralized meanings for centuries in Glastonbury. It has this in common with other pilgrimage centers that frequently generate distinctive economies and are sites of contestation. Glastonbury is now an example *par excellence* of a contemporary pilgrimage center, with traditional and new forms of religion, traditional and new goods and services, producing a distinctive economy. Pilgrims try to capture some of Glastonbury's charisma through a range of goods purchased there, which they may then further personalize according to their perception of Glastonbury's essence. Notwithstanding the elements of continuity, however, changes in methods of spiritual consumption, the range of goods and services available, and the contemporary impetus for consumption all must be taken into account.

We may be far from "a post-modern resanctification of the market" (York 2004: 375), but studying the development of Glastonbury's spiritual economy furthers more granular understanding of some aspects of contemporary spiritual consumption. Redden's insights concerning the role of "intermediary spaces," the importance of value-relativism, and the operational significance of commodification and marketization are particularly relevant. There is diversity not just in the goods, services, and experiences available but in the meanings and nuances attributed to consumption, as Possamai points out: "Aquarian perennists (paradoxically) consume in a way that justifies an evolutionary perspective, presentist perennists focus mainly on the present and neo-pagan perennists consume in such a way that it valorizes neo-pagan values and lifestyles" (Possamai 2002: 214).

As Olav Hammer (2004), Sutcliffe (2003), and others have noted, although there is strong emphasis on the personal quest and individualism within contemporary integrative spirituality, the books on the shelves of individuals following these paths are often remarkably similar, they have frequently attended similar workshops, belong to a variety of overlapping networks, have an interest in and awareness of alternative forms of community, and so on. As a number of parallel clusters of consumption coexist in Glastonbury, the spiritual seeker often feels at home there. This sense of community is significant; that people on "personalized" spiritual journeys appreciate fellow travelers is sometimes overlooked.

It is important to pursue the relationship between the regular economy and the spiritual economy, to see how new patterns of consumption and production, the structures of late capitalism, and the severe financial forecasts for the coming years affect both the alternative economy and mainstream business models and working patterns. With around 40 percent of the High Street now occupied by "alternative" shops, and a hinterland of spiritually related businesses, healing practitioners of many sorts, specialized bed and breakfasts, diverse devotional communities, and myriad spiritually inspired events and activities, spiritual consumption has a clear impact on the economy and population as a whole.

2 The economies of Charismatic Evangelical worship

Pete Ward

The success of Charismatic worship music was directly related to specific economic pressures and opportunities. In the first instance this meant that the evangelistic orientation of the Jesus Rock Music and Music Gospel Outreach's (MGO) Christian beat groups gave way to more mainstream worship music. The impact of the much smaller British Christian youth scene on the development of Evangelical worship culture, however, should not be underestimated. At the same time worship leaders had a major advantage in that they could be employed directly by churches for the regular weekly worship. The numbers of churches making this commitment to fund a full-time worship leader is a measure of growing significance of Charismatic worship at this time. Christian record companies and music publishing companies soon found a new way to support their activities. MGO entrepreneurs Geoff Shearn and Nigel Coltman were to lead the way in seeking new sources of revenue to support their activities. The Christian Copyright License was an invention that rewarded artists, record companies, and publishing companies who focused on worship music. The importance of a range of publishing opportunities for individual songs and the complexity of the global worship market led to initiatives such as CopyCare, which managed all aspects of royalties for song writers and publishers in the Christian scene. This kind of exploitation of varied streams of funding was a major factor in the success of Charismatic worship.

The economic context of worship

The Christian music scene in Britain was shaped by its size. The limits of the Christian market acted to privilege worship music over contemporary Christian music. This means that despite the efforts of MGO and the activities of Youth for Christ and the existence of festivals such as Greenbelt, very few Christian musicians have been able to make a living as professional artists in the UK. In 1979 Norman Miller, at the time one of the largest promoters of Christian artists, was very clear on this fact. "Britain is just not big enough to support full-time gospel artists. Some of our artists are literally living on the bread line," said Miller.[1] Cummings points out that in 1972 the average contemporary Christian music album would sell around 2,500 copies. In the 1980s albums sold a similar number (Cummings 1995: 24). Cummings reveals the extent of sales was very low even with what might be widely regarded as a successful record: "Christian music hits sell between 3,000 and 6,000 and anything over 6,000 sales in the UK is both a mega hit and a rarity" (ibid.).

This meant that contemporary Christian music could not be supported through the usual sources of record sales and touring. This was a market-based reality. What was also a market reality was that worship leaders were able to develop a larger and more viable market for their records. In the 1980s Spring Harvest were able to increase their impact through the sale of worship books and recordings. Between 1984 and 1989 Word Records sold 100,000 units linked to Spring Harvest. In addition to these sales, the Spring Harvest 1989 Celebration Album sold 20,000 copies.[2]

These kinds of sales made the activities of Christian music companies just about viable in this country. What they did not do was support the worship leaders themselves. Graham Kendrick is one of the few exceptions to this. As a gospel artist, Kendrick made a fairly modest and perhaps precarious living. He was essentially a missionary being supported by the charitable funding of British Youth for Christ. When he began to focus upon worship this situation changed and he was able to support not only himself but also his whole organization, Make Way, on the basis of record sales and income from publishing. Kendrick's success as a worship leader was what made this level of activity and income possible (Cummings 1992: 52). That said, Kendrick was something of an exception in being able to support himself in this way.

For the majority of worship artists, a wide range of diverse activities were required if they were to be able to earn a realistic living. Chief among these was a salaried post working with local congregations. As well as being based in churches, worship leaders were also taken on full time by evangelists, preachers, and Christian organizations. While Christian musicians who specialized in performance and evangelism tended to suffer financially, those involved in worship were able to develop relatively secure careers by receiving regular financial support from these kinds of relationships. In the 1980s Andrew Maries was one of the first of this new breed of worship leader to be employed by an Anglican church. Maries was supported in this ministry by David Watson's church, St. Michael le Belfry in York. In the 1990s, when he was still a teenager, Matt Redman was employed as worship leader by St. Andrew's, Chorley Wood, where David Pytches was the vicar. From here he was able to develop his ministry by working with Mike Pilavachi of Soul Survivor.

Gradually worship leaders became a regular fixture in Charismatic churches throughout the country. For many of these artists a regular income from the local church, supplemented by fees for appearances at other events, made the full-time worship leader a realistic, if somewhat modest possibility.[...]

Publishing and recording

For companies such as Kingsway and Thankyou Music the developing worship scene involved a varied range of activities. While the sales of contemporary

Christian music were extremely modest, sales from products associated with worship were relatively successful. The commodification of worship songs, however, also led to the slow development of a number of other opportunities to create income. These developments are a characteristic of the economics of worship music and they are a major factor in the ability of companies and artists to sustain their activities in the British evangelical subculture.

In the area of record sales, Kingsway Music and others were able to develop sales strategies that maximized income from both artists and individual songs. Within the developing genre of the worship album, four main categories emerged. First, there were albums that were branded and linked to particular worship books. The *Songs of Fellowship* albums would be an example of this kind of recording, where the record was linked by a brand name to a particular collection of songs that are published in a songbook. Second, there were worship albums that were made by live recordings at particular events. The *Spring Harvest Live* worship albums would be an example of this type of recording. These kinds of albums benefit from the branding of the event and they have a sense of integrity that comes from this association. Third, there were albums that were recordings, usually made in a studio, by an individual worship artist or band. Kendrick's various albums would be an example of this kind of recording. These albums represented the latest offering from the artist, providing a collection of their work at that time. Finally, record companies found that they were able to draw upon all of this material to produce compilation albums. The development of these different kinds of recordings meant that a successful worship song or artist might be packaged and sold in at least four different ways.

A similar strategy to maximize the way that songs were made available can be seen to have developed in the area of music publishing. Following the success of *Songs of Fellowship* a number of publishers brought out collections of worship songs and songbook series. Physically, Graham Kendrick was not able to be the worship leader in every Charismatic church in the country, but in the mid-1980s there was a very high probability that his songs would have made an appearance. This was made possible because his songs were made available in a number of different songbooks. Basic to the use of songs in churches, therefore, was their publication in these songbook collections. Kingsway had their *Songs of Fellowship* series, but there were a number of other publications from which churches might choose. The main competitor to *Songs of Fellowship* was the *Mission Praise* series published by HarperCollins. The first *Mission Praise* book was published in 1984 as a songbook linked to the visit of Billy Graham for Mission England. The explicit aim of the book was to produce a collection of songs that reflected the breadth of Evangelical worship. Thus it included a number of standard hymns alongside worship material associated with Charismatic Renewal.[3] As well as the major collections of songs there was also the annual publication of song collections linked to events. These included the songbooks published by Harvest Time linked to the Dales Bible Week and the Spring Harvest Songbooks.

Songbooks were essential for worship leaders and musicians in local churches, since they not only included the musical notation for the songs but also generally included guitar chords and sometimes directions on how these chords should be played. Songbooks linked to events were particularly important because they tended to be updated every year. So new songs were introduced and of course more royalties were distributed. The range of worship songbooks and their regular updating meant that royalties would be earned on the same song from a variety of different sources. One of the main functions of Christian music publishers soon became the management of the placement of songs in books. It was also their role to encourage artists to record songs and then to collect royalties on both of these activities. A publishing company would generally receive one-third of all income gained in this way (but it could be as much as 50 percent) (Law and Lives 1982: 8). The multiplication of royalties from individual songs being published represented a significant stream of income for a music publishing company such as Thankyou Music (the publishing arm of Kingsway Music).

It soon became clear that income from royalties was potentially very substantial indeed. Cummings records the case of Karen Lafferty, who wrote the song "Seek Ye First." This relatively short, and simple song was published by the American company Maranatha Music. As a result the song was recorded and reproduced in music books many times over. The royalties from this one song, according to Cummings, ran into thousands of dollars (Cummings 1984). It must be remembered that Lafferty's success was generated out of the US market, rather than the UK. That said, within a few years British artists were also participating in the global charismatic scene and the publishing companies were right at the heart of these developments.

In fact, the diversity of possible royalties to be generated worldwide through the publishing of worship songs is a very complicated business. Nigel Coltman used his specialist knowledge of the Christian worship scene to launch another new initiative. In 1996 he set up CopyCare. This was a new venture that allowed him to use his knowledge of this complex field to manage songs on behalf of publishers.[4] This kind of initiative was necessary because of the range of publishing and other activities generated by the increasingly vigorous and global evangelical culture. A similar initiative was to significantly boost the growth and development of worship music around the world. This was the unique scheme to collect royalties directly from churches for the reproduction of song lyrics and music.

The Christian Copyright Licensing Scheme

[...] With numbers of churches seeking permission for the use of songs, the Christian Music Publishers Association set up a scheme to simplify the use of copyright material in churches. In 1985 the Christian Copyright Licensing Scheme (CCLS) was launched.[5] Under the scheme, the major Christian music publishing companies joined together to offer a single license which allowed churches, organizations, and those running events to reproduce the lyrics of songs specifically for use in worship. The companies involved in setting up the scheme included Thankyou Music, Springtide, Scripture in Song, Word Music, Jubilate Hymns, and Celebration Services. Licenses for churches were charged according to average attendance; for example, churches with around fifty regular worshipers were charged £28.75; those with 100 were charged £143.75.[6] By 1987 the scheme had issued 2,000 licenses and a new organization was launched linked to the scheme, which was called the Christian Music Association (CMA). The CMA published its own magazine, *Worship*, which carried articles on worship-related matters, as well as an update on the publishers associated with the CCLS.

The revenue was distributed to the songwriters and publishers on the basis of detailed forms filled in by each license holder indicating which songs they had copied that previous year. Licenses could not be renewed without this completed form being supplied. On the basis of these returns a chart of the most popular songs was published in each issue of *Worship*.[7] By 1990 the scheme was issuing 7,000 licenses annually in the UK, and plans were developed to extend the scheme to the USA. In 1991 the results of the returns showed the percentage of each denominational group among license holders—Anglican, 29 percent; Baptist 21 percent; Methodist 9 percent; Pentecostal 9 percent; Evangelical 7 percent; United Reformed Church (URC)/Brethren/Presbyterian/Salvation Army/ Catholic/other 17 percent. It was also found that 90 percent of Pentecostals and house churches used their own overhead projector transparencies.[8] In the 1990s the license was taken over by the now established American company Christian Copyright Licensing International (CCLI).[9] According to the publicity material in 1997 there were 27,000 license holders in the UK: these included schools, churches, and organizations. Fees ranged from £52, for groups 0–15, to £543, for those over 1,500.[10] In 1997 CCLI issued a total of 135,000 licenses in Australia, Canada, Great Britain, Ireland, New Zealand, South Africa, and the USA.[11]

Innovations such as the CCLI indicate how the worship scene was creatively financed. The scheme created a new source of revenue from song royalties that previously did not exist. The Christian music publishing companies were able to support their claim for these royalties by emphasizing the way that many churches were routinely acting in an illegal manner by reproducing song lyrics for use in worship. This source of funding was to be very significant in creating an economically viable market for Charismatic worship. The licensing scheme should be seen alongside the other practices which companies developed to use songs in a variety of publications and recordings. These practices not only spread the influence of a particular song or artist, they also maximized revenue from royalties. These developments demonstrate how a viable market was created and sustained for charismatic worship. These economic strategies exploited the market, but, at the same time, if they had not come about it is very likely that Charismatic worship would not exist, at least in its current form. The economics of worship is therefore essential to its production and also to its consumption.

The rise of the internet

[...] Evangelicals have always been keen to embrace any new communication possibilities (Sweet 1993). For the various organizations and individuals promoting worship music in the UK, the internet has been a significant advantage. For contemporary Christian music groups such as Delirious? it has meant that they have been able to communicate directly with their fan base, effectively bypassing the secular press in the UK and the religious press in the USA, both of which, for different reasons, tend to ignore British Christian bands. For the record companies, book distributors, festivals, and organizations the web has also offered a chance to offer their products to a wider audience.

The network of Christian bookshops has often struggled to keep the range of stock associated with the growing number of worship artists. In contrast, on their websites organizations such as Vineyard or Soul Survivor are able to present their whole range. The internet, along with new and cheaper recording technologies, has led directly to the proliferation of titles and the release of more specialized and targeted CDs. Direct sales through the internet are important also because they represent a larger profit for the organization or company than sales through the traditional bookstores. That said, sales associated with an appearance at one of the major festivals such as Soul Survivor remain the most important factor in UK success.

Alongside sales, many groups have sought to use the internet as a means of developing their ministry. In the late 1990s, Soul Survivor transferred its youth oriented magazine on to the internet. The online magazine seeks to support young Christians in their spiritual lives. *Youthwork Magazine* has continued to publish hard copy but it also has developed as a web-based magazine offering articles and materials on youth work to a much wider and more international audience, with the website also including more interactive content, including the possibility of uploading videos. Spring Harvest and New Wine have used the web to promote their festivals but they also use it to sell their materials and in recent years people have been able to book into the festivals online.

Selling out to the culture?

The problems that have arisen from the economic and business side of the worship scene have been largely unacknowledged within Charismatic churches. In particular, the weaknesses and failings of individuals, organizations, and companies, whilst evident to many, are very often glossed over by the need to appear successful, or Christian or morally correct. Part of the problem here is that the various mechanisms of the culture and the market are generally regarded as being used by God. What God is doing is often seen as expressed in sales figures, or the numbers attending a festival or indeed a local church. The anointing of a worship leader may be linked to how many people come forward for ministry at an event. This raises difficulties, for whilst it may be possible theologically to say that God was often at work in the business side of worship, one should be wary of too close an identification between sales and the Spirit. [...]

The Charismatic movement has given rise to a number of powerful organizations such as Spring Harvest, Alpha, and Kingsway. The way that these organizations act to promote and defend their particular franchise and business interests has led many to feel uneasy about the commercial nature of the worship scene. The widespread unease among Christian people about television and the film industry has been to some extent reflected in the way that some see Charismatic worship as manipulative and commercially led.

On the whole I am unsympathetic to this analysis of the wider Charismatic scene. There seems to be some truth in the idea that Christian organizations act in a similar manner to commercial companies being driven by the desire to promote their own products. These may be sold as "resources" but they are nevertheless sold. This means that at a festival such as Soul Survivor, worship artists linked to the "brand" are generally featured, and the songs in the songbook, the CDs in the record store, and the other books and merchandise necessarily reflect this fact. Where organizations develop significant alliances the openness to those outside the "cartel" has sometimes been even more limited. Partly this comes from the need for every stakeholder to feature their own speaker or worship band or latest initiative. The effect of this on the wider church, however, is that it tends to cut out the independent or grassroots initiative.

The size of the British scene naturally lends itself to monopolies. Because the market is so small, any significant success in the UK will almost inevitably create a large fish in what is really a very small pond. Over the last thirty years organizations such as Spring Harvest, *Buzz*, Authentic Media, Kingsway, and others, through their own success and the acquisition and merger of companies, have at times threatened to establish a near monopoly in their fields. In the wider secular scene, business practices are regulated through government intervention and through the regular scrutiny of the media. When the Christian media are owned by the media companies, or when they begin to promote events and their own resources, clearly problems may emerge. This makes it imperative that we develop an appreciative but also critical culture among the worshipers in the churches.

To be critical, however, does not mean that we should not be aware of the immense value in the activities of Christian organizations and businesses. It is simplistic, in my view, to dismiss all commercial or business activity as some form of manipulation. As I have argued throughout this piece, the adoption of particular forms of communication simply represents the means to contextualize Christianity. In developing a critique of the worship culture of the church we should not focus solely on the activities of the "producers." We also need to examine the way that people consume the product and make something of it in their own spiritual lives.

Notes

1 News item, *Buzz*, January 1979, p. 4.
2 News item, *Worship*, Autumn 1989, p. 14.
3 News item, *Buzz*, March 1984, p. 53.
4 News item, *Worship Together*, November 1996, p. 18.
5 Chuck Fromm, of the American publishing company Maranatha Music, maintains that such a license was first pioneered by his company. Shearn then introduced the scheme in the UK.
6 News item, *Buzz*, September 1985, p. 15.
7 News item, *Worship*, Winter 1990, p. 16.
8 News item, *Worship*, Winter 1990, p. 16.
9 This was the successor to the company first started by Chuck Fromm.
10 CCLI "Congregational Worship and Copyright," p. 2.
11 CCLI (1998) "Reference Manual," p. 1.

3   Mecca Cola and burqinis

Muslim consumption and religious identities

Nabil Echchaibi

Halal. It is a centuries-old guide to how life should be lived. It alludes to a quality of life that is reflected in the way food is processed, clothes are designed, medicine is prepared, commerce is carried out, and how our personal and social relationships are conducted. Halal is a way of life for over a billion Muslims living in over 148 countries. In business terms, this is a huge consumer base spread out all over the world ... The Halal industry is bolstered by the demands from the world's Muslim population that is getting younger, more educated, and affluent, who are embracing the Islamic contemporary and global lifestyle.[1]

(Halal World Forum 2010)

This is an excerpt from the promotional video of the Halal World Forum, an annual transnational economic summit inaugurated in 2006 in Malaysia. Since its first meeting in Kuala Lumpur, the summit has set an ambitious agenda to harmonize a fragmented global halal (Islamically permissible) industry that now includes sectors beyond the food market such as pharmaceuticals, cosmetics, toiletries, and services such as banking, insurance, and tourism. Unifying this global market and creating common standards for the label "halal" has become a clarion call as Muslim and non-Muslim entrepreneurs realize the untapped potential of a huge consumer base that demands a market more in compliance with its religious beliefs. The halal marketplace today includes a vast array of products and services from Mecca Cola, Fulla (the Islamic response to Barbie), the MacHalal at the Beurger King Muslim,[2] design collections for Muslim chic,[3] Muslim Apps,[4] to Islamic banking and halal-friendly tourism resorts in Dubai, Istanbul, and London.[5]

The stunning growth of the global halal industry (with a market value estimated today at US$2.3 billion) has been accelerated by a wave of religious fervor among a social class of young, educated, and affluent Muslims who, according to the organizers of the World Halal Forum, wish to embrace an "Islamic contemporary and global lifestyle." It is still unclear what this Islamic lifestyle is, but a new market of consumer products, advertising, and commercial media programming is increasingly labeled "Islamic" and slowly contributes to the rise of an alternative culture industry. Like all forms of consumption, such an elaborate Islamic consumer culture has deep implications for identity construction and constitutes a prime stage for the production and reproduction of what it means to be a modern Muslim in the twenty-first century.

This chapter explores the significance of emerging modes of Islamic consumerism through an analysis of religious identity politics and the dialectical encounters between Islam and Western modernity. Muslim consumption is interrogated as a dynamic discursive practice invested not only in the ethical cultivation of piety, but also in the edification of an Islamically inflected modernity. I argue that the Islamic marketplace, with its emphasis on disciplined consumption and dialogic connection to secular culture, has become an ideal site for the study of Islam as a religious tradition in constant motion and deliberation. My concern here is not only to address the impact of consumer culture on Muslim piety, but also to examine the implications of the steady and creative appropriation of secular and modern spaces for the sake of creating an Islamic ideal and a distinct identity.

Islamic consumer culture

The presence of Muslim commodities in the marketplace is not new. Muslims have always shopped for such items as prayer mats, clothing, rosaries, religious self-help books, audiocassettes, and pamphlets. There is, however, a marked change in the scale and nature of products available for pious consumption in Muslim societies and among Muslims living in the West. While consumption of older religious products may have been related to Islamic movements and their call for the preservation of virtues such as modesty, obedience, and piety, the emerging consumer culture presented here is also concerned with safeguarding the same virtues, but it deploys new commodified cultural forms and spaces for this purpose. Increasingly, these forms and spaces are borrowed and inventively re-worked from global (Western) consumer brands and practices.

In 2002, Tawfik Mathlouthi, a French-Tunisian entrepreneur, launched Mecca Cola as a protest product against what he called "American imperialism." With 20 percent of profits pledged to charitable projects in the Muslim world and with the cola made from the water of Zamzam, a holy water source in Mecca, each Mecca Cola bottle comes with the message "Don't shake me. Shake your conscience" or "Drink with discipline." Mecca Cola and other variants like Qibla Cola and Cola Turka may well be about a political statement against American cultural hegemony or a perceived American pro-Israeli foreign policy—10 percent of the revenue from Mecca Cola is sent to aid humanitarian work in Palestine—but the popularity of these protest brands can also be explained by their ability to imbue a desirable global product with a reverent quality and transform a trivial act of consumption into a committed act of faith. What is more striking about the successful marketing strategy of these alternative cola companies is their creative inversion—not rejection—of the flow of global cultural products and their subversion of the secular market to help foster religious identities through consuming practices. It would be naïve to overplay the market impact of Mecca Cola and others as competitors of the original and powerful Coca-Cola company because that has been negligible even in Muslim countries, but when this is placed in a larger context of how global consumer products and cultural fashions are appended with an Islamic identity, it becomes clear that the market is turned into a powerful discursive terrain where commodities not only embody but also mediate religious ideals and qualities.

Fulla, the Muslim alternative to the Barbie doll, is another instructive example of how the market is used for the discursive production of religious identity. As with the marketing of Mecca Cola, Fulla, a doll made by a Syrian couple, is contrasted with the blaring sexuality of the Western Barbie and posited as a more modest role model for young Muslim girls. Fulla comes with a hijab and full-length garment for outdoor use, but included in the package are other fashionable clothing and hair accessories for indoor use. Bearing a striking similarity to Barbie, Fulla and other Muslim dolls like Razanne only mimic the iconic figure of the Western toy to then invest it with new values, as the Fulla brand manager explains in a *New York Times* article:

> This isn't just about putting the hijab on a Barbie doll. You have to create a character that parents and children will want to relate to. Our advertising is full of positive messages about Fulla's character. She's honest, loving, and caring, and she respects her father and mother.
>
> (Zoepf 2005)

Since Fulla came out in 2003, millions have been sold in the Middle East thanks to an ambitious marketing campaign which saw the doll being endorsed by other popular products among young consumers like breakfast cereals, toys, stationery, and luggage. A series of commercials on Arab satellite television presents Fulla as a young and pious girl who prays on time, plays in the park, entertains her friends at home, and reads before going to bed. The transnational marketing of Fulla as the "better doll" for Muslim girls borrowed much of its narrative from a concerted criticism of the ethically unfit Western Barbie from traditional (and contested) centers of Islamic authority like Saudi Arabia, where the Committee for the Propagation of Virtue and the Prevention of Vice, a.k.a. the religious police, called Barbie a threat to morality. Sheikh Abdulla al-Merdas, a Saudi imam who supports the ten-year-old ban in Saudi Arabia against Barbie, said dolls "should not have the developed body of a woman and wear revealing clothes. These clothes will be imprinted on their minds and they will refuse to wear the clothes we are used to as Muslims" (Associated Press 2003). Similarly, Iranian Prosecutor General Ghorban Ali Dori Najafabadi believes Barbie and other Western toys to be "a danger to be stopped" because of their "destructive" social and cultural implications.

Far from being a progressive example of a Muslim woman's agency, Fulla and other Muslim dolls represent an ongoing struggle for the production and control of a collective identity for the Muslim female subject through the construction and market mediation of normative values of gender roles and lifestyles. Of course, Muslim women have been among the first to criticize the commodification of religious symbols such as veiling and other gender norms and their mainstreaming through the socializing effects of toys. But this struggle has to be contextualized as a power ideology through which some Muslim men and women seek to articulate their religious specificity using a modern idiom of capitalist consumption. Discussing the significance of the veiling movement in Turkey, Turkish sociologist Nilüfer Göle argues that for some years now, a culturalist Islamist ideology is publicly challenging the automatic association established by Western modernists and their supporters in the Middle East that to be "civilized" is the same as being "Westernized":

> It [contemporary Islamist ideology] promotes the return of the Muslim actors to the historical scene in terms of their own religious morality. The Islamist body politic conveys a distinct sense of self (*nefs*) and society (*umma*), one in which the central issue becomes the control of sexuality through women's veiling and the segregation of the sexes in public life. Hence the veiling of women emerges as the most visible symbol of this Islamicization of the self and society. But, in addition, other social forms such as beards worn by men and taboos regarding chastity, promiscuity, homosexuality, and alcohol consumption, define a new consciousness of the Islamic self and the Islamic way of life ... Islamism emphasizes Muslim identity and reconstructs it in the modern world. Islamic faith and the Islamic way of life become a reference point for the re-ideologization of seemingly simple social issues such as the veiling of Muslim students at the university ... censorship of erotic art, and discouragement of alcohol consumption in restaurants. Activism regarding these issues demonstrates the Islamist problematization of a universalistic construction of Western civilization and criticism of the "secular way of life."

(Göle 1996: 16)

While the women described in Göle's research use Islamism as a narrative of empowerment to gain access to modern spaces such as the university and the workplace, a recent wave of Islamic television programming effectively targets the world of entertainment and popular culture not simply to fend off the assaulting impact of cultural imperialism, but most importantly to construct an alternative model of modernization and a new Muslim subjectivity. Building on the success of his vision to modernize religious programming, Ahmed Abu Haiba, an Egyptian television producer, recently launched 4Shbab, the first Islamic music video channel on Arab satellite television. Funded by Saudi investors, 4Shbab features various Muslim artists and bands (only men) from Muslim countries, Western Europe, and the US who sing in Arabic and English about their love for the prophet, the importance of religious piety, and the value of charity and filial obedience. A promotional video used at the time of the inauguration of the channel in 2009 invites young Muslims through a strong and confident voiceover to create "a new vision for art, for beauty, and for the human," while a silhouette of a muscular young man walks determinedly toward the camera, suggesting the beginning of a new era where Muslim youth are supposedly in control of their own cultural production. In an interview with AlArabiya.net, Abu Haiba said 4Shbab, which means "for the youth" in Arabic, will act as an ethical guide to help a culturally disoriented Muslim youth react more creatively to the predominance of Western popular culture and go beyond a passive mimicry of its value system. "A divided identity is what Muslims are experiencing in these times," he said. "Young Muslims are bombarded with a slew of non-Islamic cultural values through music that contradicts their life-styles, and forces them to believe one thing and watch another" (AlArabiya 2009). In contrast, 4Shbab features the popular music of British singer Sami Yusuf, a prolific Muslim singer of Azeri origins who studied music at the London Royal Academy of Music. Yusuf's slick music videos use high production standards and his lyrics celebrate the compassion of God and his forgiveness. In his repeatedly shown music video "Asma Allah" ("Allah's Attributes"), Yusuf, dressed all in white, sits at a white piano with a white background as he sings the nintey-nine attributes of God while an array of Muslims from various ethnic and racial backgrounds, men and women (veiled and unveiled), old and young, take turns lip-synching the lyrics of the song. The video bears some similarity to pop star John Lennon's music video for his song "Ordinary People."

Music videos in the case of 4Shbab become an apt site for producers and artists to re-script the terms of engagement with the world of pop culture. In 2005, Amr Khaled, a famous Egyptian tele-Islamist whose show *Sunae Al Hayat* (*LifeMakers*) was produced by the same Ahmed Abu Haiba, introduced his viewers both on satellite television and online to an aggressive social agenda he called "Faith-Based Development." The modern Muslim man for Khaled is someone who takes the initiative even if the odds are against him, because his faith is not only his rallying cry but also the source of his creativity (Echchaibi 2011). In one episode of *LifeMakers*, Khaled bemoans the fact that men spend hours in cafes smoking and lounging around aimlessly. He then calculates the hours that could be saved each day by avoiding unproductive activities and the amount of constructive work that could be achieved instead. If his audience is short on ideas about becoming productive, Khaled is always resourceful in providing concrete examples and charting specific strategies which he introduces on air and develops further on his highly interactive website. In an episode entitled "Culture, Art, Media and Making Life," Khaled invites his audience not to stop at simply denouncing music videos on Arab satellite television which objectify women's bodies. He explains that

> the problem with video clips is not only the dissolute words and movements, but the biggest problem is, in fact, the importation of something that has nothing to do with our own culture. The picture is Western and the voice is ours, what would the clip look like? It is useless and aimless. In that way, it is not art that will exalt the soul; it is directed to desire and

lust; this is the result of blind imitation ... I ask all those who are with us today, please don't accept the obliteration of the identity of our nation, preserve our culture and our arts.

(Khaled's website, http://amrkhaled.net/newsite/index.php)

Khaled then urges everyone to write letters to artists and television channels and complain about the overt sexualization of women and their denigration. A few days later, it was reported that some of these channels received thousands of letters from across the Arab world and from others living in Western Europe and in the US. What is worth noting in Khaled's faith-based initiatives is his up-to-date familiarity with pop culture and his ability to relate to young Muslims' ambiguous fascination with Western culture without completely rejecting it. This is strikingly apparent in his latest show on Islamic satellite television, which adapts the reality format of Donald Trump's *The Apprentice*. *Mujaddidun* (The Reformers) aired in the summer of 2010, but instead of the pugnacious demeanor of the highly competitive contestants in the American version, *Mujaddidun*'s contestants help each other to succeed and work more as a team rather than as combative individuals overzealous in their the-end-justifies-the-means quest to wipe out their competitors. Khaled's contestants, both men and women from nine Muslim countries, work only on charitable projects with meager budgets and the winner of the show is not rewarded with a high-paying managerial job at a successful firm, but a prize of $140,000 to lead a socially conscious development project in their home country.

In a strong critique of *Mujaddidun* on *Elaph*, a daily online publication in Arabic, columnist Deema Tariq Tahboub asks if Muslims should innovate on their own or simply mimic what's already there and plaster a religious theme on anything Western. "Not everything that glitters is gold," Tahboub said. "Should we subject Islam to the logic of marketing, advertising, profits and losses, commodity exchange, demand and supply?" (Tahboub 2010). It would be naïve to think that the producers of shows like Khaled's *Mujaddidun* or television channels like Abu Haiba's 4Shbab are solely motivated by the cultivation of Muslim piety. The world of Islamic entertainment has become a lucrative segment of the television and advertising markets, and Saudi investors have been flocking to fund creative programming that could generate revenue while serving a "higher purpose" of religious education. But symbolically, the same market-driven world of business and entertainment becomes a powerful metaphor to mark what Göle described as "the return of Muslim social actors to the history from which they were expelled when the idea for society was progress defined by the Western world" (1996: 137). In fact, much of the narrative of this Islamic renewal reveals that there are no qualms about using the material symbols of Western progress as in technology and specific cultural forms as long as the ultimate purpose is to purge those symbols of their secular values, invest them anew with Islamic ones, and empower Muslims to think that they participate in the market on their own terms.

Consumption and the Muslim modern

The examples described so far all indicate a desire by some Muslims to use their faith as an ethical compass for a safer navigation of modern life and its material articulations. It is a conscious quest to reassert control at a time when Muslims feel stripped of their agency to define and produce social and cultural progress on their own terms. The examples also reveal the way in which Mexican theorist of urban culture Garcia Canclini (2001: 47) thinks of consumption "as a site of cognitive value," not a site of unreflexive, compulsive behavior:

> *consumption is the ensemble of sociocultural processes in which the appropriation and use of products takes place.* This characterization leads us to understand our acts of consumption as something more than the exercise of tastes, whims and unreflexive purchases, as is presumed by moralistic judgment, and as something that goes beyond individual attitudes explored in market surveys ... To consume is to participate in an arena of competing claims for what society produces and the ways of using it ... If consumption was once a site of more or less unilateral decisions, it is today a space of interaction where producers and senders no longer simply seduce their audiences; they also have to justify themselves rationally.
>
> (Canclini 2001: 38–9, emphasis in original)

Consumption in contemporary Muslim culture industries, then, reflects an ongoing search for an authentic Islamic identity that reformulates cultural heritage to free itself from the weight of uncritical mimicry of the West. Certainly, the producers of Muslim-inflected commodities must convince their target audiences that their act of consumption is a meaningful act of articulating their cultural distinction in a market of inchoate flows of ideas and values. Both production and consumption within these culture industries also become a politically significant lever to usher in the conditional entry of Muslims into modern spaces of social life. Their condition is to embrace those spaces while retaining their capacity to resist the meta-narratives of Western modernity— itself a discursive construct—and its mainstreaming of Enlightenment values such as individualism, secularism, pluralism, and equality.

This religious and political function of consumption, therefore, is constructed around a discourse of resistance and "taming of modernity" (Kraidy 2009: 192) which ultimately becomes prescriptive of what constitutes an alternative Muslim modernity. As clearly articulated in Ahmed Abu Haiba's targeting of young Muslims, the choice today is between two models of modernity, a good model of an ethical Muslim modernity and its opposite bad model of secular modernity. Of course, defining these models, as happens frequently in the literature on alternative modernities, is a highly essentialist enterprise which easily reifies a one-dimensional understanding of both the Western modern experience and the questioning of its doctrinal substance (Gaonkar 2001). But this kind of cultural particularism not only helps boost the marketing impact of Muslim commodities, but also arguably elevates its producers and consumers to the ideal position of critical social actors, consciously engaged in an ideological critique and assessment of modernity.

The source of appeal in this carefully constructed narrative of resistance lies primarily in its invitation to continue using the toolbox of modernity as an integral part of the process of reconstructing a "true" modern identity. While other forms of Islamism, like Osama bin Laden's, challenge the West from outside of its hegemonic structure by seeking to neutralize (through bombing) the very nerve center of its economic and material progress, the kind of culturalist Islamism presented here calls into question the normative values of Western modernity from within that hegemonic framework. The culturalist turn in Islamist politics is in fact a response to the intellectual failure of political Islamism in its various manifestations to offer a viable alternative to Muslims and produce durable socio-cultural changes in Muslim societies (Roy 2004). The fact that autocratic regimes are still ruling undisturbed in many Muslim societies amidst high unemployment figures, low literacy, and religious polarization is a good case in point. This doesn't mean that the political strand of Islamism, which offers the Islamic State as the only framework to re-Islamize society, will cease to exist, but, as Roy says, it seems like its rhetoric is louder than its accomplishments, and Muslim youth are increasingly disaffected by the staleness of the political Islamist and secular solutions alike. In contrast, the heightened sense of religiosity that has swept through many Muslim societies and Muslim communities in the West bespeaks a desire to approach the question of change and progress from the bottom up and as a transformative process that is equally critical of the normative values of Western modernity and those of traditional Islam. More and more, educated middle and upper class youth deploy their understanding of Islam to mark a clear rupture with traditionalist, anti-modern articulations of their own religion, using market-driven media to express this differentiation (Nasr 2009). The media and the market are privileged as effective agents to eventually enable a pious revalorization of the individual.

It is important to study these emerging Muslim consumer cultures as significant loci for the construction of contemporary Muslim subjectivities beyond the deterministic binaries of traditional religious and modern secular identities. I argued in this chapter that consumer patterns could be instructive in revealing how Muslims discursively engage modernity as a source of both contention and identification, in which apparently mundane objects such as soft drinks and toys become an important medium through which such engagements take place.

Notes

1 The Halal World Forum started in Kuala Lumpur in 2006 and has become ever since the prime halal industry event attended by hundreds of senior industry executive and government delegates representing more than fifty-seven countries.

2 In 2005, two French entrepreneurs of North African origin opened the first halal burger joint in France. Beurger King Muslim (BKM) (Beur is the name used in the Parisian slang of Verlan to refer to Arabs born in France) sells burgers, fries, and

sundaes using Islamic dietary laws. Many of the BKM sandwiches are referred to as "koul," a play on words which combines the English word "cool" with the Arabic word "koul" ("to eat" in Arabic). Muslim female employees at BKM have the option of wearing a hijab, a strong statement against the French ban on ostentatious religious symbols. BKM also closes on Fridays around the time of prayer (Smith 2005).

3 Sophia Kara, a British Muslim fashion designer, launched Imaan clothing collections for Muslim women who wish to dress modestly and still be fashionable. Kara's design is a fusion of Western, Asian, and Islamic fashion which seeks to offer creative alternatives to the black abaya and the single-colored veil. Her fashion shows are often followed by a fundraiser to benefit local charities in London (Heatley 2007).

4 A number of Muslim applications for smart phones have been recently released, ranging from supplication apps, through Mecca Qibla direction apps, to call for prayer alerts (Bunt 2010).

5 The halal tourism industry has been growing steadily in the past few years, generating increasing revenues for hotel chains in Muslim majority and Western capitals. Guests in luxurious hotels can expect prayer mats, Korans, Mecca direction indicators for prayer, a variety of halal menu options, and in some cases gender-segregated sport and entertainment facilities. Crescentrating.com, a search website, was recently launched to help customers find halal-friendly tourism options worldwide (Byrd 2010).

4 The spirit of living slowly in the LOHAS marketplace

Monica M. Emerich

Introduction

Fast world, meet the slows.

Around the world, individuals and organizations are taking aim at the iconized and canonized notion of speed, the golden child of globalization, neo-liberalism, and late modernity. Speed connotes innovation, intelligence, success, and excitement. Forced into comparison with its glitzy antonym, the word "slow" has become the semiotic poster child for the undesirable, labeling everything from kitchen drudgery to dull-witted people. But slow—and its aide-de-camp, simplicity—are marshaling new respect, refashioned (in some cases by the most fashionable amongst us) with a new international cachet.

The marketplace known as LOHAS, or Lifestyles of Health and Sustainability, is an umbrella descriptor for a wide variety of industries that produce products and services marketed as environmental, natural, organic, socially responsible, sustainable, and healthy. There is no certifying agency or standard-issuing central committee for LOHAS; there are only media that articulate what LOHAS is, a reformed capitalism with a healthier, more socially just, more balanced worldview. Key to the ideology of LOHAS are the tenets of slow living, now formalized in such organizations as Slow Food and Slow Money.

The idea of slow living has become the darling of the lifestyle empires of Oprah Winfrey and Martha Stewart. Celebrities (Prince Charles is a supporter), activists, foodies, non-profits, cooks, and moms find slow to be at least a partial answer to our various modern ills, a way to reinstate the *art* of living. Slow aficionados aren't advocating swapping your car for a horse and buggy or spearing a fish for dinner. That is, slow living isn't about slowing time as much as it is about savoring time.

In this essay, drawing on my own fieldwork, I explore the ways in which LOHAS media and LOHAS consumers construct and interpret slow-living practices and beliefs as an artful way of living and what that represents.

About LOHAS

"LOHAS may sound like a disease," said the *New York Times*, "but it may be the biggest market you have never heard of" (Cortese 2003: 4). Since then,

LOHAS has penetrated Wall Street and the global market lexicon, even though most consumers have probably never heard the word, and it remains mostly a "trade" term.

LOHAS was the brainchild of eco-goods and healthy-living products retail giant Gaiam Inc., owned by Jirka Rysavy, once a runner-up for *Inc.* magazine's prestigious Entrepreneur-of-the-Year award. Rysavy coined the term "LOHAS" with a handpicked group of advisors and investors in the mid-1990s and circulated it as an in-house market strategy. But in the late 1990s Rysavy approached Natural Business Communications, a small publishing firm, to propose a business magazine based on the LOHAS concept. The proposal worked and in 2000 Natural Business not only published *The LOHAS Journal* but also produced an annual conference, the LOHAS Forum. Both still operate, under different ownership.

Natural Business and Rysavy believed LOHAS provided the necessary logic to both explain and support the wildly expanding natural and organic products industry. Through the 1990s, that small industry had boomed, attracting new consumers, generating larger stores, and propagating national regulation. Increasingly these customers were demanding more than just healthful ingredients in their groceries, dietary supplements, personal care, and household goods—they wanted the goods they purchased to also be socially just, humane, and environmentally safe.

Around the same time, sociologist Paul Ray produced interesting research that further supported the logic of LOHAS. His study showed 24 percent of the adult population in the United States "made a comprehensive shift in their worldview, values, and way of life—their culture, in short" (Ray and Anderson 2000: 4). Ray called these individuals the Cultural Creatives. Influenced by the 1960s social movements, Cultural Creatives' reformative values formed a root-stalk of beliefs about the sanctity, meaning, and balance of life, which informed their politics and everyday lives, from the clothes they wore to the foods they ate. Natural Business consulted with Ray, and the profile of the LOHAS consumer—the Cultural Creative in the marketplace—was born.

From its inception, the term LOHAS has been primarily articulated by the media, including magazines, websites, radio, television, marketing materials, and conferences. There is no LOHAS store, no LOHAS headquarters, and no LOHAS patent (at least, not in the US; LOHAS is treated differently around the world). I understand LOHAS as a discourse that advocates products and practices marketed as Fair Trade, socially responsible, natural, organic, mind/body/spirit, "green" or "eco," sustainable, integrative medicine, and spiritual. At LOHAS conferences, this conceptual menagerie springs to life in the convening of hippies-turned-millionaires, global industrialists, entrepreneurs, yogis and yoginis, media moguls, scientists, spiritual authors and visionaries, medical doctors and scientists, activists, and celebrities (including Raquel Welch, Daryl Hannah, Amy Smart, Joan Baez, Ed Begley Jr., some Olympic athletes, and rock and roll stars), all supporters of overarching LOHAS concepts of health and sustainability.

It falls to the media to thread these varied people, visions, industries, products, services, and beliefs into a single string, into a cohesive "lifestyle of health and sustainability."

Live slowly, live mindfully

The first "slow" social movement to gain international attention was the Slow Food Movement, a cleverly named counterpoint to fast food. Today, there are other successful slow ventures, including Slow Money and Slow Cities. The products, practices, and visions promoted by these movements align with those articulated within the LOHAS marketplace, which is why LOHAS media make explicit references to "slow" living, treating the notion as an essential component of a lifestyle of health and sustainability. LOHAS publication *Experience Life* says simplicity can be a "means of fostering greater life freedom, personal integrity or social justice" (Hart 2009: 82); an *Organic Style* magazine article says simple living is meant to "slow us down" and provide us with "natural pleasures" (Erney 2004: 88); and the *Yoga Journal* says we can have those while leaving "less of an ecological footprint" (Colin 2004: 113). The idea is to "look beyond the dollar value of every purchase to its deeper value and leaving wasteful consumption patterns behind," says *Experience Life* (Hart 2009: 82).

In their book *Slow Living*, Wendy Parkins and Geoffrey Craig say the "desire for slow living [is] manifested in a range of social phenomena" and there is "no prescriptive checklist of activities which comprise slow living, nor would a 'slow subject' necessarily engage in all of the practices which we mention" (2006: 3–4). Ditto the LOHAS marketplace. Slow has a natural porosity to it that is appealing to LOHAS media because it can be pasted onto almost any activity or product without risking advertiser displeasure.

When I asked an experienced journalist who had worked in senior management at two LOHAS publications about how the idea of "slow" living fitted into that of LOHAS, he responded, "All of the Slow movements—Slow Food, Slow Money, Slow Thinking, Slow Fitness—incorporate the concepts of awareness, consciousness and concern for the greater good." He went on to say that slow movements "understood the bigger picture of what is important, just like LOHAS," by which he meant living in ways that respect the needs of all people and ecological systems. To him, slow meant being mindful, just as "LOHAS is about learning to be conscious of our every action and its impact on the world."

Infusing time with value

"Daria" is a LOHAS consumer, a mother of two small children, and an international marketing consultant who telecommutes from home. When I asked her how she practiced "slow" living, she replied, "I try to live in each day and not get caught up in speed." She strives to "be present" and says that "a lot of it has to do with food and consumption of things." Even though Daria's husband commutes to his job and even though she subscribes to advanced digital technology—both activities dependent on speed—it became clear in our interview that there is a range of acceptability in the expenditure of time and speed for timesavings in Daria's mind.

As we spoke, a truck delivered sand for her children's new sandbox. Daria was explaining why she would not buy processed, convenience foods; why she made her own laundry detergent and bread; and why she used cloth rather than disposable diapers. For her, the time that might be "saved" by using the commercial products actually robbed her family of their quality of life. These products undermine her family's health and even the essence of what family is about, she told me. When I asked how they did so, Daria explained that cooking with whole grains and natural foods represented security, love, environmentalism, and good parenting. Her mother had prepared meals from scratch and Daria's recollection of that was a happy one.

Wendy Parkins writes in *Time and Society Journal* that it's important to understand that the notion of "slow" in slow living is not a simple bid against late capitalism, but rather is formulated around the "desire for 'time for meaningful things'" (Parkins 2004: 364). Parkins adds:

> Slow living involves the conscious negotiation of the different temporalities which make up our everyday lives, deriving from a commitment to occupy time more attentively. Implicit in the practices of slow living is a particular conception of time in which "having time" for something means investing it with significance through attention and deliberation.
>
> (Parkins 2004: 364)

"Slow means being present, being mindful," Daria said. "I'm a Christian. I'm also incorporating meditation mindfulness into my beliefs. That all seems to me to fit into slow living." She added, "In modern society, once you've tasted convenience, it's hard to go back, but I feel better doing these things, even though it's a pain, just to know that I am doing the best thing for earth and family."

Another informant, "Laura," found herself living a slow life by force rather than choice. "I was living in the suburbs when the economic downturn happened and I lost my business," she says. But at her core, she had always loved rural life and the real or imagined simplicity of a life connected to the land. "Although [my] actual moment of change came about because of a financial crisis, I think now that it pushed me to do what I always wanted to do," she says.

For Laura, that meant selling her 3,300 square feet of living space in the city and moving to a rural town fallen on hard times. She rented a 480 square-foot house with a small yard, but one large enough to grow most of her family's food. The downsizing required parting with most of her worldly possessions, which she ultimately found cleansing in a way she had not expected. Material things, she says, "cloud our thinking of what is possible. I feel like I could lose any material thing now and be fine. It's an emotional process; it makes you redefine yourself."

As Laura explains it, redefinition meant reuniting parts of her identity. Where her suburban life was "compartmentalized," with work life segregated from leisure and parenting, she now sees her life as holistic. She works from home as a freelance writer (writing on simple living) and Laura says this role blends seamlessly with other roles as homemaker, gardener/farmer, and parent. Time, or the way in which she spends her time, has become her identity touchstone.

This was the same for "Katherine" and for "Emilie." Katherine told me she was groomed to live fast. Growing up in a suburb of a major U.S. city, young Katherine felt pained over the excavation of local wild lands for strip malls. At age 18, she had her "aha" moment when attending a Rainbow Gathering, a countercultural collective emphasizing non-hierarchical community, non-violence, and sustainability initiatives.

"There were thousands of people living off the land using basic skills," she says, adding, "When I saw women making soymilk from scratch, it galvanized something in me." At age 42, Katherine has lived in a small cabin in the country for much of the time since. She grows most of her food and chops her own wood for heat.

Another informant, "Emilie," heads her own marketing firm in the LOHAS market, work she is passionate about. But when she found herself at a cross-roads in life, she found herself yearning for something more. She thought about opening a restaurant based on organic agriculture and the traditional, artisanal foods of Italy and France, but realized she lacked the necessary food-service experience. Instead, she joined her local Slow Food chapter.

"It was everything I wanted—preserving artisan traditions at the table, supporting local and organic farmers, enjoying good food and wine in community, and culture," Emilie says. Slow Food represented for her a way to desegregate her work and leisure interests, similar to what Laura experienced. And, like Katherine, Laura and Daria, Emilie found she was also reclaiming a nostalgic part of her childhood. Her European family, she says, "dressed for dinner!"

For Emilie the joy of dining mindfully and fashionably goes hand in hand. She derives deep pleasure from the community and fine food in Slow Food meetings and she is pleased that she is supporting local farmers and cooks. She noted that mainstream media often accuse Slow Food of being an "elitist dining club," but she says the charges make her "bristle" because the media overlook the fact that Slow Food represents a long-term commitment to organic agriculture, local economic development, Fair Trade, and social responsibility.

Reconnecting with social and natural worlds

Daria and I were speaking about the benefits of slow living for society. She believed there were far-reaching consequences to the cultural addiction to speed. "There's this idea that if we use convenience products, we save time and we'll be able to do good things with that time, but it is the opposite," Daria said. "There are very negative consequences for our health and the planet of using convenience items."

Each of my informants reiterated that it was important to infuse each moment with meaning, to "live" in the moment by being "mindful"—and that included considering how others might be affected by the ways in which we live. Emilie believes everyone should be mindful of their consumption and production and how market practices can harm people, cultures, and environments locally and globally.

Similarly, Laura says that after changing her lifestyle she realized how she'd become disconnected from the natural world, a relationship that was keenly important to her as a girl. As an adult, she said she had "spent most of [her] time dealing with human culture," but when she downsized, she found that she "stepped out of the rigidity of my former life—it was freeing. I was learning to experience a wider world."

Just as Laura believes her former life in the city actually stunted a genuine life experience, Katherine says when she made the earth instead of popular culture her orienting principle, she was freed from artificial cultural mandates that "dictate that we need this job or that house."

In *Slow Living*, Wendy Parkins and Geoffrey Craig say time is "increasingly becoming a key indicator of core values of people's lives, what they spend time on, not money, better indicate their values and priorities—their ethics of living" (2006: 39). Just so, Laura, Katherine, Emilie, and Daria see their lives as enriched by slow-living practices. They're "happier" by shifting their orientation to life and infusing it with more meaning.

Slow as consciousness in LOHAS

The principles of slow living are useful conduits through which LOHAS media articulate a multifaceted concept of consciousness. The practices are seen as capable of representing for consumers a remonstration of late capitalism while also posing as one solution for its reform. In this sense, "arts of the self" can stand "as ethical strategies that do not simply aim at self-expression or self-indulgence" but rather "cultivate the capacity for critical responsiveness to the world" (W. E. Connelly, in Parkins and Craig 2006: 14).

This is key to understanding LOHAS discourse. First, LOHAS is a sensual market encouraging consumers to seek out improved flavors, delightful tactile pleasures, enriching family experiences, more visually beautiful landscapes or bodies and more. Second, consumers and producers who do so following the auspices articulated as "LOHASian" are referred to in the marketplace as "conscious." They adhere to LOHAS memes: balance the mind, body, and spirit; correct the course of neo-liberalism that puts profit before the health of people and planet; and understand that modern science ignores other important aspects of true wellness.

This discourse takes on a distinctly spiritual tone; individuals are exhorted to recognize the holistic nature of social, environmental, and personal sustainability, to see that one leads to and from the other (see Emerich 2006). Living simply or slowly is consciousness, we are told in LOHAS, because it incorporates these three tiers of sustainability. And, "simplicity leads to spirituality; spirituality leads to simplicity," states an article in the LOHAS publication *Natural Solutions* magazine (Crawford 2005).

When I asked Emilie if she regarded her membership in Slow Food as having a spiritual aspect she replied, "Definitely!" She said, " ... there is something about the whole Slow Food thing that plays into that idea of healing." She said Slow Food linked up with her identity as a yogini, as a professional in the LOHAS marketplace, as a child of European parents, as a cook, as a wife, and as a mother. "This is my work," she said.

Katherine said slow living was spiritual because it honored the planet, the sun, and the moon. "These are our providers, what Christians think of as their sky God," she said. "They sustain us." When I asked her what spirituality meant to her, she replied "gratitude for life, witnessing our source with an open heart, and living in proper alignment with that. We need to change society because it's stupid and deeply wrong. It's what Christians call a sin," she said.

When I asked Daria the same question, she responded, "The core Christian belief is the golden rule and doing these [slow] things are a better way to treat our community." She said that it felt "funny to say this stuff out loud because I haven't thought about it," but she added, "I have a sense that these things [slow-living practices] are the right things to do; that they are all connected even if they might seem kind of minimal or unimportant."

A body-centered spirituality

In their article about the Slow Food Movement, Allison Hayes-Conroy and Deborah Martin write that perhaps certain "political ideas, beliefs and self-definitions require a bodily kind of resonance in order to activate various kinds of environmental and social activism" (Hayes-Conroy and Martin 2010: 271), and they refer to this resonance as "visceral processes of identification" (ibid.: 269).

Laura reiterated this notion. Modern life, she said, "cuts us off from our humanness." "When you put technology or anything between people and direct experience, then that person disengages and is diminished or unable to reach full potential," she said. Laura gave the example of growing her own food. "I have a relationship with my food. Without that I wouldn't really understand what it takes to get that food there. That probably gets to the spiritual because what is this life all about other than beauty, appreciation, love, truth, honesty and non-material things?" For her, the art of life lies within the consciousness she expresses through slow living.

For Emilie, knowing she is supporting local economies, which she says is a "grassroots movement from the heart," heightens the joy of good food. "We know we all need to do something—here is something we can do in our own neighborhood," she says.

All my informants experienced a genuine change in their lives when they adopted slow-living philosophies. Laura put it this way: "What has happened internally to me has exceeded my expectations. I didn't expect how profoundly that would change me as a person ... it is hard to come up with the words for it. Paring life down to the essentials is whittling away at ego. I'm getting to the core of who I am."

Conclusion

Living more slowly for my informants means carefully considering everything they do, buy, eat, and use. This has reinvigorated their everyday life not only as a site of meaningful pleasure but also as a site of empowerment and of social critique.

Along these lines, Parkins and Craig say the "extraordinary proliferation of lifestyle television" and even "recent political debates about the urgency to find 'work/family balance'" all point to the fact that the everyday is "no longer the background against which important public issues are considered, it is itself the issue" (2006: 8). In LOHAS discourse the site of the everyday has always been the core of that market focus. As *Experience Life* put it, "By making personal choices that respect the principles of sustainability, we can interrupt the toxic cycles of overconsumption and overexertion" (Gerasimo 2009: 53). The goal of LOHAS has always been to bring about broad-scale social and environmental change through the private labor of consumer and producer.

This labor isn't just altruistic or philanthropic but rather presented as self-healing, as a step toward rediscovering the right and natural way to live. Health and sustainability represent the axes of "truth"—a natural law linking our own survival to that of the survival of all. By mending the divisions and dualism among mind, body and spirit, the holistic self is able to go on to heal the world. The media's job is to articulate this holism, the non-dualism of physicality and spirit; of global and local; of self, society, and the natural world. For LOHAS discourse, the language around slow living has become a useful tool. The tenets serve a dual purpose: they anchor the Self by providing concrete links between act and outcome (save the environment by eating organically grown food or nurture local economies by buying locally made products, for example) and they critique the homogenization of advanced capitalism. For LOHAS, this supports and justifies niche markets in ways that also reduce human suffering, protect local cultures, and reduce environmental destruction.

By sanctifying and desanctifying various acts, beliefs, products, and organizations, the LOHAS media and market organizations serve as what Pierre Bourdieu referred to as "cultural intermediaries" in that they generate meanings about what constitutes a "lifestyle of health and sustainability" (Bourdieu 1984: 359). The texts attempt to neutralize competing narratives about consumption in the culture—namely, that consumerism is narcotizing and narcissistic, at best, and imperialistic and oppressive at worst. This is metonymic work, articulating some actions and objects (organic or locally produced foods, for example) as stand-ins, symbols, or representations of other beliefs, such as "consciousness," "wisdom," and "sustainability."

By consciously labeling some or all of their lifestyles as "slow" or "simple," my informants "cultivat[e] a subjectivity based on affirmation of values like attentiveness as daily pleasures," while also finding "opportunities for modest shifts in broader articulation of social organization and public culture" (Parkins and Craig 2006: 14). For Daria, Laura, Katherine, and Emilie this subjectivity only manifested when they erased boundaries they perceived in their lives among their roles as parents, citizens, spiritual beings, activists, and workers, for example.

If we regard ritual as "a mechanism for communication and social coordination" (Winkelman 2009: 462), then these individuals ritualize deeper values about how one should live using slow-living practices. Eating, spending money, making household goods, and gardening serve my informants as potential transformative acts that supply immediate pleasure through taste or feeling and feed a deeper source of meaning that they translate as healing of the self, society, and the natural world, a tying to the universal order and answering a universal spiritual question: how are we to live?

5 Burn-a-lujah!

DIY spiritualities, Reverend Billy, and Burning Man

Lee Gilmore

Sporting a bleached blond pompadour, a polyester leisure suit, and a clerical collar, Rev. Billy stood at the foot of an immense red and gold pyramid in the middle of a vast desert, its tiers, niches, and location simultaneously invoking Mayan temples, Indonesia's Borobuder, and Egyptian pyramids. Perched atop this "Great Temple" was a humanoid effigy—its skeletal wooden frame outlined in bright blue neon—destined to meet its end in a blazing sacrifice the following night. Arrayed behind Rev. Billy was a glittering choir adorned in bright gold satin robes, belting out powerful gospel tunes. Speaking in an impassioned tone—distinctly reminiscent of the great bible thumpers of classic American Evangelism—Rev. Billy cried out to the crowd gathered before him:

> We call out to the great "burn-a-lujah" God! We need your help tonight. We need to stop our shopping. We gotta help each other deal with our flagrant consumerism. Isn't that right? And we're gonna do it right now. Give us the power right now.[1]

The symbolic pastiche of this moment—pyramids, preachers, and neon idols—should surely pique the interest of any student of religion. What on earth is going on here?

Welcome to the Burning Man festival and the Church of Stop Shopping. Held in the middle of an utterly barren Nevada desert since 1990, Burning Man describes itself as a communal celebration of "radical self-expression" and "radical self-reliance," drawing tens of thousands annually.[2] Participants, colloquially dubbed "Burners," create artwork and ritual for this event that often creatively appropriate motifs from a vast global well—crosses, devils, labyrinths, buddhas, gods, goddesses, priests, corporate logos, and more—all are here patched together in a heterodox hodgepodge through which participants play with the stuff of popular culture. The festival's numerous ritual and ritualistic elements cast the event as a semi-religious cultural happening that its organizers hope will "produce positive spiritual change in the world," even while they explicitly deny that it constitutes a new religious movement as such.[3] To this end, many participants describe Burning Man as providing a sense of "spirituality," although they too would not characterize the event as "religious" and generally resist the institutions and doctrines of traditional "religions."

For its part, the Church of Stop Shopping—which changed its name to the Church of Life After Shopping in late 2008, reflecting the changing economic climate and consumer ethos following a global fiscal meltdown—is a New York-based performance group led by Bill Talen, a.k.a. Rev. Billy. He is not ordained, nor does he possess any formal background in ministry or liturgics; rather, his training is in the theater, and his "revival meetings" preach a progressive gospel of anti-consumerism. Performing in small independent theaters, parish halls, college classrooms, parking lots, street corners, and (on occasion) the Burning Man festival, Billy and his Church strive to defend small-scale economies and promote environmental sustainability. Urging individuals and communities to resist corporate homogeneity in favor of local diversity and cultural independence by transforming their purchasing habits, Rev. Billy also urges people to wake up to what he sees as a more authentic life by "putting the odd back into God," invoking "the God that is not a product," and calling for "change-a-lujah," "peace-a-lujah," and (when at Burning Man) "burn-a-lujah."

Both Burning Man and Rev. Billy make for fascinating case studies of what I term "DIY (do-it-yourself) spirituality," in which concepts and symbols originating within diverse cultural and religious traditions are playfully combined in order to forge individualistic and idiosyncratic yet sincere quests for meaning and spirituality. At Burning Man, it can seem as though the random flotsam of human history and global cultures has washed up in the desert only to wash back out at the festival's end, often changing participants' sense of themselves and their place in the world. In the case of the Church of Life After Shopping, its appropriated "evangelical revival" ritual mode—in combination with an intense desire to connect with and create change within communities—deliberately blurs the lines between irony and spirituality, thereby destabilizing normative assumptions about religious structures, religious behaviors, and religious experience.

Creative bricolage is nothing new in the history of religions, and indeed can be said to have long played key roles in religious change through what has commonly been called "syncretism." While traditionalists may see such developments rather unfavorably, it is indisputable that whenever diverse cultures and religions come into contact they inevitably adopt ideas, symbols, and performative modes from one another. A difference here is that DIY spiritual frameworks are not constructed on cultural scales, but rather are expressions of individual agency as people cobble together ad hoc spiritualities based on a patchwork of global religions. Yet DIY spiritualities are neither constructed nor performed in solipsistic or a-cultural bubbles. Rather, signs, beliefs, and identities are extracted from resources made available and visible through popular culture. Furthermore, as demonstrated by the cases of Rev. Billy and Burning Man, people imaginatively utilize this material within communities that are intimately and actively connected to one another, drawing upon and reinforcing longstanding sub-cultural networks. Yet even while freely borrowing from the "symbolic inventories" of mass media and popular culture, in the cases of both the community of Burning Man and the activism of Rev. Billy, the hegemonic and homogenizing elements of corporate-controlled and consumerist-oriented cultures are critiqued, resisted, and parodied, as individuals and communities seek alternate ways in which to function within the capitalist mechanisms and religious options of late modern society.[4]

DIY spiritualities have tended to be criticized as inherently shallow, amoral, and disconnected "cafeteria religions." I wish to sidestep such debates for the time being and instead examine the "everyday religious life" of DIY spiritualities on their own terms, as illustrated in these examples. Where some have expressed concern that individualistic spiritualities portend an increasingly superficial and troubled religious future, I suggest that DIY spiritualities need not result in socially detached or theologically degenerate individualisms, but are instead often grounded within strongly tied, ethically reflexive, and sophisticated communities, constituting a particularly late modern response to perceived ills inhabiting both consumer culture and traditional religious options.

Both Burning Man and Rev. Billy's Church provide apt demonstrations of the extent to which advocates of DIY spiritualities may be genuinely connected to one another in substantial communities with emergent ritual traditions that can motivate participants to make real and radical changes in their own lives, as well as to take actions towards building a more just and sustainable world. In illustrating these cultural systems in operation, this essay considers the character of Rev. Billy and the community of Burning Man, highlighting their ritual and spiritual overtones, their mutual resistance to consumer culture, and their social activism.

Meet Rev. Billy

Reverend Billy was born in the wake of then-Mayor Giuliani's controversial redevelopment of New York City during the late 1990s. Inspired in part by his friendship with the Rev. Sidney Lanier, an Episcopal priest with strong ties to the New York theater community, as well as by the preachers, doomsayers, and other oddballs that were being slowly swept out of Manhattan, Rev. Billy first took to the streets in protest at the newly opened Disney Store on Times Square. Calling out the Disney corporation as a purveyor of goods produced by exploitative sweatshop labor, as emblematic of encroaching gentrification, and also as a colonizer of the American public imagination, he began to preach his own unique gospel on the dangers of consumerism and multinational corporations, raising aloft a large Mickey Mouse doll stapled to a makeshift cross, which he would humorously yet pointedly proclaim to be "the anti-Christ."

With the help of his wife Savitri Durkee—who serves as the group's director and producer—Billy's mission expanded by the early 2000s from a one-man street performance into a full fledged "Church," featuring over two dozen members of the "Stop Shopping Gospel Choir" and the "Not Buying It Band." Seeking to stretch artistically beyond one-dimensional satire, Talen discovered that his work was becoming both serious and transformative in ways that he had not foreseen, as the character of Rev. Billy began to enlist some of the mythic and symbolic power inherent in the ritual genre to become something much more profound.

My first encounter with Billy was at Burning Man in 2003, as briefly described above. At one point, Rev. Billy revisited the still painful collective memory of September 11 and spoke of the hypocrisy of the U.S. administration's response to this tragedy, forcefully proclaiming:

> George Bush tried to persuade us that *beyond* was revenge. And now he's killed three or four times as many people as died on September 11th. He's killed many more people. And in so doing, he said that he was representing the people who died there and their relatives. That's a lie. We know what the people in the towers said in last few seconds of their lives, on the phones and in email … They said, "I love you. I love our children. Tell them I loved our life together. And we will see each other again." There's a kind of *beyond* going on here. Beyond the World Trade Towers! Beyond the hatred. Let's go *beyond*. We're looking to go tonight, children. Are you with me? Burn-a-lujah![5]

That moment was poignant and deeply moving, and I began to sense that there was more going on here than the superficial caricature I had anticipated. As I observed this spirit also apparently moving through the crowd around me, I began to understand that Rev. Billy's mock-preacher was *for real*.

Raised in a Dutch Calvinist tradition, Talen is at times suspicious of mainline religious institutions, even in cases where their progressive politics may be aligned. Likewise, I have spoken with Christians of varying political and theological orientations about Billy and some have expressed their dislike and distrust of his work, taking offense at his sarcastic appropriation of the preacher's collar. But as Rev. Billy's public profile has grown, other Christians have come to celebrate his work and see its parallels to their own traditions. For example, Walter Brueggemann wrote in the progressive Christian magazine *Sojourners*:

> Rev. Billy is a faithful prophetic figure who stands in direct continuity with ancient prophets in Israel and in continuity with the great prophetic figures of U.S. history who have incessantly called our society back to its core human passions of justice and compassion.
>
> (Brueggemann 2007)

When I interviewed Talen in late 2003, I asked him how he understood the spiritual resonance of his work. He replied:

> Because the word "spiritual" is bankrupt, because of religion, because the word "religious" is bankrupt, because of churches, we tend to not return to

those words ... Dead language makes a dead experience. It's better in a
Rev. Billy performance for us to walk to the edge of the abyss, beyond
which is silence, and to stand there and say, "Alright, we're gonna jump."
And that's the point in the sermon where I start to stutter and I'll say,
"Somebody give me an amen, help me, help me," and somebody will say,
"We're with ya, we're with ya." And I haven't said anything, but we've
walked to a place together.[6]

The Church's anti-consumer ethos is framed—with Billy's usual combination of
irony and sincerity—as a unique spiritual practice of sorts: "Buddhists sit. Sufis
twirl. We here at the Church of Stop Shopping have our own practice. We back
away." As the choir sings:

Mother, Father, that Godly Mystery
Will you come here and teach me?
When the lowest prices hit me
Walmart will it always reach me?
Mother and Father, that Godly mystery
Back away from the Walmart, back away
Back away from "big box," back away
It's a union busting sweat zone
Our neighborhood's our home
Back away, back away, back up and pray.[7]

In mobilizing a widely held contempt for Walmart's exploitive corporate policies this rhetoric positions the relatively simple activism of shopping elsewhere
as a heartfelt prayer.

In late 2007, just before the annual Christmas spending orgy, the Church
released a film entitled *What Would Jesus Buy?* documenting a 2005 cross-
country bus tour from New York to Disneyland.[8] Obviously playing off the
popular Christian aphorism "What would Jesus do?" the film sought to interrupt popular media symbols and producers—particularly Disney, Walmart, and
other ubiquitous corporate retailers—by illustrating the realities of sweatshop
labor and educating consumers about the hidden consequences of their shopping, thereby transforming these icons from signs of indulgence to sites of
oppression. In 2009 Billy's campaign became explicitly political when he ran for
mayor of New York City as the candidate of the Green Party. In so doing, he
and his supporters utilized email, Facebook, and Twitter to send out frequent
campaign updates and invitations to events such as petition drives, block parties, and weekly Sunday "BBQ Revivals" in a park in the Bronx. Programs
featuring topical discussions and music were streamed online at voterevbilly.
org, as well as via a low-power FM radio station. These various tools served
not only as means of communication, but also as means of serving larger goals
to resist corporate monocultures, support diverse neighborhoods, and create
genuine human ties and communities.

Meet Burning Man

Like Rev. Billy, Burning Man is an apt illustration of how DIY spiritualities playfully converge and transform global symbol systems in seeking alternatives to corporate hegemony and cultural homogeny. Rev. Billy and his Church first made their way to Burning Man in 2003 at the behest of the festival's organizers, who invited them to perform there in recognition of a shared ethos. By this time, Burning Man had grown considerably from its humble origins as an impromptu gathering among a handful of friends on a San Francisco beach in 1986 into an internationally renowned event drawing nearly 50,000 by 2008. The event takes place in an otherwise obscure corner of Nevada called the Black Rock Desert— where the principal feature is an absolutely flat and desolate plane of crackled clay called the *playa*—and situated every year at the center of the event site is the Burning Man itself. Fondly known to participants as "the Man," it is a towering 40-foot wooden sculpture lit with multicolored shafts of neon, standing even taller atop sizeable and variously designed pedestals, such as 2003's "Great Temple." Ostensibly genderless and void of any specifically stated meaning, the effigy is ultimately filled with explosives designed to detonate in a carefully orchestrated sequence as the figure is consumed in flames at the festival's climax, a rite that participants have come to call simply "the Burn."

An elaborate civic infrastructure is built, destroyed, and rebuilt each year by thousands of volunteers and organized by two dozen year-round staff members. These organizers eventually articulated a set of key "principles" intended to reflect the community's ethos, centered around ideals of participation, decommodfication, immediacy, communal effort, and gift economies, among others that are likewise shared by Rev. Billy's community.[9]

Participants also produce hundreds of often monumentally scaled artworks for the event, many of which are fated to be consumed by fire. Among the most prominent of these are a series of *Temples* (distinct from the "Great Temple" that served as a base for the Man in 2003 and that would share that moniker only once), which became a beloved annual feature of the festival beginning in 2000. Initially designed by artist David Best—who after a few years turned responsibility for the Temples over to other members of the Burning Man community—the various incarnations of the Temple aptly illustrate the festival's characteristic hybridity. Amalgamating iconography and architectural styles originating in numerous cultures, traces of Southeast Asian temples, Russian Orthodox churches, Islamic mosques, and Shinto shrines can all be observed taking shape in these structures, mixing intricate filigree with towering, onion-shaped domes, repetitive mosaic patterns, and gothic spires. Each Temple serves as a chapel in which participants are invited to honor the dead by inscribing names and memories upon the walls and by leaving behind photos and assorted mementoes. Visitors to these structures discover intensely introspective spaces devoted to remembrance and forgiveness, and the sense of grieving is often palpable.[10] Ultimately, on the final night of the festival, each annual Temple is set aflame. The general tenor of participants' celebration tends to be markedly low key, standing in stark contrast to the ebullient and boisterous displays of the Burn, which is traditionally held the previous night. Once the Temple catches fire the several thousand in attendance fall absolutely silent and the only sound is that of the crackling flame.

The Temples are but one of the more obvious sites that Burners describe as spiritual and transformative. While most participants would probably agree that the event can "be whatever you want it to be," Burning Man is for many a venue in which to express and ritualize individualized, eclectic, and anti-institutional DIY spiritualities. My research on this festival—entailing a decade of partici-pant observation, dozens of interviews, and an online survey—found that almost half of those asked variously described their experiences of Burning Man as "spiritual," while nearly three-quarters affirmed an experience of significant life or perspective change through the event, and two-thirds reported that these experiences were tied to a sense of "community" (see Gilmore 2010). The rigors of surviving in the stark and harsh desert environment also contribute drama-tically to a sense of catharsis and transformation. In its seemingly endless and otherworldly terrain, the playa stirs up themes of hardship, sacrifice, mystery, and boundlessness that are deeply ingrained in the Western cultural imagination, and participants often speak of being "on the playa" in a way that references this sense of environmental and cognitive "otherness," helping to set the stage for transformative experiences and a potent sense of the sacred.[11]

Rev. Billy meets Burning Man

In 2005, Rev. Billy and a few choir members returned to Burning Man, where they ended up leading an impromptu memorial service at the Temple for the victims of Hurricane Katrina, which had devastated the Gulf Coast just days before. Approaching the Temple to the strains of New Orleans' famous anthem "When the Saints Come Marching In," Billy called for contributions to huma-nitarian relief funds that were being collected by festival organizers. Addressing the crowd, Billy spoke movingly of life, death, and ritual:

> Throughout the week I know many of you—I know I have—brought to the Temple our artifacts, our pictures, our fragments of conversation, our shared dreams, with people that passed this year, and I know that to simply walk through this dusty red Temple is to feel the accumulated power of the conversation, the prayer, that we're sharing with our loved ones over the week. And the Temple has the pictures and notes—our memories of our loved ones. And we will ask the earth and the sky to take those memories up and out. And we know that we will join those mem-ories when we become ashes and smoke ourselves.[12]

In the light of the death and destruction left in the wake of Katrina, the Temple seemed a fitting place for those attending Burning Man that year to gather and express their concern and grief.

At the conclusion of that year's Burning Man event, several participants traveled immediately to the Gulf Coast, where they quickly established an ad hoc relief effort. Setting up tents and shelters still dusty from the desert, over the course of eight months more than 200 volunteers distributed food, water, and other critical supplies, demolished damaged buildings, hauled away debris, rebuilt a Vietnamese Buddhist Temple in Biloxi, Mississippi, and a home in Pearlington, Mississippi.[13] Initially dubbed the "Temple to Temple" project, as several members of the Temple construction crew were among the first to be involved, the momentum generated by these efforts would be maintained with support from Burning Man's organizers to spearhead a variety of volunteer projects—including environmental restoration, community support, and disaster response, under the auspices of a new affiliated organization called "Burners without Borders."[14]

In this instance, the raw human tragedy and grief wrought by Katrina, the common human urge to alleviate suffering, the unique ritual, environmental, and social context of Burning Man, along with Rev. Billy's message of compassion and social justice, all converged to create an impetus to action that would have far-reaching consequences. Spurred not only by Rev. Billy's ritual at the Temple, but even more by the ritual of the larger Burning Man event, the spirit of transformation experienced by many Burning Man participants in this case expressed itself as a desire to create meaningful change in service of a much wider community.

Conclusions

Reverend Billy and Burning Man are what David Chidester would call "authentic fakes." In examining the ways in which pop-culture phenomena like baseball or rock and roll are analogous to religion through their rhetoric, symbolism, and rituals, Chidester argues that even these fake "religions" are doing *real* religious work if they are "engaged in negotiating what it is to be human" (Chidester 2005: 18). Billy is not a "real" preacher. But although his characterization is satirical, his message is genuine. With a ritual mode that aptly captures the essence of the "fire and brimstone" evangelical tradition, Rev. Billy draws upon the popular American Protestant tradition of itinerant, extra-ecclesiastical ministry, while simultaneously resisting and realigning that symbolic heritage with a performative style that rises above simple parody. The Church of Life After Shopping invites its congregations to experience their efforts as an ironic brand of DIY spirituality without explicitly labeling its intentions as such. In so doing, Rev. Billy retains his appeal to a wide audience, enabling people to have uplifting and inspiring experiences, and mobilizing them to embrace and act on his ethos without requiring adherence to a particular theology or institution.

Furthermore, the ritually complex field of Burning Man is also not a "real religion," yet it showcases a brand of DIY spirituality that challenges convenient categories. People go to Burning Man to express their truest senses of self and to feel connected to something larger than that self. In so doing, they create, perform, ritualize, and play with this sense—freely pillaging from a global treasure trove of cultural and religious symbols as they do. In inviting people to play with the stuff of diverse cultures, reshaping them to one's likings or whims, both Burning Man and Rev. Billy serve to render the constructedness of cultures transparent, highlighting their native hybridity, adaptability, and plasticity. Rather than pointing towards empty, isolated, and antisocial "cafeteria religions," these DIY spiritualities cultivate their own routes toward the participatory and the collective through ritual—which can motivate people not only to create change in their own lives but also to share their ideals in the service of others.

Rather than pointing to either "spirituality" or "religion" as essentially distinct categories or binary opposites, as they are often treated in popular discourse, on closer examination Burning Man and Rev. Billy subvert these concepts, offering a window onto the dialectic between the two. Religious institutions have historically long been subject to innumerable critiques stemming from desires for authenticity and transformation, in turn spawning new institutional (and anti-institutional) structures. Thus, contemporary tensions between "organized religion" and "DIY spirituality" may be productively framed in terms of ongoing and dialogic exchanges between the individual and the collective, inspiration and institution, spontaneity and liturgy, prophecy and tradition. In this regard, the experiences held by participants in either the Burning Man festival or a Rev. Billy performance to be sacred or transformational are no less—and, from their perspective, perhaps even more—authentic than many of the basic encounters that have long been taken to constitute "religion." Ultimately, for those who embrace DIY spiritualities, what matters more than academic quibbles about what properly constitutes spirituality, religion, or authenticity are individuals' own immediate and idiosyncratic experiences, their cathartic and visceral rites, their resistance to corporate monoculture, their creative cultural convergence and playful hybridization of culture, their personal spiritual agency, and the community formed and challenges met and overcome in the crucible of the desert.

Notes

1 Performance of Rev. Billy and the Stop Shopping Gospel Choir, August 29, 2003.
2 See http://www.burningman.com/whatisburningman/about_burningman/principles.html (accessed June 29, 2009).
3 See http://www.burningman.com/whatisburningman/about_burningman/mission.html (accessed August 5, 2009).
4 For more on "symbolic inventories," see Hoover (2006).
5 Performance of Rev. Billy and the Stop Shopping Gospel Choir, August 29, 2003.
6 Interview with Bill Talen, October 16, 2003.
7 "Back Away," composed by Bill Talen and William Morris. Available at: http://www.revbilly.com/work/music/songs/back-away (accessed July 29, 2009).
8 Directed by Rob Van Alkemade and produced by Morgan Spurlock.
9 See http://www.burningman.com/whatisburningman/about_burningman/principles.html (accessed June 29, 2009).

10 For more on the Temples, see Pike (2005: 198).
11 For more on the geography of the Black Rock Desert, see Goin and Starrs (2005).
12 Performance of Rev. Billy and the Stop Shopping Gospel Choir, Rev. Billy, September 4, 2005.
13 See http://www.burningman.com/blackrockcity_yearround/misc/katrina_thumper.html (accessed January 5, 2009).
14 See http://www.burnerswithoutborders.org (accessed June 20, 2007).

6 Spirituality and the re-branding of religion

Jeremy Carrette and Richard King

God is dead but has been resurrected as "Capital."

From feng shui to holistic medicine, from aromatherapy candles to yoga weekends, from Christian mystics to New Age gurus, spirituality is "big business." There has been an explosion of interest and popular literature on mind, body and spirit and "personal development." We now see the introduction of modes of "spirituality" into educational curricula, bereavement and addiction counseling, psychotherapy, and nursing. Spirituality as a cultural trope has also been appropriated by corporate bodies and management consultants to promote efficiency, extend markets, and maintain a leading edge in a fast moving information economy. For many people, spirituality has replaced religion as old allegiances and social identities are transformed by modernity. However, in a context of individualism and erosion of traditional community allegiances, "spirituality" has become a new cultural addiction and a claimed panacea for the angst of modern living. Spirituality is celebrated by those who are disillusioned by traditional institutional religions and seen as a force for wholeness, healing, and inner transformation. In this sense spirituality is taken to denote the positive aspects of the ancient religious traditions, unencumbered by the "dead hand" of the church, and yet something which provides a liberation and solace in an otherwise meaningless world. But is this emergence of the idea of "spirituality" all that it seems? Is something more complex and suspicious at work in the glorification of the spiritual?

To contest some of the dominant readings of "spirituality" within western societies and their silencing of traditions will require some examination of how these discourses operate in the contemporary socio-economic world. Our argument emerges from a frustration with the lack of clarity and critical discussion of the concept of "spirituality," a notion that has become pervasive in contemporary society in the consciousness of its advocates and its detractors. The concept therefore represents on the one hand all that is banal and vague about "New Age" religiosity, whilst on the other signifying a transcendent quality, enhancing life and distilling all that is positive from the "ageing and outdated" casks of traditional religious institutions.

Our argument attempts to uncover what amounts to a silent takeover of "the religious" by contemporary capitalist ideologies by means of the increasingly popular discourse of "spirituality." We seek to challenge the contemporary use of this concept as a means of reflecting and supporting social and economic policies geared towards the neoliberal ideals of privatization and corporatization, applied increasingly to all spheres of human life.

Questioning modern spirituality

What is neoliberalism and what exactly does it have to do with spirituality?

> Neoliberalism is the defining political economic paradigm of our time—it refers to the policies and processes whereby a relative handful of private interests are permitted to control as much as possible of social life in order to maximize their personal profit. Associated initially with Reagan and Thatcher, neoliberalism has for the past two decades been the dominant global political economic trend adopted by political parties of the center, much of the traditional left, and the right. These parties and the policies they enact represent the immediate interests of extremely wealthy investors and less than one thousand large corporations.
>
> (McChesney 1999: 8)

For many, spirituality would seem to have little to do with questions of economics and politics. The roots of this modern attitude go back to eighteenth century European thought (the Enlightenment), where the underlying principles of liberalism were born. In challenging the traditional social, moral, and philosophical authority of the Church, European intellectuals sought to establish a framework for society and politics that avoided the religious conflicts of previous centuries. The solution, outlined most notably by philosophers such as John Locke, was to relegate the religious to the private sphere of life—to clearly demarcate it from the public realms of politics, science, and philosophy.

The Enlightenment is also a period characterized by attempts to define the specificity of these different aspects of cultural life. This led to an intellectual *obsession* with defining the precise characteristics of religion (a preoccupation that continues to this day). This is a misleading enterprise because it takes conceptual distinctions with a specific history of their own and treats them as if they are features of the world rather than of a culturally specific way of understanding it. It is clear, for instance, that it makes little sense to draw a sharp distinction between the secular (politics, economics, science, philosophy) and the religious dimensions of human life in any other culture than those conditioned by modern liberalism and the European Enlightenment philosophies of the eighteenth century. We should also make our position on this question clear from the start: *there is no essence or definitive meaning to terms like spirituality or religion.* The attraction of defining an essence is that it clearly demarcates a field for the purposes of analysis. Such a move, however, leaves the impression that spirituality is somehow *really* divorced from other spheres of human life such as economics, culture, and politics. The desire to attribute a universal essence to the meaning of spirituality also ignores the historical and cultural traces and differences in the uses of the term. Searching for an over-arching definition of "spirituality" only ends up missing the specific historical location of each use of the term. There is no view from nowhere—no Archimedean point outside of history—from which one could determine a fixed and universal meaning for the term "spirituality."

This book seeks to shift debate about religion and spirituality away from a misleading emphasis upon truth and authenticity ("What counts as real spirituality?") towards a consideration of the socio-political consequences of such claims ("Who benefits from particular constructions of 'spirituality'?"). Our approach is to pay attention, following William James, to the "fruits not the roots" of contemporary uses of the term. What are the socio-political *effects* of the decision to classify specific practices or philosophies as "spiritual" and who benefits from such constructions? However, where we differ from James—a primary exponent of a psychological definition of religious experience—is in wishing to displace the individualization of the spiritual, since it is precisely this which allowed consumerist and capitalist spiritualities to emerge in the late twentieth century.

There are two features of this relatively new phenomenon that we seek to contest. First, we wish to challenge constructions of spirituality that promote the subsuming of the ethical and the religious in terms of an over-riding economic agenda. We do not do this out of some attempt to privilege some pure realm known as "the religious" or "the spiritual" and separate it from apparently "worldly" concerns. In our view there is no distinct realm known as "the religious" that exists in isolation from the social, political, and economic world (King 1999; Carrette 2000). This is not to reduce "the religious" out of existence but to refuse to isolate it from those other dimensions of human life (except for the purposes of analysis). There may be no pure *homo religiosus* but there is also no *homo oeconomicus*, despite the increasing dominance of the economic as an apparent indicator of fundamental human motivation and action.

Those traditions classified as "religions" in the modern consciousness have always been bound up with economics and modes of exchange. However, a fundamental ground shift has taken place in American and British culture in the last twenty years, related to the deregulation of the markets by Ronald Reagan and Margaret Thatcher in the 1980s, and this is changing the relationship of cultural forms to the market. With the development of organizations like the World Trade Organization (WTO) and the emergence of neoliberalism as the dominant economic ideology of our time, this cultural and political shift has already gone global. With the emergence of *capitalist spirituality* we are seeing an attempted takeover of the cultural space traditionally inhabited by "the religions" by a specific economic agenda. Entering public institutions that provide education, health-care, and professional expertise within society as a whole, the ideologies of consumerism and business enterprise are now infiltrating more and more aspects of our lives. The result of this shift has been an erasure of the wider social and ethical concerns associated with religious traditions and communities, and the subordination of "the religious" and the ethical to the realm of economics, which is now rapidly replacing science (just as science replaced theology in a previous era), as the dominant mode of authoritative discourse within society.

This represents the second feature of dominant conceptions of spirituality that we wish to challenge, and this is their essentially accommodationist orientation. In a sense, the most troubling aspect of many modern spiritualities is precisely that they are not troubling enough. They promote accommodation to the social, economic, and political mores of the day and provide little in terms of a challenge to the status quo or to a lifestyle of self-interest and ubiquitous consumption.

One response to the emergence of capitalist spirituality might be to argue that this is not "true" or real spirituality. Such a move would imply that there is something easily identifiable as "spiritual" in the world that would correspond to the real or proper usage of the term. In any case, whose construction of the term are we to take as the normative standard by which all others are to be judged? Rather, we wish to challenge the individualist and corporatist *monopoly* of the term "spirituality" and the cultural space that this demarcates at the beginning of the twenty-first century for the promotion of the values of consumerism and corporate capitalism. We do this, not because we wish to appeal to some kind of ancient "authentic" or "true" spirituality to which they do not conform (as if that or any definition could encompass the historical phenomena captured by the diverse uses of the term "spirituality"), but rather to open up a contested space that will allow alternative, more socially engaged, constructions of the term to express themselves.

What is being sold to us as radical, trendy, and transformative spirituality in fact produces little in the way of a significant change in one's lifestyle or fundamental behavior patterns (with the possible exception of motivating the individual to be more efficient and productive at work). By "cornering the market" on spirituality, such trends actually limit the socially transformative dimensions of the religious perspectives that they draw upon by locating "the spiritual" firmly within a privatized and conformist space. Sadly, not only have the primary exponents of "the spiritual" generally failed to address this issue, but academic commentators upon these new forms of spirituality, even when noticing such trends, have generally preferred the language of so-called "neutral description" rather than that of cultural critique. Most have emphasized the 1960s and 1970s context, and ignored the spread of market ideology within culture in the 1980s and 1990s. What we saw emerge in the last few decades of the twentieth century was a form of "New Age Capitalism" (Lau 2000) and it offers a fundamental challenge to our global cultural heritage that it is in the process of colonizing. [...]

The two phases in the privatization of religion

It is often recognized that, since the Enlightenment, "religion" has been subjected to an erosion of its social authority with the rise of scientific rationalism,

humanism, and modern, liberal democratic models of the nation-state (a process often called secularization). In modern western societies, to varying
degrees, this has usually manifested itself as the relegation of "the religious" to
the private sphere. What has not been sufficiently appreciated by contemporary
social theorists, however, is that the later stages of this process have become
intimately intertwined with the global spread of corporate Capitalism. We can
describe both of these trends as the privatization of religion, but in two distinct
senses. In the first instance, the European Enlightenment led to an increased
tendency to exclude religious discourse from the public domain of politics,
economics, and science. In the main this was achieved by representing "the
religious" primarily in terms of individual choice, beliefs, and private states of
mind. For philosophers such as John Locke and Immanuel Kant, it was
important to demarcate the precise domain in which religion should be located,
in order to preserve the secular space of liberal political governance from the
conflicts, intolerance, and violence arising from the conflict between competing
religious ideologies and groups within European societies. Religion in this context becomes a matter of personal assent to a set of beliefs, a matter of the
private state of mind or personal orientation of the individual citizen in the
terms set out for it by modern (i.e. Enlightenment-inspired) liberalism. A consequence of this approach is that, in different ways and variegated forms, religion has been formally separated from the business of statecraft in
contemporary Northern European societies (though with different inflections
and degrees of smoothness). We can call this process the *individualization* of
religion.

This cultural shift has allowed a much greater degree of individual experimentation and freedom to explore religious alternatives and has been crucial in
the development, for instance, of the melting pot of religions and spiritualities
that is often called "the New Age." The individualization of religious sensibilities,
however, has caused some to worry about the erosion of a sense of community
and compassion for others in modern societies. These concerns are picked up by
leading religious figures, such as the current Archbishop of Canterbury Rowan
Williams, who argued in his 2002 Richard Dimbleby lecture that

> the future of modern liberal democracies depends heavily on those per-
> spectives that are offered by religious belief. In the pre-modern period,
> religion sanctioned the social order; in the modern period it was a potential
> rival to be pushed to the edges, a natural reaction. But are we at the point
> where as the "public sphere" becomes more value-free, the very survival of
> the idea of public sphere, a realm of political argument about vision and edu-
> cation, is going to demand that we take religion a good deal more seriously.
>   (Rowan Williams, Richard Dimbleby Lecture, December 19, 2002)

However, there are problems with Williams's understanding of "religion." It is
already the case that the "religious" is seeping into the public domain of
modern secular societies. First, this is occurring in the commodification of

religion as spirituality—a trend that this book seeks to address. Second, it has entered the twenty-first century public discourse of western nations in a violent way through the appropriation of "Islam" by certain radical groups from the Middle East and South Asia. Moreover, Williams does not express an awareness of the problems in deciding what exactly counts as a "religion." The secular space of modernity, that which is deemed to exclude the religious, is itself a product of a particular "religious" history (that of European Christianity) and the Enlightenment reaction to it. It is also far from clear that one can map the "secular–religious" division onto non-western cultures without severe distortion occurring (King 1999). Nevertheless, we agree with Williams in his view that the traditional perspectives and ethical orientations of the "religious traditions" are essential for the very preservation of the values of tolerance and respect that secularism and liberalism sought to preserve in the initial attempt to exclude the religious from the public domain.

In the late twentieth century, however, there was a second form of privatization that took place. It partially built upon the previous process, but also has important discontinuities with it. It can be characterized as a wholesale *commodification* of religion, that is, the selling off of religious buildings, ideas, and claims to authenticity in service to individual/corporate profit and the promotion of a particular worldview and mode of life, namely corporate capitalism. Let us imagine that "religion" in all its forms is a company that is facing a takeover bid from a larger company known as Corporate Capitalism. In its attempt to "downsize" its ailing competitor, Corporate Capitalism strips the assets of "religion" by plundering its material and cultural resources, which are then re-packaged, re-branded, and then sold in the marketplace of ideas. This re-selling exploits the historical respect and "aura of authenticity" of the religious traditions (what in business terms is often called "the goodwill" of the company) whilst at the same time separating itself from any negative connotations associated with the religious in a modern secular context (re-branding). This is precisely the burden of the concept of spirituality in such contexts, allowing a simultaneous nod towards and separation from "the religious." The corporate machine or the market does not seek to validate or reinscribe the tradition but rather utilizes its cultural cachet for its own purposes and profit.

Like the selling of public utilities and services in our modern neoliberal economies, such as gas, electricity, water, health-care, and transport systems to private companies, the material and cultural "assets" of the various religious traditions are being plundered, "downsized," and sold off as commodities. "Religion" is facing a "takeover bid" from the business world, and without the protection of the state, which increasingly recedes from social welfare and public service initiatives in a neoliberal context. Today in most British cities you will find old church buildings that have been sold off to become business offices, supermarkets, public houses, nightclubs, and private apartments. However, it is not primarily the sale of buildings that we are concerned with here, but rather the exploitation of the "cultural capital" of the religious for the purposes of consumption and corporate gain. From the branding of perfumes using ancient Asian concepts and the idea of the spiritual ("Samsara" perfume, "Zen" deodorant, "Spiritual" body-spray) to clothe the product in an aura of mystical authenticity, to the promotion of management courses offering "spiritual techniques" for the enhancement of one's work productivity and corporate business efficiency, the sanitized religiosity of "the spiritual" sells. However, this use of spirituality involves a number of complex levels of engagement. Whilst appearing to endorse the values of the ancient traditions that it is alluding to, such moves represent little more than a silent takeover of religion. Marketing "the spiritual" allows companies and their consumers to pay lip-service to the "exotic," rich, and historically significant religions of the world at the same time as distancing themselves from any engagement with the worldviews and forms of life that they represent. Religion is re-branded as "spirituality" in order to support the ideology of capitalism.

A typology of spiritualities in relation to capitalism

When trying to understand the nature of what we are calling capitalist spirituality, it is necessary to make a number of distinctions in order to appreciate the various relations that exist between contemporary forms of spirituality and capitalism. Although we are not claiming that spirituality should (or indeed could) be separated from economic questions, we do believe that *it should not be fundamentally shaped* by an economic ideology. We wish to challenge the way in which the concept of spirituality is being utilized to "smooth out" resistance to the growing power of corporate capitalism and consumerism as the defining ideology of our time. We do this not out of some misguided belief that traditional religious institutions and systems have been free from authoritarian and oppressive strictures of their own, but rather out of a concern that cultural diversity is being eroded by the incessant march of a single worldview—an economically driven globalization—driven by a triumphalist and corporate-oriented form of capitalism.

The spectrum of spirituality–capitalism relations: the different types

For the purposes of our analysis, one can make a distinction between four degrees of relative accommodation to the ideology of capitalism.

Revolutionary or anti-capitalist spiritualities

Such movements reject the capitalist ideology of neoliberalism (life determined by market forces alone) and the pursuit of profit as a goal that can be combined with a recognition of a spiritual, religious or ethical dimension to life. Many of these groups have emerged from within specific religious traditions. They ground their spiritual approaches in a "this-worldly" commitment to social justice and appeal to a wide range of ancient traditions and movements such as the social critiques of the early Israelite prophets, the Christian Social Gospel movement, Islamic notions of a just economy and universal brotherhood, Buddhist notions of enlightened re-engagement with the world for the sake of alleviating the suffering of others, the radical egalitarian strands of bhakti and Sufi movements in India, etc. Examples of movements and trends that build upon such historical precedents include the various philosophies and theologies of liberation amongst subaltern groups across the "two-thirds world," socially engaged Buddhism, the deep ecology movement, etc.

Business ethics/reformist spiritualities

Such movements accept the pursuit of profit as a legitimate goal and therefore do not reject the capitalist system in its entirety, but believe in restraining the market in terms of fundamental ethical principles deriving from a particular religious or spiritual perspective on life. There is a long tradition of religious reform of business activities, as found, for instance, in the various religious co-operative movements and the Quaker tradition of ethically oriented business enterprises, as put forward by such authors as Georgeanne Lamont in *The Spirited Business* (2002). These forms of spirituality, like Tom Beaudoin's Catholic social ethics and his idea of "economic spirituality" in his work *Consuming Faith* (2003), seek to find ways of synthesizing traditional "religious" understanding with the values of business and consumer culture. Such approaches accept, with some ethical modification, the *status quo* of the market and business world, and do not seek to question the underlying basis of its ideology. The emphasis is upon the integration of ethical values into the dominant culture, rather than a radical exploration of how the ethical demands of the religious tradition might require a substantial re-evaluation of the economic system. The ideology of neoliberalism is never placed under radical scrutiny in these forms of spirituality, which therefore, in many respects, provide indirect support for a consumerist culture. Such forms, therefore, can easily venture towards and hold aspects of both consumerist and capitalist spirituality, as seen in Tom Beaudoin's work *Consuming Faith*:

> There is an authentic spiritual impulse at the heart of our branding economy ... We live out our relation to our ultimate meaning through what and how we buy. Let the integration of faith and economy be the mark of the true spiritual seeker today, a consuming faith.
>
> (Beaudoin 2003: 106–7)

Individualist/consumerist spiritualities

This trend represents an aspect of what is sometimes called "prosperity religion" (for instance US tele-evangelism), but in a modern de-traditionalized setting. The linkage between religious practices and the profit motive is as old as history itself, but "prosperity religions" is a term generally used by scholars of religion to refer to movements that emerged in the nineteenth century and developed in response to the Industrial Revolution and the rise of modern capitalism. They have tended to be modernist in orientation and are complicit with the capitalist system at the same time as maintaining strong links to tradition, scripture, and religious specificity. As Woodhead and Heelas note,

> Prosperity religion, of course, is bound up with what would appear to be an ever-more significant feature of modern times: the growth of consumer culture and the associated "ethicality"—if that is the right term—of people intent on satisfying their consumeristically driven desires. It could well be the case that prosperity religion is (characteristically) about the sacralization of utilitarian individualism.
>
> (Woodhead and Heelas 2000: 174)

What we are here calling "individualist or consumerist spirituality" relates to a late twentieth century development within the broader historical phenomenon of "prosperity religions." It refers to those who embrace capitalism, consumerism, and individualism, and interpret their religious or spiritual worldview in terms of these ideologies. Whereas the nineteenth century prosperity religions were generally modernist in origin, the consumerist spiritualities emerged in the late 1960s and are generally "post-modern" in orientation, with an emphasis upon eclecticism, individualist experimentation, and a "pick and mix" approach to religious traditions. There is much within the "New Age" and "Personal Development/Self-Help" movement that exemplifies this trend. [...]

Capitalist spiritualities

Capitalist spiritualities involve the subordination and exploitation of religious themes and motifs to promote an individualist and/or corporate-oriented pursuit of profit for its own sake. Capitalist spiritualities are emerging in response to the rise of global finance capitalism. Like the individualist or consumerist spiritualities upon which they have fed, they are "post-modern" in the sense that, grounded in an information age and the transfer of electronic data across national boundaries, they tend to disavow explicit association with traditional religions, promoting instead a highly eclectic, disengaged, and de-traditionalized spirituality. This conforms to emerging social trends and the contemporary social *Zeitgeist* of late capitalist societies. Such trends, however, manifest an uncritical assimilation of business values into their rationale. In many cases, what characterizes such trends is a subtle shift beyond an exclusive emphasis upon the individual self and towards a concern with making the individual employee/consumer function as effectively as possible for the benefit of corporate organizations and the "global economy."

Traditional religious appeals to the importance of "community" and social connectedness are here "re-branded" in terms of the desirability of working for the corporate community or buying more of this or that product. Such a move allows advocates of *capitalist spirituality* to use the traditional language of "belonging" but this time orient it towards the need for employees to align themselves with the corporate mission statements of their employers, or to reinforce the ideology of consumerism. Examples of this trend include Deepak Chopra, Osho Rajneesh, and a variety of authors such as Jesper Kunde ("Corporate Religion"), Carayol and Firth ("Corporate Voodoo"), and John Grant ("The New Marketing Manifesto"). [...] Some movements maintain an affiliation to a specific religious tradition whilst expounding a corporatist ethic (such as the Catholic movement Opus Dei and some forms of Neo-Pentecostalism). For a fairly comprehensive list of the literature in this genre to the mid-1990s, see Heelas (1996: 66–7).

We offer the above interpretive grid as an alternative to the typology offered by Roy Wallis (1984), which classifies new religious movements in terms of their *world-affirming*, *world-denying*, or *world-accommodating* orientation. Wallis's approach is built upon older (Weberian) classifications of religious attitudes towards the world ("this-worldly" vs. "other-worldly") and remains useful at a certain level of analysis. However, the typology naïvely assumes unanimity about what "the real world" is like (to which each group is said to have a particular orientation), yet this is precisely one of the major points of contention between different traditions and worldviews. Moreover, for the purposes of our current discussion, Wallis's typology is insufficiently focused on attitudes towards capitalism and consumerism to pick out the trends that we wish to explore.

Using our fourth category as our point of orientation, one can classify contemporary forms of spirituality according to the various degrees of accommodation or resistance they exhibit to the following features of what we are calling capitalist spirituality:

1 *Atomization*: the individualization of responsibility with no consideration of society.
2 *Self-interest*: an ethic of self-interest that sees profit as the primary motivation for human action.
3 *Corporatism*: placing corporate (not community) success above the welfare and job security of employees.
4 *Utilitarianism*: treating others as means rather than ends (e.g. seeing humans as consumers to be persuaded, other businesses as competitors to be overcome, or employees as resources to be used).
5 *Consumerism*: the promotion of unrestrained desire-fulfillment as the key to happiness.
6 *Quietism*: tacit or overt acceptance of the inevitability of social injustice rather than a wish to overcome it.
7 *Political myopia*: a claim to political neutrality—the refusal to see the political dimensions of "spirituality."
8 *Thought control/accommodationism*: use of psycho-physical techniques, described in terms of "personal development," that seek to pacify feelings of anxiety and disquiet at the individual level rather than seeking to

challenge the social, political, and economic inequalities that cause such distress.

This list is far from exhaustive, but we hope that it gives the reader a sense of the particular orientation that is associated with capitalist spiritualities. In terms of our fourfold typology, one can read examples of contemporary spirituality in terms of the degree to which they demonstrate conformity or resistance to the above eight characteristics. It is important to appreciate, however, that the typology that we have outlined is an analytic abstraction for the purposes of classification. It should not be read as referring to fixed types, but rather as four points on a dynamic cultural continuum. There may also be some movement along the spectrum of possibilities in the case of specific movements and individuals at different times. No person or movement, for instance, can claim to be free from all of the eight features highlighted above as characteristic of capitalist spirituality. Rather, it is a question of where one can be placed on the spectrum at any given time in terms of one's complicity with such trends. We are not claiming to be able to step outside the influence of consumerism and inhabit some "pure" realm of ethical or spiritual practice. [...]

Part II
Media and the transformation of religion

Introduction

In one episode of the BBC Radio 4 series *A History of the World in 100 Objects*, the director of the British Museum, Neil MacGregor, describes in detail "a lavishly gilded ceremonial sword." Known as an *alam*, it is described, on the accompanying BBC website, as "an Iranian Shi'a religious parade standard." This is an older, pre-electronic, form of religious media. *Alam* were "originally battle standards, designed to be carried like flags into the fight, but in seventeenth-century Iran they were used in great religious processions, and rallied not warriors, but the faithful." MacGregor reflects on how a material object can be used to evoke and to mediate memories of martyrdom, which lie at the heart of Shi'a Islam. At the end of the program he goes on to claim that:

> Despite Iran's recent reputation for intolerance, the religious legacy of Shah 'Abbas is still evident in the country today. The state is of course officially Shi'a, but the Armenians still worship in their cathedral, and Christians, Jews and Zoroastrians are all free to practise their religion in public, their rights enshrined in the constitution.[1]

This statement provoked several respondents, writing in various on-line contexts, to criticize vigorously these claims about modern-day Iran. They beg to differ. For these writers Iran is an authoritative theocratic regime, which is intolerant of other religious groups. McGregor's use of this object to emphasize the roots of Iranian freedom of worship provoked several readers to become writers and contest his claim publicly on-line. Millions can now not only hear the broadcast again but also view and scrutinize this 300-year-old artifact with a few clicks on a computer. It was originally used as a symbol to evoke devotion, though now in a new digital context it leads some to question digitally the religious authority of the current Iranian regime as well as the interpretation of the director of one of the world's most visited museums.

This is one example of how the meaning of a religious object can be transformed and contested through contemporary media. Since the early 1990s increasing numbers of scholars have examined such processes, analyzing the relation between media and religion. This has resulted in a number of new scholarly developments. First, there is an increased awareness of how media go beyond electronic or digital forms and can include historical or contemporary objects. As we shall see in Part III, material objects matter. They can take on symbolic power and significance. Second, researchers are analyzing the implications of how the authoritative pronouncements of religious or scholarly figures can be challenged on-line or through other digital media. Third, scholars are reflecting further on the cultural, communicative, and historical contexts as significant factors for understanding both how media are used and how religious traditions evolve. Finally, researchers are examining how the ability of audiences to move from being consumers to producers of media productions has significant implications for the transformation of religious traditions. Some scholars have related this to what has been described as the "participative turn" in practice or the "cultural turn" in scholarship (see Mitchell and Marriage 2003: 337–8; Hoover 2006: 213). The chapters in Part II explore these and related themes.

The first chapter in Part II is taken from Stewart Hoover's *Religion in the Media Age* (2006) (Chapter 7). At the heart of Hoover's ground-breaking book is the argument that "media and religion have come together in fundamental ways" (2006: 9). His case is supported by detailed reception research investigating the relation between media and religion. This is explored through careful interviews and observational studies. These largely concentrate upon the everyday experiences and lives of people in their homes. This research reveals how audiences experience media, interact with others around media, and express divergent accounts of the media. His discussion of the events of September 11, 2001, provided here, illustrates his argument that media have "brought religion to the fore in new and unprecedented ways" (Chapter 7, p. 75). He suggests that different media became a source of experience of the events on 9/11, a source of knowledge about the other, and a source of Islamist critiques, as well as a location for mourning and grieving.

Such concrete discussions find theoretical development in David Herbert's chapter on media and the re-publicization of religion (Chapter 8). By re-publicization he means "a heightened public presence for religion" (p. 89) and a growth "in the public circulation ... of symbols and discourses" (p. 90). His argument draws upon Habermas's idea of the "post-secular,"[2] where the earlier belief that religion would decline or evaporate has been replaced with an awareness that religion continues to play a significant role even in supposedly "secularized" settings. According to Herbert this has been heightened through the mediated diffusion and circulation of religious symbols. This is a theme that Herbert has explored in a different way in relation to development of the public sphere and the popularity of "sacred soaps" in India (see Herbert 2003: 112–14 and the discussion of Gillespie's chapter here, pp. 103–8). One result of the "re-publicization" of religion is the pluralization of religious authority. The decline of institutional religious authority, accentuated through fragmented media use, production, and experience, is a recurring argument found through several essays in this book.

This can be seen in Marie Gillespie's discussion of "The role of media in religious transnationalism" (Chapter 9). Taken from Gillespie's ethnographic study of *Television, Ethnicity, and Cultural Change*, which explores the "role of television in the formation and transformation of identity among young Punjabi Londoners" (1995: 1), Gillespie's chapter, like Hoover's, investigates the everyday practices and conversations surrounding specific media productions. Her research reveals both the ties of tradition and the breaking of customs, shedding light on the phenomenon of "cultural hybridity." Two experiences stand out from her essay. First, one Punjabi family, living in Britain, watch Peter Brooks's adaptation of the Indian epic *Mahabharata* on television. They find it both frustrating and irritating because of their avid following of the "sacred soap operas" of the *Ramayana* and *Mahabharata*. As a result Brooks's revised portrayal of individual gods leads to consternation and confusion. Their loyalty to the *Mahabharata* and the *Ramayana* as foundational stories has been reinforced by their viewing habits and appears to have little room for more radical theatrical or televisual translations. They are made uneasy by a production that undermines their own received performative tradition. Gillespie neatly contrasts this desire to preserve a mediated tradition with the actions of a group of teenagers who break with a traditional *Diwali* dance, replacing it, to the horror of their more traditionalist Sikh teacher, with their own interpretation of a *Dirty Dancing* sequence. Gillespie's study illustrates the "re-creative" power of both young and old audiences as they consume and interact with mediated narratives.

The creative and productive interactions of audiences is a theme highlighted by Lynn Schofield Clark's essay on "Religion and authority in a remix culture: how a late night TV host became an authority on religion" (Chapter 10). This nuanced account of authority in a media age focuses on the North American comedian Stephen Colbert. Drawing upon Max Weber's threefold definition of authority (charismatic, traditional, and rational-legal), Clark analyzes how, despite hostility towards authority figures, forms of cultural authority persist. Through his humor, irony, and subtle insider religious language Colbert is an example of a celebrity who develops a relationship with a growing audience, which draws upon *"consensus-based interpretive authority."* This authority is not necessarily permanent and can evolve, increase, or dissipate over time.

The account of how individuals or groups can grow in authority and public respect through their representation in public media is well told in the final chapter of Part II. Diane Winston's essay on "The Angel of Broadway: transformative dynamics of religion, media, gender, and commodification" provides a valuable historical insight into how "a small, marginal evangelical mission" transformed "from ragtag street preachers to multi-million dollar social service providers" (p. 124). In the extract here (Chapter 11), which draws upon her book *Red-Hot Righteous: The Urban Religion of the Salvation Army* (1999), Winston illustrates how the initial suspicion towards the women who joined the Salvation Army was overcome. Her account of how these "lassies" (as they were described) moved from being perceived as "ladies of ill-repute" to "angels of the slums" highlights how portrayals in news, advertising and film can both reflect and contribute to public perceptions about religious groups. As Winston demonstrates in *Red-Hot and Righteous*, "between 1919 and 1950 the Salvation Army's status changed from an outsider sect to an almost mainstream denomination" (ibid.: 249), and "a highly respected provider of social services" (ibid.: 3). With respectability and skilful use of popular communicative tools the Salvation Army developed the magnetic authority to become one of the USA's most successful charities at fundraising. According to Winston one of the main ways in which this religious authority was developed was through a series of films that "introduced Salvationists to the wider public," bringing them into the "cultural mainstream" (p. 127). Significantly, this process ensured that the Salvationists lost control of their public image and found their distinctive theology was defined largely by their actions of compassion. Film, like other media, has the potential not only to reinforce public religious authority, but also to transform religious meanings as well.

Taken together, the chapters in this part of the book illustrate the value of paying careful attention to which images are promoted (cf. Winston, Chapter 11), how symbols are mediated and interacted with (cf. Hoover, Chapter 7), how mediated narrative forms can become authoritative (cf. Gillespie, Chapter 9), how media can be used to challenge traditional authority structures (cf. Clark, Chapter 10), and how religious themes and symbols circulate around the public sphere (cf. Herbert, Chapter 8). Perceptions about religious belief and practice are constantly evolving and these chapters illustrate how active audiences and creative producers can contribute to such developments.

Notes

1 See Episode 81, http://www.bbc.co.uk/ahistoryoftheworld/about/transcripts/episode81/ (accessed December 7, 2010).
2 Jürgen Habermas, "Notes on a post-secular society," June 18, 2008, http://www.sign andsight.com/features/1714.html (accessed December 7, 2008).

7   Religion, the media, and 9/11

Stewart Hoover

It is trite to say that the events of September 11, 2001 were unprecedented in their scope and effect. No major city in the "Group of Eight" industrialized countries had experienced such a major loss of life from an intentional act of violence in peacetime.[1] A strike at the heart of American commerce and media with such surprise galvanized the world and the nation. Throughout the world, at least the Western world, it is now conventional to use the term "9/11" to describe the events, and to think of international relations and global politics in "pre-9/11" and "post-9/11" terms. A great deal of public and scholarly comment has followed, focusing on everything from the security implications of the attacks to their impact on public consciousness, locally, nationally, and internationally.

The religious subtext of the attacks has also been an important, if problematic, element of discussion and debate. The barbarism of the events scandalized the world, and there has been an ongoing effort to reconcile them with their claimed roots in religion. A much-feared anti-Arab or anti-Islamic backlash did not materialize to any great degree (Ismail 2001), but it could be argued that in a more subtle way, smaller-scale reactions against Islam and against people of Middle Eastern and/or Muslim descent continue, and underlie certain political debates and repercussions that continue to gather force both in the USA and elsewhere (Said 1997).

In keeping with the theme of this book, however, it is important to understand the attacks as significant for the interaction between religion and media that they represented and continue to represent. They simply would not have had the same force or effect without the media. At the same time, they brought religion to the fore in new and unprecedented ways, ways that have forever shaped the way we see its contributions to politics, public discourse, social change, and political struggle. Further, the fact that religion and media *interacted* in these events is also significant.

The media, religion, and religion and media together were important in the events and their aftermath in four ways. First, *the media were the source of national and global experience of the events*. They were for all intents and purposes *media events*. Second, the media were and are *the source of "our" knowledge of "them" and "their" knowledge of "us."* Third, American media exports such as films are an important basis *for the Islamist moral critiques of U.S. and Western culture.* And finally, 9/11 illustrated and confirmed the role of the media as central to a new "civil religion" based in *public rituals of commemoration and mourning.* Let's look at each of these in turn.

The media as the source of the experience

One of the most unprecedented things about the 9/11 attacks was when and where they occurred. Subsequent political and security analyses of the strategy behind them noted that Bin Laden had a penchant for choosing targets for their political and symbolic value, and for sticking with targets once they were chosen. On one level, then, the 9/11 attacks on the World Trade Center were nothing more than a second attempt following the less "successful" 1992 bombing there (Juergensmeyer 2001). On another level, though, the 9/11 events were exponentially more significant in that they were so spectacular. Their spectacle was an effect of their timing. The two airplanes arrived at their targets approximately eighteen minutes apart. In the most media-saturated city in the world, hundreds of cameras were trained on the smoldering north tower when the second airplane struck the south tower, ensuring that millions of people throughout the world saw that strike live on television.[2]

What the city, the nation, and the world saw, in living color, was a horrible spectacle. Victims of the attack waved from windows above the smoldering floors, and in acts of unimaginable desperation, many of them flung themselves to their deaths to avoid the flames. And then, the most unimaginable sight of all: two 110-story buildings—the very symbols of the modern triumph of metropolitan civilization—crumbling to rubble. All of this was captured, shown live, repeated, and commented upon by media observers during hours and days of coverage. Every reader of this book no doubt has these images forever imprinted in memory. The immediacy—and, more important, the visuality—of the spectacle defined it and continues to define it. Other incidents of violence and horror before and since have also been visualized. War, genocide, natural disasters, and accidents are visually documented. In the case of 9/11 we all *participated* in the events, knowing that these things were happening, in real time, to real people, in a place where—our intellect told us—such things should not happen, as we were watching them.

In her thoughtful work on the role that visualization and depiction play in the process of "bearing witness," media scholar Barbie Zelizer points out that the ability to picture and represent events such as the Holocaust has changed the way witnessing is seen and done in modernity (Zelizer 2005). Visual records play an ever more significant role in our collective experience of our common humanity, and in our personal and political relation to suffering. It has been widely observed that those events that are pictured achieve a place in public consciousness not shared by events that are merely reported upon by other means. For example, the Boxing Day Tsunami of 2004 galvanized world attention to the plight of hundreds of thousands of casualties and millions of survivors while unpictured events going on at the same time, such as the massacres in the Darfur province of Sudan, received less attention.

I contend that, in addition to the visuality of 9/11, there was also its instantaneity. We all knew that these things we were watching were happening at that very moment. I do not want to ignore a more troubling aspect of these matters that has also been widely observed as a reason for the relative prominence of the 9/11 events. That is that, while disasters and catastrophes have come to be coded as commonplace in the developing world—something that happens to "those" unfortunate people "over there"—events such as 9/11 (where the total number of victims was in fact only around one one-hundredth the number who died in the Boxing Day Tsunami) become news because they are happening to white people in the developed world (Mitchell 2007).[3] On one level, it can be said that in the global media landscape not all human lives are of equal worth. On another level, we should also remember that in the conventional journalistic calculus, things are news because they are unusual or unprecedented, and a major terrorist attack within the borders of the United States was unusual and unprecedented.

The instantaneity of the 9/11 depictions and reception did serve to draw viewers into a common experience in a new and galvanic way. It became an event and an experience that was widely shared on a moral and emotional level, as evidenced by the global outpouring of sympathy and support. It thus had the makings, at least, of a binding experience that transcended its immediate surroundings. Many communities and contexts and interests have tried to "claim" it, leaving aside the unquestioned claims of the victims and their families. Did it "belong" to New York (hundreds also died at the Pentagon and in a field in western Pennsylvania)? To the firefighters and police on the scene? To America and patriotic American ideas about justice and right? To the West? To the Christian world? The right to define its moral, political, and religious meaning continues to be an issue of great debate to this day, and will no doubt be so for decades to come. The point of interest to our discussion here, though, is the nature of the event and the experience. The attacks of 9/11 were a turning point in history that was experienced in a deep and profound way because they were mediated in real time. Their relationship to religion is perhaps less obvious, but as we proceed to reflect on them, religion will become a more and more important dimension of the story.

Our knowledge of "them" and their knowledge of "us"

The afternoon of September 11, 2001 was a regularly scheduled lecture day in an introductory course in mass media and society. Like many of my colleagues, I chose to offer the two hundred-odd students in the class an opportunity to process the events of the morning, and opened the floor for questions, responses, and discussion. One of the first questions asked was "Why didn't we know someone hated us that much?" Other students chimed in with similar wonder that we could have been so blind to such sentiments about the USA. Implicit in these questions was the assumption that, in a modern, mediated world, saturated with journalism, we should be more knowledgeable about "others" out there, and their attitudes about "us." This was compounded in subsequent days by the growing sense that immigration, globalization, and global social and cultural change were making it ever more important to know about the rest of the world, to try to understand it, and (in the case of the U.S. foreign policy establishment, at least) to try to project a more favorable impression of the USA to the rest of the world.

These discourses are rooted in one of the most significant functions of media in modernity: their role in transcending geography, bringing once vastly separated individuals, groups, and communities into closer contact with one another. Marshall McLuhan's widely noted aphorism that the media age would usher in a "global village" is now thought to be overdrawn and overly optimistic. The media do have the capacity to cross space and erase time, and as geography becomes less of a barrier, we do increasingly know more about the "others" from whom we are separated by great distances. The instantaneity of the electronic media has made it possible for us to know much more about events across the world as they happen, and to have a contemporaneous grasp of events abroad. The visuality of the electronic media has added a sense of credulity to this knowledge, as pictures are taken to be more real and credible than oral or written accounts.[4]

Whereas McLuhan is taken to have expected that this mediated connection would bind disparate communities and peoples closer together, things don't seem to work quite that way. There is evidence, for instance, that increasing knowledge about others can lead as readily to mistrust and misunderstanding as to trust and understanding (Kellner 1992: esp. pp. 1–11). A major reason for this has to do with the context and framing of reception of media messages. In a classic international and cross-cultural study, Tamar Liebes and Elihu Katz showed that viewers of the 1980s U.S. soap opera *Dallas* read the show in ways that were more dependent on those viewers' own contexts and life situations than on the central themes and messages of the program (Liebes and Katz 1990; see also Lull 1988; Mandel 2002). Viewers can and do make new meanings out of the things they view from "other" contexts, meanings that they are as dependent on their own situations as on the manifest values or messages in those media materials (Ginsburg *et al.* 2002: 14–16).

More specific to the challenges of 9/11 and its aftermath, though, is the particular way the East is represented in the West, and vice versa. My students expressed the feeling that they had not been well served by media that have been shown by their nature to be inordinately focused on the developed world and myopic about international news beyond a few key areas of U.S. special interest, such as Israel (Said 1979, 1997; Gans 1979; Tuchman 1980; Epstein 1972). Also significant is the obverse, the issue of how American and Western lives, interests, and values are portrayed in the other direction. At the root of these concerns, of course, is an issue near to McLuhan's concerns, that is, how global understanding is or is not served by the media we consume. There is no doubt that in all respects the events of 9/11, their precursors, and their consequences were rooted in a mediated knowledge base. This makes 9/11 a media issue in a fundamental way, to the extent that we are concerned about its roots in ideology and values and about ways it might have been avoided or its causes and consequences ameliorated. That so much of its motivation and its reception were *framed by religious ideas* makes it by definition an issue of media and religion, something that we'll look at in more detail next.

Media as the source of Islamist critiques

In their early coverage of the attacks, the so-called "mainstream media" of North America and the West attempted to describe for the first time in a comprehensive way the roots of Islamist ire against American and Western culture. While we should not forget that, for most critics, fundamental political realities of U.S. foreign policy and historic international behavior are at the root of the problem (Ajami 2001), there is no denying that a cultural/moral critique also motivated the 9/11 attackers (Singer 2001). Press reports of Al Qaida and its motivations stressed this moral critique. Simply put, Al Qaida and Islamist movements more generally identify their challenge to the West in historic terms, and identify Western values, particularly Western *moral* values, as an important underlying motivation for their particular *jihad*. A press report at the time of the attacks quoted a young Islamist seminary student from Pakistan: "We are happy that many *kaffirs* (infidels) were killed in the World Trade Center. We targeted them because they were *kaffirs*, unbelievers" (ibid.).

This was echoed in the instructions given to the attackers themselves. Referring to the passengers they would encounter—and ultimately kill—on the planes, the instructions carried by Mohammed Atta and others referred to them as sacrificial animals. "You must make your knife sharp and must not discomfort your animal during slaughter," they said.[5] There was of course concern that some of the attackers might have become enculturated during their time in the USA, and Atta felt it necessary to remind them that their basic struggle was against the apostate and depraved West. It was essential to think of the victims of the attacks in these terms, and these terms were rooted in a sense that the overall struggle was between the moral claims of the two worlds: Al Qaida's particular (and to most Muslim authorities heretical) claims about Islam—morally superior to the depraved West.

Where do these ideas about the West come from? As has been widely noted, the media are of course the primary context within which "they" could know about "us." In an analysis of the influence of satellite broadcasting in the Arab world, Middle East scholar Fouad Ajami describes an advertisement for a Western product appearing on Al Jazeera, the satellite network widely viewed across the Arab world:

> One ad offered a striking counterpoint to the furious anti-Westernism of
> the call-in program. It was for Hugo Boss "Deep Red" perfume. A willowy

Western woman in leather pants strode toward a half-naked young man sprawled on a bed. "Your fragrance, your rules, Hugo Deep Red," the Arabic voice-over intoned. I imagined the young men in Arab-Muslim cities watching this. In the culture where the commercial was made, it was nothing unusual. But on those other shores, this ad threw into the air insinuations about the liberties of the West—the kind of liberties that can never be had by the thwarted youths of the Islamic world.

(Ajami 2001: 48)

As anyone who has observed the media scene in non-Western contexts knows, this is but one example of the kind of anachronism one regularly encounters there. The political economy of Hollywood-based media production is such that foreign distribution is often the most profitable outlet for films or videos that would never make it in their home markets (Sturken and Cartwright 2001: 319). Most often, these films—along with the major features that have a life both at home and abroad—contain large amounts of sexuality and violence, things that sell well globally (Mattelart *et al.* 1994). What this means is that in much of the developing world—and significantly in the Middle East—what is seen of the West is a picture that few people in the West would wish to have identified as emblematic of Western values of either sexuality or violence. The ubiquity and instantaneity of global media mean that we are no longer able to have a private conversation, or to keep our national cultural material to ourselves. Others are looking in, and they are drawing their own conclusions. This plays into the events of 9/11 in a profound and fundamental way, in that Al Qaida's critique of the West is less theoretical and more concrete to its followers and potential followers. Combining the Islamist reading of history in terms of a global struggle between two worlds[6] with a moral critique that provides followers and supporters with concrete and galvanic images of the West, clerics and other leaders have given their masses some powerful ideas and motivations.

These trends should not be difficult for those of us in the West to understand, parallel as they are to our own reactionary and Fundamentalist movements. However, the moral critique should not be seen in terms of its consumption by followers "in the street" as an ephemeral matter. Mark Juergensmeyer, author of a definitive work on religious terrorism, observes, of the images of the West consumed in the Islamic world, "It is difficult for those of us in the West to appreciate how these people [Islamists] feel *shamed* by what they know of the West. They feel *personally* responsible to do something about it" (Juergensmeyer 2001).

This echoes of course the kind of moral critiques that frequently erupt in the USA, and to a lesser extent elsewhere in the West, over "immoral" film, television, books, or other media. Religiously inflected critics here are seemingly highly motivated to address such things. That people several steps removed from this context are also watching, are also similarly offended, and are moved to action is a new and unprecedented reality of the media age. Islamists also share in common with certain of their Christian Fundamentalist counterparts a sense of persecution. Religion scholar Elizabeth Castelli's recent work on the so-called "Persecuted Christians" movement has demonstrated how legitimate cases of persecution have been conflated in some Christian circles with presumed "oppression" of Christians in the *Christian* West (Castelli 2004). For Islamists and Christian Fundamentalists alike, claims to oppression and persecution can be powerful in building common purpose and solidarity.

In both cases, the media can be powerful contexts for the realization of the condition of oppression. Fouad Ajami quotes an Islamic preacher, Sheik Muhammad Ibrahim Hassan, commenting on the connection between this sense of oppression and 9/11:

> "Oppression leads to an explosion," he said angrily. "Under the cover of the new world order, Muslims in Chechnya and Iraq have been brutalized ... Any Muslim on the face of the earth who bears faith in God and his Prophet feels oppression today. If a believer feels oppression and thinks that no one listens to him and that power respects only the mighty, that believer could be provoked to violent deeds. We saw things—horrors—in Bosnia that would make young people turn old ... Where were the big powers and the coalitions and the international organizations then? Where are they now, given what is going on in Palestine? The satellite channels have spread everywhere the knowledge of this oppression."
>
> (Ajami 2001: 48)

What is most significant about this situation is not, of course, the politics and balance of power, things that are immemorial and universal. Nor is it surprising to hear such a critique of U.S. and Western policies and practices from a religious figure in the Muslim world. What is just beneath the surface is the reality that the media age has made these symbols and these issues real in a way that brings them directly to the fore in the lives of individuals and movements. As the sheik notes, the media have made these images, symbols, and struggles available everywhere. The two valences of this situation—the knowledge of the exercise of real power by the West in political contexts in the Muslim sphere of influence and the spreading through entertainment media of images of the West that shame conservatives there—work together, and worked together in the bill of particulars carried by Al Qaida in 9/11.

The new "civil religion" of commemoration and mourning

No one who watched the coverage of the events on 9/11 on U.S. television could escape the sense that this was more than a mere "news" story. Admittedly it was, and one of the most significant and striking of all time. Like earlier moments in television history, "being in the right place at the right time" made the careers of some previously less well-known reporters and anchors. What soon emerged, though, was a kind of rhythm of representations, narratives, accounts, and remembrances.[7] The nearly incessant replaying of the images soon became problematic for some, especially children.[8] But, there is a sense in which such coverage, and conventions of coverage that emerged with 9/11 were part of a larger media landscape.

That landscape is a long tradition of mediated public experiences stretching back at least to the Kennedy assassination in 1963. That event was a major turning point in American media and journalistic history. Occurring at a time when television was just coming to its own as a news medium, the events in Dallas provided an unprecedented opportunity for the visual, real, and instantaneous power of the medium to emerge. As with 9/11, there were technical and logistical reasons for this, including the presence of so many media to cover what was a politically significant event, the recently perfected ability to send television images back and forth across the country, the eventual emergence of actual amateur film of the shooting itself, the live-on-camera shooting of the assassin himself, and the fact of the "media-friendliness" of the Kennedy administration. Also as with 9/11, the overarching reality of the event played the key role. A young, popular, charismatic president, known to the public because of television, was killed so unexpectedly and publicly. The shooting occurred on a Friday. The American (and, indeed, the world) public thus had a whole weekend to watch and to try to come to terms with the events. And, as they unfolded, there was continuing drama: the search for the killer, his eventual arrest and then killing; followed by the hurried inauguration of the new president. The return of the body to Washington the same night, with live images from the tarmac as the casket and the young widow, still wearing her blood-soaked clothing, entered the hearse. The statement from President Johnson attempting to reassure the public of a stable transition. And then, later, the lying-in-state, the state funeral, and the burial. Few who were alive at the time can forget the images and the emotions.

And, significantly to our considerations here, it was all televised. Television reporters and anchors struggled to find their footing in this new reality. Anchors such as Walter Cronkite served to guide the viewing world through the events, offering words of sorrow, comfort, hope, and consolation. It forever changed the way we think about television news, and imprinted on a generation of television news people (and on succeeding generations) the expectation that at certain times, and with certain events, their role would be to step up and act in real time and with real emotion. There are simply those times when emotional detachment is difficult, particularly when journalists are experiencing the same events at the same time as their audiences. The years since 1963 have seen many debates in professional circles about "personality journalism" and about the tendency for television journalists to become entangled with their stories. Behind many of these debates is a cultural memory of the JFK assassination.

It is my argument that this event ushered in the beginnings of a new form of public ritual linked to collective national and international processes of commemoration and mourning. In the years since 1963, there has been a series of such events. These include the tumultuous year of 1968, which saw the assassinations of Martin Luther King and Robert F. Kennedy, as well as the Chicago Democratic Convention. Television of course played an important role in public experiences of the Vietnam War and its aftermath, and some of the same issues and trends might be seen in the coverage of Watergate. But, commemoration of loss is the key ingredient of the rituals I have in mind, linking the JFK assassination with subsequent events such as the Challenger explosion, the shootings at Columbine High School, the bombing of the Murrah Federal Building, and of course 9/11.

Cultural scholars Daniel Dayan and Elihu Katz have described the role of television in the emergence of global forms of what they call "media events." These collective events are "real" in the sense that they are rooted in actual political, religious, or civic processes, but they are also important and unique because they are televised and interrupt the flow of television. Television, say Dayan and Katz, has introduced new contexts, processes and conventions to these forms, seeing in them an underlying taxonomy composed of contests, conquests, and coronations. They would not be structured in the same way without television, they argue, and television makes them national, even global, in scope and character. Religion may play a role in the events described by Dayan and Katz, but its presence or absence is not a central feature of their analysis (Dayan and Katz 1992).[9]

I wish to take things in a different direction than Dayan and Katz, looking more directly at how 9/11 can be seen as an expression of a kind of "civil religion" of commemoration and mourning. This differs from Dayan's and Katz's view in two key ways. First, I see in events such as the Kennedy funeral, the Challenger explosion, Oklahoma City, and 9/11 the dimension of mourning, of contention with shared fear and loss. Critical questions about the legitimacy of the state, not just about the status of a leader such as Kennedy, are in play, and the whole question of the function of such an event in support of social order is also in question [...] Second, whereas Dayan and Katz tend to side-step the implicit religiosity of these events (while very persuasively describing the role that explicit religious form plays in them), I want to look more directly at the way that religious sentiments, sensibilities, and meanings come into play in them.[10] Dayan and Katz tend to see the role of religion in such events either as a legitimating authority or as a source of formal elements that are brought into play in the structuration of the events. So the approach here is at some distance from their analysis, following instead Robert Bellah's influential ideas about the function of civil religion. To Bellah, civil religion is something that, while existing in secularized public contexts, nonetheless seeks to infuse those contexts with deeper and more profound meanings. Bellah notes: "American civil religion is not the worship of the American nation but an understanding of the American experience in the light of ultimate and universal reality" (Bellah 1974: 40).

Bellah's own work outlined ways in which formal and informal contexts of public ritual have traditionally been infused with such themes and values.[11] Often these have been seen as somewhat denatured, including things such as seemingly rote prayers and invocations at sporting and political events. A vibrant debate has continued in popular culture over whether and what kind of popular-cultural materials might be serving such civic piety, and whether it would be delegitimated by its commodification or diluted by its over-application (see, for example, Forbes and Mahan 2000: particularly pp. 1–20; Chidester 2000; see also Chidester and Linenthal 1995). I want to contend that, in events like 9/11, the media have come to play a central role in civil religious practices that are authentic to critical moments in national self-understanding.

Powerful political and national narratives and sentiments, such as those which might be invoked by an event like 9/11, have been traditionally thought of as stable, firm, and consistent. Newer ways of thinking about culture have begun to question such assumptions. We now think of fundamental cultural ideas as evolving and as significantly rooted in contemporary experience. Reflecting on the way commemoration invokes significant memories of the nation and its values, historian John Gillis observes,

> we are constantly revising our memories to suit our current identities. Memories help us make sense of the world we live in; and "memory work" is, like any other kind of physical or mental labor, embedded in complex class, gender and power relations that determine what is remembered (or forgotten), by whom and for what end.
>
> (Gillis 1994: 3)

It is interesting to note that it has only been relatively recently in American culture, at least, that ideas about the kinds of meanings rooted in consensual understandings of where we've come from have concerned the broad swath of public discourse. Traditionally, only the cultural elites cared. Gillis notes that in addition to this sort of democratic disinterest in the past, the American project was originally conceived of as very much about the future, with figures such as Jefferson specifically eschewing the idea of narrativizing a national "past" (ibid.: 7).

Yet there are some received notions available to us from the earliest days of the republic, ideas that can be seen to still be in play (though not necessarily determinative) in the way that tragic events such as 9/11 are remembered, interpreted, and understood. In his comprehensive study of the *physical* sites of American violence and tragedy, cultural geographer Kenneth Foote cites an early expression of American ideas of civil religion in a quotation from Joseph Galloway published in 1780:

> The fundamental and general laws of every society are the lessons of instruction by which the subject is daily taught his duty and obedience to the State. It is the uniformity of these lessons, flowing from the same system of consistent polity, which forms the same habits, manners, and political opinions throughout the society, fixes the national attachment, and leads the people to look up to one system of government for their safety

and happiness, and to act in concert on all occasions to maintain and defend it.

(Foote 1997: 267)

The fundamental idea that collective interest underlies a sense of duty and obligation to public order is nearly generic in American civic education. One way of thinking about civil religion, then, is through ideas like these, where the religion is not sectarian, but underlies a sense of duty to a state whose legitimacy is both underscored and justified by its relationship to public sentiments, duties, and obligations. The system is in a way self-justifying when it works smoothly. That is why it is so fundamentally unsettling (and might so readily invoke ideas of—and defense through—civil religion) when catastrophes seem to befall the nation and its people. Both its provision of security and its legitimacy are under assault.

In late modernity, it seems, this theme of legitimacy is paired with questions of unity, of shared and common purpose. In an era defined by self and self-identity, our relations and senses of empathy with other "selves" becomes a prominent issue and concern. Such unity is also under siege in events like the JFK assassination or 9/11. It becomes necessary to rebuild a sense of commonness and unity out of a sense of disruption and loss. As Foote points out, there is a malleability to the social practices that address such concerns. Citing Eric Hobsbawm's notion of "invented tradition," he echoes Wade Clark Roof's invocation of the same idea, and thus allows a linkage to ideas of religious practices that are constituted by such invention (ibid.: 267, n. 10). The overarching project of commonness or common purpose is, as I said, under assault in events like those described by Foote, the bombing of the Murrah building, and of course, the September 11 attacks.

[…] Events of common suffering and victimization are, as we've seen, dramatic moments of relatedness, with connection and commonality the whole point. This is a dimension of the "new civil religion" that separates it from received notions. On a level more related to the media, though, is the simple fact that the experience is, in the first instance, one that is experienced through the media: 9/11 was instantaneous, real, and visual. In a long and established line of such events, a "priesthood" of media figures, including reporters and anchors, held important roles in the experience, conveying important ideas about its meaning and providing a narrative of its unfolding across time. As Dayan and Katz point out, this is a well-established and long-accepted role, where conventional practices and expectations are suspended for the sake of a larger purpose (Dayan and Katz 1992: 7). The ritual vocabularies through which the media narrate events like 9/11 have become complex, routine, and conventional. While a detailed study from this perspective remains to be done, there is evidence of one important element of these conventionalized media narratives in Edward Linenthal's accounts of the Oklahoma City bombing. Too quickly, he notes, voices in the media began to speak of "healing" and "closure." Whereas it can be argued that such violence can never truly be healed,

Linenthal contends, newspaper columnists, television anchors, and reporters all began talking of closure for the events (Linenthal 2001: 94–5). "Closure" and "the healing process" (a term heard frequently in the local television coverage of the Columbine massacre) are concerns of a priesthood oriented toward conventionalized rituals more than they are concerns of journalists covering a process that might never (as Linenthal argues) come to closure.

In Oklahoma City, at Columbine, and near the World Trade Center, Pentagon, and western Pennsylvania sites, the "democratic" claiming of a role in commemoration involved the physical claiming of a location, typically a fence.[12] Fences surrounding the World Trade Center site and a nearby church became the site of spontaneous shrines filled with the objects of the "vocabulary of memorialization." Flags, poems, teddy bears, news clippings, posters, banners, clothing, and more conventional paraphernalia, including candles and wreaths, covered the site. Many of these came from outside the USA, a testament to the global nature of the events.

The notion that there is an evolving trajectory of such commemoration is supported by the seeming emergence of such practices in smaller, more localized events. For example, the tragic murder of a young shop attendant in my home town stimulated a familiar response. Within hours of the news, a spontaneous shrine appeared at the storefront where the killing occurred. It grew and developed over the coming days, and contained many of the familiar elements of the "public vocabulary of mourning" we've been talking about: flowers, teddy bears, poems, etc.[13]

The intermixture of the media-experienced and the direct relationship to the events invokes ideas about the nature of media experience that ring true with the evolving perspective we have been describing here. Media sociologist John Thompson speaks of "mediated quasi-interaction," where communication mediates between audience experience and events. Thompson intends to refer to the experience of day-to-day life more than to such singular events as 9/11, but his description is still apt:

> For many individuals whose life projects are rooted in the practical contexts of their day-to-day lives, many forms of mediated experience may bear a tenuous connection to their lives: they may be intermittently interesting, occasionally entertaining, but they are not the issues that concern them the most. But individuals also draw selectively on mediated experience, interlacing it with the lived [direct] experience that forms the connective tissue of their daily lives.
>
> (Thompson 1995: 230)

If I am right, the components of this emerging civil religion of commemoration and mourning involve both media practice and "real life" practice. A set of conventions of media coverage of events like 9/11 has emerged, with journalists taking roles that link them personally and morally to the events, and at the same time function to narrate the experience for the broader public. The mediation of the events connected people to them in ways that gave the events a sense of reality and instantaneity. The unique horror of the events gave them a particular power to motivate action. The actions moved in the direction of finding commonality and connection rather than of crafting narratives of triumph or transcendence. The unique facticity of the experience further motivated people in disparate locations remote from the events to take ritual action, even actions as trivial as lighting candles and attending prayer services. The nature and extent of the evolution of these cultural forms will no doubt continue to evolve. What is clear, though, is that the events of 9/11 provided a unique and particular moment of interaction between ideas of religion and practices of the media.

Notes

1 The signal precedent for a time was the bombing of the Murrah Federal Building in Oklahoma City in 1995. In a haunting passage, Edward Linenthal wrote of that event in 2001, "Will a future terrorist act that inflicts even more death consign Oklahoma City to a less prestigious location on the landscape of violence?" (Linenthal 2001: 234).

2 The planners could not have anticipated that film footage of the first plane strike would also surface, shot by a French cameraman working on a documentary about New York firefighters, and that a security camera also would capture the crash at the Pentagon. But, in an increasingly media-saturated world, we have come to expect that, somehow, pictures of such things are more and more routinely available, from either surveillance cameras or the ubiquitous amateur videographer.

3 See the chapter on "reframing news," in particular, where Mitchell asks, "why is it that when about 3,000 people died on September 11 most news broadcasters and newspapers around the world provided saturation coverage for days and sometimes weeks afterwards, while when over 3 million die in the D.R. Congo it is largely ignored by the media?" (2007: 73; also Mitchell, Chapter 19).

4 This is, of course, a problematic notion. For a thoughtful discussion, see Sturken and Cartwright (2001: ch. 8).

5 "Focus Special: The Atta Document in Full," (London) *Observer*, September 30, 2001, p. 17.

6 We should not overlook that this "clash of cultures" interpretation of the West's confrontation with Islam (widely credited to historian Bernard Lewis) is echoed by influential voices in the West as well (Hirsch 2004).

7 For a description of this form of broadcasting, see Dayan and Katz (1992: 4–7).

8 Linenthal cites a study by psychiatrists at the University of Oklahoma which found that children were depressed by the images, and that pre-schoolers "thought that each time they saw the ruins of the Murrah Building a new building had been destroyed" (Linenthal 2001: 75). Anecdotal reports at the time of 9/11 suggested similar effects on children. A colleague of mine recounted that she'd realized that her young son had concluded that each time he saw the 9/11 footage, another building had been attacked.

9 For a discussion of their taxonomy, see pp. 25–39. I am indebted to Nick Couldry for his thorough and thoughtful critique of Dayan's and Katz's work. On the whole, I agree with his analysis, and to the extent that what I have to say about the rituals of commemoration and mourning needs to be seen in the sort of totalized terms he problematizes, I see no problem with calling them, to paraphrase Couldry, "event-based narratives where the claims of a central set of concerns is particularly intense" (2002: 67). I further acknowledge here the consonance between Couldry's tentative analysis of the 9/11 events (2003: 72–4) and my own here.

10 This difference may of course be rooted in differing scholarly paradigms. Dayan and Katz's analysis is historical and formal, whereas I am speaking here as an audience researcher.

11 Therefore, my approach also differs significantly from Bellah's in that he did not envision popular culture as playing a role, focusing, like Dayan and Katz, on the formal elements of the events and practices.

12 See, with regard to the Columbine site specifically, Pike (2001).

13 There also seems to be a growing and developing public practice of memorialization at sites of highway fatalities, requiring state highway departments to institute new rules regulating them. Linenthal and Foote note that, while there has been a longer-standing Catholic practice underlying this, it appears to be spreading more broadly in the culture.

8   Why has religion gone public again?

Towards a theory of media and religious re-publicization

David Herbert

Introduction

A combination of the rapid development and dissemination of media technologies, the liberalization of national media economies, and the growth of transnational media spheres is currently transforming the relationship between religion, popular culture, and politics in many contemporary societies (Meyer and Moors 2006; Campbell 2004). Indeed, these processes are combining to produce a heightened public presence for religion—a phenomenon I propose to name "re-publicization"—albeit in different ways, across different societal milieux, of which I discuss here three types—"post-colonial,"[1] "post-communist," and "Western." My argument is that while religion in each of these types of society faces a similar "structural predicament related to the globalization of mass societies and the porous pluralism of late modernity" (Hefner 1998: 83), and to which media change is central, these structural changes are articulated in different ways in different societal contexts, with varying consequences for the relationship between religion, politics, and society. This plurality of outcomes and renewed public prominence of religion runs contrary to the expectations both of earlier media scholars, who anticipated that the spread of electronic media would result in flattening of cultural forms (McLuhan 1964), and of secularization theorists, who predicted that the spread of modernization processes would produce a decline in the social significance of religion (Bruce and Wallis 1992). Hence, after an outline of interactions between media, culture, and politics, which I argue produce re-publicization, I conclude with a discussion of the implications of the processes identified for more general theories in the sociology of media and religion.

Post-colonial societies, communications change and the de-differentiation and functionalization of religion

Under colonial systems religion was routinely subjected to regimes of control and categorization (van der Veer 2008). Nonetheless, it often provided a resource in anti-colonial struggles, and in the post-colonial period has remained socially significant in shaping public law and in other aspects of social organization. At the level of political society, however, it was often less publicly prominent in the immediate post-colonial period, as secular nationalist ideologies dominated (Ayubi 1991). Then, as Meyer and Moors (2006) demonstrate, since the early 1990s there has been a marked growth in the public circulation and visibility of religious symbols and discourses in many post-colonial societies in Africa, the Middle East, Latin America, and the Asian subcontinent. Because religion was never privatized in a Western liberal sense, the term re-publicization is more appropriate here than de-privatization (Casanova 1996: 559). Meyer and Moors (2006: 18) link this proliferation to changes in media production, regulation, and (relative) political liberalization. For example, in the case of Ghana, "the marked public articulation of Pentecostalism ... was facilitated by the retreat of the state from control over the media and the easy accessibility of cheap media technologies" (ibid.).

In this process, the ties which linked religious symbols and discourses with the traditional contexts and institutions through which they have been transmitted and which have sought to control their use are loosened. Thus it becomes necessary to distinguish between "religion" as "the distinctive way of life of communities of followers shaped by their particular system of beliefs and practices that are oriented towards the supernatural" (Smith 2003: vii), and "the religious" as "more diffuse articulations ... [in which religion] is significantly transformed as it spreads throughout the surface of social life, disseminating signs yet having to accommodate to given formats" (Meyer and Moors 2006: 16–19).

I call this process de-differentiation, as religious symbols and discourses ("the religious"), enabled by the diffusion of electronic communications systems, spread out across other social systems, including commerce and entertainment (Rajagopal 1999), welfare (Sullivan and Abed-Kotob 1999), education (Starrett 1998), and politics (Wickham 2004). Contrary to the expectations of secularization theory that religion will become ever further confined to its own specialized sphere (Wilson 1982), religion instead becomes more widely distributed across modern systems, often functionalized—that is, doing work—within them (Starrett 1998: 153). As Meyer and Moors suggest, this "having to accommodate to given formats" (2006: 19) has consequences for the "content" or character of religion, which will be discussed more fully here pp. 95–7. For now, we note one aspect of this change, which Starrett has termed "functionalization" (1998: 153).

Starrett uses the term in the context of the Islamization of Egyptian public life since the late 1980s, a process which has included the spread of Islamic symbols and discourse across a range of fields of social life, including law, welfare, media discourse, and fashion. But he focuses on the role of education in this process, arguing that the transformation of Egyptian public education systems, and especially religious education, beginning under Ottoman reformers in the nineteenth century but influenced by British Protestant Sunday school pedagogy, produced a mode of understanding Islamic knowledge as useful for practical purposes. This way of understanding Islamic knowledge is the key to its adoption across other social systems, summed up in the Muslim Brother-hood phrase "Islam is the solution," and it has inspired the appropriation and legitimization of Islamic discourse for welfare, legal reform, and politics.

These processes of de-differentiation and functionalization of religious sym-bols and discourse are not confined to post-colonial contexts, but rather also found in other societal contexts, including in post-communist and Western societies.

Post-communist societies and the structural transformation of religious authority

Many observers have described the growth in the public presence of religion in post-communist societies, following its forcible exclusion under Communism (Borowik and Jablonski 1995; Froese 2001; Sarkissian 2009: 488). The dynamics of re-publicization are complex here, because while communist regimes sup-pressed and forcibly privatized religious actors and institutions, the same attempt to control the public sphere also politicized culture, including religion, creating a complex dynamic between public and private. As Ramet explains,

> In communist times, religion was defined as "the private affair of the indi-vidual" and efforts were made to exclude it from the public sphere except insofar as religious leaders were prepared to endorse communist leaders and programmes; today, the religious communities routinely play promi-nent public roles and speak out on public policy issues. Or again, in com-munist times, such matters as a student's haircut, T-shirt, or other apparel were defined as matters for the authorities to censor; today, such things are considered the private affair of the individual.
>
> (Ramet 2009: 88)

Like the student haircut, acts of religious ritual such as open air Papal masses on John Paul II's visit to Poland in 1983, or the tour of the image of the Black Madonna in the Great Novena became political acts, but today may be more matters of devotion, if not entirely de-politicized. So the inflation of the poli-tical meaning of cultural symbols under Communism means that post-Communism is characterized by a complex mixture of the de-politicization of religion (the performance of public religious ritual, or membership of a reli-gious organization, is likely to carry less political "charge"), accompanied by a re-publicization in which religious symbols and discourses are more widely distributed and mobilized in the public sphere, and religious institutions exer-cise more public influence—or at least are more vocal, and in some cases have re-established close connections with the state (Sarkissian 2009; Damian 2010). Aspects of this re-publicization include the growth of religious media (Radio Maryja and TV affiliates in Poland—Czubkowska and Raczkowski 2006; the Trinitas radio and TV stations in Romania—Damian 2010: 23), the growing role of religious organizations in commenting on public issues and securing state funding (e.g., in the Hungarian case, Enyedi 2003), and significant intervention at the level of state, political, and civil society, for example in the case of the Polish Catholic Church (Herbert and Fras 2009).

As elsewhere, this increased public presence does not necessarily correspond to growth in religious practice. For example, church attendance dropped in Hungary from 23 percent once monthly or more in 1993 to 17.4 percent in 1999, and this pattern is common in other Central European contexts. However, in other cases religious practice has increased. In Romania, for example, monthly or greater church attendance increased from 29.7 percent in 1993 to 46.5 percent in 1999, showing only a slight decline in 2006 (45.9 percent), with more frequent attendance (once weekly or more) higher in 2006 than in 1999 (World Values Survey 2010). This complexity suggests the need for an explanatory framework that can deal with both growth and decline in different aspects of religion's public presence and vitality. Again, in these cases re-publicization is a more appropriate term than de-privatization, because the process of enforced exclusion under Communism, often accompanied by confiscation of property and sometimes state propagation of rival atheist institutions and ideologies, and the related suppression of civil society, has produced quite different religious (and social) fields to those in Western societies.

The aspect of religious re-publicization that we will highlight here to illustrate the structural transformation of religious authority is the growth and influence of religious media producers, using the Polish case of the Radio Maryja group.[2] As in post-colonial societies (Meyer and Moors 2006), the context is one in which a combination of some relaxation of state control and new technologies reducing production and broadcast costs, and increasing broadcast space have enabled religious producers to enter an increasingly plural mass media marketplace. Radio Maryja was created in 1991, growing under the leadership of Taduesz Rydzyk of the Polish Catholic Redemptorist order to become Poland's fourth largest radio station, in terms of weekly listeners (Radio Maryja website 2007). The organization has expanded to include other media outlets (including a newspaper, Nasz Dziennik ["Our Daily"], and television channel, Trwam), universities and other educational institutions, and a museum.

This media group has maintained close connections with nationalist politicians, which were particularly influential during the 2005 elections and subsequent PiS (Truth and Justice) led coalition government of 2005–7, during which several key agenda items for Radio Maryja were pursued by the government, including embedding the model of heterosexual marriage in the constitution, blocking pilot research for introducing the morning after pill, and abolishing a government post for gender equality (Fras 2011). But arguably, its greater influence is in linking religious symbols and discourses in the public imagination to a particular nationalist agenda, narrowed from their mobilization in the anti-communist opposition, and often in spite of the policies of the official Catholic Church. Thus, in the case of the controversial prominent positioning of crosses at a Carmelite convent at the site of the former concentration camp at Oswięcim (Auschwitz), the station mobilized popular support for the Carmelite convent and crosses, in spite of opposition from the Vatican and Polish Catholic hierarchy (Wollaston 1994). Again, in 2010, following the death of Polish president (and former PiS leader) Lech Kaczyński and many Polish government officials in a plane crash, the group supported the unofficial erection of prominent crosses as a form of commemoration at a controversial public site, in spite of opposition from the church hierarchy.

The case illustrates two points. First, Radio Maryja mobilizes as an interest group independent of the Catholic Church, and is not afraid to oppose the church hierarchy, or indeed the Vatican—yet at the same time it depends for its popular mobilization capacity on Catholic symbolism and discourse. It is thus a case of religious symbols being mobilized independently of their traditionally authorized religious interpreters. This process has also been observed in post-colonial, including Muslim-majority, societies, where Islamic symbols and discourses are increasingly mobilized by Islamist opposition groups independently of (often state-sanctioned) traditional religious authorities, or *ulema* (Starrett 1998: 232–3). Both in classic secularization theories (Berger and Luckmann 1967) and in more recent neo-secularization theories (Chaves 1994), it has been argued that pluralization of religious authority weakens religious authority as such, but these cases suggest another possibility, in which "Authority is now more a characteristic of products themselves ... than productive processes ... Who the producer is—when that can determined—is less important than the marketability of what he [*sic*] has to say" (Starrett 1998: 233). While it may be an exaggeration to state that authority is shifted entirely from producer to product, from institution to discourse, not least given increasingly close and powerful ties between church and state and some post-communist settings (Sarkissian 2009; Damian 2010), it would seem that the pluralization of media, media producers, and markets is altering the way that religious authority (amongst other forms) is being produced.

This leads to a second point that can be drawn from the Polish case. While the close connections between Radio Maryja and the PiS-led government may be the most obvious example of religious influence on politics in post-communist Poland, the discursive and visual imaginary created by Radio Maryja may be more significant in the long term. As Rajagopal has argued in the context of India after the fall of the first BJP-led coalition:

> Even in the absence of a Hindu nationalist domination then, we may have in India a Hinduized visual regime, evidenced for example in commodity consumption in everyday life, acting as a kind of lower order claim than national identity and continuing to have a force in politics, albeit of a more dispersed subtle and less confrontational kind.
>
> (Rajagopal 2001: 283)

So in Poland, although the electoral fortunes of particular nationalist parties may ebb and flow, the presence and growth of the Radio Maryja group continue to provide a symbolic and discursive reservoir for such movement, and other populist causes, to feed on. As one commentator put it, "one pope, two presidents and seven prime ministers have changed ... since the creation of Radio Maryja ... but the Father Director endures and plays an ever greater role in Polish politics" (Czubkowska and Raczkowski 2006).

Western societies and diasporic intensification

In Western Europe, much of the increased public visibility of religion is due to conflicts arising between secular or laïcist institutions and secularized majority populations, on the one hand, and those immigrant and ethnic minority groups for whom religion plays a more prominent public role. This situation has been called "post-secular" by Habermas (2008), not because the age of secularism has passed, but rather because forms of secularism which expected religion to decline as a social force are discovering that they need to adapt to the ongoing public presence of religion. The same broad characterization works to an extent in the United States, although here levels of religious vitality are generally thought to be higher, as is the political mobilization of more longstanding religious groups. Here, the separation of church and state is also thought to have stimulated religious activity in civil society (Casanova 1996), and other factors, such as low levels of state-funded public provision of welfare (Norris and Inglehart 2006) and the strength of private religious broadcasting (Smith 1998), have all been seen as factors which have led to the development of thriving religious subcultures; the latter may also be seen as a forerunner to the growth of religious broadcasting in post-communist and post-colonial societies.

Here I argue that a significant factor in the strength and visibility of religion amongst migrant communities and ethnic minorities in Western societies is the increasing volume and speed of transnational connections between populations in the West and countries of origin. Communications technologies enable geographically dispersed groups to feel part of global communication communities which interact in real time. For example, Beck and Lau describe "Turkish and German speaking transmigrants who, while they may live in Berlin, are living out their expectations, ambitions and cultural disruptions elsewhere as well, namely in transnational networks" (Beck and Lau 2005: 554).

Beck and Lau's concern is with how to study such spatially dispersed social worlds, but the point is that new media and cheap international transport enable transnational religious networks to function much more intensively, creating what we term "diasporic intensification." This process, involving the increased capacity of kinship networks and transnational religious networks (such as Sufi orders—Werbner 2002) to function across geographically dispersed locations, significantly alters the impact of societalization as envisaged in classic secularization theory (Bruce and Wallis 1992: 9). While the latter envisages a shattering of the disciplinary hold and attenuation of the imaginative power of the life-worlds into which religion is woven in the often rural "sending societies" of migrants, revolutions in transport and communications transform the capacity of such systems to be reproduced, albeit in altered forms, across migratory pathways. Such networks can have significant political consequences, in both migratory hubs and sending societies, as the case of the transformation of the imagined community of the "suffering ummah" illustrates.

Evidence from Muslim communities since the mid-1990s suggests that the media's circulation of images and discourses can produce some quite radical reconfigurations of religious identity. For example, images of (and discourse on—Hirshkind 2006: 29) Muslim suffering in different parts of the world (especially Bosnia, Palestine, Iraq, Kashmir, and Chechnya) made available through the electronic media since the 1990s have arguably transformed the historically diverse meanings of the Arabic term *umma* (Ayubi 1991: 18), politicizing and inflecting it to invoke a suffering community, much more akin to the Shi'ite theology of martyrdom than the Sunni theology of "Manifest Success" in which the concept first developed (Geaves 2005: 96–117). While the initial disseminators of these images (transnational, Western-based broadcasters such as CNN) produced this effect unwittingly, the advent of Arab satellite broadcasting (e.g. Al-Jazeera) significantly altered the semantic framing of their dissemination, and *jihadi* websites self-consciously promote it (Awan 2007).

There is evidence that this sense of being part of a suffering *umma* is now very widespread, from studies of Muslims both in the West (Mandaville 2001; Cesari 2004; Al-Ghabban 2007) and in the Middle East (Hirshkind 2006). In this case, then, structural change (e.g. the advent of media technologies enabling instant transnational broadcasting, and lower access costs enabling wider transnational dissemination) is implicated in the increased political salience (and semantic transformation) of religious discourse, in turn producing change in an aspect of religious identity.

"Internal" secularization and media circulation

In secularization theory the process of the transformation of the meaning and felt sense of "ummah" would be categorized as "cultural defence" (Bruce and Wallis 1992: 9). This reductive characterization is entirely inadequate to grasp the dynamics of this process, which is not simply a defense of tradition, but rather a radical reinterpretation of it, and represents an active and adaptive transformation rather than a rearguard action against the secularizing force of modernization. However, there remains the question of what happens to religious "content" in the process of circulation through electronic media and participation in media culture; in particular, is religion's distinctive content somehow lost or "internally" secularized?

Meyer and Moors (2006: 13) ask if the adoption of new media technologies by religious groups might not turn out to be a "Trojan Horse," in which the logics of media formats and commodification might turn out to subvert religious purposes, and Ohm argues that "commercialisation ... appears to vindicate [communitarian and pious] fears by being at odds with any group consistency and identity in the longer run" (Ohm forthcoming). While they have different origins, such concerns about the corrosive or subverting influence of media transmission on religious cultures and communities have a long history. McLuhan (1964) famously argued that media content is subordinated to the sensory effects of "hot" media, Wilson (1982) that American Evangelicalism's apparent vibrancy concealed an "internal secularization" of its content, while more recently Roy (2004) has made a similar argument in relation to the Islamization of society in Muslim-majority cultures:

> Islamization of society led to the Islamization of secular activities and motivations which remain secular in essence: business, strategies of social advancement, and entertainment (like the five-star Islamic resorts in Turkey, where the real issue is fun and entertainment, not Islam).
>
> (Roy 2004: 40)

However, closely observed ethnographic work, like that of Starrett (1998) in Egypt, suggests that functionalization does not necessarily entail disenchantment:

> functionalization occurs without the desacralization of the material, so that the process described by Durkheim earlier in this century as one of the goals of the modern education system is subverted. Naturalistic and materialistic explanations coexist with supernatural ones, for Muslims perceive them as non-contradictory. The "real" reasons for religious practices do not strip off their theological cloaks. Since God is concerned with the welfare of the Muslim community, the prescriptions of Islam are not only beneficial, but manifestly rational.
>
> (Starrett 1998: 153)

Indeed, it seems that in certain contexts the reproduction of religious symbols and discourse can intensify their potency in mediating the divine to the devotee. For example, in an Indian and Hindu context, Pinney (2002) analyzes the use that Hindu devotees make of postcard reproductions of deities, which serve as a focus of domestic devotion. Pinney argues that reproduction intensifies the "aura" of the original:

> The mass dissemination of postcard reproductions serves to reinvest originals with a new aura. The original artwork now comes to embody what the reproduction lacks and must be enclosed in shrine-like security structures to protect them from the admiring, and sometimes hateful, gestures of their devotees.
>
> (Pinney 2002: 356)

He argues that *darshan*, the core Hindu devotional practice of "eye contact" with the deity achieved through sight of the image (*murti*) and reproduced in Hindi cinema and photography, offers an example of a cultural practice which taps into this optical unconscious to create a powerful bodily aesthetic sensibility. Indeed, he argues that *darshan*, while culturally specific, is "not strikingly unlike a whole range of culturally diverse practices that stress mutuality and corporeality in spaces as varied as those of religious devotion and cinematic pleasure" (ibid.: 359). Furthermore, the emotional intensity developed through such engagement is not confined to private devotion, but may also find public and political expression, from the mob storming of a power station when the transmission of an episode of a popular Hindu religious epic is interrupted to its more organized channeling by the BJP (Rajagopal 2001). Such evidence suggests that the process of interaction between religious culture and new technologies is best seen as a dialectical one, in which religious and public spheres are both altered, rather than simply subsumed within a more powerful logic, whether that of capitalism or of secularization.

Conclusion

In this chapter I have presented evidence which suggests that the growth and dissemination of electronic media technologies, in the presence of the liberalization of media economies and increases in transnational migration, is producing a "re-publicization" of religion across a wide range of contemporary societies, post-colonial, post-communist, and Western. Across these intersecting landscapes, religious symbols and discourses are being contested and reconfigured in ways that basically linear paradigms of secularization and mediatization are unable to narrate. Rather, what is needed is a "multiple modernities" (Eisenstadt 2000; Hefner 1998) approach that recognizes the diverse range of outcomes that the dynamic interaction of media change and religious tradition in late modernity produces. Its development will require close collaboration between scholars across the fields of religious studies, media studies, anthropology, sociology, and political sciences.

Notes

1 "Post-colonial" is used here primarily to denote societies which achieved independence after 1945, in which the majority of peoples are of a different ethnic group to the original colonizers, and where modernization processes were initially imposed on society from above by colonizers or by indigenous elites. However, Meyer and Moors (2006) also use the term to refer to Latin American societies.
2 My thanks to Max Fras, Ph.D. candidate at the Open University, for his contribution to this section of the paper.

9 The role of media in religious transnationalism

Marie Gillespie

Globalization/localization

It is now commonplace to argue that the interconnectedness of cultures brought about by the transnational flow of images, commodities, and peoples is leading to the formation of a global culture, dominated by transnational corporations, and increasingly Americanized and commercialized (Mattelart *et al*. 1984; Schiller 1969, 1973). The acceleration of global flow by communications technologies means that cultural forms (for example the Indian "sacred soap" the *Mahabharata*) are available for worldwide consumption on a mass scale. Anthropologists and cultural historians, in response to the development of cultural studies in advanced capitalist societies, are now beginning to analyze how consumers in all sorts of settings create or conform to personal and social identities through acts of consumption, and how commodities provide a resource for developing shared, collective frames of reference (Appadurai 1986; Douglas and Isherwood 1979; Miller 1987, 1992). Indeed, Miller only came to study the reception of the American soap *Young and Restless* in Trinidad (Miller 1992) because no one would talk to him while it was on, and so he was forced to watch with his informants.

Tradition/translation

It is possible to observe both a proliferation and a polarization of identities, both a strengthening of existing local identities and a formation of new identities. As Robins argues:

> The continuity and historicity of identity are challenged by the immediacy and intensity of global cultural confrontations. The comforts of Tradition are fundamentally challenged by the imperative to forge a new self-interpretation based upon the responsibilities of cultural Translation.
>
> (Robins 1991: 41)

These challenges are felt most powerfully by diasporic groups, such as black Britons and British Asians, some of whom have made a "strategic retreat to more defensive identities [...] in response to the experience of cultural racism" (Hall 1992: 308)—in response, for example, to the rise of a "morbid celebration of Englishness" (Gilroy, quoted in Morley and Robins 1989: 16) in the 1980s. Hall claims that this strategy has been developed in a variety of ways, including re-identification with: "cultures of origin"; the construction of strong "counter-ethnicities" as forms of symbolic identification (e.g. cultural Rastafarianism); revivals of cultural traditionalism, religious orthodoxy and political separatism; and the formation of "new identities" around terms (such as "Black" or "Asian") chosen and inflected to encompass differences (Hall 1992: 308). Hall concludes that globalization does have the power to contest and dislocate national identities, in that it has a pluralizing impact, opening up new possibilities and positions of identification. But its general impact is highly contradictory, as different groups, let alone individuals, respond in a range of different ways to the diversification and concomitant politicization of identity.

Robins (1991) provides a scheme for thinking about these responses. Some gravitate to what he calls "Tradition," in the attempt to restore their former "purity" and certainty. Others gravitate to what he calls "Translation" (following Bhabha 1990; cf. Rushdie 1991), exploring their identities as transformative processes in the interplay of history and politics, representation and difference. And yet others oscillate between tradition and translation (cf. Bhabha 1990). It is this oscillation that is becoming evident on a global scale today. Identities are in transition, involved in a multiplicity of crossovers and mixes. Thus globalization may mean neither universal assimilation into one homogeneous culture, nor a universal search for roots and revival of singular identities, but a complex, highly uneven process of many-sided translation.

The term "translated" has been adopted by cultural critics to describe

> those identity formations which cut across and intersect natural frontiers, and which are composed of people who have been dispersed forever from their homelands. Such people retain strong links with their places of origin and their traditions, but they are without the illusion of a return to the past [...]. They bear upon them the traces of the particular cultures, traditions, languages and histories by which they were shaped. The difference is that they are not and never will be unified in the old sense, because they are irrevocably the product of several interlocking histories and cultures.
>
> (Hall 1992: 310)

Members of such "'cultures of hybridity'" are "irrevocably translated"; as "the products of the new diasporas created by the post-colonial migrations," translated men and women "must learn to inhabit at least two identities, to speak two cultural languages, to translate and negotiate between them. Cultures of hybridity are one of the distinctly novel types of identity produced in the era of late-modernity" (ibid.).

Translated, or hybrid or syncretic cultures, emerging out of the fusion of different cultural translations, may constitute a powerful creative force. But

LEEDS TRINITY UNIVERSITY

they can also encounter fierce, often violent, opposition where they are perceived as threatening fundamentalist projects of cultural "purification" (as in the case of Salman Rushdie, and as in the case of the new ethnic nationalisms in Europe). And there is perhaps little reason to hope that "new ethnicities" have any less destructive potential than "old" ones. But translated cultural identities are the inevitable consequence of the simultaneous globalization of media communications and growth of migration and transnational diasporic "communities." Two researchers, Appadurai and Hannerz, have recently advanced the analysis of this new type of formation in important ways.

Appadurai (1990) addresses the cultural politics of "deterritorialisation" and the sociology of displacement that it expresses. The tension between homogenization and heterogenization, in his analysis, is the central problem of today's global interactions, and the key to its analysis lies not in homogenization but in "indigenization." Inasmuch as "one man's imagined community is another man's political prison" (ibid.: 295), Appadurai diagnoses a widespread and increasing fear of "cultural absorption" by larger polities and cultures. It is thus the "central paradox of ethnic politics" today that "primordia (whether of language or skin colour or neighbourhood or of kinship) have become globalized," such that sentiments of intimacy and localized identity may ignite as political sentiments across "vast and irregular spaces, as groups move, yet stay linked to one another through sophisticated media capabilities" (ibid.: 306). Such "primordia" may well be the "product of invented traditions" (Hobsbawm and Ranger 1983) or "retrospective affiliations." But,

> because of the disjunctive and unstable interplay of commerce, media, national policies and consumer fantasies, ethnicity, once a genie contained in the bottle of some sort of locality (however large) has now become a global force, forever slipping in and through the cracks between states and borders.
>
> (Appadurai 1990)

Appadurai describes a global process of "disjunctures and conjunctures" between "ethnoscapes" (the landscapes of living persons) and "mediascapes"— "image-centred, narrative based accounts of strips of reality" which

> offer to those who experience and transform them [...] a series of elements (such as characters, plots and textual forms) out of which scripts can be formed of imagined lives, their own as well as those of others living in other places. These scripts can and do get disaggregated into complex sets of metaphors by which people live (Lakoff and Johnson 1980) as they help to constitute narratives of the "other" and proto-narratives of possible lives, fantasies which could become prolegomena to the desire for acquisition and movement.
>
> (Appadurai 1990: 299)

Appadurai therefore asks us to examine empirically which sets of communicative genres are valued in which ways, and "what sorts of pragmatic genre conventions govern the collective 'readings' of different kinds of text" (ibid.: 300). This is the task which this chapter undertakes; it is one which is all the more urgent because of the major political implications of these cultural processes.

"Deterritorialisation [...] is one of the central forces of the modern world, since it brings labouring populations into the lower-class sectors and spaces of relatively wealthy societies" (ibid.: 301), and one of its results has often been to create an intensified sense of critical attachment to the politics of the home state. "Deterritorialisation [...] is now at the core of a variety of global fundamentalisms including Hindu and Islamic fundamentalism." The Hindu example is most pertinent here. Appadurai argues that the Hindu diaspora has been exploited by various "interests both within and outside India to create a complicated network of finances and religious identifications, in which the problem of cultural reproduction for Hindus abroad has become tied to the politics of Hindu fundamentalism at home" (ibid.: 302). Such links are illustrated below, where I focus on Southall's local video culture and its role in the "reinvention of traditions" through a case study of the "devotional viewing" of Doordarshan's (Indian national TV) serial version of the *Mahabharata* in a Southall family. As Appadurai puts it: "Deterritorialisation creates new markets for film companies, art impresarios and travel agents, who thrive on the need of the deterritorialised population for contact with its homeland" (ibid.: 302). Both through media representations and through experiences of touristic travel as "return to the homeland," ethnically specific "mediascapes" of "invented homelands" are constructed. These mediascapes then often, through the processes described above, become the site of desires for change which are transferred to the living "ethnoscape." Thus Appadurai argues that "The creation of 'Khalistan,' an invented homeland of the deterritorialised Sikh population of England, Canada and the United States is one example of the bloody potential in such mediascapes, as they interact with the 'internal colonialisms' [...] of the nation-state" (ibid.).

As we shall see, however, most young people in Southall tend to reject these forms of cultural politics, associating them with their parents. Some young men appropriate the symbols of Sikh fundamentalism as a style, in order to present a "hard" (macho) image; but their Sikh peers often regard this as posturing, with little if any real political significance. The great majority aspire not to reterritorialize their ethnic group, but rather to transcend it in a mode of being described by Hannerz (1990) as "cosmopolitan."

Hannerz explores cosmopolitanism as "a state of mind" and "a mode of managing meaning" (1990: 238) in the context of globalization. It involves both a certain "orientation," which he describes as "a willingness to engage with the Other" and an "openness toward divergent cultural experiences, a search for contrasts rather than uniformity"; and also a set of competences (ibid.: 239). These general and specific competences include the ability to adapt flexibly to other cultures, and skill in maneuvering in and between particular cultures. The acquisition of such competences is, in fact, a central concern for young people in Southall.

The growth and proliferation of transnational communications and social networks "generate ... more cosmopolitans now than there have been at any other time" (ibid.: 241). Cosmopolitans experience transnational and territorial cultures as "entangled" in a variety of ways: "the real significance of the growth of the transnational cultures [...] is often not the new cultural experience that they themselves can offer people—for it is frequently rather restricted in scope and depth—but their mediating possibilities" (ibid.: 245). Transnational media play an increasing role in providing people with experiences of other cultures, helping to make cosmopolitans of them. Media mediate cultures; and as cosmopolitans read media, they translate between territorial, local, diasporic, national, and global cultures and identities:

> The transnational cultures are bridgeheads for entry into other territorial cultures. Instead of remaining within them, one can use the mobility connected with them to make contact with the meanings of other rounds of life, and gradually incorporate this experience into one's personal perspective.
> (Hannerz 1990: 245)

Cosmopolitans are, Hannerz suggests, perhaps "never quite at home again" (ibid.: 248), as their plural cultural experience makes them unable to enjoy the "untranslated" local's sense of the "natural" necessity of specific cultural forms. But he suggests, citing McLuhan, that "the implosive power of the media may now make just about everybody a little more cosmopolitan. And one may in the end ask whether it is now even possible to become a cosmopolitan without going away at all" (ibid.: 249). In this sense, too, the experience of migrants and diasporas is far from being marginal: it may well represent an imminent global/ universal future. Yet, as Hannerz observes, there can be no cosmopolitans without locals, since for the former the experience of diversity depends on access to varied cultures, just as locals increasingly feel the need to carve out special niches for their cultures and preserve them from the threat of assimilation and homogenization (ibid.: 250). In negotiating ethnic and cultural identity, locals and cosmopolitans may thus have a common interest, one which is potentially at odds with that of nation states. [...]

Local uses of the media: negotiating culture and identity

TV offers powerful representations of both Indian and British culture for the youth of Southall, who, though British citizens, do not always feel themselves to be part of the British nation and, though of Indian heritage and Punjabi background, are often less than willing to embrace all aspects of their cultural heritage. One of this chapter's key arguments is that the juxtaposition of culturally diverse TV programs and films in Punjabi homes stimulates cross-cultural, contrastive analyses of media texts, and that this heightens an awareness of cultural differences, intensifies the negotiation of cultural identities, and encourages the expression of aspirations towards cultural change. In short, the consumption of an increasingly transnational range of TV and films is catalyzing and accelerating processes of cultural change among London Punjabi families. But it will also be argued that Punjabi cultural "traditions" are just as likely to be reaffirmed and reinvented as to be challenged and subverted by TV and video viewing experiences. [...]

Devotional viewing: "sacred soaps"

As I indicated earlier, films serve the purpose of language learning, and elders also use them to impart religious knowledge. Parents encourage their children to learn their mother tongue at school, but students, by and large, are not keen. Resources are scarce and few are eager to take up Hindi, Urdu, or Punjabi as an examination subject. Literacy in these languages is not regarded as a useful skill. However, many young people are keen to develop oral/aural skills in order to communicate effectively with their elders and with relatives in Britain and in India, and films provide a way of doing so. Language is also a potent symbol of collective identity and often the site of fierce loyalties. In the context of a British society which constructs linguistic difference as a problem rather than as a resource, the desire to defend and maintain one's linguistic heritage becomes strong. Furthermore, in a community faced with religious diversity and at times division, it is not surprising that cultural identity is often construed as being based not only on linguistic but also on religious continuity. Religious or "mythological" films are viewed for devotional purposes, particularly (but not only) in Hindu families, and their viewing is often integrated into daily acts of worship.

In recent years India's government monopoly TV channel, Doordarshan, has screened serial versions of sacred texts of Hinduism, the *Ramayana* and the *Mahabharata*. They have enjoyed unprecedented popularity not only in India, where some 650 million viewers regularly tune in, but also in the Indian diaspora, where they are followed on cable TV, on video or, as with the *Mahabharata* in Britain, on broadcast TV. Some argue that these TV epics have exacerbated the trends towards Hindu fundamentalism and been exploited for political purposes: the BJP, the Hindu nationalist party, used several actors in these epics as candidates in various state elections (Chatterji 1989; cf. *We Have Ways of Making You Think*, BBC2, November 27, 1992). However, in Southall, Hindu families have found them useful for helping their children deepen their religious knowledge and beliefs.

During my fieldwork in Southall, I was fortunate enough to be welcomed into the home of the Dhanis—a Hindu family—in order to watch the Channel 4 broadcast of Peter Brook's stage adaptation of the *Mahabharata*, which occupied six hours on a Saturday evening in November 1990. A few weeks later BBC 2 began broadcasting Doordarshan's ninety-one-part serialized version of the *Mahabharata*. So over a two-year period I visited them regularly on Saturday afternoons to watch it. The juxtaposition of the two versions, one Indian and the other "western," led the Dhanis to perform a contrastive analysis. Our conversations and my observations during viewing formed the basis of a detailed case study of the reception of these two TV versions of the *Mahabharata* by the Dhani family (Gillespie 1993, 1994). Here I shall highlight some of the key insights of this case study and summarize its findings.

The *Mahabharata* and the *Ramayana* are the foundation myths of Indian society. They are said to permeate every aspect of Indian social life and to enshrine the philosophical basis of Hinduism, and for centuries have served as an *ithisa* or a fundamental source of knowledge and inspiration for all the arts. In Sanskrit, *maha* means "great"; *Bharat* is the name of a legendary family, which in an extended sense means "Hindu," or—extended further—"mankind." The *Mahabharata* is thus variously translated "The Great History of India" or "The Great History of Mankind." It tells the story of a long and bitter quarrel between two groups of cousins: the Pandevas and the Kauravas. It recounts the history of their divine origins and the conflict over who will rule the kingdom. Towards the end of the epic Krishna, one of the most revered of Hindu deities, incites the Pandevas to go to battle against their cousins to restore order and achieve justice. The *Bhagavat Gita*, one of the most sacred Hindu texts, which contains the essence of Hindu philosophy, records the advice which Krishna gives to Arjuna, a Pandevas, in a moment of self-doubt and weakness before going into the battle which is to decide the fate of the earth. Although few Hindus in Southall are familiar with the *Mahabharata* in its entirety, many know the *Bhagavat Gita* and, like the Dhanis, have acquired knowledge of its characters and story-line through its serialization in popular cartoons and filmic versions.

The Dhani household consists of nine people: the mother and father in their late forties, five daughters aged 12 to 23, and two sons aged 11 and 18. They emigrated to Southall from Calcutta in 1978. The father and mother are employed in local catering firms. The family regularly views religious films and Mrs Dhani, in particular, will often stay up until the early hours of the morning to view them. She claims that religious films provide her with comfort and solace from life's everyday anxieties. There is a tone of playful guiltiness in her voice when, sometimes, she admits to having watched religious videos for some fifteen hours at the weekend.

The devotional viewing of religious films involves taboos, prohibitions, and rituals, similar to those surrounding sacred places and objects. It is incorporated into the Dhanis' everyday lives, as are their domestic acts of worship. For example, at the start of a religious film incense is lit, and when a favorite god such as Krishna appears, the mother will encourage her children to sit up straight and make a devout salutation. An extra *puja* (an act of worship which is generally performed three times a day: before dawn, at noon, and in the evening) may be performed before or after viewing. Once a religious film has been switched on it must be viewed until the end out of respect. Food should not be eaten whilst viewing, except *prasad* or holy food that has been blessed. Viewing religious films is seen as a pleasurable act of devotion in itself and devotional viewing is arguably a mark of transformation in religious practices.

However, these "new" modes of TV consumption are nevertheless deeply rooted in Indian religious and cultural traditions, especially the iconographic conventions associated with the representation of deities (Guha-Thakurta 1986), and devotional modes of looking, seeing, and worshipping images deemed sacred (Appadurai and Breckenridge 1992).

My first visit to the Dhanis to watch Peter Brook's production of the *Mahabharata* was marked by confusion and a crisis. I shall briefly describe the evening in order to set the scene. From the outset confusion reigned as the international casting and bleak, sackcloth costumes had the immediate effect of rendering their dearly loved gods unrecognizable:

RANJIT: That's Ganesha!
SEFALI: No it isn't, be quiet.
LIPI: That's Vishnu!
MALATI: Don't be silly, that's Vyasa.
RANJIT: But Vyasa is Vishnu.
SEFALI: No he's not, he's Krishna.

After twenty minutes or so Mr Dhani and his elder son went out, proclaiming: "It's no good, it doesn't carry the meaning." Mrs Dhani, her five daughters, youngest son, and myself continued watching half-heartedly. A sullen and solemn atmosphere reigned and their lack of interest in the program was evident. They began telling me of their love for the god Krishna and their delight in the TV serial the *Ramayana*, which they had watched on video—which portrays the childhood of Krishna and tells the story of Krishna's incarnation, Lord Ram, and his wife, Sita. After a couple of hours, part three of the production opened with preparations for the battle and with Krishna encouraging Arjuna to go to war. Silence fell and intense viewing began. The children appeared to become increasingly alarmed: "Mum, why is Krishna telling Arjuna to kill his cousins? Why is he telling them to go to war?" asked Ranjit, the younger boy. "You don't know who the goodies and the baddies are in this one," said Malati. "Why are we watching this anyway?" exclaimed Sefali. "Tell me, who's enjoying it? Shall we switch it off?" All eyes fell upon me: "Yes, please do if you want to."

It is difficult to convey the sense of relief and change of atmosphere that occurred the moment the set was switched off. I was troubled that they had been putting up with it because of my presence and, as I later discovered, indeed they had. Mrs Dhani and her two eldest daughters disappeared upstairs. I heard the sound of bells ringing and a horn blowing. Sefali explained: "Oh, that's all right, they're just doing a *puja*." Their displeasure in and distaste for Brook's production were passed over quickly. "Terrible rubbish!" Malati muttered. Soon Mrs Dhani and her daughters reappeared: "Let's put *Sita's Wedding* on" (a film which tells of the wedding of Rama and Sita which occurs in the *Ramayana*). "Yeah!" cried the children. "Wait till you see it! it's fantastic!" By this time it was 10.30 p.m., so, fearful of overstaying my welcome, I replied that maybe I should come back: "No! No! Mum says you must stay!" There was a joyful atmosphere as *Sita's Wedding* was put on. "Why didn't we think of this before?" Munni cried. The mother sat on the floor with her two youngest children tucked under each of her arms as they all sang along to the opening song. When Ram appeared, they sat up and made a salutation: "Thank God, I have my taste back again!" said the mother as we continued watching into the night.

The drama of this first evening at the Dhanis reached its crisis at the moment, highlighted by Ranjit, when Krishna's divinity and moral integrity seemed to be thrown into question. After performing the *puja* the Dhanis became receptive to viewing *Sita's Wedding*. This is perceived as a sacred text and was viewed accordingly in a devotional manner. However, the reasons why Brook's production was so distasteful to the Dhani family only became apparent to me in subsequent weeks, as we began watching Doordarshan's version and the Dhanis began doing a contrastive analysis of the two versions which was to last for several weeks. This contrastive analysis was quite spontaneous on their part but it was also, of course, encouraged by my presence—by their desire to understand the story themselves and to be able to explain it to me. I was an outsider being gently ushered inside their family, their home, and their religion, and this dynamic triggered an exchange between us of unparalleled depth and intensity in my fieldwork. We reviewed parts of Brook's production as they were curious to resolve the moral dilemma that confronted them as a result of Krishna's exhortation to the Pandevas to go to war against "their own flesh and blood," as Ranjit put it. Malati got a copy of R. K. Narayan's shorter version of the *Mahabharata* and a text of the *Bhagavat Gita*, and so began our journey into resolving the enigmas and moral ambiguities it posed.

Brook's production was so distasteful to the Dhanis because, first, it flouted the iconographic conventions associated with the representation of Hindu deities. Certain visual codes, such as the use of color to symbolize the personal and moral qualities of the gods, had not been respected in their eyes:

SEFALI: You can't even recognise Krishna. Normally he's blue.

MALATI: Gunga and Bhisma normally wear white because it's a symbol of purity and truth.

RANJIT: Duryodhana should wear red, shouldn't he, because of his anger and the blood that gets shed?

Such systems of color classification and symbolism are to be found in many ancient religions; according to Turner (1966) they provide a kind of primordial classification of reality. In fact the visual codes associated with the representation of Hindu deities have developed over centuries, but it was the introduction of popular, mass-produced prints which resulted in more fixed and stereotypical portrayals of the gods. Guha-Thakurta (1986) has traced the changing iconography of popular, religious picture production in India. He describes how the introduction of lithographic presses and color printing led to the increased production of prints with "gaudy and flamboyant colours, dazzling costumes and majestic backdrops." The deities acquired a new solidity and roundedness. Theatrical postures and expressions also became part of the fixed stereotype of the gods. He argues that these developments contributed to the increasing humanization and domestication of divinity.

However, for the Dhanis, more disturbing than the flouting of visual codes in Brook's production was the transgression of yet more deeply rooted cultural codes, such as the primary distinction between gods and humans. In their view the gods were not portrayed with due dignity or respect.

SEFALI: All gods are born into royal families. In the Indian one you can tell the gods from humans [...] and who is a king from the way he talks and behaves, you can tell by his strength [...] when like Krishna appears there's always joyful music. There are other things, like the king will always wear gold and the prince silver.

SEWANTI: Like in the Indian one you can tell a baddy because he will be wearing dark clothes and the music will have an evil feel to it [...] in the English one they've left it all to the language. In the Indian one everything contributes to the meaning—the way they speak and how they are spoken to, how they behave, what they wear, their clothes, their jewelry, everything.

MALATI: The respect is missing, like you would never hear Krishna being called by his name like that, it would always be Lord Krishna or Krishna ji. You would never hear someone call their elder by their name [...] people show Krishna respect in the Indian one by kneeling and kissing his feet [...].

SEWANTI: They've spoiled the picture of the culture [...].

MUNNI: There's no feeling in it.

MALATI: They borrowed the story but not the culture.

In contrast, in the Indian version, the representation of the Hindu deity conforms to traditional iconographic conventions and therefore can be worshipped on the screen, as are the gods in the popular prints which adorn every room in their home. Thus, for devotional viewing to occur, the image must be perceived as sacred, as entitled to and worthy of veneration. Brook's production violated the sacred aura of the gods as represented by conventional iconography. [...]

In many aspects of their everyday lives the Dhanis apply religious ideas and beliefs which were undoubtedly developed and refined by their viewing of the *Mahabharata*. Specific notions of time, fate and free will, destiny and reincarnation frame their everyday perceptions, but in their contrastive analysis of the two versions of the *Mahabharata* the Dhanis explicitly articulated their understanding of the Hindu philosophical and religious tradition in a way which illuminated, for them perhaps as much as for me, key aspects of this tradition and so contributed to a further shaping of their values and beliefs.

The highpoint of the entire epic came during the *Bhagavat Gita* sequence when Krishna shows his universal form. The sheer awe with which this sequence was viewed by the family was as remarkable as the images on the screen. A low-angled tracking shot follows Krishna, surrounded by a golden aura, and, as he moves gracefully through the air, his figure expands to dominate the screen and his multifarious incarnations successively appear around him amidst flames and shafts of water. This represents for the Dhanis a divine vision. It is as if Krishna makes an appearance in the living-room. For the Dhanis, full of awe and wonderment, it is like *nirvana* on TV: devotional viewing at its fullest intensity. [...]

Dirty Dancing at Diwali

Diwali, the Festival of Lights, is celebrated with great rejoicing in October each year in honor of Lakshmi, the goddess of wealth. It marks the beginning of the New Year for Hindus and Sikhs alike. In most families, a ritual purification by water is followed by much dancing and music. In Southall, on the night of Diwali every house in every terraced street places candles along the low outside wall which separates the front garden from the pavement, and the skies are lit with magnificent firework displays. These firework displays are themselves an innovation in customary practices at Diwali, facilitated by the close proximity of Guy Fawkes Night, celebrated on 5 November throughout England: this is the only time in the year when fireworks are widely available in shops. Local schools usually close to enable families to celebrate, but most schools organize Diwali concerts, not unlike Christmas concerts in form, where performances of "traditional" Indian dancing, singing, and music are conventional. Typically, groups of girls learn the dances from a popular Hindi film and mime to songs, while boys play a range of Indian musical instruments.

At the high school where I worked, the deputy head, regarded by his students as a very "strict" Sikh, had made himself unpopular because of his attempts at "preserving religious and cultural traditions." According to many students, he was "going too far," chastizing students for cutting their hair, condemning girls who wore skirts or the slightest touch of make-up, and generally imposing a very strict regime. He also placed great emphasis on Indian performing arts, especially at Diwali. One year (1990) a group of 14- to 16-year-olds surreptitiously decided to change the Diwali concert repertoire and to perform a dance routine from the film *Dirty Dancing*—a "rite of passage" film which had maintained an unparalleled degree of popularity since it hit the box offices in 1987.

Dirty Dancing is set in an American holiday camp for teenagers in 1963. It traces a girl's passage from innocence to sexual maturity, and from ugly duckling to beautiful dancing princess, through a romantic encounter with the dancing instructor. Freed from parental constraints, dancing, especially sexually suggestive "dirty dancing," is enjoyed each night by the kids at the camp. The essential values of the film concern loyalty and friendship, and its major crisis occurs when the girl faces a conflict between loyalty to a friend and to the values of her parents—a theme to which most young people in Southall can easily relate. Patrick Swayze, an extremely popular film star among local girls, is the star dancer. His dancing partner gets pregnant several weeks before the final concert which marks the end of the summer camp and in which they are due to perform their star turn. Jennifer Grey, the female star of the film, obtains the money for an abortion from her father, refusing to tell him what the money is for out of loyalty to the girl. She simply asks her father to trust her.

Much of the film is about the preparations for the concert. Without his partner Swayze is at a loss, but Grey, of course, steps in. Initially they are simply dancing partners but soon they become intimate. They devote every waking hour to practising the dance for the final night. Further problems arise when Grey's father, a doctor, is called to the scene of the girl's botched abortion. Thinking Swayze is the father and that his daughter used the money to protect him, he forbids his daughter to have anything to do with him. Swayze is then sacked after being accused of theft by a jealous admirer. Grey stands by him and pleads his innocence to her father and the manager. When they refuse to believe her, she reveals that he could not have been responsible for the theft since she slept with him on that night. Her father is appalled.

All is very gloomy when the final night comes and the concert proceeds in a very dull manner. But Swayze returns, making a dramatic entrance. With all eyes upon him, he spots Grey sitting in a corner with her parents, declares that "No one puts Baby in a corner," takes her hand, and leads her up onto the stage. He stops the proceedings, grabs the mike, and tells everyone that they will do the last dance together. He publicly declares his love for her, saying that their love is not based on instant attraction but grew from their mutual respect and loyalty—values very close to the hearts of Southall youth. The dramatic climax arrives as they perform their duet to "I've Had the Time of my Life"—a lively flamenco/rumba mix involving intricate steps and an intense erotic charge. The high point of the dance is the "lift": he jumps off the stage, she runs down the aisle and makes a dramatic leap to fly up into his arms. The party takes off and everyone starts dancing—including two apparently staid old ladies in fur coats. All misunderstandings are cleared up as the father admits to them both that he was wrong, thereby declaring his approval of the romance.

Just as in the film, Amit and Jaspreet, who were chosen to do the dance routine, rehearsed every night after school for six weeks. They learned the steps from the video by repeatedly watching it. The whole process of rehearsing began to emulate the film itself—especially the problem of getting the steps right and doing the "lift." They could not practise the lift standing waist-deep in a lake, as in the film, but went to Southall Park, and practised it using park benches. Their performance was an outstanding success. The school audience went wild; students whistled, shouted, hooted, clapped. They had never seen such a skilled and daringly erotic performance by a boy and girl together. Boys do not usually dance at concerts and so Amit was considered brave and was praised for this, especially as he performed so well. The lift was met with cries of delight, and as Jaspreet twirled around in the air, the deputy head (rather than throw off his turban and dance, like the old ladies in furs, as someone jokingly suggested later) stalked out in disgust and rage—a triumphant victory for all youth present.

This appropriation of a western popular film was both unusually planned and unusually confrontational, setting out to challenge the culture of authoritative elders through a public performance and celebration of allegiance to the values of an idealized version of "western youth." As I have indicated, the choice of *Dirty Dancing* for this purpose was far from accidental, since the film itself is centrally concerned with conflicting loyalties to peer group and parental values. The jokingly suggested alternative response by the deputy headteacher might indeed be taken to imply a wish for this conflict to be resolved as in the film: a desire for the bearer of paternal authority in the school to emulate the filmic father's final acknowledgement of the legitimacy of the young stars' behavior. In many respects the differences between peer and parental cultures, and various kinds of attempt to negotiate between "Indian" or "Asian" and "British" or "western" systems of representation, values, and beliefs structure the viewing patterns reported by young people in Southall. Certainly this process can be conflictual. But as the aspects of the local media culture which I have outlined in this chapter indicate, outright confrontation is much rarer— certainly in domestic settings—than processes of debate, accommodation, and adaptation, in which young people, mothers, fathers, and grandparents take up contextually variable positions in response to their viewing. What can be discerned overall is a complex process of many-sided negotiation between the cultures actually and televisually present in Southall, a negotiation which is reflected in patterns of TV talk in youth culture.

10 Religion and authority in a remix culture

How a late night TV host became an authority on religion

Lynn Schofield Clark

Introduction

When late night talk show comedian Stephen Colbert testified before a U.S. Congressional Subcommittee in September of 2010 about the plight of migrant workers, the mainstream media were paying attention. But Colbert's audience arguably wasn't the members of Congress in attendance or the reporters who covered the event. The intended audience seemingly included those who saw the video once it went viral thanks to YouTube, Facebook, and blog mentions. Colbert noted in interviews that he testified because, like U.S. Democratic Representative Zoe Lofgren, who had invited him to testify, he wanted to raise awareness regarding the human rights violations that migrant workers experience (Grier 2010b). Colbert and Lofgren were betting that Colbert's celebrity would garner attention for the plight of migrant workers, and might raise awareness about the issue among his vast audience. And indeed, within two months, the video of his testimony available on YouTube had reached one million views.[1]

Colbert's testimony included some barbs for the U.S. Congress, such as when he noted that he trusted that "both sides would work together in the best interests of the American people as you *always* do."[2] He also utilized irony, noting that the "obvious answer" to the charge that "too many immigrants" are engaged in U.S. agricultural work is to "stop eating fruits and vegetables." But notably, Colbert broke character when he was questioned after his opening statement before the subcommittee, indirectly referencing his religious identity in explaining why he was using his celebrity to advocate for migrant workers:

> I like talking about people who don't have any power. It seems like the least powerful people in the United States are migrant workers who come and do our work, but who don't have any rights ... And you know, "whatsoever you do for the least of my brothers," and these seem like the least of our brothers right now ... Migrant workers suffer and have no rights.
>
> (Kandra 2010)

Audience members who were a part of Christian congregations, as well as those knowledgeable about that religious tradition, might be familiar with the "least of my brothers" reference as a call for justice attributed to Jesus in the New Testament (e.g. Matthew 25). In making this reference, Colbert was identifying himself as an insider to that tradition who would be recognized as such among other insiders. And this insider status, as will be discussed below, is a key facet of how Colbert has come to assume a somewhat unlikely mantle of religious authority among many in his growing U.S. audience.

Indeed, many of the reports covering Colbert's testimony in Congress implicitly questioned what right comedians might have to take their acts outside the realm of comedy.[3] Catholic commentator John W. Kennedy panned Colbert's Congressional testimony (Kennedy 2010), and Fox News decried it as a waste of time. But many saw the Congressional testimony as consistent with earlier messages in Colbert's comedy.[4] Colbert's television program, after all, has often referenced religion and the incongruities between stated faith commitments and actual practices in social and political life.[5]

Stephen Colbert first garnered a wide audience with a segment titled "This Week in God" that aired on Jon Stewart's *The Daily Show* on the U.S. cable channel Comedy Central. The segment, created by Colbert, featured "everything God did" in the prior week, often highlighting the inconsistent acts of religious or political leaders who attempted to lay claim to religious authority. And ever since *The Colbert Report* began airing on Comedy Central in late 2005, Colbert has included an average of at least one reference to religion in each week of his programs, including editorial comments on the Vatican and Pope Benedict XVI, U.S. Islamophobia, and evangelical and mainline Protestant groups.[6] The program has hosted the Roman Catholic gay activist and former *New Republic* editor Andrew Sullivan, Catholic League President William Donohue, evangelical Baptist minister and author Tony Campolo, Jesuit Father Jim Martin, and Religious Studies scholars Elaine Pagels, Randall Balmer, Steve Prothero, and Bart Ehrman, among others. Playing a newscaster in the model of conservative Fox News talk show host Bill O'Reilly, Colbert's persona embodies a fundamentalist Catholic perspective that often expresses little interest in understanding non-Christian religions.[7] At the same time, Colbert's "real life" identity as a Catholic is well known, and has been referenced in interviews with *Rolling Stone* magazine, NPR's *Fresh Air* with Terry Gross, and the Religion News Service.[8]

Colbert has been widely recognized as an influential figure in popular culture and in journalism, as he has been on the cover of countless magazines and served as guest editor of a special issue of *Newsweek* in June 2009.[9] His appeal is particularly noteworthy among well-educated young adults under 30.[10] Given his popularity among a small yet influential audience and the fact that his program is increasingly prominent in the public realm, the irreverent and morally perceptive views he espouses are particularly relevant in a discussion of how celebrities might attain a form of consensus-based interpretive authority.[11] By focusing on the emergence of a cultural figure who has no direct power to wield and no official capacity from which to lead, yet whose media platform enables him to offer social commentary about religion through satire, in this chapter I aim to shed light on how individuals attain religious authority in relation to the emergence of the prerogatives of remix culture.

In this chapter I will explore why a comedian and celebrity such as Stephen Colbert needs to be considered seriously as a source of authority in relation to religion. I argue that it is not that media figures such as Colbert are replacing traditional religious authorities such as rabbis, priests, or ministers, or that the media are displacing religion's authoritative role in culture more generally.[12] Rather, in a culturally plural context, members of society need not only leaders of religious traditions, but also interpreters of how various players in our societal fabric operate in relation to one another. Those who are positioned to serve as interpreters of religion's role in society, and whose views articulate those that are consensually accepted, thus emerge as authoritative figures in contemporary culture. Colbert, therefore, is here considered for what will be termed the consensus-based interpretive authority he wields, albeit without intention and without power, when it comes to the relation between religion and politics in the United States.

It is important to note that Colbert is not an authoritative voice for all people even in U.S. society, let alone in other locations. Yet examining his popularity and the frequency with which he refers to religion in his programs and publications raises a key question: in today's religiously plural and politically divided western societies, who has the right to speak about religion publicly? Some who take the authority of state and institutional religion seriously might invest religious authority in traditional religious and state leaders, but others who are more skeptical of these traditional sources of authority might invest authority elsewhere. Thus, through this discussion I raise the question: what happens when that investment of authority "elsewhere" seems to be in the form of a media celebrity? How, then, is authority constituted, enacted, and made manifest?

To consider these questions, I begin by considering what authority is, and what modern society's discomfort with authority has meant in terms of theorizing the emergence and challenging of authority in contemporary culture. I then consider how scholars have thought about the role of media in relation to authority, with some writers exploring how media have supported and challenged traditional authority whereas others have considered how media have replaced traditional authority. In recent years, scholars have been rethinking authority in relation to digital media, arguing that rather than seeing media in relation to traditional authority, we need to consider how new media participate in managing and producing consensus that, in turn, provides legitimacy to authority. In the final section, therefore, I explore how Colbert's authority is manifested in and through his articulation of irreverence as that stance has emerged as a consensually accepted approach to religion in a religiously and culturally plural society.

The question of authority

Sociologist Adam Seligman has noted that modernity is hostile to authority; this is why we have difficulty understanding its persistence in our contemporary society (Seligman 2000). Yet a desire for traditional authority does persist, as is particularly evident in the ethnic and religious identities of the Islamic world and in neo-conservative movements such as the U.S. Tea Party.[13] Yet even those who affirm traditional sources of authority believe that *individuals* have the capacity to decide for themselves whether or not a particular organization or individual warrants authority. And this belief in the individual's power of reason is what Seligman calls "modernity's wager." Individuals now look to themselves—rather than to God, nature, or church—as sources of moral authority, and this morally conscious self has become the foundation for the civic order.

Authority within the civic order has been a topic of interest within sociology since the writings of Max Weber in the nineteenth century. Weber was interested in how people granted legitimacy to three types of political leadership in which people grant leaders the right to speak for and lead others. Weber identified religious, sacred, and spiritual forms of authority as *traditional* authorities, along with what Hannah Arendt later termed the "pre-political" authorities of parents, family, or tribe. As George Ritzer noted, "traditional authority is based on a claim by the leaders, and a belief on the part of followers, that there is virtue in the sanctity of age-old rules and powers" (Ritzer 1999: 132). The traditional leader's authority, therefore, rests on something related to his or her identity (age, status within the family, education), but is also dependent upon the leader's ability to adhere to and embody traditional principles.

Many scholars have been interested in how media present a challenge to traditional sources of authority (Hjarvard forthcoming; Hoover 2006; Campbell 2007). In contemporary times, the Catholic clergy sex scandal is the most prominent example of how traditional leaders lose their authority when exposed for failing to embody traditional and widely accepted principles.

Weber noted that some leaders were granted authority based on *charisma*, or how a group of people viewed a particular individual personality as extraordinary. Charismatic authority is often seen as revolutionary, in that such personalities can challenge traditional authority. In recent years, religious charismatic leadership has been seen as highly suspect, as it tends to be associated with leaders of new religious movements such as David Koresh and Jim Jones (McCloud 2003; Arweck 2006).

What Weber termed *rational–legal authority* refers to the fact that as societies grow in size and complexity, their method of rule tends to become more routinized, rational, and bureaucratic. Society's members thus place their trust in a set of uniform principles encoded into law and practice, which, in Weber's view, can over time function as an "iron cage" that traps people into systems of increasing efficiency and control (see, e.g., Beniger 1986). Notions of authority are codified and recodified, as Anthony Giddens has noted (Giddens 1990).

Unfortunately, not many scholars have considered how media and religion relate to rational/legal authority and the rise of what has been termed algorithmic authority, or the authority that rests in such consensus-based collective evaluation systems as one finds in Amazon's recommendations, populist television programs such as *American Idol* and the Eurovision song contest, and Google's search engine. In this chapter I argue that Colbert's authority is most closely related to an outgrowth of rational–legal authority, as his authority must be understood in relation to the prerogatives of a profit-driven media system that thrives on amassing large audiences that give their attention, and thus their consensus, to particular persons or programs.

Consensus-based authority

Consensus-based authority is not new, even to religion. A shift to consensus-based authority dates to the ascetic-Puritans of the sixteenth and seventeenth centuries, as Seligman points out (Seligman 1990). Prior to that time, traditional and moral authority were rooted in the hierarchy of the church, and were seen as something that was passed down through the offices of that church. Yet the Puritans of England and later America resisted this institutionalization of authority, instead prioritizing the "community of the elect." The community of Puritans viewed themselves as covenanted together in pursuit of the moral life, and thus saw the ministry as "based on consent, collective agreement and the fundamental equality of believers and ministers before God" (ibid.). Rather than a priest whose authority derived from his relationship with the church, therefore, the Puritan minister's authority was localized and defined in relation to one congregation. Moral and religious authority came to be rooted in *consensus*, as the group had to agree to grant authority to a leader. Once the individual leader lost the consent of his flock, his authority was no longer legitimate, and thus he was no longer recognized as an authority within that congregation or elsewhere.

Just as religious leaders came to be recognized and "called" in relation to consensus, so communities also came to be bound together in relation to collective pride and shame. Thus, authority also came to be related to what we *sacralize* as a society: we invest authority in people who can articulate or embody what we hold most meaningful, truthful, and valuable. Long before the consensus-based media of today, therefore, societies were granting authority to those who were able to articulate what its members found meaningful. The media industries, however, have deepened and propelled this process further. As profit-based industries, media such as newspapers, music recordings, and television must appeal to the largest number of people possible, thus reinforcing popular ways of seeing the world as a means of garnering attention. This system has resulted in the rise of celebrity as well as a related populist approach to culture.

Celebrity, as Frank Furedi has pointed out, offers an alternate means of validation to traditional and charismatic authority. Celebrity "signifies that someone possesses the quality of attracting attention," and in garnering this attention, they can attain some of the deference that was once afforded to more traditional authorities (Furedi 2010). The rise of the celebrity authority, in fact, has come about as a byproduct of society's uneasy relationship with authority.

Unlike traditional elites whose authority rests on specialized education or relations to political or religious authority, or charismatic leaders viewed as extraordinary, celebrities often achieve their celebrity based on their ability to
articulate and represent *ordinariness*. They serve as a reference point for others;
they are seen as "like us" rather than in some way superior. Celebrities become
"an exalted version of ourselves," as Furedi argues, offering an alternative to
the privileged elite, the superhuman, or the traditional authority. But celebrity
authority has one other advantage in the consumerist context in which it
emerges: it is easily replaceable, certainly much more so than either familial ties
or the political authorities within the rational–legal system who are granted the
right to represent us for a pre-established period of time. Like consumer goods,
if a celebrity fails us for some reason, we can simply look for a new celebrity to
elevate. Celebrities who fall from grace have seen consumer attention wane,
hence limiting their ability to speak and act authoritatively. Such failed celebrities have in effect demonstrated their lack of ordinariness and relatability,
whether due to their moral failings, their elite privileges and self-perception, or
their marginal views.

Media celebrities, whether of television, film, music, or sports, are given
attention as long as they are found to appeal to a significant audience. But not
all celebrities can be considered authorities, of course, particularly in relation to
the political order. Many celebrities benefit from some combination of physical
attractiveness and relatability and make little attempt to provide social commentary on political, religious, or cultural occurrences. Some media celebrities,
such as Sean Penn, Timothy Robbins, and Charlton Heston, become known for
their use of celebrity to promote political views that are not necessarily mainstream; others, such as Barbra Streisand, J.K. Rowling, Eddie Izzard and Michael
Caine, use their celebrity and funds to support largely mainstream politicians
and positions. Some personalities, such as Michael Moore, Michael Franti, and
Ani DeFranco, have built their celebrity upon the appeal their political and social
messages hold for a particular audience. Well-known political news commentators have similarly built audiences that come to identify with and appreciate
their commentary, from the US's Frank Rich and David Brooks to E.J. Dionne
and the UK's Peter Oborne, and from Rachel Maddow and Keith Olbermann to
the more controversial Rush Limbaugh, Anne Coulter, and Bill O'Reilly. These
celebrities are *consensus-based interpretive authorities* in the sense that their
very celebrity rests upon their ability to articulate perspectives that are widely
appreciated and that provide what is taken as a reasonable interpretation of
current events. A few missteps may be forgiven, but if audiences sense that their
commentary or ethical lapses step too far outside the acceptable mainstream,
they may eventually find their celebrity waning, along with their ability to
speak authoritatively on the issues that concern them—as commentators such
as U.S. right-wing talk show hosts Michael Savage and Rick Sanchez and the
liberal-turned-conservative comedian Dennis Miller have found.

Although some celebrities have suffered loss of popularity when their
outspoken religious views differ from those of the U.S. mainstream, as witnessed

most spectacularly with Tom Cruise's promotion of Scientology, many media celebrities seem to be permitted a wide berth when it comes to their religious inclinations. Of course, for commentators whose authority rests on articulating widely accepted views, the situation is slightly different. Those who are known for speaking about issues with religious dimensions tend to be seen as simpatico by the tradition's insiders and as more or less partisan by outsiders to their traditions; the Mormon Glenn Beck and U.S. Middle East commentator Thomas Friedman come to mind. Yet Beck and Friedman, like Colbert, embody specific religious affiliations and simultaneously give voice to perspectives that are widely accepted both within those traditions and among those who do not embrace them. Their ability to speak to the mainstream therefore contributes to their positions as consensus-based interpretive authorities, but they do not speak authoritatively for all, or without resistance from some. The authority these celebrities wield also rests on the fact that they are not understood to be seeking or claiming authority, particularly in the traditional sense. Rather, they are claiming to be entertainers and interpreters, seeking audiences. They might seek to provide interpretations in what they view as the public good, but due to their position within the media system, they are only permitted to do so indirectly.

Media studies and cultural authority

Media studies has long been interested in persons who utilize media to establish their authority within a culture. Early studies of propaganda viewed mass media as a key player in establishing Hitler's authority in the Weimar Republic, but subsequent work challenged this simplistic view of media, noting that the media were a series of institutions, not a singular force that could be wielded with intention. Mass media came to be viewed as a part of the rational/legal authority within society, as it was a system of institutions, professions, and practices that reflected as well as shaped public opinion, even as it often privileged the perspectives of those in power. If messages in the media did not find resonance with an audience, they were dismissed as marginal. In the profit-driven media environment of the west, this meant that those in power who sought to craft media messages that were well received would do well to pay attention to the taken-for-granted views of the audiences with whom they wished to establish authority. And indeed, beginning with the Reagan administration, U.S. officials approached the construction of media messages with a great deal of intentionality and sophistication.

Yet in addition to political authority, media studies has also been interested in issues of *cultural* authority, or the right of some to express the perceived norms of the whole. The roots of such studies date to the unlikely figure of Matthew Arnold, who in 1869 bemoaned the fact that the new urban dwellers of the English industrial age had little appreciation for the traditions of great literacy and culture as the English elite defined it. At that point in history, a few well-trained authorities were trusted to identify cultural texts worthy of preservation and celebration, and their authority was very much rooted in class position as well as education. But the selection of certain cultural artifacts as more worthy than others meant that those cultural materials produced by people outside of the elite were largely ignored or, worse, viewed as destructive and inferior to the culture that was deemed worthy of preservation. This was the genesis of the term "popular" culture: it referred to the culture "of the people," but also assumed that such culture was morally inferior to the culture of the elites (Clark 2008). During the industrial era and after, of course, cultures apart from the elite flourished. They remained largely unrecognized and under-appreciated until the spread of mid-twentieth century social, intellectual, and educational movements, when such traditions came to be recognized and eventually appreciated as important contributors to a diverse and democratic culture (Du Bois 1986; Hoggart 2009). Celebrity authority, as described above, is clearly a legacy of the populist desire to elevate attractive yet seemingly ordinary individuals. As these individuals become reference points for members of society, they are endowed with the attention and deference once reserved only for traditional elites.

As the media have come to be viewed as cultural institutions that are distinct from and yet influential in relation to other institutions such as those of politics, education, the family, and economics, journalism historian Barbie Zelizer has argued that authority emerges out of ritual, symbol, and narrative in the context of communities. She argues that journalists have been cultural authorities, or persons granted the authority to tell the stories society is then to recognize as meaningful and important, because they have formed a professional culture and a set of practices that echo consensus-based norms. Authority, Zelizer has noted, is "a construct of community, functioning as the stuff that keeps community together" (Zelizer 1992: 4). Yet professional journalists are not the only ones to lay claim to the cultural authority to tell the community's stories. Zelizer illustrated this in her review of how Oliver Stone's feature film *JFK* contributed to reshaping a culturally authoritative story, giving credence to conspiratorial myths that, prior to the film, had been considered marginal by most in society (including the traditional journalists covering the assassination). Through Stone's use of narrative, imagery, symbol, and an ability to tap a deeply resonant theme of government conspiracy that had predated the Kennedy assassination, Stone was able to create a new version of history, much to the dismay of those who understood the assassination's facts differently. Thus, this kind of cultural authority was consensus-based and interpretive, providing a narrative that differed from that of elites yet was popularly accepted and reinforcing of what people sacralized.

With digital media, our likes and dislikes have become even more systematized. We are constantly providing inputs to systems of information, whether in the form of purchases we make, stories we read, or videos we view online. Through these impersonal systems of data collection, we are providing expertise about culture. We rely now upon an algorithmic authority, as digital entities such as Amazon or Google produce a statistical determination of what is culturally worthy (Shirky 2009). This is foundational to what Lawrence Lessig,

Adrienne Russell, and others have termed a *remix culture*, as new technologies enable people to participate both passively and actively in creating and evaluating culture (Russell 2011: ch. 4). Termed "participatory culture," this ability to become involved in cultural production and hence to exercise cultural authority is widely celebrated for its democratizing potential (Jenkins 2006; Lessig 2008; Manovitch 2001). Today, we recognize that we each can participate in creating cultural systems of order, and therefore we grant authority to people like Stephen Colbert, or to people like Glenn Beck, as they speak about the role of religion in relation to culture in a way that echoes our own beliefs (Wesch 2007a, 2007b). As we participate in watching their programs, purchasing their books, contributing to their fan websites, and sharing clips from their programs with others in our social circles, we are contributing to their consensus-based interpretive authority in a remix culture. We participate in a process of remixing cultural elements in a way that reinforces some perspectives and narratives and deemphasizes others. In this sense, then, it is not the media that undermine traditional or promote charismatic authority, but rather it is the collective uses of the media in a remix culture that enable a new form of authority to emerge and become reinforced.

Conclusion

Weber's description of authority as traditional, charismatic, and rational–legal is still applicable today, yet it does not fully account for the rise of cultural authority as it has come to be contested in the mediated realm of the twentieth and twenty-first century. In this chapter I have argued that with the institutionalization of rational–legal authority in the profit-driven media systems that increasingly rely upon consensus, a seemingly democratic culture promotes sometimes-unlikely candidates for its authorities about topics of concern.

Colbert's religious authority is not universal, nor is it permanent. Indeed, like the leaders of the Puritan flocks of centuries earlier, Colbert's authority to speak about religion is granted through consensus as his audience continues to find his humor and interpretations relevant and insightful. Yet Colbert's status as a member of the U.S. Catholic community also contributes to his authority. He is a meaningful voice within a specific interpretive community that appreciates irreverence, particularly when it comes from one of "our" own. Were he to make statements about Catholicism or other faith groups that were considered offensive, blasphemous, or simply tasteless, his popularity would probably wane. But irreverence continues to fit well with a population that's increasingly skeptical of authority and its institutions, and with a young adult population that is increasingly tolerant of difference and intolerant of intolerance. Irreverence recognizes that there are no easy answers for the relationship between U.S. religious identities and politics, and anyone in a position of power who acts like there is, and who tries to impose his or her will on others, is open for parodying. Irreverence also helps an audience recognize that anyone who tries to define what religion is and what it means is also open to parodying.

This is why the atheist Richard Dawkins is as likely to come under criticism as the Pope on Colbert's program. In a time in which young adults in particular want to be accepting and tolerant, and yet some also want to be at least nominally religious, irreverence gives this particular segment of the population a stance: they can be faithful in recognizing that these issues of which rules are appropriate and who gets to decide are not easily resolved issues.

One final irony that is worth noting with regard to the rise of consensus-based interpretive authority in the realm of religion is that even as religiously conservative young people are questioning the traditional sources of authority within their religious organizations, religiously affiliated viewers are respectful, even reverent, of Colbert. In large part, this is because Colbert does identify as a Catholic and interacts knowledgeably and often sympathetically with religion and religious persons in a way that makes sense for his audience.

It is relatively easy for some who agree with Colbert politically to applaud the fact that today the ability to speak authoritatively about religion no longer rests within traditional religious institutions. Yet Colbert's story seems more a cautionary tale when those same people consider his talk show rivals. Glenn Beck similarly gives voice to religious perspectives, and he, too, has demonstrated the ability to exercise consensus-based interpretive authority among his own interpretive community.

Just as a feature filmmaker was able to undermine the traditional authority of journalism, in the context of new media others have challenged or claimed journalistic authority, as well, raising the question noted at the beginning of this chapter: who has the right to speak publicly and authoritatively about topics of concern? And, moreover, how is this right justified philosophically and morally, particularly in the increasingly anti-authoritarian environment that the Internet has wrought? In this chapter I have not attempted to provide justification for the promotion of Colbert as a religious authority, but I merely point out that, given the importance of both consensus and interpretation in contemporary society, Colbert has come to take on an authoritative position regarding religion as he has critiqued religion from the position of a well-placed insider. As the process of mediatization means that collective uses of media push popularity and consensus above other criteria of cultural authority, so the authority to articulate common perspectives will continue to shift into more diverse locations and will be found in operation in perhaps increasingly brief forms. Together, audiences, taken-for-granted perspectives of certain powerful interpretive communities, and the institutional forces of the media are working together to reconstitute the field of cultural production in relation to religion and authority.

Notes

1 As of November 15, 2010, YouTube reported 955,919 views of Colbert's Opening Statement posted by CSPAN, 50,000 views via the Daily Beast, and more than 100,000 views from various sources, including RussiaToday, KrayolaTop, Fire-DogLakeTV, and others.

2 The hearings were broadcast on C-SPAN3. C-SPAN1 offers uninterrupted coverage of the House of Representatives and the live program *Washington Affairs* every morning; C-SPAN2 provides uninterrupted coverage of the U.S. Senate; C-SPAN3 features live public affairs events and airs historical archived programming. The three C-SPAN channels are noncommercial public affairs programming channels that receive no government support. They are operated by the National Cable Satellite Corporation and are funded through the subscriber fees charged to cable and direct broadcast satellite operators.

3 See numerous reports from Fox News: http://www.foxbusiness.com/markets/2010/09/ 23/stephen-colbert-testimony-migrant-workers-spokesperson-says/; http://www.foxnews. com/politics/2010/09/24/stephen-colbert-appears-capitol-hill-hearing-illegal-immi- grants/; http://www.huffingtonpost.com/2010/09/25/megyn-kelly-outraged-at-c_n_738567. html; http://www.examiner.com/political-buzz-in-national/rep-king-goes-on-fox-news- to-object-to-stephen-colbert-s-testimony-video. See also Grier (2010a). Making this point about the fact that reporters are less interested in Colbert's content than in the authoritative controversy it generates is Sconce (2010).

4 Fox News cohost Gretchen Carlson promised to feature the testimony and dismissed it as "a stupid waste of time," September 30, 2010. But see also Jackson (2010).

5 Several blogs have been devoted to following Colbert's references to his Catholic identity, notably http://CatholicColbert.wordpress.org.

6 This figure is based on looking at the references to religion on the Colbert Nation website, as well as research on Colbert from 2008. See Brehm (2009).

7 See, e.g., "A Colbert Christmas: The Greatest Gift of All," debuted on Comedy Central, November 23, 2008.

8 Rolling Stone, "The Joy of Stephen Colbert: The New Issue of Rolling Stone," *Rolling Stone*, September 2, 2009; *Fresh Air with Terry Gross*, National Public Radio, November 19, 2008; Winston 2010. An outtake from the television program "Strangers with Candy" features Colbert doing a joyously frenetic dance to the Catholic folk mass song "The King of Glory," which is a video that has since gone viral.

9 "Stephen Colbert: King of Magazine Covers," *Breaking the News*, December 17, 2009. Online. Available at: http://www.breakingthenewnews.com/blog/2009/12/17/stephen- colbert-king-of-magazine-covers.html. Newsweek, June 5, 2009.

10 Pew Report on young adults.

11 I am using the word "prophetic" to reference the fact that his critiques of religion often imply that religion should lead to social justice and compassion.

12 The claim that media are replacing religion is central to mediatization of religion theory as articulated by Stig Hjarvard. (See Hjarvard forthcoming.)

13 Pew study, 2010.

11 The Angel of Broadway

The transformative dynamics of religion, media, gender, and commodification

Diane Winston

How did a small, marginal evangelical mission become one of the most successful charitable organizations in the United States? The transformation of the Salvation Army from ragtag street preachers to multi-million dollar social service providers is a story of religious dynamism, canny leadership, and strategic planning. But it is also a case study of how a network of actors, ideologies, and technologies—in this case, media producers, news managers, religious leaders, gender practices, consumerism, and the mass media—enacted a shift in perceptions and a change in attitudes. Drawing on theories of mediation and mediatization (Hjarvard 2008a) as well as actor-network theory (Latour 2005), this chapter focuses on how film served as a catalyst for changing public opinion about the Army, and why lassies, living symbols of the Army, were key. A cautionary tale, at least for believers, the fate of Army illustrates, in Stig Hjarvard's words, how the "the media—as conduits, languages and environments—facilitate changes in the amount, content and direction of religious messages in society, at the same time as they transform religious representations and challenge and replace the authority of institutionalized religion" (Hjarvard 2008a: 14).

Crucial to this process are the ways in which gendered religious representations are rendered, then circulated, by the secular news and entertainment media. Within the media's commercial logic (Jansson 2002), lassies (the popular term for Salvationist women) were the most apt embodiment of the Army because they could be depicted as sexual female figures.[1] Initially, the secular news media sensationalized lassies as emblematic of the Army's shortcomings. The storyline engaged readers and helped sell newspapers. Later, the secular entertainment media cast the lassie as a melodramatic heroine, whose virtues trumped masculine vices—and propelled ticket sales. In both cases, the aims of media—telling compelling stories and making money for owners and advertisers—colluded in the commodification of the lassie. Symbolizing the frisson of religion and sexuality, she sold the media product. But, at the same time, she also imparted a new vision of the Army's mission and identity.

It's an advertising truism that sex sells, and in the news business religion and sex sell very well. For most world religions, the female body is a contested site. Within Christianity, the longstanding tension between the "good" maternal body and the "sinful" sexual body has had a profound impact on both women's individual and cultural identities. The Madonna, the good woman and the ultimate mother, was a virgin. There is no archetype for a good and sexually active woman and mother. For centuries, sexually active women fell into the Magdalene's camp, and at best might repent for their sins. The problem is obvious for a religious movement in which women play a visible public role. How to create a new image that transcends a very old, very powerful dichotomy?

The dilemma, as potent in the twenty-first century as it was in the first, reflects the titillation generated by the tension between sanctity and sexuality: Can a "good" woman be sexual and a "sexual" woman be good? This question played out in the context of the nineteenth century news media, an industry bent on using scandal and sensation to sell newspapers (Winston forthcoming). Salvationist publications might try to compete but their circulation could not match that of the secular press; the negative image of Army lassies lasted almost a decade. Only through perseverance and good public relations did it change.

Refashioned as "slum angels" by Salvationist leaders and, in time, secular newspapers, lassies enabled the Army to be seen in a positive light. The new identity also appealed to entertainment media that valued heroines whose wholesomeness could be telegraphed by a plain blue uniform. That wholesome image, subsequently deployed in Broadway's musicals, transferred easily to the fledgling film industry. Film made possible the widespread circulation of the image of the virtuous lassie, and concomitant aspects of media logic, including commodification and entertainmentization,[2] influenced public perceptions not only of lassies but also of their Army. The public's low opinion of the Army as a scandalous outlier was transformed into widespread appreciation for its work as a humanitarian social service provider. In this chapter I explore how the confluence of media, gender dynamics, and human agency made that possible. It reviews the Army's mission and its deployment of women; religious and secular depictions of Army lassies; and the impact of film on the lassies' and, by extension, the Army's image.

The Salvation Army, American news coverage and Army counter-attacks

The Salvation Army, an evangelical missionary organization, began in late nineteenth century Britain.[3] Its founder William Booth believed material security was a prerequisite for successful evangelism. His "army" was a living metaphor, and Booth courted public notice—if not notoriety—as a branding and marketing strategy. Soldiers held services in pubs and graveyards, used brass bands to attract attention, and encouraged women to publicly preach. Critics called these female troops "Hallelujah lasses" and the Army adopted the name as a badge of pride. In 1880, when the Army launched its official American "invasion," the landing party was made up of one man and seven women. Many of its earliest American recruits were women and its initial leadership, from 1886 to 1934, included two Booth daughters and a daughter-in-law.

During its first years in the United States, the Army's enthusiasm attracted curiosity-seekers. Yet the obvious excitement, evident in rollicking open-air services and spirited meetings, drew criticism. Both the secular press and the ministerial elite condemned Salvationists as vulgar, sensationalist, and un-Christian. Much of the censure was directed at Army women. Both secular and religious publications accused female Salvationists of sacrificing their respectability. According to allegations, women became hysterical at Army services and were compromised by living in co-ed barracks. It was even claimed that male officers routinely seduced female recruits. Women who joined the movement were characterized as low class, and if daughters of the middle and upper classes enlisted, their families often went into mourning. The *New York Times*, singling out a society girl from her co-religionists, noted: "An air of breeding [makes] her conspicuous among her coarse-faced companions."[4]

When Maud Charlesworth Booth, daughter of a respectable English clergyman, took command of the American Army with her husband Ballington, she had to overcome the notoriety spread by the news media. Months before the Ballington Booths arrived in New York, the local press headlined their romance, informing readers about the religious zealots who came between a father and his child. (Maud's father, an Anglican cleric, did not approve of his daughter joining the Booths' Army.) The consequences were duly noted:

> The real moral of this story is that parents who do not wish their children to become officers in the Salvation Army had better forbid attending meetings in the first instance. The part the Army assigns to women has extraordinary attraction in these times ... By the side of such experiences as this career opens to them, the ordinary routine of home must appear intolerably dull.[5]

Maud and other women may have wanted to be religious leaders, but most Americans did not approve. The *New York Times* declared: "whoever joins the Salvation Army from the nature of the case bids good-bye to respectability."[6] But Maud's words and deeds, as well as her plummy accent and genteel manners, challenged the perception that becoming a Salvationist meant an end to a woman's good name. Her weekly column in the *War Cry*, the Army's newspaper, fortified female officers who worried that preaching in bars and storming brothels compromised their natural modesty. Booth argued that the desire to save sinners bestowed the "power to rise above" one's circumstances. She championed the "Woman Warrior," a soldier who wed gentleness and loving kindness to courage, strength, and action. Most women warriors came from small towns and modest means. In *War Cry* fictions, unworldly females realize the emptiness of their lives when confronted by the Army. But the heroine dies before she is saved and, with her last breath, regrets her ill-spent years.

Real-life stories were less dramatic. Recruits were the daughters of church-going farmers or small businessmen. Most had fallen away from organized religion or found it unfulfilling. Few careers were open to them unless they left home, but many lacked the will to strike out on their own. The Army offered an alternative. Even if her family disowned a young soldier, she had little time to grieve. She was expected to move to a new city, build up a corps, and make it self-sufficient. After a few months, she would be assigned elsewhere. Throughout the 1880s, Army women serving in small towns and cities were whipped and beaten because they were not considered respectable. They challenged gender roles at a time when social and economic changes were upending cultural conventions and creating a backlash. For many Americans, the lassies' public role placed them beyond the bounds of acceptable gender behavior and they were treated harshly. After Maud and Ballington Booth resigned in 1895, there were no further mentions of women warriors. Maud's female successors, sisters-in-law Emma Booth-Tucker and Evangeline Booth, were more conventional.

Emma Booth-Tucker, for example, projected a "mother's heart"—an image resonant with the cult of domesticity—the nineteenth century valorization of the female as nurturer. She epitomized the "womanly woman" whose implicit moral authority won her a place on the public stage. Emma juggled work and family: she led a national movement, traveled extensively, and cared for seven children. Methodically overseeing even the smallest details, Emma cut her children's hair, sewed their clothes, and led them in Bible study. Likewise, she encouraged Salvationist women to focus on tasks associated with the domestic sphere. Instead of woman warriors, Salvationist women embodied a softer, more maternal persona. Slum sisters, living among the urban poor, modeled Christian virtues by "mothering." They nursed, scrubbed, cooked, and took care of tenement children. Their mix of daring and self-sacrifice enchanted female reporters, who wrote about "slum angels" toiling amidst urban squalor. In one such article for the *New York World*, reporter Julia Hayes Percy enjoyed tea and plum cake at the Army's barracks before setting out on her night of revelation ("revelations of such misery, depravity, and degradation that, having been gazed upon, life can never be quite the same afterward").[7]

In 1903, Emma Booth-Tucker was killed in a train accident. The *War Cry* eulogized her as "the incarnation of true womanhood," and the secular press agreed. During her tenure, lassies gained a new respectability alongside deep admiration for their work. In Emma's stead, William Booth sent his daughter Evangeline to head his U.S. troops. An unmarried woman who enjoyed authority, Evangeline lauded new opportunities for women while supporting traditional notions of female moral superiority. Although she supported suffrage and women's rights, Evangeline maintained the home-centered language of mothers and sisters when describing the lassies' role. During the First World War, Evangeline drew on this mix to justify sending lassies overseas. Sensing that American soldiers needed "mothering," she deployed her girls to the French front. Sallies staffed huts where they read to the troops, sewed their buttons, and served coffee and doughnuts. As one soldier wrote to his family, "These good women create an atmosphere that reminds us of home, and out of the millions of men over there not one ever dreams of offering the slightest sign of disrespect or lack of consideration to these wonderful women."[8]

Celebrated in letters as well as newspapers stories, the Sallies ensured the Army's popularity stateside. But what was described as Christian witness in Army publications became humanitarianism in secular coverage. Lassies were likewise re-imagined by the news media. The *War Cry* ran photos of sturdy women working in wartime conditions: plainly clad in helmets, long skirts, and military jackets, they wear broad smiles on tired faces. Secular outlets presented a prettier picture. A wartime cover of *Cosmopolitan* featured a sloe-eyed Sallie with an enigmatic smile and a distinctly unArmy-like hair bob. Framed by the Stars and Stripes, she is as much a patriotic figure as a religious one. With its evangelical identity overshadowed by a humanitarian mission and its public face synonymous with a pretty girl, the Army began fundraising in earnest. The organization was increasingly reliant on public donations to fund its growing network of social services, and the new image was crucial for success.

Celluloid lassies and the Army's counter-offensive

In the Army's early days in the USA, the secular entertainment media, like the news media, depicted members as crazed religious enthusiasts. Satirists parodied the military metaphor, making fun of uniforms and parades. Popular ditties made fun of the low-class religious zealots. In one early film, the 1900 *Soubrettes in a Bachelor's Flat*, three chorus girls carouse with a young man. When the police stage a raid, the nearly nude women jump into Salvation Army uniforms. The film drew on the sexually promiscuous image of Salvationist women for comic effect. But by the turn of the century, that portrayal was the exception. More often, the lassie, easily recognizable by her uniform, was a symbol of feminine virtue. In the 1897 musical *The Belle of Broadway*, a young playboy is converted when he falls for an Army lass.[9] A decade later, theatergoers likewise embraced *Salvation Nell*. Nell, a scrubwoman whose lover is sent to jail, considers prostitution but instead joins the Salvation Army. When her man is freed, he wants to return to their old ways but she prays for his conversion. He finds God, joins the Army, and the two are wed. The conceit behind these plays suggests that early twentieth century audiences believed that Army lassies could save both rich playboys and poor scoundrels.

At a time when cultural elites, social reformers, and religious leaders were concerned about the mores and morals of working class women, as well as the growing numbers of middle and upper class women choosing careers, the lassie embodied traditional feminine values for the modern age. She upheld the primacy of religion and family, yet she also worked in the public square. Most important, she was an appropriate love object. Unlike Roman Catholic nuns, another identifiable group of religious women, lassies embraced marriage and motherhood. Thanks to the uniform, they were feminine without being overtly sexual, radiating a fresh-faced attractiveness that suited secular melodramas. Lassies continued to play this role in early movies. In *The Salvation Army Lass*, a 1908 D.W. Griffith film, a moll-turned-lassie saves her gangster boyfriend from a life of crime. Of the fifteen movies made between 1911 and

1920 that feature Salvationists as main characters, eleven depict lassies saving recalcitrant men.

The Army's first and only attempt to work with Hollywood was the 1919 film *Fires of Faith*. While other movies depicted Salvationist efforts, this was the only one to have full Army cooperation; Evangeline Booth even appeared in several scenes. The movie dramatized the Army's war efforts in France, including its heroic efforts to supply soldiers with homemade doughnuts. No prints of the film are extant, but publicity stills, reviews, and the studio press book suggest that *Fires of Faith* was the best that the Army could expect from secular moviemakers seeking a mass audience. Paramount called the movie a "tribute" to the Army, but the marketing campaign toned down the religious angle in favor of a love story. Its heroines served as Sallies, but their religious work was secondary to their romantic travails. Fresh from her war service, the lassie made a thoroughly modern and highly marketable heroine.

But as celluloid lassies overshadowed flesh-and-blood Salvationists, Army leaders had to decide whether losing control of their image was worth the attention. William Booth preached that any publicity was good publicity, and he zealously cultivated good relations with the secular news media while findings ways to co-opt its forms for religious content. Evangeline Booth, looking to Hollywood in the early twentieth century, was no different. Salvationists in America and Australia had early on experimented with making movies, but they were unable to produce and distribute them on a commercial scale (Winston 1999: 169–70). Since many early commercial movies also had religious themes, Booth may have thought that Hollywood could do what the Army alone could not accomplish: use this new media for evangelism.

The success of commercial films transformed notions of mass media distribution and consumption. Unlike newspapers and journals geared to particular audiences and specific regions, movies were simultaneously available to audiences nationwide. Unlike plays, operas, or concerts, movies were local and affordable. The markers for industry disruption—ease of use, cost to consumer, and ubiquity—were Hollywood's hallmarks. Men, women, and children who had never read a newspaper or attended a theater went to movie palaces in small towns and big cities, immigrant neighborhoods and upmarket shopping districts. For a few cents, they enjoyed a novel spectacle: moving images depicting a larger-than-life story. Providing "a new, shared national realm of experience," film did not simply offer a common context; rather it superseded older assumptions about identity and culture (Hjarvard 2008b: 127). Accordingly, film representations helped reshape perceptions of people, places, ideas, and movements (see, e.g., Niderost 2010). In the Army's case, movies introduced Salvationists to the wider public, a development that helped the group become part of the cultural mainstream. But the result was not the spread of the Army's evangelical message, the outcome leaders sought. Rather, the celluloid lassie, heroine of romantic melodramas, represented the Army as a do-gooder group, living its religion in practical ways. The practice outweighed the preaching, and the image of the pretty lassie trumped both.

Even the most sympathetic portrayals did not match Salvationists' self-image. Adhering to the underlying rationale of the movie industry, gendered film representations focused on looks and personality—qualities that served the interests of a market that used pretty girls and their over-the-top romances as commodified entertainment. Celluloid lassies were vibrant and appealing, but their religion less so, reversing the emphasis that the Army wanted. The Army initially resisted—first by ignoring Hollywood, then, with *Fires of Faith*, hoping to change the system from within.[10] But a religious movement could not compete with commercial media's economic power and concomitant ability to control. However, the Army could capitalize on the commodification of its lassies for its own fundraising. Building on their wartime popularity, Salvationists had extended the size and scope of their social service delivery, but the movement's down-and-out membership could not provide a solid financial base. As a result, they "sold" their vision to the public at large. Army leaders permitted Broadway showgirls to collect money for its annual appeal, and posed models for fundraising posters. The logic of commodification inherent in the new medium of film transformed not only the way that the public saw the Army, but also the ways in which the Army branded and marketed itself. As mass entertainment shaped perceptions of the Army, Salvationist leaders shifted their public message and marketing, appearing less as an evangelical outreach than as an action-oriented faith, fronted by a pretty face, in need of funds for helping the less fortunate. Although this perspective was never communicated to members through the *War Cry* or other publications, among the public at large Salvationists were compelled to concede the power of self-definition to the very cultural forces they had hoped to reform.

Those forces turned treacherous as, over the next decade, religious images that were initially positive grew more ambivalent. The cumulative effect of the "roaring 20s," talkies (film with sound), and the Great Depression led Hollywood producers to make films darker and more sexually explicit than their earlier efforts. In movies such as *The Angel of Broadway* (1927) and *Laughing Sinners* (1931), characters wavered when confronted with Army strictures. Worse, some Salvationists appeared to be morally ambiguous. In *The Angel of Broadway*, a cabaret performer burlesques the Army in her act. When she decides to learn more about the group, she puts on a uniform and helps in the work. She doesn't join the Army and the uniform is less a religious marker than a costume change. In *Laughing Sinners*, a jilted showgirl becomes a soldier but when her former beau wants her back she mocks her newfound faith and casts off the plain blue suit. When she realizes her mistake, her conversion is telegraphed by her return to uniform. In *She Done Him Wrong*, an upright Army officer is revealed to be an amorous undercover policeman. Once again, the uniform serves as a costume instead of signifying a commitment. The *War Cry* made no mention of the entertainment industry's appropriation of the uniform for prurient purposes, but Army leaders could not stop moviemakers from speculating whether good girls (or boys) turned bad when they shed the uniform or, conversely, if bad girls became good when they put it on.

Though official Army sources never mentioned these tensions, the leadership's attitudes can be seen in the case of Captain Rheba Crawford. Her brief Army career demonstrates how the Army sought to control its image by enforcing conformity (Winston 1999: 203–6). Crawford, a popular evangelist, was placed on rest furlough because of her "unorthodox theology and dress" (McKinley 1995: 174). (She welcomed a reporter to her Greenwich Village flat in "dainty slippers" and black satin lounging gown.) But it was more likely her independence and outspoken personality that disturbed Army leaders. Celebrated in the secular press as "The Angel of Broadway" and enshrined in Damon Runyon's short stories, Crawford was feisty and attractive: the living embodiment of the celluloid lassie. Through her friends in the theater and admirers in the press, she attracted a following that paid more attention to her looks and personality than to her testimony and service, an inversion that angered Army leaders. Ordered to stop preaching, Crawford quit the movement and was feted in a "Farewell to Broadway" revue packed with socialites, celebrities, and theater folks.

After Rheba, there were no more star soldiers, and within a few decades the celluloid lassie had lost her luster. Like most commodities, she had peaked. Attractive faces still adorned Army fundraising posters, but shields, kettles, and tambourines—other aspects of the Salvationist brand—frequently replaced them. In *Guys and Dolls* (1950), the lassie's last starring role, she was embodied as Sister Sarah Brown, a fictionalized portrait of Rheba Crawford based on Damon Runyon's stories. But the movie heroine lacked the flash of the real woman. Sister Sarah was a throwback to the virtuous lassie whose love could save a scoundrel, but in 1950 her chaste demeanor seemed more fusty than inspiring.

Despite the lassies' loss of screen time, their impact on the Army's image and mission remains strong. The movement's sharp evangelical message is muted and its humanitarian services emphasized—often to the consternation of officers who signed on to be pastors and preachers, not social workers. However, the brand sells well in the American public square. Throughout the 1990s the Army was the largest charitable fundraiser in the United States and it remains near the top. The celluloid lassies had a key role in this achievement. By giving the Army an attractive face, they enabled the movement to cash in on the commoditization—and subsequent secularization and sexualization—they enabled on screen. The process was not simply a result of mediation; rather, a network of technology, ideologies, and human agency instigated an example of religious adaptation. As described by Lynn Clark, "media interact with and transform religions in particular ways, at particular moments in time, in relations to particular interests" (Clark forthcoming). At a historical moment when private faith was increasingly differentiated from public religion, when films needed virtuous female leads, and when Salvationist leaders looked to the American public for financial support, Hollywood enabled an image of the Army as a patriotic, activist religion. Now when the Army is shown in a movie, it telegraphs a non-offensive, do-gooder creed ringing in the holiday season. The lassie's pretty face originally sealed the deal, but it's sound of coins clinking in kettles that has stayed on screen.

Notes

1 Feminist film theory continues to debate the role and position of male and female spectatorship and subjectivity, but it is generally agreed that classic Hollywood films privilege the male spectator. (See Penley 1988; Thornham 1999.)
2 Entertainmentization refers to "the phenomenon that the power of entertainment is increasingly determining social and political realms" (Leberecht 2004).
3 For more on the Army, see Winston (1999), Walker (2001), McKinley (1995).
4 *New York Times*, December 10, 1892, p. 8.
5 *New York Times*, March 11, 1883, p. 5.
6 *New York Times*, February 2, 1892, p. 4.
7 *American War Cry*, March 1, 1890, p.1.
8 *American War Cry*, June 15, 1918, p. 4.
9 The play was a hit in London and revived on Broadway in 1916. A movie version was filmed in 1952 with Fred Astaire.
10 The struggle for control over mediation is discussed by Hoover (2009).

Part III

The sacred senses

Introduction

In 1939, work was completed on a replica of the Lourdes shrine in the grounds of St. Lucy's Catholic Church in the Bronx, complete with rocks, plants, and a running spring (in reality a pipe plumbed from the New York City public water mains). The site was constructed to resemble the landscape at Lourdes in which Saint Bernadette responded to the call to dig in the ground to reveal the miraculous waters for which Lourdes was to become famous. In a vivid account of ordinary people's use of the "Bronx Lourdes," Robert Orsi traces the ways in which this self-evident replica of a pilgrimage site has itself come to be regarded as a place of divine grace and healing. People come to the site to drink the water as a way of receiving a blessing, use it to make the sign of the cross on themselves, and put it in bottles to take home or even to put in their car radiators. Whilst its users know this place is a replica, they also regard it as a holy place: "everyone knows exactly where the water comes from and everyone maintains that the water is holy and powerful" (Orsi 1997: 5).

What is striking in Orsi's account is not only his description of the replica shrine itself, but what happens when he discusses his fieldwork at this site with his students:

> Students in my class on U.S. urban religions are offended by the practices that take place at St Lucy's. They are especially outraged that the people involved consider these practices "religious." The last time I introduced this material one student called what went on at St Lucy's "a lot of crap," an unusual breach of classroom etiquette and uncharacteristic of the student but indicative of the anger provoked by the images I was showing ... [For them] what happens at the Bronx grotto is literally inadmissible, intolerable, in a religion classroom, because it is not "religion" ... Religion is not preoccupied with "material things" ... Religious feelings represent a "higher state of consciousness," a "union of the one with the one," that sends "shivers down the spine" of a sort different from the shivering of wet grotto pilgrims.
>
> (Orsi 1997: 5–6)

St. Lucy's doubtless presents particular challenges to conventional ways of thinking about what constitutes "proper" religion. But what Orsi's case demonstrates more generally is the challenge of taking seriously the material dimensions of religious life when religion is often constructed as a matter of the spirit, of belief, of internal conviction. Since the early 1990s, however, there has been a significant shift towards taking much more account of how lived religion is practiced as an embodied and material phenomenon. Part III gathers together readings from writers who have been particularly influential in this development.

One of the most important emphases in this recent work on the materiality of religion has been a turn away from the study of religious artifacts themselves to an interest in how different material and aesthetic practices form the substance of religious life. This shift—from an "object-centered" to "practice-centered" approach—has meant thinking not so much about what objects symbolize (as if they were mere instruments to get at "real" religious meanings) or what traditions of representation they reflect, but about the place of objects, images, and sounds in our lives. The following chapters explore these questions in a range of different ways.

Chapter 12 is taken from Colleen McDannell's 1995 book *Material Christianity*, which along with the work of David Morgan and Sally Promey, was a pioneering text in the new writing on material religion which began to develop from that period. In this chapter, McDannell, a religious historian, argues that the ways in which the material is conceived of in relation to Christianity have been shaped by wider cultural assumptions about materiality that have influenced not only the academic study of religion, but the ways in which Christians themselves have come to define what constitutes "proper" Christianity. Such distinctions are not simply matters of abstract classification. The definition of what constitutes appropriate Christianity also relates to hierarchies in which certain social groups are associated with practices of "de-materialized" Christianity (i.e. elite, educated men) and others are placed at the margins of the proper faith by their association with material practices ("women, children and other illiterates"). As McDannell observes, the way in which the material dimensions of Christianity have been thought about in modern times reflects similar kind of hierarchical judgements that are made about the relative value of "high," "folk," and "popular" culture as well as the kinds of people that enjoy them (cf. Lynch 2005: 3–17). Taking material Christianity seriously, then, is not simply a process of re-focusing our gaze when we study lived religion, but challenges normative assumptions about "authentic" religion and culture that run both through the academy and wider society.

In Chapter 13, taken from his award-winning book, *Between Heaven and Earth* (2005), Robert Orsi asks the question of how the sacred becomes a material reality in people's lives. Whilst people's faith in sacred figures can often be a taken-for-granted aspect of religious life, Orsi observes that sacred figures only become real in people's lives by a process of cultural work. In this chapter, Orsi focuses particularly on the shape this work took in the lives of Catholic children in twentieth-century America. Central to Orsi's argument is not only his account of the cultural practices through which children were trained to experience themselves as being in relationship with sacred figures (such as imagining one's guardian angel), but the idea that the very bodies of particular kinds of people (such as children) become a medium through which sacred presence is experienced. By bringing faith alive in the bodies of children, then, the sacred takes material form for a wider community of people. This reminds us that the process of making religious worlds real does not simply involve material forms, but also operations of power expressed through the kinds of stories and practices that are employed in relation to particular bodies. This is not simply a "top–down" process in which those who are on the receiving end of such religious formation are merely passive victims. As Orsi (2005: 89–95) has commented elsewhere, the physical and symbolic importance of children in Catholic devotional settings also gave children considerable power to disrupt those settings, and thus their (bad) behavior was an ongoing source of anxiety for those who sought to control it.

In Chapter 14, the anthropologist Birgit Meyer presents another theoretical framework for thinking about the embodied and aesthetic nature of religious life. Drawing on her extensive fieldwork in West Africa, as well as her management of major research collaborations (see, e.g., Meyer 2010), Meyer observes that William James's individualistic, interiorized, and pre-social concept of religious experience is inadequate. Instead, Meyer argues that religion is always mediated in the sense that religious experience is only made possible through physical media (whether images, sound, texts, or the body itself). Rather than seeing the study of "media" as a specialist sub-field of religious studies, Meyer therefore places the issue of the mediation of religious life as a central question for understanding how people construct and maintain religious life worlds. Exploring this involves thinking about how and why certain media are seen as more authoritative mediators of authentic religious experience (including media that might seem inherently "fake," such as special effects in film), how religious life is shaped by the kind of media available at any given place and time, and how these media become meaningful through particular aesthetic, embodied ways of experiencing and acting. As with the preceding chapter by Orsi, this raises further questions about how people are trained into these ways of feeling and experiencing religious media (see also Schmidt 2000; Morgan 2005).

The subsequent two chapters explore in more detail particular kinds of media and sacred senses. In his chapter on "Finding Fabiola" (Chapter 15), David Morgan explores specific questions that are raised in relation to the use of visual images in religious life. Taking the case of St. Fabiola—a sixth-century saint, later popularized through a series of portraits and prints—Morgan asks how images of Fabiola have come to capture people's imagination to the degree that they have. The answer, Morgan argues, lies not in some kind of original source, for there was no original image of Fabiola and little original information about her life. Rather, it lies in the ways that people make use of images— and the ways that images affect people. What is important in the case of Fabiola is the ways in which people, through these images, come to identify with her as an example of pious suffering. The stories and images of Fabiola provide the basis for this identification, but this process doesn't stop with the image. Rather, the power of the image lies in the human capacity to imagine a presence beyond the image (the "real" Fabiola), who can be experienced as a source of sympathy and inspiration.

In Chapter 16, Christopher Partridge, a leading scholar of religion and popular music (see, e.g., Partridge 2005, 2006), argues that insufficient attention has been given to the embodied, emotional, and sensory nature of popular music in the study of religion. Moving beyond the study of popular music songs as texts, or the study of the religious motivations or interests of particular musicians, Partridge argues that more attention needs to be given to the ways in which music helps to create religious forms of "affective space." Rather than simply being a vehicle for the "real" meaning conveyed through lyrics, the physical and auditory properties of music create particular kinds of sensory and emotional environments that can be interpreted in religious ways. Taking the example of dub reggae, Partridge demonstrates how its sonic properties, including the emphasis on bass, lend themselves to particular kinds of experience and possibilities for interpretation. Whilst much has been written about the visual and material dimensions of religious life, Partridge opens up new questions for how we might take the sonic dimensions of religious life more seriously (see also Schulz 2008).

Finally in this part, Stephen Pattison's chapter (Chapter 17) raises important ethical questions about our relations with material objects. Summarizing central arguments from his 2007 Gifford lectures, Pattison observes the ways in which our lives and bodies are inseparable from the material environments and objects we interact with. Moving beyond the idea that material objects can be thought of as exerting forms of agency over human life (see, e.g., Latour 2005), he argues that, by bearing the marks of human intention, material artifacts can be thought of as having person-like qualities. Human beings therefore form conscious or unconscious relations with the material objects that form the stuff of their everyday lives, in which objects may become a focus of deep attachment, irritation, or indifference. Framing these relations in ethical terms, Pattison argues that good lives are not characterized by an absence of attachment to material objects, but precisely by a quality of attention and regard for the objects with which we surround ourselves. Drawing on Daniel Miller's ethnographic work on material culture and everyday life, Pattison suggests that rather than being an unhelpful substitute for ethical relations with other people, deepening our moral commitment to the objects around us is also likely to reflect a deeper ethical commitment to other people as well.

The chapters in Part III therefore show how religion and materiality are inseparable. This is not simply the case in relation to high religious art, which has already received considerable scholarly attention, but also in relation to the ordinary objects, images, and sounds of religious life that may have little intrinsic aesthetic value for art critics, but form the material ground through which religious life becomes possible.

12 Scrambling the sacred and the profane

Colleen McDannell

One of the reasons why the material dimension of American religious life is not taken seriously is because of how we describe the nature of religion. A dichotomy has been established between the sacred and the profane, spirit and matter, piety and commerce that constrains our ability to understand how religion works in the real world. In spite of the difficulty of defining "religion," scholars and theologians frequently accept a simple division between the sacred and the profane. They also see an evolutionary, modernizing trend that has caused Western societies to become increasingly secular. By looking at material Christianity, we will see little evidence that American Christians experience a radical separation of the sacred from the profane. If we look at what Christians *do* rather than at what they *think*, we cannot help but notice the continual scrambling of the sacred and the profane. Likewise, by focusing on material Christianity we can no longer uncritically accept the secularization model.

Although binary thinking has a long history in the West, we can look to Emile Durkheim's classic study *Elementary Forms of the Religious Life* as perhaps the most influential description of the division of the world into the sacred and the profane. Durkheim wrote in 1912 that all religions classify things, both real and unreal, into the two opposing and distinctive categories of the sacred and the profane. The sacred consists of an ideal and transcendental world that is set apart from ordinary life. Signaled by rites such as anointings, consecrations, fasts, wakes, and seclusion, the sacred is defined primarily by its very opposite, the profane. The profane is the everyday and the utilitarian. While awe, intoxicating frenzy, and a sense of the foreign mark the sacred, the profane is commonplace, frequently boring, and familiar. The space of the church or temple is sacred; the home and workplace are profane. The clergy, privileged leaders, and people who have been initiated into cultic rituals are sacred. Workers, children, women, strangers typically are profane. For Durkheim these two worlds are not merely separate, they are "hostile and jealous rivals of each other ... The sacred thing is *par excellence* that which the profane should not touch, cannot touch with impunity" (Durkheim 1915: 55). In various forms, this dualistic understanding of the nature of religion can also be found in the writings of Max Weber, Gerardus van der Leeuw, and Mircea Eliade. According to these theorists of religion, without this binary division there cannot be authentic religion. "The religious life and the profane life," declared Durkheim, "cannot exist in the same place" (ibid.: 347).

This theoretical construction of religion reflects one aspect of the Jewish understanding of God as developed in classical Christian thought. In this tradition, the God of the Hebrew scriptures is understood as represented as a disembodied voice that interacts with embodied human beings (Scarry 1985: 181–243; Freedberg 1989: 61f.). Humanity and divinity are presented as radically separated; God is uncircumscribable and unmanipulable. The Protestant reformer John Calvin maintained that humanity comes close to God only in our souls because God is a spirit. "Since God has no similarity to those shapes by means of which people attempt to represent him," he wrote in his *Institutes of the Christian Religion*, "then all attempts to depict him are an impudent affront ... to his majesty and glory" (Baum, ed., quoted in Michalski 1993: 62). Divinity, the wholly other and sacred, should not be brought into the profane world of bodies and art. The omnipotence and greatness of God, stressed by theologians like Calvin and Zwingli, meant that humanity could not influence the divine.

Built into Christian theology, however, are doctrines that weaken this dualism. The doctrine of the Creation emphasizes both the immanence and transcendence of God. Not only is God majestic and distant; God created and sustains the universe through power and love. The Incarnation also enables the material dimension of Christianity to assume a theological meaning. Through the Incarnation, Christians believe that God becomes intimately associated with humanity because of the divine appropriation of the human body and condition. In Christ, there is a blurring of the material and spiritual; the sacred voice and the profane human body. The longing for the physical presence of God is eliminated in the embodiment of Christ. Jesus of the Gospels is an object of touch and of vision. Although Christians hotly debate the nature of the Incarnation, the separation that Durkheim perceived between the ideal and the material was fundamentally overcome, at least this once, in Christ.

For those Christians who emphasize the bodily nature of Christ and his intimate understanding of human longings, the material world no longer could be radically profane and unattached to the sacred. Theologians like the eighth-century Syrian John of Damascus closely aligned the embodied Christ not only with matter but with the saving nature of matter. "In former times God who is without form or body, could never be depicted," he wrote in defense of using images in Christian worship:

> But now when God is seen in the flesh conversing with men, I make an image of the God whom I see. I do not worship matter; I worship the Creator of matter who became matter for my sake, who willed to take His abode in matter; who worked out my salvation through matter. Never will I cease honoring the matter which wrought my salvation.
>
> (John of Damascus, *De imaginibus orationes*, Migne *PG* 94, quoted in Kuryluk 1991: 53)

Throughout the debates over the use of images in Christian communities, whether in the eighth century or sixteenth or twentieth century, some have eagerly accepted the scrambling of the spiritual and the natural, divine and human, sacred and profane. Protestant theologians from the Reformed tradition have generally rejected the possibility that the supernatural could be so frequently manifest on earth. Lutheran and Episcopalian thinkers were more receptive to the visual and sensual world but cautioned against idolatry. As we will see, lay Protestants often ignored such warnings and included material culture in their religious lives. While modern Roman Catholic theologians criticize what they understand as superstitious excesses in devotionalism, typically Roman and Orthodox thought and liturgy have highlighted the divine connection with matter.

The study of American Christianity, however, is not modeled on the Catholic understanding of the frequent fusion of the sacred and the profane. Jon Butler cogently argues that American religious history has been unduly shaped by a Protestant understanding of what defines religious faith, community, and behavior (Butler 1991). Butler coins the term "Puritan model" to describe scholarly focus on the themes of Calvinism, evangelicalism, declension, rising secularism, laicization, democracy, and American exceptionalism. While the Puritans themselves may have experienced their lives as "worlds of wonder," this is not how traditional historians have perceived them (Hall 1990).[1] The Puritan model is a historiographical construct, not a historical observation. For Butler, Catholicism, Eastern Orthodoxy, Judaism, and Native American religions can only be "authentic" or "real" when they reflect elements of the Puritan or Protestant model. Butler encourages us to consider new models that would take into account the heterogeneity of individual religious experience, the importance of place, and the varieties of institutional authority. In particular, he argues that the Puritan model prevented scholars from seeing that demonstrations of supernatural intervention were (and are) essential to the lives of Americans. While the Puritans may have seen the divine elsewhere, the Puritan model preferred Christianity separated from home life, sexuality, economic exchange, and fashion.

The assumption that true Christian sentiments can be, must be, set apart from the profane cannot be upheld when we look at how people use material culture in their religious lives. While there are certainly Christians who disdain the material world and strive to eliminate visual representations of it from their communities, there is no compelling reason to hold these groups up as the standard to which all other Christians must be compared. The Puritan model of religious historiography denies the rich complexity of American Christianity and serves as a blindfold to the strong materialist trends in religious culture. If we immediately assume that whenever money is exchanged religion is debased, then we will miss the subtle ways that people create and maintain spiritual ideals *through* the exchange of goods and the construction of spaces.

When Christian activities seem too wedded to the profane, they are typically held up as further signs of secularization and the decline of religious influence in

America. Taking their cues from Durkheim, sociologists report that people need to have an element of enchantment in their lives that mystifies fundamental social relationships. The secularization theory tells us that within Western nations religion no longer speaks to this supernatural longing in humanity.[2] For many scholars, secular popular culture now serves this need. These scholars follow Karl Marx, who wrote in *Capital* that in order to understand the relationship between people and commodities we must "take flight into the misty realm of religion." In capitalism, products made by human beings become "autonomous figures endowed with a life of their own" that can interact with their makers, owners, and with each other. Marx described this attitude toward commodities as "the fetishism" (Marx 1976: 125). Consequently, some scholars conclude that secular objects can provide the magical dimension of life that religious objects once did. For Sut Jhally, advertising is where

> the commodity world interacts with the human world at the most fundamental levels: it performs magical feats of transformation and bewitchment, brings instant happiness and gratification, captures the forces of nature, and holds within itself the essence of important social relationships.
>
> (Jhally 1989: 218)

Ray Browne draws on religious language for his books on material culture, *Objects of Special Devotion* and *Icons of America* (Browne 1982; Browne and Fishwick 1978). America, for many historians and culture critics, is a non-religious and consumer-oriented country where CB Radios may be interpreted as meaningful icons (Pollman 1978).

The conclusion that magical mass-produced commodities or spaces substitute for religion in a secular culture can be reached only because scholars have disregarded that material dimension of religious life in America. Most historians, folklorists, archaeologists, and cultural critics focus on non-religious material culture because they do not recognize the persistent and meaningful continuation of religion in America. While they frequently call things "religious," they rarely discuss religious artifacts. I suspect they share the notion with many scholars and theologians that "real" religion cannot be materialist. It is not surprising that historians and sociologists assume that the American landscape and consumer culture are devoid of religious forms since specialists in religion fail to note the material dimension of explicitly religious culture. If social scientists see only the profane and religionists only the sacred, then both miss the ways Christians combine these concepts. We cannot speculate about the CB radio as "icon" if we have no idea about how religious icons (whether Eastern Orthodox icons or mass-produced Christian images) function in twentieth-century America.

Secularization theory has recently been criticized in light of the spread of "fundamentalism" in America and abroad.[3] Revisionists of secularization frequently postulate that what we are seeing in America is not the continuation of religion but evidence for some totally new religious configuration. At the end of her article on "The Born-Again Telescandals," anthropologist Susan Harding seems surprised to see that now the "religious mingles with secular, churches become businesses, Christ dispenses grace on TV, preachers call themselves CEOs and run for President, faith healers build ultramodern hospitals, AT&T hires New Age consultants, and churches hire religious market analysts." For her we now live in a "new world composed of preposterous categorical hodge-podges." This new world contrasts with the old world, where "the things forming these zany amalgamations were kept apart, separated, in their place, properly ordered and moving progressively toward some end" (Harding 1994: 555). Since religion is not going away, Harding concludes that it must be mutating into something new. In other words, the contemporary religious world in America does not look like a "real" religious world where, in the spirit of Calvin and Durkheim, the sacred is far from the profane. In the "old" world everything religious was in its proper place. Harding has uncritically accepted the notion that at some ill-determined period in the American past "mingling" did not occur. She has, in effect, followed the Puritan model of scholarship by describing the contemporary religious situation as "declension" from a past of theological certainty and fervent piety.

The conclusion that contemporary religions are the creation of something "new" cannot be historically justified. Rather, I show in these case studies that the scrambling of the sacred and the profane is common in American Christianity. Mingling has occurred throughout its history. The categories of sacred and profane are the constructions of scholars and not always a part of the awareness of those involved in practicing religion. What is occurring is that scholars trained in poststructural or critical theories are now finally seeing the "preposterous categorical hodgepodges" of religion. By focusing on the objects, landscapes, and arts that people use to articulate and shape their Christianity, I see complicated and interactive relationships between what has been called the sacred and the profane. To focus exclusively on the binary opposition between sacred and profane prevents us from understanding, rather than enabling us to understand, how Christianity works. The case studies I include provide various angles for understanding how Christians, of assorted types, continuously mix the supernatural, God, miracles, ethical concerns, and prayer together with family, commerce, everyday worries, fashion, and social relationships. The material dimension of Christianity shuttles back and forth so frequently between what scholars call the sacred and the profane that the usefulness of the categories is disputed.

Women, children, and other illiterates

The material dimension of American Christianity has been ignored not merely because a dualist notion of the sacred and profane privileges certain expressions of religion over others. Longstanding theological and intellectual interpretations of art, objects, and places have associated material expressions of religion with certain types of people. Paralleling the assumption that the sacred is separate from the profane is the notion that meaningful Christianity is best defined by specialists in the sacred: people schooled in theology, active in reform movements, or outstanding in church leadership. Buying bibles, visiting cemeteries, using miraculous water, wearing religious clothing, and owning religious bookstores have been ignored because scholars deem these practices less spiritual or authentic. Those who use non-literary means of expressing ideas about the supernatural and its relationship to the everyday world have not been considered fully "adult" Christians. Christians who use objects or images in their devotional lives or who feel that certain places are imbued with special powers are seen as needing spiritual helps or crutches. These "weak" Christians who require physical "aids" are separated from "strong" Christians who grasp spiritual truths directly. It is this perception, that only weak Christians express their faith by interacting with material culture, that this book hopes to counter.

The assumption that "strong" Christians do not need material representations of their faith has its origins in Platonic ideas of beauty and Hebraic iconoclasm. Christians who reject the importance of religious images and goods privilege a strand of thought that insists that the divine cannot be represented. Platonic and Neoplatonic philosophy asserted that the highest form of truth and beauty is spiritual and therefore disconnected from the earthly and the material (Freedberg 1989: 63). There is a cosmic hierarchy that proceeds from the mind and soul downward to matter. To turn from spirit toward the bodily realm is to move toward evil, the negation of the spiritual. The phenomenal world of nature and images conceals the ideal world of truth that lies beyond the particulars. The third-century philosopher Plotinus rejected the custom of painting individual portraits because he felt that the pure idea of the person's character would be obscured in the physical matter of art (Belting 1994: 132). For those critical of representation, contemplation might initially entail the use of images to assist in reaching a greater insight but the goal was to progress beyond the need for physical aids. As Augustine concluded from his and Monica's vision at Ostia, the soul's goal was to raise itself higher and higher; to have every sign silent, to hear without tongue or voice, and then, eventually, to experience "that eternal wisdom which abides above all things" (Augustine 1961: 198).

To this notion of the hierarchical relationship between spirit and matter we add the Hebraic suspicion of the arts. Biblical iconoclasm served as a continual referent for Christian thinkers. The story of the Golden Calf (Exodus 32) tells Jews and Christians that when people lose their faith in God they construct false images of the divine. The iconoclastic violence that followed the making of the Golden Calf emphasizes the difference between a wayward people looking for a material representation of the divine and their leader, to whom God directly speaks without visual mediation. God eventually commands the faithful not to make graven images or a likeness of anything that is in heaven above or the earth below. Most importantly, they should never bow down to images or serve them (Deuteronomy 5: 8–10).

The urge to image, however, is not easily quelled. The iconoclastic controversies in Christianity reveal the persistent desire to create images of God and the saints. Medieval Catholicism produced a rich array of decorative arts and devotional devices to stimulate piety. Among their arguments against the iconoclasts, Catholic theologians developed the idea that it was the illiterate who needed images to enable them to grasp the divine mysteries because they could not read.[4] Our minds, they reminded us, are oriented toward mundane matters and are largely incapable of rising to spiritual things. Images and devotional objects help people contemplate the divine and teach the true faith because not everyone can approach God through the intellect. The uneducated, women, and children were particularly responsive to sacred images, objects, and spaces (Herrin 1982; Kuryluk 1991: 65–87). For those theologians disposed to see the positive nature of images, the majority of Christians needed to use the visual world to move towards that which cannot be seen. For those who had iconoclastic leanings, such "helps" could be tolerated because illiterate Christians needed them to understand and express their faith.

The Protestant reformers of the sixteenth century reinterpreted the "illiterate argument" for the use of images in liturgy and instruction. While Luther vacillated on the issue of images (prohibiting the adoration of statues or pictures while recognizing their instructive possibilities), Zwingli and Calvin had no such reservations. Images should *not* be placed in churches because Christians were susceptible to confusing the sign with the referent; the representation with what stands *behind* the referent. Art and objects tempted a weak humanity that fell too easily into idolatry. According to the reformers, images were a part of an external cult that tried to manipulate God by placing too much trust in human activities. All Christians must place their faith in God alone and scorn those false activities that implied humanity could magically control the divine. From the Protestant perspective, an all-powerful God controlled humanity and people only fooled themselves if they thought their rosaries and pilgrimages could gain them salvation.

The iconoclastic stream within Christian history has assumed that people who are illiterate or not properly trained in religion frequently mistake the *image* of the divine for the divine itself. This skeptical attitude toward people who use images is not confined to theologians and religious leaders fighting iconoclastic battles. Like Protestants fearful of Catholic images and Catholics fearful of the "excesses" of the uneducated, some modern thinkers have felt that the "weak" easily fall prey to the lure of mass culture. During the first half of the twentieth century, cultural critics observed that a powerful "culture industry" made up of the media, popular arts, entertainment, and fashion controlled the desires and needs of the "masses."[5] The masses, according to theorists like Theodor Adorno and Herbert Marcuse, had weak egos and submissive psyches that were easily pacified. Adorno and his colleagues at the Frankfurt Institute for Social Research remembered how ordinary people were caught up in the fascist movements of the 1930s instead of acting as agents for proletarian revolution. These writers were convinced that the culture industry cheated the consumer of what it promised and turned people into unthinking zombies. American Dwight Macdonald succinctly summarized the Frankfurt School's negative attitude toward the masses and popular culture in his 1944 essay "A Theory of Popular Culture." He explained that

> mass culture is imposed from above. It is fabricated by technicians hired by businessmen; its audiences are passive consumers, their participation limited to the choice between buying and not buying. The Lords of kitsch, in short, exploit the cultural needs of the masses in order to make a profit and/or to maintain their class rule.
>
> (Macdonald 1944: 20)

For the sixteenth-century Protestant reformers, the powerful Catholic church manipulated weak people through images and trinkets; for some mid-twentieth-century critics, the culture industry did the same with jazz and best sellers.

During the mid-twentieth century, the Protestant (and increasingly Catholic) suspicion of images combined with a modernist distrust of popular culture to create an extremely hostile environment for the study of Christian material culture. For a variety of Christian theologians spiritual and cultural growth proceeded from the concrete, visual, and everyday to the abstract, literary, and unique. The more ethically and morally superior the religion, the more it presents an abstract deity who need not be approached through material "helps." The influential German-born theologian Paul Tillich called on Christians to see God as the Ultimate Concern, the "depth dimension" in all experience. He rejected the view that only traditionally religious symbols express the divine and instead believed that Christians could discover an ultimate concern in the secular world. Tillich, unlike Durkheim, saw the sacred in the profane. However, like other cultural critics of the period, he could not see authentic religion in the "Sunday school" art of the masses. "The religious art of capitalist society reduces the traditional religious symbols to the level of middle-class morality and robs them of their transcendence and their sacramental character," he concluded. Tillich preferred modern art, such as Expressionism, that

> has a mystical, religious character, quite apart from its choice of subjects. It is not an exaggeration to ascribe more of the quality of sacredness to a still-life by Cézanne or a tree by van Gogh than to a picture of Jesus by Uhde.[6]
> (Tillich [1932] 1956: 88f.)

Theologians and scholars of religion ignored the popular "religious art of capitalist society" because expressions of both art and religion that were more intellectual could be found in the achievements of a handful of artists, writers, and thinkers. "The masses crush beneath it everything that is different," summarized Ortega y Gasset, "everything that is excellent, individual, qualified, and select" (Ortega y Gasset 1950: 12).

It is not surprising that until recently scholars of American religion, following in the steps of the European intelligentsia and Christian iconoclasts, turned away from popular religion and its arts. Historians who embraced the Puritan model of American religions ignored those Christians who used images and objects because they were "less" Christian than evangelical Protestants. If scholars examined the material dimension of American religion, they opted to study either folk customs or utopian communities where religious convictions (like art) were not mass-produced but handcrafted. The material dimension of religion was acknowledged only when it reflected their scholarly preference for the abstract and individual. The fascination with the material culture of the Shakers reflects the scholarly search for an "authentic" religion that was embodied in an "authentic" material culture. According to historian Stephen Stein, popular preoccupation with the details of Shaker material culture and the exclusion of the dynamics of their historical and religious development produced an idealized and frequently Pollyanna-ish view of this community. There is something pathetically revealing in the comment of a 1984 Shaker that "I almost expect to be remembered as a chair or table" (Stein 1987).[7] We know far more about the material universe of the Shakers—a community that tried to simplify their physical universe—than we do about that of Roman Catholics, whose sacramental theology fully exploited the material world.[8] Since American Catholic "arts" were mass-produced and used by unschooled immigrants, they held little interest for scholars looking for the unique and the intangible. In the case of the Shakers, their utopian community life and design preferences marked them off from the "masses" and thus made them fit subjects for study.

In the aftermath of the civil rights movements and student rebellions of the 1960s and 1970s, "the masses" became a more appropriate subject matter. As "the masses" asserted themselves politically, they looked less like a homogeneous lump of people and more like diverse communities of African Americans, students, Native Americans, women, gays, the handicapped, white ethnics, or Hispanics. Historians in America and Europe began to explore the lives of ordinary people. Instead of focusing on politics, the activities of a few "great men," and written sources, historians now construct narratives of social change from the "bottom up." Sociologists are rejecting the Frankfurt School's pessimistic appraisal of the masses and their culture. Scholars at the Birmingham Centre for Contemporary Cultural Studies counter the notion of an undifferentiated "mass" by studying a variety of contemporary sub-cultures. Cultural studies conducted in Britain and the United States challenge the notion of a cohesive "culture industry," diminish the gap between high and low culture, question the idea that mass culture overwhelms the consciousness of the working class, and discuss how small groups of people create their own cultural lifestyle (Bigsby 1976: 17).[9] Mass culture itself is now portrayed as a "contested terrain" where various communities struggle to establish meanings. Recovering the subjective experiences of people and the small details of everyday resistance has become a legitimate scholarly agenda.

As scholars have acknowledged the ability of average people to resist, define, and express themselves through "popular" culture, they have also re-evaluated the ways Christians have used images, objects, and spaces. Historians now explain that Protestants have never been entirely free from using images and spiritual "helps" in their lives. Luther, Zwingli, and Calvin, it turns out, made certain exceptions to their distrust of religious images and objects. Luther placed twenty-one woodcuts (including Cranach's series on the Apocalypse) in his 1522 New Testament. The Augsburg Confession of 1530 said that images could be used to encourage people to lead a holy life and to restrain their imaginations (Gilman 1986: 34). Proper images could direct the mind toward historical scriptural reality and away from religious fantasy. Both Calvin and Zwingli permitted the humanity of Christ to be depicted visually in the home. While it was forbidden to have statues of the saints in church, families could display prints of biblical scenes (Michalski 1993: 56, 90). In England there was a slow process of eliminating unacceptable images from houses and inns and replacing them with acceptable ones. Painters replaced the saints with Old Testament scenes and allegorical figures (Watt 1991: 135). In the space of the home or tavern and in teaching children, images could be used. Historians of early modern Europe and America now entertain the idea that the distinctions between Protestants, Catholics, and "pagans" were less sharp than was originally assumed (Thomas 1971; Hall 1990: 71–116; Butler 1990: 7–97; Hambrick-Stowe 1982: 23–53).

Protestants in the seventeenth and eighteenth centuries might have been more open to material expressions of Christianity because Europeans were discovering the joys of consumerism. In his work on patterns of modern materialism, Chandra Mukerji revises established sociological and historical explanations of the rise of capitalism by describing the existence of a "hedonistic consumerism" in the early modern period (Mukerji 1983: 2). Mukerji and other scholars have pushed the origin of consumerism back into the sixteenth and seventeenth centuries.[10] Challenging Max Weber's theory that the spirit of modern capitalism finds its sole source in an ascetic, savings-minded ethic of Protestantism, Mukerji contends that early modern Protestants and Catholics indulged in forms of mass consumption that spurred a lively trade in books, art work, chinaware, and furniture. Even poorer Europeans bought "luxuries" such as ribbons and copper pots. Both Catholics and Protestants were exploring new ways to use material goods in their social and economic lives. Colin Campbell arrived at a similar conclusion in *The Romantic Ethic and the Spirit of Modern Consumerism* (Campbell 1987). He points out that a parallel tradition ran alongside the better-known Protestant material asceticism. Not all Protestants, as Weber has led us to believe, lived modestly in order to maximize profits from God's gifts. A more sensual Protestantism promoted free thought, Arminianism, sentiment, romanticism, and consumption. Mukerji and Campbell both conclude that modern consumerism and the sensual needs of the individual did not arise due to the weakening of the Puritan ethic but rather have been a continual part of Protestantism since the sixteenth century.

It is inevitable that a book on material Christianity will include the activities of women, children, and lay men. However, my intention is also to discredit the impression that educated men do not form relationships with pious art, use healing water, or wear religious garments. Lay men and clergy typically hold the key positions in the production and distribution of religious goods and the construction of Christian landscapes. Mormon men wear garments and Catholic men use Lourdes water. Material Christianity is a means by which both elite and non-elite Christians express their relationship to God and the supernatural, articulate ideas about life after death, and form religious communities. To gloss over, ignore, or condemn material Christianity because of its associations with "marginal" Christians is to misunderstand who uses the tangible and sensual in religion.

At the risk of perhaps overvaluing the statements of women, children, and other "illiterates," I take seriously their laconic statements on religion. I do not ask: "Is it art? Is it religion?" and then apply an external standard of religiosity to their piety. Too often such questions retard rather than promote inquiry. "What clouds our perception," David Freedberg astutely summarizes, "is exactly the compulsion to establish whether an object is art or not, and whether it belongs in a museum or not" (Freedberg 1989: 437). While I am sensitive to the times that Christians accuse other Christians of indulging in unauthentic pious thoughts or superficial religious behavior, I am more interested in what the rhetoric says about their own conceptions of Christianity. Readers may decipher my own religious and artistic prejudices but it is not my intention to evaluate Christian material culture by a set of ethical and theological standards. I am not drawn to criticize Christians who use Lourdes water or who wear "Praise the Lord" T-shirts. I reject, however, the opinions of those who find nothing significant in these religious gestures.

Notes

1 An example of traditional approaches to Puritanism can be found in Perry Miller's work on the "New England Mind" in *The Seventeenth Century* (1939) and *From Colony to Province* (1953).
2 Secularization has been the dominant sociological theory for explaining religious evolution until recently, and can be found in Wilson (1966), Wallace (1966), Berger (1967), Bellah (1970), and Dobbelaere (1987).
3 Recent revisions include Barker *et al.* (1993), Finke and Stark (1992), Roof and McKinney (1987), Stark and Bainbridge (1985), and Warner (1993).
4 Gregory the Great (600 CE) in response to Serenus, *Ad Serenum Episcopum Massiliensem*, PL 77, col. 1027f. See Freedberg (1989: 163) for other theologians who based their ideas about images on this argument.
5 See J.M. Bernstein's introduction in Adorno (1991) *The Culture Industry: Selected Essays on Mass Culture*; Brantlinger (1983: 222–48); Lunn (1990).
6 Tillich is referring to Fritz von Uhde, a late nineteenth-century German painter.
7 The works by Edward Deming Andrews and Faith Andrews on Shaker life display this "material culture" orientation. See *Shaker Furniture* ([1937] 1964) and *Religion in Wood* (1966). See also Ray (1973). For a more critical appraisal of Shaker life, see Stein (1992); and for an alternative version of their artistic vision, Promey (1993).

8 Although neither of these books focuses exclusively on Catholic material culture, both provide discussions of Catholic use of objects, images, and spaces: Kane (1994) and Orsi (1985).

9 For a discussion of the development of cultural studies, see Brantlinger (1990). Examples of the Birmingham School's concern with subcultures are Hebdige (1979); Hall and Jefferson (1976).

10 This thesis also underpins the articles collected in Brewer and Porter (1993). Economic support for an early consumer revolution is argued by Thirsk (1978) and McKendrick, Brewer and Plumb (1982).

13 Material children

Making God's presence real through Catholic boys and girls

Robert Orsi

Presence is central to the study of lived Catholic practice—the study of Catholicism in everyday life is about the mutual engagement of men, women, children, and holy figures present to each other. But presence is a human experience; how sacred presence becomes real in particular times and places is a question. That is what I begin with here. How do religious beliefs become material? How do the gods and other special beings—and, more broadly, how does the world, visible and invisible, as the world is said to be within a particular religious culture—become as real to people as their bodies, as substantially *there* as the homes they inhabit, or "as the stucco-over-chicken-wire from which these houses are made?" Anthropologist Clifford Geertz's influential 1973 definition proposed that religion is "a system of symbols which acts to establish powerful, pervasive, and long-lasting moods and motivations in men by formulating conceptions of a general order of existence and clothing these conceptions with such an aura of factuality that the moods and motivations seem uniquely realistic" (Geertz 1973: 90). Geertz was primarily concerned with the cognitive realness of religion and its emotional and intellectual viability. Religions offer and substantiate accounts of the world that render the chaos and pain of experience meaningful and tolerable. But Geertz's reference to religion's capacity to clothe—to give material substance, fabric, and texture to—a culture's vision of the way things are suggests another account of religion. Religion is the practice of making the invisible visible, of concretizing the order of the universe, the nature of human life and its destiny, and the various dimensions and possibilities of human interiority itself, as these are understood in various cultures at different times, in order to render them visible and tangible, present to the senses in the circumstances of everyday life. Once made material, the invisible can be negotiated and bargained with, touched and kissed, made to bear human anger and disappointment, as we have seen in men and women's relationships with the saints. But the question remains: how does this happen?

[...] Religious cultures offer multiple media for materializing the sacred. There are images, statues, beads, ritual objects, smells, visions, colors, foods and tastes, vestments, oils, and waters. The invisible often becomes visible as faces, in heaven (in the face of Blessed Margaret of Castello looking at my uncle

Sal) and on earth (in the face of a woman who keeps an image of the Sacred Heart of Jesus on her bedroom dresser and teaches her grandchildren how to pray to this holy figure and who is forever associated in their minds with the suffering savior). Religious rituals, with their movements, smells, sounds, and things, are privileged sites for rendering religious worlds present in the movement of bodies in space and time as well.[1]

Things do not exhaust the materiality of religion, however, and rituals—particularly major performances in the control of religious authorities—work more or less successfully to limit materialization and to bind presence. It is true that people find ways of having private experiences of presence within authorized and controlled ritual time and space that are sometimes tolerated, sometimes not. But there is a difference between Christ's presence on the altar during the sacrifice of the Mass and the Mother of God standing on a Basque hillside. The two are not unrelated, nor is this a simple matter of elite or official religion versus popular or vernacular religion; such boundaries are never absolute. But ritual is only one venue for the constitution of a religion's realness. Rituals are occasional events. How the realness of the world as enacted in ritual is carried over into ongoing everyday life remains a problem for religious theory. So ritual is not a sufficient answer to the problem of presence.

The materialization of religious worlds includes a process that might be called the corporalization of the sacred. I mean by this the practice of rendering the invisible visible by constituting it as an experience in a body—in one's own body or in someone else's body—so that the experiencing body itself becomes the bearer of presence for oneself and for others. The following example will help clarify what I mean by the materialization or corporalization of the sacred as an experience evoked, produced, or occasioned in bodies. In an article addressed to Catholic parents and educators in December 1937, a teaching sister from Detroit's Marygrove College asked her readers how the truths of Advent and Christmas—"Christmas is Jesus' birthday. Jesus is God. He made you and me and everybody ... Jesus will bless us and make us happy with Him"—could be made real to children. These abstract theological notions, Sister Mary warned, make no sense to youngsters unless somehow accompanied by "concrete experiences" (Sister Mary I.H.M. 1937: 305).

The "spiritual," Sister says again, must be "made concrete," and the way she proposes to do this is by having children make a crib for baby Jesus. At first it seems Sister is concerned to teach children by means of the *things* they actually manipulate, but her plans are more complicated than this. The boundaries between matter (the crib and its figures, straw, and animals), experience (the child's inner apprehension of the realness of Christmas), and the sacred get erased in Sister's discussion of the project. The crib must be a thing, she says, a box or basket that "will actually be the crib in which the statue or picture of the Infant will be placed on Christmas morning," but the crib "must actually be spiritual, that is, made of prayers and acts of love and sacrifice" (ibid.: 306). Actually spiritual, actually material: these are not separate in the way Sister is thinking about this classroom work.

Between the truth of Christmas and the box that stands for that truth is the child's body, and it is mostly with this that Sister is concerned. It is in the child's flesh that Christmas will be made real, tangible, and accessible. "Eating things the child does not like could make the straw," Sister advises, "being obedient the coverlet, being nice to others when playing with others, the pillow." Saying morning prayers *devoutly*, by which Sister means with a particularly attentive and focused attitude of body and mind, brings the image of the Blessed Mother to the crib; devoutly reciting bedtime prayers summons Saint Joseph to the manger:

> Special acts of love—telling Jesus he loves Him, asking Him to come on Christmas and be happy in our home, telling our Lady he loves her, giving a picture or statue a kiss, saying a prayer during the day—these could be special trimmings around the Crib in the form of flowers or snow or anything else which would show the child that he is waiting for the Blessed Babe.
>
> (Sister Mary I.H.M. 1937: 306)

The child "lives the same life as ever, but he conquers himself and does all now in the power of the Infant King." Sister means real things by coverlet, snow, flowers, and so on—the appropriate posture or attitude in the child's body leads to the literal placement of additional things on the crib—and she means what is happening in children's imaginations and bodies.

Where is the materiality of religion here? Where is presence? In the crib or in the taste in the child's mouth as she eats foods she does not like? In the straw or in the postures the child must assume for the privilege of putting the straw in the crib, in the statues or in the special acts of love that give the child permission to arrange the holy family there? Religious materiality or presence here is not things but practice. Sister Mary's intentions are clearly directed to making spiritual realities concrete in children's experience. The objects involved are media of a much larger materializing ambition. The Catholic word for the instruction of children in the faith was *formation*, but "instruction" is too pallid a word for what this process aimed at and "formation" was not simply a matter of shaping the intellect. What was formed in formation was the realness and presence of the sacred in the bodies and imaginations of children.

Sister's ambitions become especially clear in her discussion of how to treat time. Children live in an endless present, she says; the notion of time's passing has very little meaning for them. This cognitive limitation creates a special problem when it comes to Advent, a season of anticipation that requires some notion of time. Otherwise, how can a child look forward to Jesus' birth? The challenge, as Sister construes it, is to materialize time: she recommends that parents draw a vertical line across each day of a special calendar to signify that a child has said his or her morning prayer, a horizontal line for evening prayer, and in this way "each day as it passes will ... be marked with the cross ... and time will come to have a real meaning" to the child. Invisible minutes and hours acquire a solidity borrowed from the corporal experience of children, who before they know how to tell time will have known time's moral and cosmic significance in their bodies, in their praying limbs (ibid.: 306–7).

This is what Sister and I mean by "concrete experiences" of the sacred.

[...] The bodies of others may become the vehicles for the materialization of the sacred. This was especially true in the psychologically and religiously fluid domain of Catholic devotionalism. In this religious world, the bodies so used were, first of all, those of the saints. It was from the cult of saints and relics (which included matter taken from or put in contact with saints' bodies) that this orientation toward the sacred experienced in bodies was developed and popularized in Catholic cultures. A relic is explicitly an object of power taken away from the body of a holy person, either a piece of that body itself or something touched to it. Then, too, all corporal realizations of the sacred are mimeses of the presence of the divine in the body of Christ and of Christ's body present in the host during the sacrifice of the Mass.[2]

But the sacred could be present in the bodies of living persons too. The experience of persons with disabilities in their solitude and pain (as their experience was constructed in the discourse of the holy cripple) was made the site for encounters with the sacred by others who were not disabled. Just as pain may be alienated from the bodies of those in pain and made to substantiate the realness of things separate from them—this is the logic of torture, as philosopher Elaine Scarry has pointed out—so too may sacred presence (Scarry 1985: 256–68). Often enough (certainly in Catholic devotionalism but in other religious contexts as well) religion is the feelings, acts, and experiences of some people as these are imagined, imposed on them, and then taken from them by other people. Not all bodies serve this purpose, moreover, but bodies marked in some way within particular social worlds by special kinds of difference. As we saw, the bodies of the "handicapped," constructed as bodies-in-pain by the non-handicapped, became media of presence, a political and religious transubstantiation that did not necessarily help the "handicapped" live better lives.

One such medium of religious materialization—for rendering the invisible visible and present—of special importance for religious practitioners is children. Adults tell themselves (urgently and usually fearfully) that they must pass on their religious beliefs and values on to their children. To this end they organize catechism classes, Sunday school programs, after-school religious instruction, special children's rituals, and so on. The fear is that without such instruction children will be bereft and alienated on the deepest levels; in the story that adults tell about this exchange, children need religion for their own benefit.

But this is not all there is to this. Children represent, among other things, the future of the faith standing there in front of oneself; at stake are the very existence, duration, and durability of a particular religious world. Children lacking the capacity to experience Advent, as Sister Mary feared, meant that a substantial portion of the Catholic population (its *entire* future population) did not share a major religious season with everyone else. Children signal the vulnerability and contingency of a particular religious world and of religion itself, and in exchanges between adults and children about sacred matters the religious world is in play. On no other occasion except perhaps in times of physical pain and loss is the fictive quality of religion—the fact that religious meanings are made and sustained by humans—so intimately and unavoidably apprehended as when adults attempt to realize the meaningfulness of their religious worlds in their children. This is why discussions of children's religious lives are fraught with such great fear, sometimes sorrow, and sometimes ferocity, among adults, especially in times of social change or dislocation.[3]

The apparently commonsensical and straightforward nature of this enterprise—we want to pass our beliefs on to our children—naturalizes or normalizes a far more complex relationship. Children's bodies, rationalities, imaginations, and desires have all been privileged media for giving substance to religious meaning, for making the sacred present and material, not only *for* children but *through* them too, for adults in relation to them. The child addressed in religious settings and the religious world that is represented to this child are constituted in relation to each other. This is the dialectic of what is usually misnamed "children's religion."

[...] Catholic children understood that what happened in their bodies and imaginations was very powerful and could affect the well-being of others on earth and in the spaces of the afterlife. For example, Catholic popular custom held that on All Souls Day (November 2) immediate release could be secured for souls in purgatory by a special indulgence granted church visits on this holy day. It was a common practice among children to step into church, say a prayer, step immediately back outside (thus completing one indulgence visit), step back in, say another prayer, and out again (another visit), throughout the morning, with the expectation that for each "visit" powerful indulgences were secured and souls freed. Children imagined on these days that they could literally see the movement of souls up toward heaven as the result of their actions on earth.[4]

Given how important children's praying was to adults in the community it is not surprising that religious educators were forever devising strategies for ensuring that children prayed. This usually meant action upon children's bodies. Have children place their shoes beneath their beds at night, Father Henry Sullivan, a leading educator, proposed in 1937, "so that they will have to go down on their knees to obtain them the next morning" (Sullivan 1937: 739). Exactly how children prayed and especially how they arranged their bodies at prayer was carefully monitored. "Father Brown," a regular contributor to the *Junior Catholic Messenger* in the 1940s, incessantly admonished children to pray with the right physical composure. "Prayers are often said too fast," he scolded in a typical column:

> The words run together. The same program is sent too often. God gets tired of hearing, "Give me, give me!" He wishes to hear something else. Not enough broadcasts are made. God cannot be expected to be satisfied with only a few programs.
>
> (*Junior Catholic Messenger* 1942a: 36)

Among the behaviors "Manners in Church" warned against was "Dick the Dreamer," who "may *look* as if he is praying, but God on the altar knows he isn't" (*Junior Catholic Messenger* 1940: 20). Another was "Windmill Willie": "Splash go his fingers into the holy water font. Zip—goes his hand to his forehead, his breast and shoulders. The holy water flies through the air" (*Junior Catholic Messenger* 1942b: 4).

Prayer—praying in school, praying in church, and praying at home—served as another medium for making and substantiating the religious world adults and children constituted and inhabited together. The goal of Catholic prayer pedagogy and practice in its ideal expression (as this was articulated in count-less earnest and passionate articles by teaching sisters throughout the middle years of the century) was to create children who prayed unceasingly, who experienced the world across the thrumming of prayer in their bodies, and whose praying bodies could be seen by all. Adults watched children at prayer and choreographed their movements and postures. Children's inner worlds, their religious imaginations, and their understanding of the moral bonds among people and between heaven and earth were constituted in the corporal dis-ciplines of prayer pedagogy. Catholic prayer disciplines worked to embody in children the Catholic scheme of cosmic reciprocity and moral accountability. Morality was not a matter of learned rules and sanctions but of the powerfully experienced corporal connections between heaven and earth and among people on earth fully realized, enacted, embodied in the child *at prayer*. Carefully dis-ciplined to pray in particular ways, children experienced for themselves and for the adults in relation to them the realness of Catholic cosmology and the bonds between the domains of the spirit (heaven and purgatory) and the earth, as any adult would have appreciated watching children go in and out of the church doors on the day set aside for the liberation of souls from purgatory. How much more real does the cosmos get than this? Imagine what that must have felt like, to have seen the cosmos embodied in children's movements in and out of church on behalf of legions of invisible needy souls.

[...] Catholic children were taught that their guardian angels prayed with them. It is impossible to exaggerate the importance of the figure of the guardian angel to mid-twentieth century Catholic children's imaginations and spiri-tuality. The role of angels in representing the faith to children dates from the seventeenth century, when these special beings emerged as protectors of chil-dren newly identified as innocent. Angels accompanied vulnerable children on their forays out into the adult world that had been recast as a realm of danger and temptation and a place where children did not belong. (Having grown up in this world, one of the women I have already mentioned from New Orleans told me that to this day, in her older age, she never goes out without putting on an angel pin.) Guardian angels were fundamentally associated with childhood. Catholic teaching maintained that God sent every child an angel at birth to keep him or her company throughout life. Angels were said to be children's most dependable, loyal, and loving companions and protectors, and children were encouraged to speak with their angels, disclose their hearts to them, and to ask them for help as they went about their studies, did their chores, and played with friends.

Angels were everywhere. They appeared on commemorative tokens for the major transitional rituals of childhood—on the hard covers of first Communion missals, for instance—as if literally to accompany the child across these times of change. Images of angels were given to children as a reward for doing well in school. Angels turned up as characters in children's literature. There were coloring books of guardian angels for preschool children. The point of all this was to "foster greater intimacy between the child and his Guardian Angel," in Sister Angela Merici's words (Merici 1931: 350). Children made room on their desk chairs so their angels could sit beside them. They talked with their angels. Adult Catholics today warmly recall their relationships with their angels as one of the most consoling and comforting aspects of their childhoods, and they recite with obvious pleasure the little prayer they memorized as children: "Angel of God, my Guardian dear, / To whom His love commits me here, / Ever this day be at me side / To light and guard, to rule and guide, / Amen" (ibid.: 352). Angels were among the most important vehicles of communication between adults and children in the common Catholic world they made together.[5]

Although this dimension of the way that guardian angels were imagined and presented to children is lost to contemporary memory, the literature of mid-century Catholic pedagogy makes it clear that children were assured that *some* boys and girls had actually *seen* their guardian angels. This was a privilege reserved for the saints, but very obedient children (saints in their own way) might be granted such a grace. Elementary school religion teachers generally emphasized the empirical verifiability of sacred phenomena to children, teaching them that invisible holy realities could be touched, tasted, felt, and seen. Children were encouraged to have such direct sensory experiences of the sacred, and many children desired them intensely, hoping for miracles to happen to them or to experience the presence of sacred figures with their senses. Children yearned to see their angels, then, who seemed to hover just on the edge of visibility (*Junior Catholic Messenger* 1937: 20).[6]

Because angels became popular in the modern era as the companions of children who were newly understood by the culture to be vulnerable, the angels inevitably bore hints of danger and risk. Stories about angels were always stories about children in peril. A popular Catholic holy card showed an angel leading two very small children across a rickety bridge over a raging torrent just below their little feet, a horrifying vertiginous image. Adults remember this image sixty years later. Stories about angels embodied and articulated the message that children were in real danger in the world and that they needed protection all the time. Children's deaths were inscribed in angel lore. A pamphlet on "stories of the angels," for example, by the popular and prolific writer for youngsters Father Daniel A. Lord, S.J., invited children to sing a "hymn to the angels" that went, in part, "without their protection / So constant and nigh / I could not well live, / I should perish and die" (Lord 1948: n.p.). So angels were etched into children's imaginations by an implicit but deeply embedded threat of physical harm and death, and the realness of angels in children's imaginations was in part the product of this compelling dread.

Because angels went *everywhere* with their little charges (and everywhere here includes the secret places that children might slip off to precisely in order to be free of the adult supervision that was the implicit message of angel stories), they not only saw and heard what children were doing and saying, but, in a more immediately and vividly imagined fashion, they were *there* right beside children in whatever they were doing. For a child to get into a morally objectionable situation meant that he or she had brought his or her angel into it too. Children were warned that although *they* might forget "how near your angel is," their angels were always attentive to their behavior and thoughts—children were meant to know that angels knew what they were thinking and feeling and to understand that the angels knew that they knew. The angels brought a particularly intense moral self-reflexivity into children's experience.

But the connection between angels and children in Catholic imaginings was even more intimate than this. Angels did not only see what children were doing and hear their thoughts, they *felt* children's behaviors in their own angelic beings. A child's rudeness or anger caused his angel deep personal distress and sorrow, a child's kindness or generosity made his angel happy. One little girl who was specially privileged to see her angel, as reported in the *Junior Catholic Messenger* in 1937, noticed that when she did something good, her angel smiled, but when she was bad, "the angel would turn sadly away." She was doing this to her angel. She was making her angel feel this way (*Junior Catholic Messenger* 1937, 1941)!

The angels contributed in this way to the materialization of the moral life in Catholic culture. Children were taught that the good things they did and thought (their pious sentiments, when they resisted temptation, when they helped a friend, and so on) were literally borne up to heaven by their guardian angels, who returned bearing graces and gifts from God. When a child weeps for her sins, Father Brennan wrote, her guardian angel catches up one of her tears and carries it to God (Brennan 1939: 37). By their immediate connection to the child's experience and emotion, the angels bestowed a rich emotional resonance on the moral universe and rendered it imaginatively vivid and present to children. Catholic children were encouraged to experience themselves as being in two domains, natural and supernatural—there was another body out there in the world that knew and felt all the things they did. The angels thus contributed to the dissolution of children's immediate boundaries: the identification between children and angels was so immediate and intimate that children's inner consciousness, their unspoken thoughts and desires were known in their angels' bodies. In this way, then, among their many roles in human experience, the angels guarded against children's autonomy: angel lore cast children as fundamentally in need of constant supervision, moral scrutiny, and accompaniment, a need endorsed by the fear of (or the threat of) harm and death. When children moved over to make room for their angels on the seat next to them in church or in school, they were moving themselves ever more securely into the moral and cosmic world that adults were making for and with them in the media of Catholic devotionalism.

[...] Catholics today like to tell stories about their childhoods that emphasize the absurdity of them, or the brutality, sometimes the wonder and sometimes the silliness of their growing up. The impossibility of accounting for the past in one tonal register (absurdity or awe, brutality or kindness, and so on) reflects the complex and intense nature of Catholic childhood experience in the mid-twentieth century. It also reflects the fact that contemporary Catholic memory straddles the break between the working-class and rural immigrant church and the modern middle-class culture that took shape among Catholics in the United States in the 1960s and 1970s. One of the ends of Catholic religious formation in these years, as I have said, was to create passionate and disciplined children who prayed and made sacrifices, confessed their sins and went to mass, and who inhabited a radically tangible and accessible moral and spiritual universe. The *Junior Catholic Messenger*, which generally tried to appeal to normal American children with its serialized adventure stories and features on sports, interesting new technologies, and funny animals, held out the most rigorous and demanding spiritual standards for its readers. Give yourselves over to the mass, editors urged children in 1943, with the intensity of a burning candle (*Junior Catholic Messenger* 1942c: 63). But all of this was not done for children only. By the disciplining of children's bodies at mass, by forming children's limbs and emotions at prayer, and by drawing children into the circulation, association, and intimacy of bodies, destinies, needs, and feelings between heaven and earth—of the lost souls, of the guardian angels, and of earthly children (although in this world children were never merely earthly)—the world as it was said to be in Catholic doctrine became sensible, affectively alive, emotionally urgent to children and to the adults who labored so hard to represent and to embody this world in children.

Children were not passive in this dynamic. Catholic religious formation would not have been as effective had they been or had the realness of the world presented to them been merely imposed on them. Children enthusiastically embraced the cult of the guardian angel. They fervently assumed their share of responsibilities for the souls in purgatory. They dressed up as priests and played at saying mass. They struggled with their restless bodies to keep still in church to please Sister and to earn her respect and praise. They got swept up in the beauty of the church buildings and the rituals that took place there. They took their missals to mass and tried to follow along with the distant inaudible priest. They knew in their bodies their bonds to the souls in purgatory, which they experienced as love, guilt, and fear, and they experienced the intimacy with their guardian angels that linked their bodies to these other supernatural ones. Some of this was conscious, but much was also there by discipline, inference, in feelings produced in them by the stories adults told them and in which children were implicated. Bodily apprehensions are not always conscious, but they are real. Catholic reality took hold of children's bodies, was embodied in children's bodies, whether they knew it or not, and their bodies bore the realness of this world, at the same time that children took hold of the world in the idioms given them by their teachers and parents.

A former nun, now in her mid-seventies, shared with me a memory that illustrates what I mean here by a body awareness that can operate below the level of consciousness. This woman, whom I will call Margaret, became an "activist" nun (her phrase) in the 1960s, rejecting the devotional styles and methods of her childhood faith—rejecting, in other words, the very media I have been describing: memorized prayer, devotion to the saints, her imaginary angelic friend, and so on. This was all in her past. Then one day Margaret found herself trapped during a race riot on the streets of the midwestern city where she was working in social services. She was in real danger and frightened for her life. Then, all of a sudden, when her fear was extreme, she heard one of the old prayers she had memorized as a child sounding in her head. She was not "saying" this prayer, Margaret explained to me. The prayer was "echoing in my body." Her childhood prayer was saying her. The disciplined instruction in praying she had received as a child and adolescent, the determination of adults to embody praying in her, had done its work.[7]

The world made real in children's bodies did not always have such a positive enduring presence as one might expect given how prevalent guilt was in its constitution and death and pain in its sanctioning. The following account was sent me by a psychotherapist working in another large midwestern city:

> I have listened to hours of disclosure from suffering victims about the damages of pre-Vatican [II] practices. Midlife women still angry at missing their babies' Christenings because they hadn't been churched yet (cleansed of the stains of childbirth). A mother who felt guilty for years that her SIDS baby's death before baptism sent him to limbo ... Scores of mid-life women who have never experienced an orgasm because they were taught that sex was so dirty ... A woman who had an abortion after a rape and now believes that her two subsequent miscarriages are punishments from God.
>
> (SDK, Ph.D., to Robert Orsi, April 8, 2002)[8]

The making of the realness of a religious world is not a benign process; religious reality achieved in children's bodies (and reverberating in the memories of the adults these children become) did not make the world safer for these children, more comfortable, or even necessarily more meaningful. It made it real. The consequences of this achievement of sacred realness in children's bodies would only be recognized and known by people like Margaret later in life, for better or worse, as their bodies encountered new experiences and new circumstances.

The lived Catholic body was shaped in exchanges between the emergent generations of American Catholics and the adults in relation to them who sought to enact in young people's bodies and imaginations the world of Catholic meanings and possibilities. These adults had become anxious about this world in the years after the end of immigration and at the beginning of changes in American Catholic life; they worked fervently to render the interiority of Catholic faith visible and materially substantive for children—and for themselves. Children actively participated with adults in this work of cultural making and remaking. Tommy Twistneck,[9] the guardian angels, and the souls in purgatory awaiting redemption by the movements of children's bodies on Holy Thursdays, the living rosaries and the ways that adults arranged children at prayer—none of this was "children's religion." What was being formed in all this was not children's religious experience but the distinctive quality of modern American Catholicism.

Notes

1 A classic locus of this argument is Emile Durkheim (1965), *The Elementary Forms of the Religious Life*, especially Book Three, "The Principal Ritual Attitudes," pp. 337–496; Geertz also emphasizes the world-making powers of ritual. For a recent important discussion of religious ritual, see Bell (1992). The example of the woman associated with devotion to the Sacred Heart is taken from a conversation I had in Phoenix, Arizona, as part of the research for ongoing work on growing up Catholic in the United States in the twentieth century: LL-F-56-Superior, Az./Phoenix, Az.-2/13/01. The format of citations from this research is a variation of the one I have used in other studies: identifying initials for the person with whom I spoke (I have made these up to protect my sources but they are consistent throughout so readers can keep track of what particular people say), age, birthplace/location of our conversation, and its date. Most of the conversations took place in small groups of people (usually four to five) who gathered together, at my request, in a group member's home, for several discussions, over a three- or four-week period, about growing up Catholic. I taped the conversations and prepared transcripts afterwards. Participants in this work were chosen by a contact in a particular area I had made through friends, always an older woman with long connections to the community who drew on her friends and neighbors—and their friends and neighbors—in assembling the groups for me. The groups were made up of equal numbers of men and women and ranged in age from mid-thirties to mid-seventies. So far in this research I have worked in Louisiana, Arizona, Indiana, Ohio, and Nebraska. The people I speak to know that I am working on a book on growing up Catholic; I do not make composites and I quote individuals exactly. My sources are assured that I will protect their identities; they also know that they can ask me not to quote something they had said, even long after our conversations (although in all the years I have been working in this way, no one has ever made this request).

2 For a recent, useful discussion of the meanings of relics, see Schopen (1998).

3 My thinking on childhood has been influenced by a number of recent works on the history, sociology, and politics of childhood, among them Calvert (1992), Higonnet (1998), Jenks (1996), Kincaid (1992, 1998), Nandy (1983), Postman (1982), and Wullschläger (1995). See also the important collections by Fass and Mason (2000), Jenkins (1998) and West and Petrik (1992).

4 This was reported to me by adults ranging in age from their late forties into their eighties in all parts of the country and in various ethic groups. The practice was not ethnically specific or regional; it belonged to mid-century Catholic childhoods in the United States.

5 For examples of the place of angels in the way adults represented the faith to their children, see Brennan (1941) and Lord (1948).

6 Lord also holds out the same promise of seeing angels (Lord 1948).
7 MM-F-73-Cinncinnati, Oh./Bloomington, In.-3/4/97.
8 The writer also observed of her own childhood: "I have no doubts about the memories of having to wear blue dresses for Mary to school every day in May and the shame when my Mom couldn't come up with enough blue dresses in our family of six to 'break Mary's heart, turn your back on the Blessed Mother' by not wearing a blue dress. ... I remember my dad missing my brother's First Communion because he was president of the Holy Cross Alumnae Sodality and the priest moderator wouldn't excuse him from his duties there. In sixth grade I remember fainting from hunger because we had a Martyr's Club with prizes for those who practiced the most self-sacrifice—Sister suggested fasting and we even cut like stigmata and stuck thorn bushes in our school uniforms at Sister's suggestion."
9 Tommy Twistneck was one of series of cartoon figures appearing in the *Junior Catholic Messenger* in the 1940s who illustrated different forms of inappropriate and censured behavior by children in church—in this case turning his neck around to see what was going on around the church rather than focusing his gaze on the altar.

14 Religious sensations
Media, aesthetics, and the study of contemporary religion

Birgit Meyer

Religious sensations

In the study of religion, no one interested in the question of feelings can bypass the seminal work of the American philosopher and psychologist William James. James (1982: 42) circumscribed religion as "the feelings, acts, and experiences of individual men in their solitude, so far as they apprehend themselves to stand in relation to whatever they may consider the divine". Although James's attention to religious feelings and experiences is much to the point, it is also problematic for at least two reasons. First, his emphasis on feelings and experiences is predicated upon a strong distinction between the body, as the locus of senses and emotions, and the mind, as the site of intellectual knowledge. This distinction, which has had repercussions in the study of religion up to the present, reaffirms the Cartesian split between body and mind. Paying attention to religious feelings and experiences would then almost by necessity imply a disregard for more intellectual, rational dispositions (as if these would not also generate and sustain particular feelings and experiences). In my view, this is a vain, unproductive opposition, one that I seek to circumvent.[1]

Second, in James's perspective religious feelings and experiences are by definition private, subjective, and primary, whereas religious organizations such as churches and their doctrines and practices are regarded as secondary. Emphasizing the primary experience of God with the pathos typical of his writing and speaking, James did not realize that the disposition of the lonely individual in search of God is part and parcel of a discursive, and hence shared, cultural construction. The fact that he and those working in line with his ideas take the existence of a primary, authentic, and in this sense seemingly unmediated religious experience at face value is misleading. Indeed, as Charles Taylor puts it in his critical discussion of James's approach to religious experience: "Many people are not satisfied with a momentary sense of wow! They want to take it further and they're looking for ways of doing so" (Taylor 2002: 116).[2]

Without the particular social structures, sensory regimes, bodily techniques, doctrines, and practices that make up a religion, the searching individual craving experience of God would not exist. Likewise, religious feelings are not just there, but are made possible and reproducible by certain modes of inducing experiences of the transcendental. While from the insider perspective of religious practitioners religion may seem to originate in initially unmediated, authentic experiences of an entity perceived as transcendental, I propose taking as the starting point of our analysis the religious forms that generate such experiences.

In this context it is important to realize that sensation has a double meaning: feeling[3] *and* the inducement of a particular kind of excitement. This inducement is brought about by what I would like to call *sensational forms*, which make it possible to sense the transcendental. Sensational forms, in my understanding, are relatively fixed, authorized modes of invoking and organizing access to the transcendental, thereby creating and sustaining links between religious practitioners in the context of particular religious organizations. Sensational forms are transmitted and shared; they involve religious practitioners in particular practices of worship and play a central role in forming religious subjects. Collective rituals are prime examples of sensational forms in that they address and involve participants in a specific manner and induce particular feelings. But the notion of sensational form can also be applied to the ways in which material religious objects—such as images, books, or buildings—address and involve beholders. Thus, reciting a holy book such as the Qur'an, praying in front of an icon, or dancing around the manifestation of a spirit are also sensational forms through which religious practitioners are made to experience the presence and power of the transcendental. [...]

Let me start to clarify how religious sensations, in the sense of experiences and feelings, are organized by sensational forms, and hence are subject to social construction and power structures, by turning to my own research. A red thread in my work on Christianity, popular culture, and modern mass media in Ghana concerns the connection between local Africans' conversion to Protestantism and their concomitant incorporation into a modern state and a global capitalist market (Meyer 1992, 1995, 1999). This interest has also pushed me to investigate the current appeal of Pentecostal-charismatic churches (Meyer 1998a, 1998b, 2004a; see also Gifford 2004). By contrast to mainstream Protestantism, Pentecostal religiosity is far more geared to publicly expressing religious feelings. This expressive, public emotionality has pushed me to think about the question of religious sensations.

These churches, to adopt an expression from Bonno Thoden van Velzen, operate as a kind of "pressure cooker—or even microwave—of the emotions" (personal communication), in that they not only generate but also heat up and intensify religious feelings. Pentecostal services are powerful sensational forms that seek to involve believers in such a way that they sense the presence of God in a seemingly *immediate* manner and are amazed by His power. Still, the Holy Spirit does not arrive out of the blue. I have witnessed many such services, in which the pastor and congregation pray for the Holy Spirit to come. After some time, the prayers become louder and louder, and many start speaking in tongues. This is taken as a sign that the Holy Spirit is manifest. At a certain moment the pastor indicates the end of the prayer session and calls upon the Holy Spirit to heal the sick, protect the vulnerable, and expel demonic spirits. The desire for such a seemingly direct link with the power of God via the Holy Spirit is what made, and still makes, many people migrate to Pentecostal churches and to become born again.[4] Though in principle all born-again believers are able and entitled to *embody* the Holy Spirit, charismatic pastors are prime exponents of divine power. Indeed, this is what their charisma depends upon and what draws people into their churches.

The latest brand of Pentecostal-charismatic churches, which started to thrive in Ghana in the early 1990s, are run in a businesslike fashion by flamboyant pastors. Making skillful use of the modern mass media, which have become deregulated and commercialized in the course of Ghana's turn to a democratic constitution, Pentecostal-charismatic churches have become omnipresent in the public sphere (Kwabena Asamoah-Gyadu 2004; Meyer 2004b). Like American televangelism, many of them make use of the mass media to produce and broadcast spectacular church services to mass audiences. Recorded during church conventions yet edited carefully so as to ensure utmost credibility, such programs claim to offer eye-witness accounts of the power of God to perform miracles via the charismatic pastor and his Prayer Force (De Witte 2003). Featured as an embodiment—indeed an objectification—of divine power, the pastor conveys a sense of amazement and wonder. These programs address anonymous viewers, asking them to participate in the televised event with their prayers so as to feel the presence of God. Some people report that they have been truly touched by God when viewing such programs (De Witte 2005a). What emerges is a new sensational form that makes miracles happen on the television screen and seeks to reach out to a mass audience, which is invited to "feel along" with the televised spectacle witnessed on screen.

I find this incorporation of dramatized, mass-mediated performances of divine power and miracles highly intriguing. This phenomenon is not confined to Pentecostal-charismatic churches but is of broader importance. Modern media have become relevant to religious practice in many settings and shape the sensational forms around which links between human beings and the transcendental evolve. Although I will keep returning to my own research throughout this essay, I hope to be able to show that the question of religious sensations far exceeds that particular ethnographic setting. Though sensed individually, religious sensations are socially produced, and their repetition depends on the existence of formalized practices that not only frame individual religious sensations but also enable them to be reproduced. That is, again, why I talk about sensations in the double sense of persons having particular sensations *and* the inducement of these sensations via sensational forms, forms that encompass the objectifications of "the mysterious or 'supernatural' something felt" addressed by Marett, as well as Pentecostalism's televised spectacles and all kinds of less spectacular devices designed to link people with the transcendental and each other.

Modern media and mediation

Thinking about the at times spectacular reports in the daily news about the incorporation of television and the internet into religious traditions, one might be led to think that the presence of media is a distinct characteristic of contemporary religion. Pentecostals' televised performances of miracles, of which I have seen so many in Ghana and elsewhere, are no doubt highly remarkable events. Still, it is important to realize that media are not foreign or new, but intrinsic to religion. As Hent de Vries has argued, religion may well be considered as a practice of mediation (De Vries 2001; see also Meyer 2006a, 2006b; Plate 2003; Stolow 2005). Positing a distance between human beings and the transcendental, religion offers practices of mediation to bridge that distance and make it possible to experience—from a more distanced perspective, one could say produce—the transcendental. Take, for example, the Catholic icon: though it is carved from wood, painted, and set up—thus obviously manmade—to the believing beholder (and possibly to its maker) it appears as an embodiment of a sacred presence that can be experienced by a contemplative gaze, a prayer, or a kiss. In this perspective, the transcendental is not a self-revealing entity but, on the contrary, always affected or formed by mediation processes, in that media and practices of mediation invoke the transcendental via particular sensational forms. These sensational forms not only mediate the transcendental but often, and in our time increasingly so, depend on modern media such as print and electronic audiovisual devices. In order to avoid confusion, I would like to stress that, in this understanding of religion as mediation, media feature on two levels. Not only do modern media such as print, photography, TV, film, or the Internet shape sensational forms, the latter are themselves media that mediate, and thus produce, the transcendental and make it available to the senses.

For a staunch Protestant, for example, the Bible is never just a mass-produced book but is sacralized as the medium through which God has revealed himself. For Muslims the Qur'an is a holy book. Popular images of Jesus, as David Morgan has shown, are regarded not simply as mass-produced representations but as able to intimate the presence of Christ (Morgan 1998). In India, as the work of Christopher Pinney shows, mass-produced chromolithographs of Hindu gods become sites of worship (Pinney 2004; see also Babb and Wadley 1995). Similarly, mass-produced portraits of the early twentieth century Thai King Chulalongkorn play a central role in popular Buddhist worship practices (Morris 2000; Stengs 2007). In Pentecostal circles, television is regarded as exceptionally well suited to screening the born-again message for a mass public (see also Birman 2006; De Abreu 2002; De Witte 2003, 2005a; Hackett 1998; Oosterbaan 2006).

During my research in Ghana, I encountered many people who referred to televised miracle sessions as being true depictions of the power of God. Television (and video) are seen as modern media that can be used to prove the existence and efficiency of divine power and sustain the belief that "your miracle is on the way," as one popular Pentecostal slogan goes. During my stay in

Ghana in 2002, I was told about a Nigerian video that depicted a Pentecostal pastor who brings back to life a dead person, taken to church in his coffin. The idea of making audiovisual technologies reveal the reality and power of God, and affirm His superiority over the power of the Devil, is popularized by local video-filmmakers, among whom I have conducted research on the intersection of Christianity, media, and entertainment. Surfing along with the popularity of Pentecostal Christianity, many of them frame their movies as divine revelations that visualize the operation of the "powers of darkness" with the help of the camera and computer-produced special effects. Although spectators know quite well how these movies are made, many still insist that the audiovisual technologies mobilized for the sake of revelation show "what is there" yet remain invisible to the naked eye. In discussions about witchcraft, those defending the position that witchcraft is real refer to Ghanaian and Nigerian video-films, thus backing up their claims with audiovisual evidence. In this sense, these movies are viewed as offering a kind of divine super-vision that enables viewers to peep into the dark.

What all these examples have in common is a salient fusion of media technologies and the transcendental, which they are made to mediate via particular sensational forms. At the same time, precisely because media are indispensable to, and interwoven with, religious mediation, religious practitioners may find new media to be entirely inappropriate, or at least very difficult to accommodate. This is so with indigenous cults in Ghana, whose priests are adamant that cameras may not be brought into their shrines (De Witte 2005b; Meyer 2005a; see also Ginsburg 2006; Spyer 2001). Conversely, processes of religious innovation are often characterized by the adoption of new media, entailing fierce assaults against older media, as in the case of Protestant missionaries' dismissal of Catholicism and indigenous cults as "idol worship" that should urgently be replaced by a thorough focus on the true source of God's Word: the Bible as mother tongue. The sensational form evolving around the icon was to be replaced by a new sensational form evolving around the book.

These examples not only suggest that mediation objectifies a spiritual power that is otherwise invisible to the naked eye and difficult to access, thereby making its appearance via a particular sensational form dependent upon currently available media and modes of representation; they also highlight that mediation itself tends to be sacralized by religious practitioners. By the same token, the media intrinsic to such mediations are exempted from the sphere of mere technology and authorized to be suitable harbingers of immediate, authentic experiences (Van de Port 2006; see also Mazzarella 2004; Meyer 2005b). Religious sensations of a presumably immediate encounter with God, or of having direct access to his power, do not happen just "out of the blue"—however much those experiencing these sensations may think so. Such sensations, it needs to be stressed, are prefigured by existing mediation practices, which make it possible for believers to be touched by God in the first place.

Although I have emphasized that religious mediation happens in the immanent and hence depends on human activities, I would be wary of anchoring religious mediation in theoretical approaches that affirm a contrast between "real" and "made up." Certainly in the study of religion, we need to recognize the phenomenological reality of religious experience as grounded in bodily sensations. Since I am a scholar rooted in the social sciences, it is not my professional task to make statements concerning the true or imagined existence of the transcendental, or the ontological status of reality. Above all, as social scientists we have to come to terms with the *mediated* nature of experiences that are claimed to be *immediate* and *authentic* by their beholders and are authorized as such by the religious traditions of which they form part (Meyer 2005b; Van de Port 2005, 2006). It is enough neither to deconstruct and dismiss these experiences as "made up" and "faked" nor to take their authenticity at face value (Chidester 2005). I will return to this point in the section on aesthetics below.

The adoption of new media does not happen in a vacuum, but is bound up with broader social and cultural processes. By instigating the shift to the new medium of the printed book during the Reformation, for example, Protestantism also associated itself with new, modern techniques of the self and modes of perception, that is, with the emerging print capitalism that has been crucial to the genesis of the modern nation-state (Anderson 1991). The shift to televangelism, which not only occurs in Christianity but also appeals to members of other religious traditions, can be viewed as an attempt to rearticulate religion in what Walter Benjamin called the "era of technical reproducibility" (Benjamin 1977; see also Önçü 2006; Schulz 2003). If only what is shown on TV truly exists, then the power of God has to appear on TV. As belief becomes thus vested in the image, it becomes hard to distinguish between belief and make-believe, miracles and special effects, or truth and illusion (De Certeau 1984: 186ff; De Vries 2001: 23ff.). The accommodation of such new media and the new sensational forms that go along with them ensure the up-to-dateness of Christianity and its public presence. We could even say that television is called upon to authorize religious sensations as true, while the body of the spectator brings televised images to life, as in the Venezuelan María Lionza Cult studied by Rafael Sánchez, who shows that cult members are possessed by the spirits of TV personae and personalities (see Van de Port 2006; Sánchez 2001). The entanglement of religion, media, and the forces of commercialization, though allowing for the public presence of religion, erodes the possibility of maintaining a clear distinction between religion and entertainment (Moore 1994; see also Guadeloupe 2006). In this sense, as Jeremy Stolow puts it, media and mediation always constitute "inherently unstable and ambiguous conditions of possibility for religious signifying practices," and thus challenge the maintenance of religious authority (Stolow 2005: 125).

While the adoption of modern audiovisual media certainly transforms practices of religious mediation and the sensational forms through which the transcendental is rendered accessible, we must be careful not to overestimate the power of media per se to change the world.[5] The adoption of modern media, as we found in the context of the research program Modern Mass Media, Religion, and the Imagination of Communities, which I directed from 2000 to

2006,[6] always involves complicated negotiations, yielding processes of transformation that cannot be attributed either to media alone or to the persistence of a fixed religious message. The adoption of modern media allows for the reformation and reactivation of religion in our time. As Mattijs van de Port shows in his study of Brazilian Candomblé, cult members' practices of "visualizing the sacred"—which is supposed to remain secret—in soap-opera-style videos reveal an "inextricable entanglement of religious and media imaginaries that should guide studies of religion in contemporary societies" (Van de Port 2006: 457).

Precisely because media are intrinsic to religion, in the study of contemporary religion we need to pay utmost attention to attitudes toward modern media and their adoption into established practices of religious mediation. Given the strong visual orientation of such modern media, we are well advised to link up with the recent interdisciplinary field of research on visual culture. Important questions for further research are: how does the availability of modern media change religious mediation, and hence the ways in which the transcendental is expressed via particular sensational forms? Are there significant differences between the ways in which different religious traditions, groups, or movements adopt and appropriate different kinds of modern media? What contradictions and clashes arise from the coexistence of the interdiction on making images of God, as found in Judaism, Islam, and Christianity, and the dynamics of contemporary visual culture, which thrives on visibility? What kind of religious sensations, in the sense of feelings, are generated when religions adopt new sensational forms, such as the spectacle?

Aesthetics and *aisthesis*

Understanding religion as a practice of mediation that organizes the relationship between experiencing subjects and the transcendental via particular sensational forms requires that the material and sensory dimensions of religious mediation become a focal point of attention. For me, this understanding implies the need to pay attention to aesthetics. My understanding of aesthetics exceeds the narrow sense advocated by Baumgarten and Kant, in which aesthetics refers to the beautiful in the sphere of the arts, more or less confined to the disinterested beholder. Instead, I follow a suggestion made by anthropologists Christopher Pinney and Jojada Verrips, namely, that we link up again with Aristotle's notion of *aisthesis*, understood as organizing "our total sensory experience of the world and our sensitive knowledge of it" (Pinney 2004, 2006; Verrips 2006a: 27). To trace such an understanding of aesthetics in terms of aisthesis or sense experience back to Maurice Merleau-Ponty's phenomenology of perception (Merleau-Ponty 2002),[7] or to relate it to the phenomenology of religion as developed by Rudolf Otto, Gerardus van der Leeuw, or Mircea Eliade,[8] would be outside my present scope, not to speak of discussing the ins and outs, pros and cons, of phenomenology in general. Let me briefly explain, on the basis of some examples, why I deem it useful to consider the aesthetic dimension of religion.

[…] My plea to acknowledge the aesthetic dimension of religion is grounded in my realization of the shortcomings of more conventional interpretative or symbolic approaches in the study of religion. Sensational forms, though produced and in a sense "made up," appear as situated beyond mediation exactly because they are—literally—incorporated and embodied by their beholders. These forms evoke and perpetuate shared experiences, emotions, and affects that are anchored in a taken-for-granted sense of self and community, indeed, a *common sense* that is rarely subject to questioning exactly because it is grounded in shared perceptions and sensations. Common sense is what gets under the skin, enveloping us in the assurance "this is what really is."

[…] My ideas about the aesthetic dimension of religion have been particularly stimulated by the work of David Morgan (Morgan 1998, 2005). On the basis of his highly original investigation of the role of mass-produced images in popular American Protestantism, he proposes understanding religious images as artifacts that attribute reality to representations of the divine, making it appear as if the picture possesses "its referent within itself" (Morgan 1998: 9). Such religious images are important examples of what I call sensational forms. Being part and parcel of religious mediation, they can best be understood as a condensation of practices, attitudes, and ideas that structure experiences of the transcendental and hence "ask" to be approached in a particular manner. Far from resembling Kant's disinterested beholder of an aesthetic object, believers (have learned to) expect that images mediate the transcendental in a process that miraculously vests them with divine presence. Believers are led to engage in particular religiously induced "looking acts" so as not only to see the image but to sense the divine power that shines through it. Such "looking acts" are not confined to seeing alone but induce sensations of being touched. In this sense, religious images do not just meet the eye but have a thoroughly carnal dimension (cf. Sobchack 2004). Thus, rather than being persuasive in and of themselves, religious images work in the context of particular grammars and traditions of usage, which evoke religious sensations by teaching particular ways of looking and induce particular dispositions and practices toward them. In other words, such images are part and parcel of a particular religious aesthetic, which governs believers' sensory engagement with the transcendental and with each other.[9]

Morgan's work is not only useful for the study of religious images per se,[10] but can be extended to religious sensational forms in a broader sense, that is, the whole range of religious materials conveying a sense of the sublime, from images to texts, from objects to music. Mediating the transcendental and raising religious sensations, these material sensational forms require our utmost attention. They are the anchor points from which religious aesthetics unfold. At the same time, it is important to realize that significant differences exist between the sets of sensational forms (and the religious aesthetics that go along with these sensational forms) that are at the core of particular religious traditions, groups, or movements at a given time. Different media appeal to the senses in different ways: it makes a big difference whether a religious organization is rich in imagery and foregrounds vision or poor in imagery, or even iconoclastic, and foregrounds listening.

Of course, the aesthetic that goes along with a particular sensational form does more than just organize vertical encounters of religious subjects with the transcendental. Aesthetics is also key to the making of religious subjects in a broader sense. Religious organizations can be characterized as having distinct sensory regimes. As Talal Asad, Charles Hirschkind, and Saba Mahmood have argued, specific bodily and sensory disciplines give rise to particular sensibilities (see Asad 1993; Hirschkind 2001; Mahmood 2001). These sensibilities impart a particular sense of the self and one's being in the world—if you wish, a particular identity.[11] Religious subjects are created (ideally, that is) by a structured process—a religious didactics—in which the senses are called upon and tuned in a way that yields a habitus.[12] This process not only entails a strong emphasis on specific, privileged, sensory, and extra-sensory perceptions but also the tuning down or anaesthetization of other senses or sensory perceptions (Verrips 2006a; see also Buck-Morss 1992). We are all familiar with the fact that an overabundance of sensory perceptions may impede our—and our children's—concentration and attention (Crary 2001); techniques of meditation, for instance, are called upon to overcome such distracting perceptions and concentrate on what "really matters." Charles Hirschkind has argued that Islamic reform movements incorporate the use of mass-produced cassette sermons into an "ethics of listening," which emphasizes the importance of the ear as the key site for raising a pious Muslim subject (Hirschkind 2001; see also Schulz 2003, 2006). In the midst of the soundscape of the city of Cairo, seated in taxis or in noisy environments, young Muslims create their own soundscape by listening to cassettes. In her work on the Catholic charismatic renewal in Brazil, Zé de Abreu has shown that the priest and pop star Marcello Rossi is able to tune tens of thousands of people into "the aerobics of Jesus," which entails distinct breathing techniques to induce an exhilarating, albeit ephemeral, feeling (De Abreu 2005). [...]

The bodily and sensory disciplines implied in making religious subjects are also key to invoking and affirming links among religious practitioners. In this sense, aesthetics is central to the making of religious communities. Style is a core aspect of religious aesthetics (Meyer 2006c; see also Maffesoli 1996). Inducing as well as expressing shared moods, a shared religious style—materialized in, for example, collective prayer, a shared corpus of songs, images, symbols, and rituals, but also a similar style of clothing and material culture—makes people feel at home. Thriving on repetition and serialization, style induces a mode of participation via techniques of mimesis and emulation that yield a particular habitus. In a world of constant change, style offers some degree of continuity and stability (though style is at the same time subject to change, as styles come and go). In this sense, style is the sine qua non of identity. Sharing a common aesthetic style via a common religious affiliation not only generates feelings of togetherness and speaks to, as well as mirrors, particular moods and sentiments: such experiences of sharing also modulate people into a particular, common appearance, and thus underpin a collective religious identity. [...]

Interestingly, once implanted in a person, religious aesthetics may endure independently of exterior religious regimes or an active religious affiliation. Anyone having decided to step out of a particular religion may be puzzled about the resilience of particular religiously induced bodily disciplines and sensory practices, which it may be impossible to shed entirely (see Verrips 2006b). A good many ex-Protestants are still gripped by a diffuse feeling of awe when they hear the sound of a church organ. In Holland there are many post-Calvinists who regard themselves as secular and yet espouse an aesthetics that is deeply rooted in Calvinism. In situations of religious change, people may feel torn between the sensory modalities of the religion they embrace and those of the religion they have left behind. African converts to Christianity may still feel touched—or even get possessed—by the sound of "pagan" drums.

Conversely, encounters with a new religion often work through the body, making it difficult for researchers to maintain an outsider's position. Many anthropologists have reported how they have been sucked into the sensory modes of the religion they have studied, without even being aware of it—as in the case of Susan Harding, who found her mind to be taken over by the voice of the Baptist pastor who had been preaching to her for more than four hours (Harding 2000). Such examples stress the importance of aesthetics in underpinning people's sense of belonging and being in the world. But taking into account the aesthetic dimension of religion may also help us realize why it is that religious people may feel offended, or even hurt, when they are confronted with blasphemous images or sacrilegious acts, from Christians' being shocked by desecrating images of Mary or the crucifixion staged by pop singer Madonna in her 2006 performance, to Muslims' distress over illicit representations of the prophet, about which we now hear so much in the news (Verrips 2006b).

Precisely because religious mediations objectify the transcendental in sensational forms that call upon the body and tune the senses of religious practitioners so as to invest these forms with ultimate truth, emphasis on the aesthetic dimension of religion is indispensable. Indeed, focusing on mass media and religious mediation calls for attention to the senses and the body. Therefore, in our research we need to explore how modern media and the body, the audiovisual and the material, intersect (Spyer 2005). Important questions for further research are: what kinds of bodily disciplines and sensory regimes are peculiar to particular religious organizations, including both those that belong to major world religions and new modes of spirituality, as in New Age? What are the differences? Which senses do specific sensational forms, from the Bible to virtual sites of worship in cyberspace, from icons to mass-produced posters, address? What impact do religious aesthetics have on the making and appeal of religious identities, and on the dynamics of exclusion and inclusion of which they are part? How do religious aesthetics relate to other identities, and why and how do they survive, even though a person may leave a particular religion?

Notes

1 In anthropology, so-called intellectualist approaches, which reduce religion to a quest for knowledge (as developed by E.B. Tylor and later Robin Horton), and so-called expressivist or symbolist approaches, which emphasize the importance of feeling and experience, have long been at loggerheads. While the former tend to focus on "words" and "meaning," the latter tend to foreground "images" and "experience."

2 Taylor says this in his discussion of the appeal that James's work has today. James misrecognized formal spiritual practices, however. Peter van Rooden critiques Schleiermacher along similar lines (Van Rooden 1996). A host of approaches to religion as experience can be critiqued along the lines suggested by Taylor and Van Rooden.

3 Given that the term *sense*, contained in *sensation*, also denotes *Sinn*, or "meaning," it is important not to confine sensation to feeling alone but to see it as encompassing the formation of meaning (not as a purely intellectual endeavor, but as enshrined in broader processes of "sensing"). This allows us to transcend the infelicitous opposition between approaches in the study of religion that focus on feelings, experiences, and the body, on the one hand, and the production of meaning as a purely intellectual endeavor on the other [...]. In my understanding, the production of meaning always involves bodily experiences and emotions.

4 Because the Holy Spirit does not enter into and stay in a person just like that, Pentecostalism teaches a set of religious disciplines, such as Bible study, extensive fasting, and intense individual and collective prayer in small prayer cells. (See Van Dijk 2005.) To be filled with and express the Holy Spirit is not only a question of inward, contemplative spirituality but also a question of power: only those filled with the Holy Spirit are held to be invulnerable to evil spirits and empowered to lead a happy, prosperous life.

5 We find such a stance not only in Marshall McLuhan's famous dictum "The medium is the message" but also, e.g., in the thinking of Manuel Castells. In Castells's view, religion stands separate from the "integrated communication system based on digitized electronic production, distribution and exchange of symbols" that generates the social networks that characterize the information age (Castells 1996: 406). Referring to an eternal truth that cannot be mediated via the technologies of the information age, religion is, in Castells's view, a conservative force, and thus a matter of the past, doomed to disappear in favor of secularization. The adoption of modern mass media by religion—Castells invokes the example of televangelism—ultimately destroys religion's legitimacy: when "all wonders are online," "societies are finally and truly disenchanted" (ibid.). I disagree with Castells's view of religion as a reactive force, which can only be corrupted and rendered obsolete by taking up modern mass media. For how mistaken it is to understand the rise of public, mass-mediatized religion in this manner, see Meyer and Moors (2006) and De Vries (2001).

6 For more information on this program, see www.pscw.uva.nl/media-religion (accessed November 4, 2010).

7 For Merleau-Ponty, perception has priority over reason (Merleau-Ponty 2002). Thinking is grounded in the perceived world, that is, in experiences that precede reflection. This means that the body is central: via the body, humans are both part of and able to experience the world. This experience mobilizes all the senses.

8 As intimated in the section on religious sensations (pp. 159–61), one of the big problems with phenomenological approaches in the study of religion is the strong bias toward interiority and the assumption of a transcendent reality out there. This entails a neglect of the social construction of the transcendental in the immanent. In his stimulating article "Asymptote of the Ineffable: Embodiment, Alterity, and the Theory of Religion" (2004), Thomas Csordas critically discusses the phenomenology of religion. While his ideas about the importance of embodiment resonate with my

plea to take into account the aesthetic dimension of religion, I still find his claim that alterity forms the "phenomenological kernel" of religion problematic because it fails to include the social dimension. I agree with the point raised by Michael Lambek, that Csordas "has some way to go now to link alterity with the social and the moral" (Lambek 2004: 179).

9 Morgan's ideas resonate remarkably well with recent approaches developed in the field of cinema studies, which challenge the association of vision and the visual with the eye alone, and the concomitant disassociation from other senses. In particular, Laura Marks (*The Skin of the Film*, 1999) and Vivian Sobchack (*Carnal Thoughts*, 2004) have stressed the need to develop a more visceral, carnal approach to the visual, one that is rooted in the existential phenomenology of Merleau-Ponty (and Dufrenne 1973) and can take note of the multisensory, synaesthetic impact of images in constituting a sense of being in the world.

10 See Allen and Polly Roberts's exploration of the power of images of Sheik Amadou Bamba to sacralize space in the city of Dakar (Roberts and Roberts 2003), or Christopher Pinney's analysis of how a visual engagement with printed images of Hindu gods yields a particular "corpothetics." Pinney coins the term *corpothetics* to avoid confusion with conventional understandings of aesthetics in the Kantian sense. Entailing "a desire to fuse image and beholder, and the elevation of efficacy [of beholders' encounter with the image] … as the central criterion of value" (Pinney 2004: 194), Pinney's understanding of corpothetics and my understanding of aesthetics in terms of aisthesis converge.

11 *Identity* is a central concept in current debates. It refers to a host of meanings. I understand "identity" to mean belonging to a particular social formation that is inclusive as well as exclusive. Identity, as Peter Geschiere and I have argued in *Globalization and Identity*, creates boundaries and promises clarity and security in a world characterized by distraction and fragmentation (Meyer and Geschiere 1998). In this sense, identity needs to be placed in a dialectic of flow and closure. I would suggest that we should take into account the importance of the senses and sensations in invoking and sustaining identities that people feel to be natural and thus beyond question. I do not, of course, want to claim the existence of primordial, essentialized identities. The point is, rather, to understand why and how personal and collective identities, though constructed, are perceived as "natural" and "real." (See Meyer 2006c.)

12 For an illuminating discussion of habitus (and hexis) in the thinking of Bourdieu (and Mauss), see Roodenburg (2004).

15 Finding Fabiola
Visual piety in religious life

David Morgan

During the sixth century Fabiola was canonized and since then has been venerated as patroness of abused women. In the second half of the nineteenth century, her cult was revived among European Catholics, leading the painter Jean-Jacques Henner to produce a portrait of her in 1885, which was subsequently lost, though a photographic record remains. Hundreds of hand-made copies of Henner's portrait were made in the twentieth century by amateur artists for various reasons. Many may have derived devotional merit from honoring the saint in this way; others may have found Henner's sharp profile of the woman attractive and perhaps easy to emulate. Francis Alÿs has collected many of these, which were exhibited in 2008 as part of a project sponsored by the Dia Art Foundation in New York. The following essay first appeared in a catalogue published on the occasion of the exhibition, *Francis Alÿs: Fabiola; An Investigation* (Kelly *et al.* 2008).

Fabiola has long taught the lessons of forgiveness and charity, but her many images also have something to teach about the nature and structure of human cognition in popular piety. Empiricists are fond of asserting that knowledge is founded on concrete experience—that facts are built from the ground up, tailored to the particularities of sensation. But Fabiola in her prosaic multiplicity, in the endless iteration of her spare, quiet imagery, says otherwise. Consider her many pictures. Who are we looking at when we gaze upon any one of her many portraits? The sheer number of them destabilizes the prospect of a settled referent. Where is the fourth-century Roman lady of patrician status, befriended by Jerome and eulogized by him at her death? Finding Fabiola may not be possible, but who can resist trying when faced with so many portraits?

Fabiola and Jerome

The impulse to see images as grounded ultimately in facts is an important place to begin thinking about how pictures of Fabiola may be said to show her to the faithful. Perhaps the first thing one sees when looking at her images is not her, but what Jerome said about her. We look through the picture to the text of the bishop's eulogy, and a couple of other letters that may refer to her indirectly. This assumes, of course, that his words limned her reliably. But what is reliable?

Jerome's letters are no longer in his handwriting, but they are corroborated by contemporaries and they bear the "signature" of his style and the verification of historical circumstances. Assuming that Jean-Jacques Henner started there in order to compose his lost portrait, we too go to the letters to find Fabiola, the "real" Fabiola, seeking in the imagery correspondences to what Jerome said of her. But like the generations of Christians and scholars who have sought the historical Jesus in the documents of the New Testament, we find what the letters have constructed and we lack anything against which to test them. Jerome's epistles, like the Gospels, are not indifferent transcripts, but accounts with a purpose, rooted in the communities and circumstances that birthed them. If they are "faithful" descriptions, they are faithful to the purpose and the needs of the writer and his correspondents. Hagiography, the writing of saints' lives, is far less a description of the dead than it is the edification of the living.

Matching word to image, we see the portraits as pictorial hagiography whose message is that a sinner experienced regeneration through the regimen of penitence and contrition. Fabiola was received back into the embrace of the Church after falling away. She put aside the desire and option for marriage and undertook the work of charity. Her heavy red mantle and hood, covering her bosom and clinging like a nun's habit to all but a sliver of her fair face and long neck, signals both her penitent denial of the flesh and her patrician status. The red attire recalls the iconographical tradition of portraying Jerome in the Cardinal's red robe and hat. And since Henner also painted a portrait of Jerome (1881), the connection is even more suggestive. What the two shared was a dedication to monastic self-denial. Signaling Fabiola's asceticism was important: it mattered that the elite of her day were penitent because their rank elevated the Christian community, reaffirming its principal bonds as deeper and surer than social status, but also conferring on the group the capacity to include Rome's finest. The Christian community was happy to recognize such privilege in a society where rank meant everything.

It is a double message—one of penance and submission, to be sure. But Fabiola's beauty belies another. Let us choose one for closer inspection—no. 164 (Figure 15.1). Her classical profile, as Henner and his faithful copyists have imagined it, is etched clearly against the dark ground, rendering the ideal of grace in a long Roman nose, a Hellenic chin, and a neck that remembers the languor of a privileged life even as it vanishes modestly into the scarlet fullness of the lady's tunic. It is the contour of an imperial face on coin or medallion. So one might call it an aquiline beauty, evoking the eagle (*aquila*) in imperial insignia, echoed in the beak-like prominence of Fabiola's nose, the sharp contour of her upper lip, and especially in the determined brow that descends sternly in some images. Does it remember the hauteur of patrician rank? Or has it been baptized into the austerity of self-denial so prized by Jerome among Rome's new vestal virgins?

But this is to read the imagery in a strictly historical manner, as if the scores of images collected by Alÿs at flea markets, garage sales, and thrift stores hailed from the distant past. They don't. Their lost origin is Henner's portrait. Yet in

Figure 15.1 Francis Huys, *Fabiola*, n.d. Paint on canvas. 19 ½ × 15 ½ × 5/8 inches (49.5 × 39.4 × 1.59 cm).

the dimmest way they remember something about worlds no longer present. "Remember" may be pushing it. But vaguely encoded in the profile, in the hood and its folds is iconography that can be traced backward some distance, though not all the way back to shadowy Fabiola. What did Henner consult as he conceived his image? In the world of ancient Rome one thinks of funerary sculpture or portrait busts in which the piety of noble Roman women was registered by their gracefully covered heads. When viewed from the side, ancient Roman marble busts such as one of Livia, second wife of Augustus, observe the restrained and solemn demeanor still at work in Fabiola's countless portraits. Did Henner see Livia's bust or one of hundreds like it? He must have asked himself how Fabiola would look. She was from the upper crust, she was a person of means, one of several we know Jerome sought out to form a powerful circle of high-born women dedicated to his cause. Like each of them, Fabiola modestly put the life of privilege aside for the sake of piety. Henner would have recognized the countenance of nobility that suited Fabiola in the ancient face of Livia or any one of dozens painted during the Renaissance such as Piero della Francesca's impassive Battista Sforza (1472) or Domenico Ghirlandio's charming portrait of Giovanna Tornaboni (1488), or, in his own day, Anselm Feuerbach's *Iphegenia* (1871). After all, she had to look the part if she were to be recognized by the devout. It was a matter of probability, of the saint looking the role.

The nature of recognition

Ever since Plato, recognition has been linked to epistemology, the study of how we know. Plato contended that to know is to recognize, that is, to remember what we already knew. But if no one ever recorded a portrait of Fabiola, how are we to know it's really her? Whom do we recognize as Fabiola when we gaze upon her portrait? The cult of the saints will help us understand what people see. One Catholic website states that St. Fabiola is patroness of "difficult marriages, divorced people, victims of abuse, victims of adultery, victims of unfaithfulness, widows."[1] Those are powerful connections for the faithful who seek consolation or counsel. Fabiola is said to have suffered these difficulties: her first husband was "an adulterer and sodomite," as one letter of Jerome (Letter 55) indicates, and which has been interpreted by tradition to refer to Fabiola's husband (Jerome 2009). She divorced him, but was "compelled to take another," presumably by her family, the prominent Fabia clan. When the second husband died, she undertook public penance and was allowed to participate in Holy Communion once again. She never remarried and devoted herself to philanthropic enterprises, founding a hospital in Rome. Every saint is good for something: she will respond to petitions from the faithful precisely because she herself suffered what they do. She is inclined by sympathy to hear their prayers because she shares with them the pain and tribulation from which they seek relief.

People recognize in Fabiola what they bring to her and what they need from her. One powerful function of hagiography is to establish the basis of connection with the saint. Jerome offers bits of her story in his eulogy (Letter 77), and what is lacking there tradition makes up for by virtue of attribution. In fact, we have no evidence whatsoever that Letter 55 of the Jerome corpus refers to Fabiola when Jerome writes to his correspondent, "I find joined to your letter of inquiries a short paper containing the following words: 'ask him, (that is me), whether a woman who has left her husband on the ground that he is an adulterer and sodomite and has found herself compelled to take another may in the lifetime of him whom she first left be in communion with the church without doing penance for her fault'" (ibid.). Jerome answered unambiguously. No, she could not. And he groused about her words: "I have not been able quite to determine what it is that she means by the words 'has found herself compelled' to marry again. What is this compulsion of which she speaks?" If she does not wish "to be accounted an adulteress," he ruled, "let her do penance" (ibid.). Jerome could be a demanding, aggressive man. A fighter as scrappy as Augustine had suffered his famous invective (Brown 1969: 274–5). Whoever she was, the woman whose query Amandus conveyed kept her name out of the public discourse of a prominent and prickly bishop's official correspondence. Assuming it was her, Fabiola clearly knew that the penance Jerome mentioned was not the discreet sort, uttered quietly and privately in the pastor's study or the confidence of the confessional. It meant sackcloth and ashes in the front row on Sunday morning. Not the sort of thing a high-born Fabia took on lightly.

It requires no faith to want to recognize Fabiola. One is tugged by the pleasure of scandal in her story (if it is hers): Roman noblewoman married to a bestial lout who can't control his appetites; she walks out and divorces him. Ever cognizant of public perceptions, Fabiola's family compels her to remarry, resulting in her ostracism from the Christian community and her inadmissibility at the Lord's Table. No Eucharist meant no assurance of forgiveness of sins and therefore no salvation. Exclusion meant a metaphysical bust. Hardliners like Jerome and Augustine rigorously policed the boundaries of membership. The privileges of belonging were enforced by the agony of being kept out. The resistance made the story better, which mattered, since, among other things, sainthood consists of a story and an image. Hagiography and iconography are the media whereby the devout connect to the sacred. Fueled by need and encouraged by the fit they discern between their story and the saint's, devotees solicit the saint's help. They focus their need and hope on the cult image, which commonly bears the traces of the saint's story. They recognize her because they know her story. The hole in their heart takes the shape of Fabiola's virtues.

Copy and effigy: the cultural work of iteration

One might regard the innumerable iterations of Fabiola's image as each painter's tailoring of the saint to him or herself. She appears now angry, now nymph-like, glamorous, then unassuming, valorous, then meek, solemn, then spry. Some versions of the woman look like she comes from an afternoon television commercial selling dishwashing soap in the 1960s, whereas others, such as No. 164 (Figure 15.1) might be publicity stills from a 1940s bathrobe epic about the Bible. The suggestion is not so ludicrous when we consider the striking resemblance of many versions of Fabiola to the study of a woman from the early 1890s by Henner, now in the Hermitage Museum, St. Petersburg, Russia. The artist may have used the same model for the two portraits. All the versions differ more or less from one another and the difference, more than just the painters' technical abilities, corresponds to the many reasons people must have for painting Fabiola. Perhaps it is in fulfillment of a vow, an ex-voto, a retablo meant to be displayed in gratitude for her assistance in resolving the difficulties of domestic affairs. Her small, framed portrait is ideal for domestic display, where it celebrates victory over abusive husbands or a broken marriage. Buddhists received karmic merit for bathing images of Buddha and for copying important sutras. Hindus trace elaborate *yantras* on the steps of their homes or on pavement in temples in order to invoke the blessing of goddesses. Latino Catholics purchase small tin paintings portraying their miraculous deliverance from harm or illness by the blessing of the Virgin, then deposit them at pilgrimage sites. Pictures and copies do important religious work (see Scharf 1996; Boucher 1996; Huyler 1999: 52–3, 67, 205; Durand and Massey 1995). The very act of a lay person's making an image produces good karma, attracts blessing, conveys thanks, engages benevolent forces. This is not about art, not about personal expression, not about disinterested aesthetic contemplation, not about refined taste. Making copies is about the power of images. People make copies for the same reason they watch movies and television commercials: the lure of images lies in what they promise.

What's in a copy? A few years ago I visited a very well-known Catholic pilgrimage site at Kevelaer, Germany, where a miraculous image of the Virgin and Child is displayed behind glass in an ornate Baroque shrine. The image is an engraving entitled "Miraculous Picture of the Comforter of the Afflicted" and dates from 1640. It is not a painting or an icon, but a print produced in multiple copies and infused with the power to heal those who petition Our Lady pictured in the print. In a famous essay, Walter Benjamin once contended that the aura, the authoritative uniqueness of an image, was lost in mechanical reproduction in modern visual media. The picture at Kevelaer argues otherwise. The faithful line up to pass before the engraving. Sometimes they bring along an illustrated prayer card or a tract sold on site explaining the history of the image and its shrine. On the cover of the tract appears the miraculous image of the Virgin and Child (Figure 15.2). I was struck when I watched a pilgrim press her copy of the tract against the pane protecting the engraving. She paused to pray as she held the tract in place, as if charging it with the blessing of the Virgin. This colloquy of images did not operate as a copy meeting the original. There was no original, but two versions of the same thing meeting one another, as if like would recognize like in a bond cemented by the fervor of the pilgrim and sealed by prayer. Plato long tutored Western philosophical thought regarding the loss of reality in the copy. A reproduction, he insisted, is never equal to its exemplar. A copy is no more than a shadow of its cause, a trace blunted and blurred, half forgotten.

But the pilgrim woman might not agree. Images infused with the blessing of the Virgin are powerful media, suffering no loss of her presence. They are not copies, but iterations, one might say, "goings forth" of the sacred person to meet with the devout in the medium of her "vera effigies," her true effigies, as the Kevelaer engraving states in an ornate caption beneath the image.

Figure 15.2 Illustrated tracts of the *Comforter of the Afflicted*, 2007. Kevelaer, Germany.

"Effigy" may be the word of choice since it derives from the Latin verb "effingere," to fashion or make, with the hand or finger, as the etymology suggests. An effigy is a making or rendering, not simply a copy. But even the word "copy" has a promising past: the word derives from "copia," meaning abundance or multitude in the modern sense of copious. Medieval Latin used "copia" to designate the transcript. From there it was not far to the "carbon copy" of modern transcription. But effigy captures even more. It bodies forth the person. It is a version or rendition of the person, or a version of all its other versions. The better comparison might be to performing a musical score. The performance is not a facsimile of the composition, but a rendition—one among an infinitude of possible renditions. The need for thinking beyond the paradigm of the copy, with its long metaphysical baggage, is important to bear in mind. Plato saw images as captive to the senses and therefore bound to the lower parts of the soul. Uninformed by ideas, by the true form of thought, whose higher life arced through the mind of God, images were delusions, deceptions and nothing more.

The wily Socrates would like to work us into an interminable debate with him over what is true and false. More important, at least more useful, it seems to me, is careful attention to what believers do before images. What they do, in a word, is make the sacred present. Those who fashion a portrait of Fabiola offer her a flattering gift, and conjure in the act a relationship she is obliged to honor. Or they give her picture to another who needs the tender commiseration of one who knows what intractable husbands are like. Devotees look to her image in order to find her present in their time of need. But this returns us to the issue of likeness. If the portrait is not a copy of her face, but a true effigy, what do we see when we look at any one or any number of the images of Fabiola? What sort of recognition occurs if the image is not a copy of the real thing?

Image and epistemology

Looking at the breadth and number of Fabiola iterations, one is reminded of a number of more or less apposite types that stretch from the hallowed to the patently profane: icons of the Virgin Mary; holy cards with saints' images; portraits of Monica, mother of St. Augustine; ceremonial portraiture such as graduation pictures or official identification portraits; illustrations of Little Red Riding Hood; and Hollywood publicity head shots. As different as these are from one another, they bear at least a few compelling similarities. In every case, the image belongs to a class of images that asserts such canonical authority that what we recognize is a collective likeness rather than a portrait of a discrete person. The pictures forming the group, in other words, resemble one another, not a sitter limned long ago by a dutiful artist. Of course, there are powerful legends that assert the contrary. St. Luke was said to have been a painter as well as a physician, and to have practiced his art on the Virgin and Child (even though the first verse of his Gospel indicates quite clearly that his under-standing of the life of Jesus was not based on first-hand observation, but the literary accounts of several other writers). Veronica's Veil purports to be a kind of sacred photocopy of the face of Jesus, and therefore a portrait par excellence. The many stories recounting the *sudarium* or *mandylion* or cloth that bears Christ's features tell of different kinds of origins, some involving the painter's art perfected by angels or by Jesus himself (see Belting 1994; Freedberg 1989; Kuryluk 1991).[2] Medieval Catholic and Byzantine Christianity issued many stories like these, each of them able to warrant not only the authenticity of an original image, but the countless versions of the image in circulation, venerated in shrines from Constantinople to Rome. They were not copies of one another, but *copia*, transcripts in abundance, a multitude of images that each transmitted the honor and blessing of the sacred.

The large body of images of St. Fabiola collected by Francis Alÿs shows us this with unparalleled clarity. Examining them, one is struck by the visual fact that there is no original, no single image that emerges as authoritative, as the genesis and model of all, the grandparent from which the rest have descended. Yet one senses that there is a referent, albeit elusive, never fully present in any single image, but there nonetheless. The nearly two hundred images vary considerably but almost never so much that one does not immediately associate each with the whole (though the images that invert the profile or use green or blue instead of red put one in the mind of another type, such as the Virgin or Monica). Such variations only make the recognition stronger: we see the same face through the veil of each image's peculiarities. What we see is a juxtaposition of a consistently observed pictorial formula, virtually an eidetic schema, a mnemonic device branded on the surface of the neocortex. In virtually every instance, the angle of Fabiola's hood descends from the upper left at an angle of 45 degrees to intersect with a vertical fold located at nearly the center of the image, leaning slightly to the right. The same intense red cloth meets in a crisp contour with pale flesh. The sinuous ribbon of Fabiola's profile breaks from the red enclosure to trace itself against the dark ground of the painting. Her profile staunchly parallels the picture plane. Her lips are pursed to a plump point; her eye is watchful. A concealed hand may hold the red mantle at her chest, corralling the circumscribed flesh into a shape that almost wants to inscribe a monogram, but contents itself instead with describing the peculiar schema that viewers will not forget. Such a schema is an eidetic image insofar as it imprints itself vividly on the mind and is easily recalled by virtue of its beguiling clarity. No. 58 gathers most of the essential features into a spare template (Figure 15.3).

If we see something often enough, we form a sort of mental average from the multitude, a cognitive norm that subsumes each individual manifestation—like Fabiola no. 58. This is what Immanuel Kant argued in his *Critique of Judgment* (1790): "the imagination can ... let one image glide into another; and thus, by the concurrence of several of the same kind, come by an average, which serves as the common measure of all" (Kant 1951: 70). The stature of a beautiful man, Kant argued, was the average taken from a thousand individuals. This norm was the basis of judgment. "It is the image for the whole race, which floats among all the variously different intuitions of individuals, which nature takes as archetype in her productions of the same species, but which appears not to be fully reached in any individual case" (ibid.: 71). Kant wished to understand how aesthetic judgment operated as an intuitive form of cognition, capable of making determinations that were not rational in nature, that is, did not operate in the deductive nature of rules. Instead, he contended that aesthetic judgment was grounded in forms of apprehension that were shared by everyone and able to order perception from the basis of an original faculty called taste.

Without engaging Kant's intricate arguments, we might apply his epistemology of intuition to popular religious images since it accommodates the multiplicity or copia we face with Fabiola as well as other ubiquitous images of saints and religious figures.[3] Where do we find Fabiola? Jerome remembers her, but the faithful find her in the covenants they form through her images and in the devotional practice of fashioning her effigy. Word and image work together.

Figure 15.3 Fabiola, n.d. Paint on canvas. 11 ¾ × 9 ¼ × 3/8 inches (29.8 × 23.5 × 1.59 cm).

Her story draws a character, a plot; her image answers the need people bring to the story. By itself, what Jerome has to tell the faithful is not enough. They need more. They need to find the one spoken of, and that is where her imagery arises. The multitude of Fabiola's portraits suggests that their referent is actually the idea in the mind of the devout, which is nourished and reaffirmed each time they see Fabiola's image. To paraphrase Kant, she floats among the many different versions as the elusive model that binds them together but is never fully, finally present in any one. Hence the need for many, for an ongoing flow or cascade of images. Each iteration incants her, calls her to the moment, shaped by the peculiar requirements of those who summon the saint in the portrait they paint or display.

When art critics and art historians look at Fabiola's many pictures, they see *kitsch*. They see what their eyes need to see—a badly botched Henner or a copy of an already second-grade painting. They see what the discourse of fine art prepares them to see. But the problem with seeing kitsch is that seeing ends there—one sees nothing more, nothing but bad taste. Yet the eyes of faith see differently, according to a different set of needs. I do not propose that scholars of visual culture adopt the eyes of faith, but that they recognize how belief is a way of seeing that may be very different from their own. To see the many images of Fabiola is to look across the grain of another world. The point, it seems to me, is to see the faithful seeing and finding Fabiola where the eyes of unbelief see only kitsch.

Notes

1 See http://www.catholic-forum.com/saints/.
2 I have discussed the issue of Luke as painter and writer in *The Sacred Gaze: Religious Visual Culture in Theory and Practice* (Morgan 2005: 15–21).
3 I have considered the epistemology of recognition and mass-produced images of Jesus in *Visual Piety: A History and Theory of Popular Religious Images* (Morgan 1998: 34–50). See also the author's forthcoming study, *The Embodied Eye: Religious Visual Culture and the Social Life of Feeling* (Morgan forthcoming).

16 Popular music, affective space and meaning

Christopher Partridge

There is much about popular music that might be discussed in a chapter which seeks to convince readers that it should be taken seriously: its wider relationship to society; its problematic relationship to class identity; its contribution to the construction of an individual's sense of self; its determining of friendship groups; its ideological significance; its relationship to emotion and the reflexive self. These are all important issues, which, until relatively recently, have not been at the center of concern in discussions of popular music. Rather, the emphases have been on music production and semiotic readings of musical forms. More specifically, what has been lacking, particularly in the study of religion and popular music (an admittedly recent field of analysis), has been an appreciation of music as a dynamic medium in the construction of personal and social identities. In other words, to what extent might popular music contribute to an awareness of self and to the social and religious networks in which it is embedded? While it is enormously important to understand how music evolves, and how it is enabled and inhabited by its cultures and worlds of production, it is nevertheless important to understand the extent to which it meshes with emotion, with thought, with action, with the phenomenological and existential features of social life. As Tia DeNora has commented on the sociological analysis of music generally, "even when sociologists considered music consumption, the focus was directed less to the matter of musical experience than to the ways in which tastes, musical values, and listening practices served as symbolic boundaries for status groups and status differences" (DeNora 2001: 165). Although focusing more widely on culture, this approach was articulated cogently by Pierre Bourdieu in his analysis of "taste" (Bourdieu 1984). However, in the last decade or so,

> music's role as an active ingredient of social formation and subjectivity has been restored. Within this "new" music sociology of emotions, it is possible to conceptualize music as a device for the constitution of emotive action in and across a range of social settings.
>
> (DeNora 2001: 165)

Hence, popular music should be taken seriously because it is clear that it is *used* in everyday life to manage feeling and thought. For example, many years ago, in his Gifford lectures, the theologian H.H. Farmer identified continuities between the escapist use of alcohol or opium and the "aesthetic intoxication" induced by listening to the choir in King's College Chapel at Cambridge. The experience of being "lifted right out of the world" by choral music induced "a refreshing withdrawal and escape from the everyday pressures of things" (Farmer 1954: 190–1). More recently, writing of the album *Starfish* by the Australian psychedelic band, The Church, Robert Dean Lurie makes the following comment:

> Ah, *Starfish*. That was a big one for me. It was my introduction to The Church—*and to my new life* ... It became my constant companion, the soundtrack to my daily existence and *an escape capsule* when life became too stressful.
>
> (Lurie 2009: 172–3, emphasis mine)

An appreciation of such non-cognitive dimensions of agency is enormously important for understanding the relationship between popular music and religion. However, much current literature on religion and popular music (not that there is much) tends towards content analysis of lyrics, or discussions of the musicians' religious and ethical motivations, rather than, for example, the significance of the embodied practices of listening and dancing, or the aural properties of the music and its relation to the construction of the self. Located at the interface of Religious Studies and Popular Music Studies, this chapter seeks to go some way towards an analysis of the relationship between music and "affective space."[1] On the one hand, whether we think of listening, performance, or composition, music has a fundamental relationship with emotion. On the other hand, human emotionality, being central to meaning-making and an individual's lifeworld,[2] is important for understanding the religious and moral life (see Corrigan 2004). Hence, treatments of popular music and religion that do not attend to affective space risk failing to understand its real, lived significance.

Sociology, emotion, and popular music

While the study of the relationship between emotion, meaning, and music has been neglected, gradually things are beginning to change. From key early works in music psychology, such as Leonard Meyer's seminal study *Emotion and Meaning in Music*, which argued that "an analysis of the process of expectation is clearly a prerequisite for the understanding of how musical meaning, whether affective or aesthetic, arises in any particular instance" (Meyer 1956: 43), to more recent developments of this thesis by David Huron (2006), and to work done by musicologists, philosophers, sociologists, and psychologists (see Becker 2004; Gracyk 2007; Levitin 2007; Sloboda 2005; Thompson 2009), there is now a good body of literature and research on which to draw. However, beginning with sociological analyses, there are few better places to begin a study of the significance of popular music than with the thought of one of its most important early critics.

For good reasons, the study of popular music has found it difficult to ignore the ideas and opinions of Theodor Adorno. In placing music at the center of his critique of modernity, his work has highlighted some of the most important issues concerning the relationship between music and contemporary society (see Witkin 1998). While much of this analysis concerned classical music, he did provide some discussion of "jazz" (a term he used loosely of mid-twentieth century popular music) and Tin Pan Alley compositions (see Adorno 1990).

Adorno's work is, of course, never less than rigorous and provocative. Of particular importance to the ideas developed in this chapter is his contention that music, determined by its composition, manipulates consciousness and contributes to social management. DeNora puts the point well:

> Adorno's work explores the idea that music interiorizes and is able to instigate forms of social organization in and through the ways that it works on and configures its subject-recipient. Put bluntly, Adorno conceived of music as active, indeed formative, in relation to consciousness. In this regard, his work makes some of the strongest claims on behalf of music's power in any discipline.
>
> (DeNora 2001: 165)

However, for Adorno, the power of popular music is fundamentally malign, in that, whereas classical music is capable of fostering critical consciousness, his understanding of the overall effect of popular music was not dissimilar to Marx's thesis concerning the narcotic effects of religion. In other words, it fosters a solipsistic protection of what Marx had identified as a "false consciousness" imposed on the masses by the ruling class. That said, Adorno's insightful understanding of music's relationship with modes of subjectivity and, more widely, with social structural organization means that, not only is it a medium that "trains the unconscious for conditioned reflexes" (Adorno 1976: 53), but it can, as in the case of popular music, lead to regression and dependency (Adorno 1990). The point is that, regardless of whether we have any sympathy with his searing analysis of popular music or not, his discussion convincingly posits the thesis that it is never simply vacuous or ephemeral entertainment. Consequently, there are good reasons for taking popular music very seriously indeed.

As is now generally accepted, one of the primary problems with Adorno's work was that it always remained at the level of theory, lacking any empirical analysis. In other words, the problem with his arguments was, as Simon Frith has commented, "their abstraction. The actual use of music by pop fans is scarcely examined—passivity is assumed. The supposed effects of pop are, rather, deduced from the nature of the music itself" (Frith 1981: 45). Hence, during the 1970s, as the discipline of Popular Music Studies was beginning to coalesce, a new appreciation of its significance began to emerge. Scholars such as Paul Willis, Simon Frith, Simon Jones, and Dick Hebdige reversed the sociological gaze (see Frith 1981; Hebdige 1979; Jones 1988; Willis 1978). They were concerned to examine popular music's social presence and the subcultures it generated and maintained in an attempt to demonstrate that popular music functions as a resource in and through which agency and identity are produced.[3] In stating this, it will be clear that, while their understanding of the significance of popular music *per se* was distinct from that of Adorno, in actual fact their studies served to support his central thesis, namely that music is fundamentally connected to habits of mind, to social organization, and to modes of subjectivity. Popular music, ubiquitous in the everyday lives of most modern people—from their radio-accompanied showers in the morning, to the companionship of their iPods on the train, to the recreational spaces they inhabit—must be taken seriously as formative of social situations and of an individual's sense of identity and agency. In other words, homologies were identified between social situations, subjectivities, and music. Again, what Stuart Hall referred to as "articulations" (Hall 1980) were established between subcultures, social worlds, and popular music. For example, Paul Willis's early analysis of the social meaning of popular music, *Profane Culture* (1978), provides an essentially class-based discussion of the uses of music by middle-class hippies and working-class bikers. The latter, seeking an "antidote to boredom" (ibid.: 68), prefer rock 'n' roll, with its simple musical arrangements, because it stimulates the production of adrenaline and, therefore, the dynamism associated with their social world: "if you hear a fast record you've got to get up and do something" (ibid.: 73). Hippies, on the other hand, preferred the more complex and intricate compositions of progressive rock musicians, which articulated a more contemplative attitude of "serious listening," as well as a desire to restructure "normal time," to expand it into a reflective, affective space. Unlike bikers' preference for singles—which articulated their desire to be on the move at speed[4]—the hippie preferred the LP format, which provided extended musical worlds to inhabit, affective spaces populated by sound effects, echo, and feedback, all of which engendered an impression of "space and lateral extension" (ibid.: 157, 167–8), particularly if accompanied by induced altered states. We might also note that, supporting a lifeworld informed by countercultural concerns, instruments such as the sitar, with its easy musical reference to India and "the East," introduced particular spiritual content into the affective space of the hippie (see Partridge 2005: 100–2). As such, the early ethnography of popular music subcultures began to reveal music as dynamic, "a kind of aesthetic technology, or an instrument of social ordering" (DeNora 2000: 7) capable of informing values and shaping habits.

If popular music generates agency and shapes identity in and through the ways it is used, referred to, and thought about in everyday life, then, as Frith has argued,

> the question we should be asking is not what does popular music *reveal* about "the people" but how does it *construct* them ... Because of its qualities of abstractness (which "serious" aestheticians have always stressed) music is an individualizing form. We absorb songs into our own lives and rhythms into our own bodies.
>
> (Frith 2007: 261, 263, original emphasis)

Making a related point, David Hargreaves, Dorothy Miell, and Raymond MacDonald have argued that music is, for many people, a principal form of communication:

> it provides a means by which people can share emotions, intentions and meanings even though their spoken languages may be mutually incomprehensible ... One result is that music can be used increasingly as a means by which we formulate and express our individual identities. We use it not only to regulate our own everyday moods and behaviours, but also to present ourselves to others in the way we prefer. Our musical tastes and preferences can form an important statement of our values and attitudes.
>
> (Hargreaves *et al.* 2002: 1)

Musical likes and dislikes communicate and shape the self. It is now generally accepted that "the self," rather than being static, is always becoming, always in process, always being negotiated according to daily experiences and relationships with other selves. Hence, because popular music structures the everyday experience of listeners, placing them, for example, in affective alliances with performers and communities of taste, it plays an important role in the construction of the self.

Identity, intertextuality, dub and bass

Popular music is "like all devices or technologies," in that "it is often linked, through convention, to social scenarios, often according to the social uses for which it was initially produced—waltz music for dancing, march music for marching and so on" (DeNora 2000: 11). In other words, music can be used to contextualize or give meaning to situations. This is so because of its intertextual relationship to compositional conventions (Gregorian chant suggests a form of Christian worship and the sitar a form of Indian spirituality), as well as its relationship to sound structures evident in the natural and social worlds (for example, echo can give the impression of space and a trickling sound can communicate the impression of a stream) and past social and cultural associations (for example, Eric Coates' "Dam Busters March" from the 1955 film *The Dam Busters* might signify a nostalgic form of post-war British patriotism, or "stabbing" violin sounds similar to those in Bernard Herrmann's score for Hitchcock's 1960 film *Psycho*, which, as the music accompanying the scene when actress Janet Leigh is murdered in the shower at Bates Motel, will always signify menace). The point is that, because of its intertextuality, whether we think of the theme from *The Twilight Zone* or Bob Dylan's "Mr Tambourine Man," popular music carries social and cultural content. It contributes to the creation of a particular affective space, it communicates particular values, it instills certain attitudes, it encourages certain emotional states: aggression and calm, patriotism and subversion, Indian spirituality and Christian worship, sober attention and altered states. Hence, while we may attach particular meanings to specific pieces of popular music because of their intertextuality within our own histories, those pieces of popular music will also convey meanings because of their articulations to wider culture and society, meanings which will, in turn, shape our reception of those pieces of music. In this sense, as Frith argues, "we are not free to read anything we want into a song." He continues: "the experience of pop music is an experience of placing: in responding to a song, we are drawn, haphazardly, into affective and emotional alliances with the performers and with the performers' other fans" (Frith 2007: 263) and, therefore, with wider social and cultural contexts. In order to explore some of these issues in more detail, the following discussion analyzes a particular genre of popular music: dub reggae.

Dub is a form of reggae that has had a significant influence on the emergence of ambient, post-punk, and chill-out forms of popular music since the 1970s (see Partridge 2010). Typically characterized by echo, reverb, and bass, the reception of dub is often described in terms of the mystical and the ethereal. As the post-punk/dub experimentalist musician Jah Wobble recently put it, "dub [is] ... the form of music that I think best symbolises our yearning for the infinite, for what lies beyond the material world" (Wobble 2010). Such "spiritual" interpretations are perhaps heightened by the use of cannabis, which often accompanies its reception in dub culture. As many users have told me, the genre seems to produce atmospheres conducive to cannabinoid-induced psychological effects. The use of echo and the offbeat, it would appear, opens up spaces that encourage states of mind very similar to those induced by cannabis use. In other words, aesthetic and mind–body technologies are combined to produce a particular affective space. As Mark Kidel comments, "whereas jazz and rock often reflect an amphetamine frenzy, reggae tunes in to the slowness of ganga" (quoted in Hebdige 1979: 30). Added to this, much reggae, particularly "roots reggae" or "rockers," explicitly articulates the ideas of Rastafari. While it needs to be remembered that homologies can lead to reductionism, we are on fairly safe ground in claiming that dub is correlated with an eclectic mix of Rastafari-informed political and spiritual ideas, as well as aspects of Western counterculture, including cannabis culture and experimentation with altered states (see Partridge 2010; 2005: 82–134). As to the sonic qualities of the music itself, as noted above, dub often evokes ethereal, otherworldly, even explicitly spiritual interpretations:

> Dub music is like a long echo delay, looping through time. Regenerating every few years, sometimes so quiet that only a disciple could hear, sometimes shatteringly loud, dub unpicks music in the commercial sphere. Spreading out a song or a groove over a vast landscape of peaks and deep trenches, extending hooks and beats to vanishing point, dub creates new maps of time, intangible sound sculptures, sacred sites, balm and shock for mind, body and spirit.
>
> (Toop 1995: 115)

As with the hippies discussed by Willis, dub creates space and lateral extension, it generates a sense of reality shift which can be used contemplatively as a way of restructuring time and, because of its articulations with Rastafari and altered states, this sense of reality shift contributes to the generation of sacralized affective space, as is apparent in the titles of many albums and tracks: *Meditation Dub* (Winston Riley 1976); *The Sacred Art of Dub* (Alpha and Omega 1998); *Rebirth* (the Disciples and the Rootsman 1997); Bill Laswell's "Sacred System" or "Divination" projects (for example, *Roir Dub Sessions*); "Mystical Dub" and "Spiritual Dub" (the Hazardous Dub Company, *Dangerous Dubs, Vol. 2*, 1993); "Immortal Dub" and "Mystic Dub" (Jah Shaka, *Dub Symphony*, 1990); "Spiritual Dub" (Jah Warrior, on *Shake the Nations! A New Breed of Dub 4*).

While much could be discussed about dub (see Partridge 2010; Veal 2007), for the purposes of this chapter it will be interesting to look at the dominance of bass, which has been a central feature of not only dub's "genre world" (Frith 1996: 88), but also that of much subsequent dance music. As the Bass Lo-Ryders declare on their *Ryder Style* album, "Our God, in a Way, is Bass." To a large extent, bass functions as a stamp of authenticity. Consequently, dub culture can be understood as, to quote Linton Kwesi Johnson, "bass culture" (2002: 14–16). Accompanied by an increased emphasis on the beat, not only are the bass and the drums central, but there has been a growing emphasis on the sheer "weight" of the bass, which has, in turn, been invested with a significance that elevates it above purely aural pleasure and invests it with particular meanings. Again, this is, to some extent, intertextually determined, in that, for example, it articulates meanings developed in the rhetoric of Rastafari. Hence, for the most part, we are not here referring to those intrinsic qualities of sound that, for example, evoke feelings of sadness or joy, or to what Leonard Bernstein terms the "affective" theory of musical expression—"why is the minor 'sad' and the major 'glad'?" (Bernstein 1976: 177)—but rather to broader social meanings and cultural codes, just as "it is by now a deeply rooted commonsense assumption that a funk beat necessarily *means* sex" (Frith 1996: 102).

When examining the signification of bass, first, it is evident that it was, to some extent, gendered, being indicative of, initially, masculinity. As in many cultures, this is largely because the vocal register is gendered. As the typical male gets older, so the tone of his voice lowers and, consequently, the more masculine it is understood to be: "singing voices become identifiably more 'masculine' as they get older" (Welsh and Howard 2002: 108—on interpretations of the high male voice, see Kopf 1995). This is certainly true of Jamaican and West African cultures. For example, in Jamaican Burru and Nyabinghi drumming, the skin of the bass drum is, ideally, that of a ram goat—because, according to Count Ossie (one of the founding fathers of Nyabinghi), "the ram goat is less vociferous than the ewe by nature, and its bleat is of a lower tone. Hence, the skin when hit is of a desirable low pitch" (Reckford 1977: 3). While the musicological rationale is dubious, the cultural point is important.

Second, related to the above, the somatic impact of the bass is explicitly related to power and aggression. Descriptions of dub music rarely fail to comment on the fact that attending a sound-system event is a physical experience:

The first thing that strikes you in a reggae sound-system session is the sound itself. The sheer physical force, volume, weight and mass of it. Sonic dominance is hard, extreme and excessive. At the same time the sound is also soft and embracing and it makes for an enveloping, immersive and intense experience. The sound pervades, or even invades the body, like a smell. Sonic dominance is both a near overload of sound and a super saturation of sound. You're lost inside it, submerged under it … Sound at that level cannot but touch you and connect to your body. It's not just heard in the ears, but felt over the entire surface of the skin. The bass line beats on your chest, vibrating the flesh, playing on the bone, and resonating the genitals.

(Henriques 2003: 451–2)

The sheer physical impact of dub, interpreted largely in terms of the "weight" of the bass assaulting the body, is, again, evident in album titles: *Dub Assault* and *Dub Strike* (Sism-X); *Bass Terror* (Bill Laswell and Nicholas James Bullen); *Dub Massacre (In a Murder Style)* (Twinkle Brothers).

Third, central to these meanings is the intertextual relationship bass has with the cardiovascular system, with the pumping of blood through the veins common in heightened emotional states. Such cardiovascular articulations might be relational, religious, or political. For example, the political significance of bass is evident in Johnson's poem "Bass Culture" (2002: 14–16). The weight and depth of the bass signifies the seriousness of the black person's plight. Bass culture is the culture of the oppressed, the sound of violence and suffering: "bass history is a moving, hurting, black history" (Gilroy 2003: 391). It is, to quote Johnson's poem, "muzik of blood, black reared, pain rooted, heart geared." It is also, however, "di beat of di heart, this pulsing of blood that is a bubblin bass" (Johnson 2002: 14). In the poem, this is related to racist violence, the spilling of black blood, and the pounding of the adrenaline-fueled heart. The bass speaks of a "dread" situation.

Fourth, from a different, more comfortable and meditative perspective, the impact of the bass is sometimes related, more ontologically and even spiritually, to the deep rhythms of life. While there is not space to explore the implications, it is worth noting that this articulation is more typical of dub produced by white musicians, rather than dub that can be legitimately considered to be part of "a moving, hurting, black history." A good example of this is Smith and Mighty's *Bass Is Maternal* (1995), the cover of which has a photograph of a child standing by the sea, listening, presumably, to the heartbeat regularity of the tide. Again, the booklet accompanying the album includes four ultrasound scans of fetuses and an illustration of small child reaching out to a bass speaker, underneath which are the words "bass is maternal … when it's loud I feel safer." Although, like Johnson, Rob Smith and Ray Mighty are drawing on the experiential dimension of the bass and its perceived relationship to the beat of the heart, they have now subverted the interpretation of it in terms of suffering, or even, as in early sound-system culture, the gendered interpretation which references masculinity and aggression. Indeed, while there are always exceptions, generally speaking, in principally white, middle-class dub (particularly "ambient dub"[5]), bass becomes more relational and nurturing.

Drawing on and developing these emphases—particularly the relational, the maternal, and the primal—it is not unusual for people to articulate Romanticized, even spiritual interpretations of the sonic affect of bass in dub. For example, Greg Whitfield describes bass, "if played loud enough," as feeling like

> a wind, literally, punctuated by eerie shards of searing guitar, and melancholy piano, which seemed to invite the mind to a deep cavernous space, a sad and lonely place of lost chances, memory, or at other times an optimistic, positive spiritual uplift, resolute and strong.
>
> (Whitfield 2002)

Again, he relates Bunny Wailer's understanding of the significance attaching to bass—when filtered through an occulturally[6] informed affective space:

> this deeply dread riddim, the unifying of a dread bass and drum *physically felt* rather than heard, was a bass vibration that had been set in motion at the time of creation, and resonated onwards, like a heartbeat, primal and compelling. The vibration had echoed from source, from creation. From that time onward, it wove its mysticism, its physical, gnostic spell.
>
> (Whitfield 2002)

As we have seen, for a spiritually oriented dub musician such as Jah Wobble, the aesthetics of dub and especially its use of bass are particularly significant. Thinking, for example, of the gendering of bass, for Wobble, although bass does have male characteristics, it is, again, principally a maternal, nurturing energy. Bass, he argues,

> tends to be a feminine power, but it can be a male power as well. It's a feminine power insofar as it comes from earth and it's all-pervasive. It also has male qualities, it can penetrate and it can also be very dynamic. But the main thing for me is that it's all-supporting. It's very much the quality of the Divine Mother.
>
> (Wobble, quoted in Shapiro 1995: 34)

The point, however, is that, regardless of lyrical content, sound can have a sacralizing impact on the affective space of listeners, particularly those au fait with its genre world, including its occultural content. (Typical in this latter respect is the prolific, multigenre output of Bill Laswell.) However, there are good acoustical reasons to speculate a little further about the affective impact of bass and its link to a sense of the sacred.

Following the Island label's refusal to release his more experimental work, Wobble set up the 30 Hertz label. Thirty hertz is significant because it is close to the lowest frequency that humans can hear. That said, although hearing varies from person to person, with numerous factors influencing the range of frequencies that any one individual can detect, generally speaking humans can hear frequencies as low as 20 hertz and as high as 20 kilohertz. However, as we approach these frequency limits our hearing ability gradually fades. Hence, for most people, clear bass sound is limited to around 30 hertz—a piano's bottom note C vibrates at roughly 33 hertz. However, the point is that beyond this limit lies bass infrasound, which is *felt* rather than heard. Of course, feeling is very similar to hearing, in that both are ways of detecting sonic vibration. Research has shown, for example, that congenitally deaf people process sound vibrations in the auditory cortex—the same part of the brain that hearing people use to process sound (see Phillips 1998; Klarreich 2001). Research has also shown that during exposure to such low frequencies, infrasonic tones increase the emotional impact of the music. For example, concertgoers report higher emotional states during the times when infrasound was present. Hence, it is not difficult to understand why pipe organ music, which produces notes as low as 16 hertz, might elicit powerful feelings. Put bluntly, following one experiment it was suggested that "because some organ pipes in churches and cathedrals produce infrasound this could lead to people having weird experiences which they attribute to God" (Amos 2003). In other words, encountered in the context of cathedral worship, which is typically focused on the invisible energies described in pneumatological discourse, bass infrasound can generate sacralized affective space within which lifeworld-shaping meaning-making takes place.

Bearing this in mind, if we think of the dub sound system, "bass extension" down to lower frequencies, such as 20 hertz, may also have a powerful impact on affective space. Indeed, because human hearing is far less sensitive in the bass range than in the midrange, to be perceptually as loud as midrange sound, bass actually needs to be substantially louder. Put simply, powerful bass requires moving lots of air. This is why, as indicated above, sound systems are preoccupied with the size of speakers—large speakers will move more air than small speakers with the same excursion (i.e. the same amount of back and forth motion). The point is that, this, again, goes some way to explaining, not only dub's bass-oriented focus on power and size, but also the very physicality of dub, the empirical sense of being somatically enveloped and handled by an invisible force. Such an experience, when linked to a sense of reality shift induced by the use of found sounds, echo and reverb, as well as the related perception of space and depth engendered by reggae's offbeat, leads to a feeling of transcendence, which is often interpreted occulturally. Luke Ehrlich puts it well:

> With dub, Jamaican music spaced out completely. If reggae is Africa in the New World, then dub must be Africa on the moon; it's the psychedelic music I expected to hear in the '60s and didn't. The bass and the drums conjure up a dark, vast space, a musical portrait of outer space, with sounds suspended like glowing planets or with fragments of instruments careening by, leaving trails like comets and meteors.
>
> (Ehrlich 1983: 106)

Conclusion

This chapter has shown that there are good reasons why popular music should be taken seriously by scholars of religion. It makes a particular attempt to articulate why this should be done, not simply as content analysis of a song's lyrics (since much of the music discussed in this chapter cannot be analyzed in this way), or as a form of auteur criticism, interesting though the results of such approaches can be, but rather as an interdisciplinary analysis of sonic environments and affective space. For example, we have seen that, because of its intertextuality, popular music carries social and cultural content, which, in turn, contributes to the construction of personal and shared meanings. Sometimes such meanings are explicitly religious and/or occultural. An excellent example of this is dub reggae, which encourages a sense of reality shift through its use of echo, delay, reverb, and bass. Likewise, the looped found sounds and samples used by dub producers tend to provide a re-enchanted interpretation of the everyday; the familiar is made exotic. The consequent transition into an occulturally informed affective space is heightened by dub's conspicuous intertextual relationship with the religio-politics of Rastafari and, frequently, the effects of cannabis use. Added to this, we have seen that dub culture is "bass culture." That is to say, not only is bass emphasized, but it also carries meanings related to depth and power, which are subsequently often linked to occultural signifiers. Bass, particularly at a sound-system event, becomes a felt, unseen force. Again, this contributes significantly to the sacralization of affective space. Hence, within dub culture, there is nothing odd about speaking of "the sacred art of dub" (Alpha and Omega) or referring to the genre as a "sacred system" (Bill Laswell), and interpreting its effects in terms of "divinization" (Bill Laswell and Jah Wobble) or even myalism[7] (see Partridge 2010).

Music communicates meaning and emotion in much the same way as language does; the two share deep and important connections (see Patel 2008). Hence, future research at the interface of religion and popular culture cannot afford to avoid sonic environments, particularly those created by popular musicians. In other words, in seeking to understand the significance of the continuities between religion, popular music, and everyday life, a good understanding of the relationships between music, the cultures in which it is embedded, the values and ideas it communicates, and the emotions it evokes will facilitate analysis of how it contributes to self-understanding, identity formation, and meaning-making.

Discography

Alpha and Omega, *The Sacred Art of Dub* (A & O Records, 1998).
The Church, *Starfish* (Arista, 1987).
The Disciples Meet the Rootsman, *Rebirth* (Third Eye Music, 1997).
Hazardous Dub Company, *Dangerous Dubs, Vol. 2* (Acid Jazz, 1993).
Jah Shaka, *Dub Symphony* (Island, 1990).

Linton Kwesi Johnson, *Bass Culture* (Island, 1980).

Bill Laswell, *ROIR Dub Sessions* (ROIR, 2003).

Bill Laswell and Nicholas James Bullen, *Bass Terror* (Sub Rosa, 1995).

Winston Riley, *Meditation Dub* (Techniques, 1976).

Sism-X, *Dub Assault* (Assault Dub, 2003).

Sism-X, *Dub Strike* (Sounds Around, 2004).

Smith and Mighty, *Bass Is Maternal* (More Rockers/STUD!O K7, 1995).

Chris Spedding, *Chris Spedding* (Rak Records, 1976).

Twinkle Brothers, *Dub Massacre (In a Murder Style)* (Twinkle, 1983).

Various Artists, *Shake the Nations! A New Breed of Dub 4* (Dubhead, 2004).

Notes

1 I am indebted to Clive Marsh for this particular use of the term "affective space." Whilst thinking through ways to articulate the personal "space" within which music and emotion generate ideas and shape identities, I came across this term in the title of his Fernley-Hartley Lecture, delivered several days previously at the University of Leicester: "Adventures in Affective Space: The Reconstruction of Piety in an Age of Entertainment" (May 7, 2010). He kindly sent me the text. Although our understandings are, I think, a little different, there is significant overlap. For Marsh, "affective space" refers to "any practice or activity which entails significant emotional engagement. This could, therefore, be listening to a piece of music, going to a concert, watching a film, attending a major sporting event, watching a TV programme, attending a religious act of worship." As will become apparent, my own understanding of "space" is identified more closely with the internal world of the individual, with the "reflexivity of the self" (Giddens 1991).

2 "Lifeworld" is used here in broadly the same sense as Jürgen Habermas uses it (1987: 113–98): the latent, taken-for-granted core values, beliefs, and understandings about who we are, how we relate to others, what the world is like, and how we fit into it.

3 The study of popular music has, for the most part, been undertaken by sociologists, anthropologists, and cultural theorists, rather than musicologists.

4 A song which communicates well the principal features of the affective space referred to here is Chris Spedding's 1975 single "Motor Bikin'" (from the 1976 album *Chris Spedding*).

5 "Ambient dub" is a genre that began as a term coined by Beyond Records for their four-volume compilation of contemporary dub-related electronica compositions in the 1990s.

6 "Occulture" refers to those social processes by which particular meanings relating, typically, to spiritual, paranormal, esoteric, and conspiratorial ideas are produced, circulated, and exchanged. As such, it includes an enormous, constantly evolving and recycled range of theories and practices. Popular culture is central to the efficacy of occulture, in that it feeds ideas into the occultural pool, develops, remixes, and disseminates those ideas, thereby generating new seeds of occultural thought. Hence, I have argued that popular occulture is, in various ways, sacralizing the Western mind (see Partridge 2005, 2006, 2009).

7 With roots in West African religion, *myal* and *obeah* were techniques which enabled a person to communicate with the spirit world. Generally speaking, *obeah* was used to curse individuals and to manipulate events malevolently, and *myalism* was understood to be the remedy, in that it enabled one to remove hexes and provide immunity to spiritual attack.

17 Living relations with visual and material artifacts

Stephen Pattison

While artifacts, things designed and made by human beings, owe their existence entirely to their creators, most of us, most of the time, think of them as having very little to do with us beyond functional utility. There seems to be a clear, if invisible, line through reality whereby humans regard most of the works of their own hands as being dead and completely alien from the animated human world—even though that world is populated and significantly shaped by those very same objects.

Animals, wildernesses, seas, rivers, even rocks, which owe nothing directly to human creative agency whatsoever, are often regarded as being of great concern; people can even feel that they have a relationship, mystical, romantic, or other, with them. But while rare or extraordinary objects of high art or culture, such as the *Mona Lisa* or the Sistine Chapel, can be objects that people are overtly interested in, and with which they hope to have significant relations, when it comes to the ordinary artifacts surrounding and supporting us—pens, tables, bicycles, shoes, houses, cars—we are inclined to reject the idea that we might or should have some kind of conscious living relationship with them, even if it may be theoretically acknowledged that, as much as genes and ideas, they help to shape us culturally socially, psychologically, and even physically (Dant 1999, 2005). Witness the fact that many Western adults have bad backs because of the curious modern habit of sitting in chairs that raise us above nature, the earth, and the beasts, but also distort our spines and skeletons (Cranz 2000).

In this chapter, I question the assumption that humans live in a world that can be completely separated off from the realm of artifacts. Indeed, I argue that artifacts are full of person-like attributes—unsurprisingly, since they have been created by persons. Furthermore, it might make our lives and relations more rewarding if we actively cultivated more loving, friendly, relations with ordinary, everyday artifacts. These are the sorts of things that probably surround you now as you read (in a book, on an e-reader, through spectacles or contact lenses, by the light of an electric light, with a pencil in your hand, in a chair—all artifacts).

The idea of forming person-like relations with "dead" artifacts can seem bizarre, controversial, even worrying. Orsi (2005: 158) notes in the context of the study or living religion that "what may be upsetting about the study of lived religion is that such research appears to align itself with the realness of religious worlds, with presence, thereby threatening to reawaken presence." I would contend that all kinds of "presences" (including those recognized in artifacts) demand relationality, response, and responsibility. Presences and personal relations are both enticing and limiting. They root us to particular places and things so that while we may have more stable identities rooted in attachment and belonging, we are less detached from our worlds. This is highly inconvenient in late capitalist society, which prizes lack of resistance, material and other, and requires people to be mobile, flexible, endlessly acquisitive, and unattached to localities and things. Presences and person-like relations with all kinds of objects restrain and detain us, causing us to turn aside, sometimes even assaulting us, whether in everyday life or within religion.

Formal monotheistic Western religions, often officially hostile to deep relations with material as opposed to spiritual beings, have been an important locus for intimate and significant relationships with artifacts. So this is where I now begin.

Religion

Many people are aware of the importance of material images and objects in Eastern religions. Hindu and Buddhist temples are often full of statues that receive very personal reverence from worshippers who come to see and engage in visual relationship with the gods (Eck 1998). The Jewish, Christian, and Muslim traditions are often perceived officially to be less sympathetic to the relations with artifacts within and outside main religious contexts (Assmann and Baumgarten 2001). This is mainly ascribed to the teaching that God is invisible; believers are therefore discouraged from making images of the deity and even, in the case of Muslims, living things, that might become the objects of fascination and worship (Barasch 1992).

Prohibitions against practices often indicate that those practices are widely prevalent. And so it proves in the Western scriptural religions. The Jewish Temple in Jerusalem was full of artifacts—some think there might even have been an image of Yahweh within it (Edelman 1996; Mettinger 1995; Van der Toorn 1997). Some Jews contemporary with Jesus probably possessed small clay household god images, and some of their synagogues were heavily decorated with human and animal images (Kuhnel 2001). Once early Christians became wealthy enough to do so, they, too, started to create images and build elaborate churches full of artifacts as an aid to devotion and instruction (Jensen 2000). Rather like Hindus experiencing *darshan*, Christians would go into mosaic-clad churches like Santa Sophia in Istanbul to be seen by, as well as to see, the objects of their devotion (Belting 1994). Icons, carefully selected and painted images of the saints and of Jesus and Mary, have continued to be regarded as in some way embodying and providing an access point to divine presence in the Greek and Russian Orthodox traditions, being given the reverence that is due to an honored person in being kissed and genuflected to by devotees (Barasch

1992; Ouspensky 1992). And in the Western Catholic tradition, physical relics of the saints have been seen as embodying person-like powers to heal and to intercede (Belting 1994).

In medieval times, it was not uncommon for believers to experience holy statues coming to life and doing the sorts of things that humans do—one image of Christ was reputed to have been made to bleed by being pierced with a lance, while another, the *Volto Santo* in Lucca, apparently slipped off and threw a silver shoe as a gift at a poor minstrel (ibid.: 305). The ministry of St. Francis to reform the Catholic church in the thirteenth century started with his encountering a painted crucifix that spoke to him, telling him to rebuild the church (Francis of Assisi 1963: 211). Here, then, the distinction between inert object and living person was effectively nullified.

Even subsequent to the Reformation and Enlightenment in the West, when images were downgraded in Protestantism and scientific rationalism pushed the "spiritual" realm to become much more ethereal and distant from earthly materiality, person-like relations with artifacts of all kinds in religion are still to be found. The Protestant churches started to revere the Bible itself as an object, giving it personal respect and attributes, so that damaging a physical copy of the book was almost an injury to God. Protestants may not have had the statues and artifacts that continue to fill Catholic churches and attract reverence, but they had pictures of Jesus and of former ministers, banners, architectural embellishments, and other material things that mediated the divine to the human (Harvey 1995, 1999). David Morgan (1998) has charted the complex relationships that twentieth century Protestants have had with a widely reproduced picture, Walter Sallman's *Head of Christ*, which have included healing miracles and other wonders. Meanwhile, Robert Orsi (1985, 1996), working on modern American Catholicism, has highlighted the ways in which statues and images, for example of St. Jude and of the Blessed Virgin Mary, are essential for people's relationships with the divine. One of Orsi's respondents even threw a statue of St. Jude into the back of a car and gave it a bumpy ride to punish the saint for what he had failed to do for her—she clearly thought the image and the saint were in some sense connected and one (Orsi 1996: 113). William Christian (1992) has collected experiences of moving crucifixes and other images in twentieth century Spain, while a brief visit online will reveal the many ways in which people miraculously find apparently salvific and effectual images of Jesus in various artifacts, vegetables, and other phenomena.

In the UK, in 2007 a sculpture of Christ cleansing the Temple, created by atheist sculptor Brian Burgess, and displayed in a secular art gallery in Liverpool, was seen by some viewers to be emitting sparks from its eyes and became an object of devotion in the place it was displayed. And at around the same time, a number of people in Carlisle, including the bishop, petitioned for a granite block, inscribed with an ancient curse to celebrate the millennium, to be removed from a roundabout in the city or to be destroyed because it was thought to be bringing bad luck to the city in the shape of floods, football match defeats, and other disasters.

All this evidence, ancient and modern, demonstrates that religions have never been free of material, person-like entanglements and mediations. Even anti-iconic religious traditions like Judaism and Islam have succumbed to the material and sensual at times (Bland 2000). To have meaningful personal relations with the transcendent, material artifacts can be essential (McDannell 1995; Morgan and Promey 2001). Pictures, icons, relics, and statues continue to be treated not just symbolically, but as personal embodiments of the transcendent. In the right circumstances, they act as personal agents of communication and transformation.

Ever since the Israelites turned aside to look at the golden calf in the desert, humans have been aware of the seductive power of some kinds of artifacts and have engaged in important personal relationships with them (Mitchell 1994: 2). While this can be condemned as primitivism, idolatry, or animism (all very pejorative and judgmental terms), this might give us pause for thought. What exactly is wrong with extending person-like relations to the artifactual world? And why is that world one in which person-like relations are possible and important anyway?

I will return to these and other related questions soon, but first I want to discuss the person-like experience of a very prominent theologian with an artifact to demonstrate that it is not just the poor, ill-educated, suspicious, and women who can fall into significant relations with religiously related artifacts, the view often taken by well-educated contemporary intellectuals who see artifacts as safely dead and living in a different kind of world from the human race (see McDannell, Chapter 12).

Paul Tillich (1886–1965) was one of the most famous liberal-rationalist Christian theologians of the last century, brought up in Eastern German, word-centered, aniconic Protestantism, and perhaps best known for his propagation of a non-personal definition of God as the "Ground of Being" (Tillich 1953). So he was not religiously naive or intellectually unsophisticated; nor was he much given to the idea that physical objects, especially Catholic-inspired images, were important sources of religious experience. However, one of the most important experiences of his life occurred with an inanimate material object, a picture of *The Virgin Mary and Singing Angels* by Sandro Botticelli, in the German national art gallery. He saw the picture as a returning chaplain from the First World War, during which he had studied it, amongst others, huddled in dug-outs, by candlelight:

> Gazing up at it, I felt a state approaching ecstasy. In the beauty of the painting there was Beauty itself. It shone through the colours of the paint as the light of day shines through the stained glass windows of a medieval church.
>
> As I stood there, bathed in the beauty its painter had envisioned so long ago, something of the divine source of all things came through to me. I turned away *shaken*.
>
> (Tillich 1989: 234–5, emphasis mine)

This moment affected Tillich's whole life, giving him "the keys for the interpretation of human existence."

Tillich's experience of being "struck" by a picture in a very personal way is not uncommon. Indeed, arguably, one of the reasons that people go to art galleries is to put themselves in the way of having intimate, personal, and revelatory experiences with artworks. Visitors to Florence and Venice have been found to suffer from "Stendhal's syndrome," fainting or weeping before the images that they see and experience intimately (Elkins 2001: 43–7).

Person-like relations with everyday artifacts

Within religious traditions, even those that claim formally to be non-materialistic and anti-iconic and anti-idolatrous, there are rich veins of person-like relations with artifacts that help to mediate and make real religious reality. People become imbricated and tangled up with artifacts, sometimes surprisingly or accidentally, in such a way that it becomes possible to say that they are having meaningful relations in which many of the qualities of relationship that characterize relations with humans, including intentionality, agency, and affection, are apparent. Indeed, some people become more engaged with intimate artifacts and possessions than they do with other people.

Mostly, the artifacts I have talked about thus far in the context of art and religion are quite humanoid in shape and form (pictures depict faces, statues represent figures), so perhaps it is not surprising that people are taken up in relations with them. These kinds of person-like relationships are not confined to the realm of art or religion; furthermore, they can spread out to include non-humanoid, ordinary objects in daily life. Here, for example, is English playwright Alan Bennett musing about his kitchen artifacts:

> Note how personalised and peopled the material world is at a level almost beneath scrutiny. I'm thinking of the cutlery in the drawer or the crockery I every morning empty from the dishwasher. Some wooden spoons, for instance, I like, think of as friendly; others are impersonal or without character. Some bowls are favourites; others I have no feeling for at all. There is a friendly fork, a bad knife and a blue and white plate that is thicker than the others which I think of as taking the kick when I discriminate against it by using it less.
>
> (Bennett 2005: 284)

Bennett is not alone in his attachment to, and personalization of everyday things. Informal research reveals that friends of mine have leather handbags, jugs, pots, knives, teapots, and all manner of other artifacts that are precious to them and with which they feel they have person-like relations of affection and worth. More broadly, musicians, especially string players, seem to have very intimate relations with their instruments so that they may name them, and they worry about them, weeping over them if they are lost or broken. And others seem to have very personal relationships with cars and motorcycles, particularly old ones. When this is recognized or pointed out, they often feel a bit embarrassed. To enjoy intimate relations with artifacts can seem to be childish and immature, as if one had not grown out of dolls or toys (Gell 1998). But if negative judgment can be withheld for a moment, it can be asked why these intimate relations grow up.

One simple answer to the question of why we can potentially become involved in all kinds of person-like relations of different degrees of intimacy and affection with artifacts is that they themselves are full of humanity. They owe their existence to human beings, and so floridly manifest signs of emotion, intentionality, agency, and purpose. They *index* the people who made them, i.e. they embody their intentions, agency, emotions, etc. (ibid.). All the works of human hands and minds index their creators, some, like oil paintings or handcrafted stools, more obviously than others.

A friend of mine tries to collect artifacts that have no purpose. After a life-long quest, he has thus far only managed to collect one artifact that falls into this category. This illustrates the point that most artifacts index their creators, embodying person-like qualities; this is usually very apparent to other human beings, sensitive to these same qualities. Some artifacts manifest more person-like and relational qualities than others; they have a greater susceptibility to relationships with humans. Thus an oil painting of a human subject indexes and contains not only the features of the person concerned who may have commissioned it, but also the aims, purpose, and craft of the artist who painted it—you might even be able to see the artist's brush strokes or finger prints on the canvas.

Complex objects that are difficult to comprehend (like people) and which bear signs of complex intentionality and purpose (like people) can acquire a kind of autonomous secondary agency that affects and shapes their users (like relations with people) (ibid.). So when we encounter even superficially simple objects, like chisels, we also encounter all the generations of people and their intentions that have helped to make the chisel what it is today. The chisel then allows certain possibilities or affordances for us, but, equally, its indexical shaping prevents us from doing other things—chisels are useless for spreading butter or painting pictures, but very good for carving wood (Gibson 1986). And it is in this sense that they have secondary agency and can "do" things that shape and constrain the people who encounter them (Latour 2005).

There is, then, a set of latent person-like features within any artifact that can impinge upon us, constraining or enabling certain kinds of actions and determining to some extent who and what we can be with them. When we encounter very complex features in an object like a computer or a car, we may then be inclined to attribute a great deal of "personhood" to it; we can become engaged, even enchanted, in a kind of living complex relationship with it, both materially and symbolically. This might lead to an object becoming almost part of ourselves, a "biographical" object that shares our life over time and becomes part of us, changing its user/owner even while the owner/user is changed by the

LEEDS TRINITY UNIVERSITY

relationship also (Hoskins 1998; Kopytoff 1986). For example, I have several ancient pens which now bear the clear signs of my use on their shells and nibs, even as I have the dents in my fingers that they have helped to form as I have held them.

Humans do not form person-like relations with every artifact, any more than they develop complex, intimate relations with every person encountered in the street. Many factors influence our engagements with them (Pattison 2007a). There are external factors such as narratives, stories, and reputations surrounding objects (have you heard about the new iPhone?), their uniqueness, their complexity, their nature, and function. Some objects seem to become almost charismatic (Apple computers), even iconic and sacred. We are also influenced by more intrinsic factors: material, size, shape, line, color, texture, movement, dimensionality, heft (how it feels), apparent beauty or ugliness, ingenuity, and the affordances offered (what they allow or prevent you from doing). For some people it will be where they first encountered an artifact, their history with it, or the person who gave it to them that will give it personal value and charisma (Csikszentmihalyi and Rochberg Halton 1981). Many people have objects of no financial value around them, but because of their associations they would not change or get rid of them for the world. For others, it will be long usage that has bound them in person-like loyalty to an artifact—they have grown old together.

Relations with artifacts can be as complex as those with other members of the human race, sometimes even more so. It may even be the case that some people would be prepared to die for artifacts like cathedrals or great artworks while they might be more hesitant to lay down their lives for their human friends. And let it be remembered that in time of war some artifacts, like stained glass windows, may be protected and removed from danger before the human population. These artifacts are treated as more important than human persons—VIPs, if you like.

Designers and manufacturers are becoming increasingly aware of the need to create "sticky" artifacts with which humans can become entangled in satisfying relationships. Objects that are more rather than less person-like are easier to work with and tend to work better (Norman 2004). So commercial companies hire social anthropologists and other kinds of researchers to study how people live and work with artifacts to bring about a better design fit. Of course, in a capitalist world there is also a need to ensure that objects are not so satisfying that people want to keep and use them forever.

There can be no doubt of the depth and value of the symbolic and material relationships people have with some artifacts, at least some of the time. In a study of twenty-nine households in a street in London, anthropologist Daniel Miller found that people's relationships with their possessions directly reflected their relations with other people. Perhaps surprisingly, "usually the closer our relations are with objects, the closer our relationships are with people" (Miller 2008: 1). Indeed, far from being a kind of neutral backdrop to life, relationships with artifacts and possessions such as ornaments, clothes, CDs, pets, and furniture help people to create a habitable world of identity and morality that allows them to function.

Material relations with artifacts and other objects thus mediate and form part of all human relationships, and not just within formal religion. They vitally inform the tiny cosmologies of meaning whereby modern people create the material and moral patterns from which identity and a capacity to judge and act in the world are derived. Miller found that one woman who pierced and tattooed her own body had "created her own material order, seeing the potential of her increasing attachment, successively, to clothes, piercings and tattoos to devise something which is as internally consistent and as meaningful to her as a religion" (ibid.: 290). Thus, people create an authentic moral and aesthetic order for themselves with and around everyday artifacts.

Arguably, then, personal relations of depth with artifacts are not a kind of optional extra or something for children, but a vital part of general human flourishing and fulfilled living. Adults may not need dolls, but they do need other kinds of artifacts, objects made and circulated by human hands and intentions, if human life is to be fully human in the material world.

Conclusion: getting personal with artifacts

Person-like, friendly relations with artifacts, the works of human hands, are possible, necessary, and inevitable. Such relationships have been part of Western religions, even when they have tried to deny or minimize them in the name of spiritual ethereality or aniconism. They can also be part of everyday life as people fall in and out of love with the objects around them, for all manner of reasons. That this occurs is not unusual because artifacts themselves index human emotions, intentions, and agency. Perhaps it is surprising, then, that we are not more engaged with such relationships that so fundamentally help to structure our physical and social being at least as much as genes, language, and other aspects of culture. As Dant (2005: xi) argues, if you remain unconvinced of the importance of artifacts in human life, "just try to remember the last time that you were not engaged in some kind of 'material interaction.'"

In this last part of the chapter, I advance some reasons for nurturing more actively and consciously person-like relations with artifacts, for befriending them, as it were. But before that, it must be acknowledged that not all Western moderns will be comfortable with this. For some, perhaps particularly religious people, there is suspicion that this kind of thinking might be a throwback to so-called primitive religion and animism—this is the kind of thinking that ascribes danger to becoming attached to artifacts that might become "idols" (Harvey 2005). Becoming more attached to artifacts might seem then to displace the invisible, moral God of spiritualizing Western monotheism while at the same time attempting to re-enchant the world with a fixation on the wonderful but unnecessary "toys" that spew forth every day in a market economy. Materialist philosophers, too, though mostly positively atheistic, have tended to see material "goods" as "bads" because they represent the alienation of human reason and energy into things that then inappropriately obsess and control their living creators (Molotch 2003). This sort of suspicion would also be congenial to humanists, who might argue that rather than being bothered about deepening relations with things, we should be worried about our fellow human beings.

It is salutary, then, to be reminded of Miller's perhaps contra-intuitive finding, replicated in some other studies, that people who care about things and their relationships with them also tend to care more, not less, about their relations with persons (Csikszentmihalyi and Rochberg Halton 1981; Miller 2008). Far from being anti-humanistic, acknowledging, even deliberately deepening, our relationships within the artifactual world might then be very important in realizing our potential for relationships generally. It would almost certainly increase our pleasure and wonder in the material world, encouraging us to take it more seriously, to become more attached to it, and perhaps also to value individual artifacts more profoundly. This might mean that we made more of the artifacts that we have, rather than continually wanting to change them and acquire new ones—a very useful ethical stance in a world that is gradually running out of resources. It is right that humans should reflect ethically on this matter, because they are solely responsible for artifacts existing at all. Everyday artifacts, as well as great works of art, need human appreciation and care if they are to survive. And if humans are fully to recognize and respect their own humanity and culture as embodied in artifacts, they should seek to cultivate more careful and appreciative relations with ordinary objects of all kinds. Jane Bennett (2001: 171) asks, "Why must nature be the exclusive form of enchantment? Can't—don't—numerous human artefacts also fascinate and inspire?"

The kind of wondering, appreciative, and attentive relationship of "responding responsiveness" (Steiner 1988: 8) that it is sometimes possible consciously to experience with artifacts, whether religious or secular, great or small, old or new, mass produced or unique, is well captured by French philosopher Gaston Bachelard. He observes that "whenever we live close to familiar, everyday things, we begin once again to live slowly, thanks to their fellowship" (McAllester Jones 1991: 157). Bachelard writes of an oil lamp as a "kindly object" that "keeps faith" with humans as it does its "good deed" for us every evening. Adopting this kind of attitude to other kindly artifacts, humble or famous, that closely share human existence might not only help us to have richer, more interesting lives, but also allow artifacts to have a place in the world that transcends human selective blindness and exploitative convenience. Moving beyond an objectifying subject–object approach to "dead" artifacts, that maintains them in a state of isolation from their "living" creators, to entertaining the possibility of more phenomenological, relational, subject–subject approaches to understand relations between beings inhabiting the same material world would, then, seem to be a fruitful direction for developing human self-understanding and ethics, within both the study of religion and the study of popular culture (Latour 1993; Tamen 2001).

Part IV

Religion and the ethics of media and culture

Introduction

The British television journalist Martin Bell spent several years covering the conflict in the Balkans during the 1990s. He was wounded by shrapnel while recording a piece to camera in Sarajevo in 1992, but recovered and later became an independent MP (Member of Parliament) in the House of Commons. Later in a speech at Chichester Cathedral he raised significant questions relating to what he describes as the "journalism of attachment."[1] This challenges the assumption that journalists should always remain objective when there is clearly violence being carried out against a vulnerable group, such as the murder of several thousand Muslim men and boys in Srebrenica in July 1995. His suggestions provoked considerable debate as many journalists rejected his advocacy for a "journalism of attachment" view, arguing, instead, for a "journalism of detachment." From this point of view journalists should attempt to cover both sides of any conflict rather than attach themselves to one or other of the belligerents. Bell's argument was more nuanced than it was often given credit for. Consider, for example, his use of a story which "went the rounds" among other journalists in Sarajevo to illustrate the complexities of attaching yourself to either side of a story. This account, which he admitted might be fictional, describes a newspaper reporter in Sarajevo "who wished to write a profile of a sniper," which "both sides had and feared as much as they valued their own":

> He [the journalist] fixed it up with the man's commander and went to visit the front line. "What do you see?" he asked the sniper. "I see two civilians walking in the street," said the sniper. "Which of them do you want me to shoot?" At that point the journalist realised his mistake, pleaded with the sniper to shoot neither of them and turned to leave. As he did so, he heard two shots from the position just behind him. "That was a pity," said the sniper. "You could have saved one of their lives."[2]

Bell recognizes the difficulties posed by becoming too attached to the subject of a report. Many other journalistic autobiographies, especially of war reporters, reflect on the dilemma between becoming involved to aid or even "save" a victim, and covering a conflict dispassionately. Such a journalistic dilemma is a typical example of the kind of quandary analyzed by media ethicists. Less common, until recently, is attention towards the role of the audience, and the ethics of viewing such violent news.

Many media ethicists prefer to focus on the role of the journalist, drawing on books such as Philip Knightley's classic study *The First Casualty: The War Correspondent as Hero and Myth-Maker from Crimea to Iraq* (2004). It is striking how few references to religion or news about religion are to be found in Knightley's book. He twice observes how exaggerated or fictional atrocity stories (during the First World War and the Spanish Civil War) were used to justify religious support for fighting. And he once observes how army chaplains in the Vietnam War demonstrated little sensitivity towards the ethics of conflict. As in *First Casualty*, the ethics of covering stories about religion or the religious implications of news stories have rarely been analyzed by media ethicists. Similarly, the "cultural turn," described briefly in the introduction to Part II of this Reader, may have resulted in more sensitive cultural analysis but, with the exception of the inheritors of the school of critical theory (Lynch 2005), it has not developed extensive ethical evaluation of what is being described. Likewise, until recently few media ethicists have examined the role and responsibility of the audience.

This lack of critical and ethical reflection upon mediated religion, the role of the audience, and the covering of stories about religion is slowly being challenged. It is important to underline that the essays in Part IV, while relevant to media ethics, go beyond this field and represent a number of attempts to reflect normatively on contemporary media and culture from different disciplinary perspectives. The essays in this final part of the book therefore illustrate how the discussions around media, religion, and culture invariably have ethical implications and how some scholars are now critically reflecting on these interactions. Several of the earlier chapters also attend quite self-consciously to ethical questions. This can be discerned in a number of contexts. For example, the essays by Pattison (Chapter 17), and Carrette and King (Chapter 6) provoke a range of questions, including: What are the ethical implications raised by the actual form in which religion is mediated? Or consider the essays by Orsi (Chapter 13), McDannell (Chapter 12), and Meyer (Chapter 14) as they critically reflect upon the question: What are the values implied in the scholarly framings of the relation between religion, media, and culture? The nuanced descriptions of earlier chapters have implications for how we live, and are rich seams for teasing out ethical questions. This is also true of the chapters in this final part of the Reader.

In the first chapter in Part IV Nick Couldry reflects on media, ritual and the myth of the center of society. This is part of his book *Media Rituals: A Critical Approach* (2002), where his aim is to analyze "the media's role in ordering our lives and organizing our social space" (p. 1). In Chapter 18 of this book Couldry provides a case for demythologizing two closely related claims, what he describes as the "myth of the center" and "myth of the mediated center." The second is rooted in the claim that different media can reconstruct the center of social and political life. His account is a challenge to the claim that media accurately describe reality. Drawing on the work of other scholars, he argues that the "symbolic resourses are very unequally distributed" (p. 208) and that many groups are excluded from the power of naming. Who describes reality and how they go about the process, as well as who is "in" and who is left "out," can reinforce social hierarchies. For this reason Couldry encourages a hermeneutic of suspicion towards mediated public spectacles, celebrities, and the complex world of media rituals. Drawing on the work of Emile Durkheim and Pierre Bourdieu, he highlights the potential for "symbolic violence" when media rituals are used to reinforce social structures and perceptions of reality.

This hermeneutic of suspicion towards the presentation of reality through different media is developed further in the second essay in Part IV. Jolyon Mitchell's chapter (Chapter 19) is drawn from a detailed argument in his *Media Violence and Christian Ethics* (2007). In the first half of this book he makes a case for analyzing not only the producers and contents of news, but also the responsibilities of audiences. His chapter, entitled "Remembering news about violence," investigates which images of violence from the news audiences remember and why. This leads on to a discussion of both how audiences respond to such news images and why audiences forget certain stories. In an argument that resonates with Couldry's discussion, Mitchell argues that a range of stories are commonly left outside the news frame. This can contribute to forgetfulness and, a point developed further in the original monograph, the challenge for audiences to reframe what they are presented with and journalists to become involved in practices of redescription.

One striking characteristic of contemporary journalism is how often religion proves to be a blind spot among journalists. Recent edited collections such as *Blind Spot: When Journalists Don't Get Religion* (Marshall *et al.* 2009) explore this phenomenon in greater detail. One way of contributing to the improvement of journalistic interpretations of religious news would be through the growth of religious literacy. Elaine Graham, a leading practical theologian, develops this theme in greater detail in her essay entitled "Religious Literacy and Public Service Broadcasting" (Chapter 20). Like Herbert in Chapter 8, she acknowledges a post-secular setting and the role of the media and popular culture in promoting certain types of religious literacy. She then provides a critical account of several different approaches to religious literacy. On the basis of this typology she commends a form of religious literacy, which is rooted in citizenship, which may "require a greater imagination towards the 'otherness' of religion," and an awareness of the everyday nature of media production and consumption.

In the fourth essay in Part IV Catholic theologian Tom Beaudoin develops a critical theology of contemporary culture which takes seriously the everyday nature of media consumption. This is a theme he has developed in different ways in his book *Virtual Faith* (1998). In the discussion in this Reader he begins by highlighting the theological significance of the child abuse scandal within the

Catholic Church, which has recently dominated religious news. Writing as a practical and pastoral theologian, he explores in greater detail the themes of deconversion, ordinary theology, and interreligious dialogue, as a way of "rethinking ordinary sacred/spiritual identities" (p. 241). These reconfigurative practices are potentially even more radical than first meets the eye, leading to Beaudoin's challenge to become an agent of dispossession. This is a challenging vocation as it calls audiences and producers to confront powerful organizations and entrenched traditions. This process of dispossession has the potential to lead to the transforming of religious identities discussed in Part II of this book.

In the final chapter of this part and book (Chapter 22) Gordon Lynch considers the ethical implications of the mediatization of the sacred. Lynch revivifies the term "the sacred" from a *cultural sociological* perspective, which recognizes the multiplicity of expressions of the sacred. How can healthy democratic societies be sustained? In searching for an answer to this question Lynch highlights a new set of cultural conditions where different media can both heighten emotional experiences and define boundaries of moral communities. In this context individuals now both reproduce and contest sacred forms. For Lynch the result of this transformed communicative environment is the need for increased ethical and critical reflexivity among media producers.

This introduction to Part IV, on "Religion and the ethics of media and culture," began with a similar challenge and the kind of story commonly used in many media ethics books. It focuses on a dramatic incident to explore how journalists make difficult decisions or act in complex settings. Less common is attention to the structures that contribute to the environment in which such decisions are made. Similarly, many media ethics texts concentrate on difficult situations or dilemmas, rather than on how habits and routines shape journalists' characters, which in turn contribute to certain decisions being taken. There are several examples in Part IV of writers who are taking these factors into account, as well as exploring the normative issues raised by the analyses found in the kind of work represented earlier in this book. Authors, therefore, explore the significance of media rituals (Couldry, Chapter 18), remembering and forgetting (Mitchell, Chapter 19), developing religious literacy (Graham, Chapter 20), critical engagement with established religious traditions (Beaudoin, Chapter 21), and the mediatization of the sacred (Lynch, Chapter 22).

Notes

1 Martin Bell, unpublished Chichester Cathedral speech, July 10, 1996; see also Bell 1996.
2 Martin Bell, July 24, 2008, "Radovan Karadzic and the Bosnian conflict: 'We could have ended it sooner,'" *The Telegraph*, and at http://www.telegraph.co.uk/news/features/3637415/Radovan-Karadzic-and-the-Bosnian-conflictWe-could-have-ended-it-sooner.html (accessed December 7, 2010).

18 Unraveling the myth of the mediated center

Nick Couldry

Beyond the myth(s) of the center

We need to isolate and name one form of misrecognition that helps frame all the other specific misrecognitions involved in media rituals. I shall call this the "myth of the center," and explain its relationship to another myth, which I will call "the myth of the mediated center."

Disrupting classic myth-making

Edward Said once wrote of the image of "centrality" in American society (Said 1988: 159). There have been countless other diagnoses of US society apparently more relevant to media culture, from Baudrillard's travelogue in "hyperreal" America to Neal Gabler's recent account of American reality "conquered" by entertainment (Baudrillard 1988; Gabler 2000), but it is Said's image which is the most penetrating, and the most useful for our analysis. The US is a society saturated by media to an extraordinary degree; and the image of "centrality," if real, must have some connection with that. But the idea of society's "center" is also at the root of all Durkheimian and neo-Durkheimian accounts of how society holds together through ritual, so there is much more at stake here than an argument about one nation's television consumption.

A classic statement of the myth of the center was Edward Shils' *Center and Periphery* (1975). Shils was the eminent sociologist working in the Parsonian tradition who with Michael Young wrote one of the earliest analyses of television's role in contemporary ritual (in Shils [1956] 1975). It is precisely such an idea of society's "sacred center" on which the plausibility of classic Durkheimian and neo-Durkheimian arguments depends. When Shils wrote it, he was still cautious because he had not yet made the neo-Durkheimian move of arguing, against the direction of Durkheim's own historical analysis, that modern media, especially television, can "reconstruct" this sense of the center. This, however, is what Dayan and Katz (1992: viii, 23) explicitly argue, quoting Shils approvingly, and insisting that media recreate "mechanical solidarity" through an entirely modern technology of social coordination (the broadcast schedule, satellite distribution, and so on).

This idea is both true and false: true, because it registers the enormous pressures in late modernity (in which the media are involved) to construct a sense of society's center, but false, in that it ignores that these are precisely processes *of construction*. The analysis cannot, however, stop there. If society's "center" is indeed a myth—or if (put another way, adopting Habermas' famous distinction between "system" and "lifeworld") contemporary media fail to speak the "lifeworld's" truth to the "system," because they are in crucial respects *part of* that "system"—then we need to explain why this myth stays in place, and how it connects with the wider legitimation of media power. For this, we need to link the concepts of "symbolic power" and "symbolic violence" to the construction of a ritual body: how are the media's ritual categories incorporated in specific ritual actions and ritual mastery?

Note that this begins to shift media analysis away from media texts and into broader questions of governmentality (Rose 1996: 42) and the regulation of social practice in late modern states. Once we drop the assumption that society has a core of "true" social values waiting to be "expressed," then we are free to re-read contemporary processes of social and cultural definition for the open-ended conflicts that they really are. Perhaps the most fundamental term of conflict is the definition of "reality" itself, although "reality" of course is registered in different ways in a range of contexts: the "reality" addressed by government policies of social control, economic "reality," the "reality" of national mood, the "reality" of the fashion and entertainment worlds. Because society's symbolic resources are very unequally distributed (with media institutions being the main beneficiaries of that inequality), these ongoing conflicts of definition are marked by symbolic violence: certain definitions have enough weight and authority to *close off* most other alternatives from view, although such closure can never be total and is always, in principle, open to challenge. It is here that the deconstruction of media rituals connects to other more specific ideological deconstructions of media outputs, because it challenges our belief in the media as *the* space where we should look for expression, let alone resolution, of specific conflicts about how to understand the social world.

Counter-codes and strategies of surveillance

If we want to grasp such conflicts around symbolic power, and the play of symbolic violence, but *without* relying on any "myth of the center" or other functionalist assumptions, then we need a further concept which captures those local definitional battles beneath the surface of apparent social "consensus." This is the concept of *naming*, introduced by the late Italian political sociologist Alberto Melucci. Operating outside the Durkheimian tradition, and indeed outside the study of ritual entirely, Melucci emphasizes the importance in late modernity of ongoing contests to "name" reality. He argues that, while we live in societies where there is no sacred at all (Melucci 1989: 62, 109), our lives *are* organized towards other, more problematic forms of consensus, through the standardization of consumption and market forces (ibid.: 55), and the strategies of governments. In such societies there are conflicts over "the production of information and symbolic resources" (ibid.: 55) and "access to knowledge becomes a new kind of power" (ibid.: 84). Individuals have a stake in these battles through their own local attempts to define themselves, by appropriating common symbolic resources. In his 1996 book *Challenging Codes*, Melucci turns more specifically to the media. Contemporary societies' domination by media, he argues, requires "a new way of thinking about power and inequality" (Melucci 1996: 179), which recognizes the importance of control or influence over what he calls the "master codes." "The real domination" he argues "is today the exclusion from the power of naming" (ibid.: 182).

Melucci's main interest is the role of social movements as contesters, against the odds, of the normal concentration of the power of "naming" in governments, corporations, and media institutions. Social movements operate, he argues, both inside and outside the system of representation (ibid.: 309). Naming, and contests over naming, opens up a very different perspective on the attempts to monopolize the "reality" of historical events that we see in "media events." These contests operate not just in local and national media, but also in the intrinsically global dispersed new medium of the Internet. Recent years have seen a number of symbolic conflicts, where the "naming" of central social realities has been at stake, for example the Seattle and Genoa anti-globalization protests in 1999 and 2000, and the protests against corporate power analyzed and championed by Naomi Klein (2000).

The concept of "naming" is productive for a post-Durkheimian account of media ritual in other ways too. If we see ritualization as involving a particular way of naming the social world, this links it to other everyday practices of apparently little relevance to "ritual." I mean the everyday categorizing practices of governments. The Israeli anthropologist Don Handelman (1998) has offered an interesting recent commentary on these issues. Instead of "rituals" he prefers to talk of "public events," because he wants to reject entirely the implication that such events consensually represent "the wider social order" (ibid.: xii). Handelman's interest lies elsewhere, in how public events come to be constructed as such, "the logics of their organisational design" (ibid.: xi). Handelman's wider aim is to analyze the coordinating patterns which make up public events and their connection with "bureaucratic logics." Quite plausibly, Handelman argues that, rather than being dazzled by the mediated show of "social togetherness" in, say, sporting events or carnivals, we should think more closely about how those events' organization depends precisely on the implementation of bureaucratic categories (ibid.: xxxviii, xxxix).

Here, and elsewhere, I want to invoke a counter-reading of the Durkheimian legacy that foregrounds not the consensual nature of "the symbolic" but the inherently contested nature of symbolic power. As Pierre Bourdieu argued in his essay "On Symbolic Power":[1]

> Durkheim has the merit of designating the *social function* ... of symbolism in an explicit way: it is an authentic political function which cannot be

reduced to the structuralists' function of communication. Symbols are the instruments of knowledge and communication ... they make it possible for there to be a *consensus* on the meaning of the social world, a consensus which contributes fundamentally to the reproduction of the social order.

(Bourdieu 1991: 166)

Don Handelman echoes this point: "the control over processes of classification is a most powerful means through which to shape and control social order" (1998: xxxi). This means that, as analysts of ritual, and especially media rituals, we should be particularly *suspicious* of public spectacle. Contemporary public spectacle, far from being a revelation of underlying timeless "truths" about social life, can be seen instead as "the representation of social order under surveillance, under control, manipulated by its compositors and auditors ... magnified through the exact, clinical, optic gaze of televised and videotaped events" (ibid.: xxxix).

Mythical deconstruction or ideological analysis?

For the sake of clarity, it is important to acknowledge one possible misreading of the argument I've developed so far. This would see the argument as a latter day Marxist debunking of media rituals as ideological processes that mystify an underlying level of domination. From such a Marxist perspective, media, and media rituals, would be the vehicle for power interests that lie outside the media, above all economic interests. [...] I am not saying, however, that media rituals work *necessarily* as vehicles for any particular ideology as that term is normally understood (messages that support the interests of particular states, corporations, or other entities such as religious institutions). My analysis focuses not on the specific messages communicated through media rituals, but on the more basic mystification inherent in the *form* of media rituals, *whatever* their content and indeed whether or not they have any content. This is the idea that society has a "center." Of course, in contemporary social life there are many parallel and linked processes of central*ization*, some operating on a national scale, some increasingly on a global scale (regulatory pressures, market pressures, and so on); we have governments, after all! But this idea goes much further than that, by claiming that *beneath* these real pressures of centralization is a core of "truth," a "natural" center (different "centers" of course depending on where we live) that we should value, as the center of "our" way of life, "our" values. This is *the myth of the center*, and it is connected with a second myth that "the media" have a privileged relationship to that "center," as a highly centralized system of symbolic production whose "natural" role it is to represent or frame that "center." Call this *the myth of the mediated center*.

In reality, and whatever the competing pressures of social centralization and (we should not forget) the rival pressures of de-centralization, there is no such social center that acts as a moral or cognitive foundation for society and its values, and therefore no natural role for the media as that "center's" interpreter, but there are enormous pressures to believe in each. So great are those pressures that it even seems scandalous to name these myths as such. Yet it is essential to do so. The idea that society has a center helps naturalize the idea that we have, or need, media that "represent" that center; media's claims for themselves that they are society's "frame" help naturalize the idea, underlying countless media texts, that there is a social "center" to *be* re-presented to us. (The reality is different and more complex. An intense (but not total) concentration of coercive power in modern states works alongside, although not always in step with, the intense (but not total) concentration of symbolic power in modern media institutions.)

These two connected myths underlie a number of categorical distinctions, boundaries, and hierarchies that help organize media discourse and are played upon in the practice of media rituals. The central principle underlying all these distinctions is the hierarchy of what is "in" the media over what is not "in" the media (cf. Couldry 2000: 17). I will come shortly to the details of these categories, but it is important first to see both how this differs from a standard ideological analysis of the media and how it might support, not undermine, that separate ideological analysis. Media rituals operate to naturalize the notion of a "mediated social order" within which all specific ideologies must compete, as well as legitimating the particular representational privilege of the media (as a centralized system for producing and distributing images, information and opinions). [...]

The media's ritual categories

The "myth of the mediated center" is a label for something more complex and more messy: the mass of practices through which media power is legitimated. Media power seems legitimate because, through all sorts of arrangements of speech, thought, and action, it is made to seem natural. There are many dimensions to this process, as I argued in *The Place of Media Power* (Couldry 2000), and only some are connected to media rituals. Those that I called "banal practices of ordering" (ibid.: 48) involve the ways in which social practice is, increasingly, organized around media sources and media access. Media have become "obligatory passing points" in many areas of public and private life (Callon and Latour 1981: 287), and this is an everyday fact of social organization. None of this, however, requires anything so formalized as media rituals.

"Media rituals," by contrast, are condensed forms of action where category distinctions and boundaries related to the myth of the mediated center are worked upon with particular intensity. In media rituals, no actual networks are directly created or strengthened, but instead categories of thought that naturalize media power are acted out. For convenience, let's call these "*the media's ritual categories.*" What are they? First, and most important, the basic category difference between anything "in" or "on" or associated with "the media," and anything which is not. There is no type of thing in principle to which this difference cannot apply; that is what it means to say that it is a *category* difference. Like Durkheim's distinction between "sacred" and "profane," it cuts across everything in the social world; anything can be "in" the media. The "difference" between what is "in" and not "in" the media is therefore not natural, but a difference which, through continual usage, is constructed as natural (cf. Couldry 2000: 41).

So far we have looked at the category difference, and hierarchy, between what is in the media and what is not. This is the primary distinction through which the myth of the mediated center is naturalized. But there are important *secondary* differences as well; these derive from the assumption that what is "in" the media must have higher status than what is not, but are distinct in their reference point. For example, the term "liveness" derives from the status of what is presented in the media, but suggests a little more explicitly that the reason media things matter more is because they are part of society's *current* "reality." That "reality" is changing from moment to moment, as media coverage changes, which means that whatever is being shown *now* must, relatively, have a higher status than what is no longer being shown: hence the status of live transmission. Even more explicit, but still naturalized, are the distinctions drawn between the "reality" of the different things media present.

The media's ritual categories, like all important organizing categories, are reproduced in countless different circumstances. They become automatic, unthinking: so you might say to a colleague or partner, "Call her, she was once in that show. She might make a difference to our profile," and think no further of the category distinction you are reproducing. In media rituals, we see these category differences internalized in particular action forms which both test out their workings and naturalize their significance. I turn next to how the media's ritual categories are internalized through bodily performance.

Ritual actions and ritual bodies

If the conventional notion of ideology involves specific contents believed as such, ritual's relation to belief is more indirect. Category differences may be worked upon in actions and embedded in the organization of, and the body's orientation in, space, but that does not mean that these categories are necessarily articulated in the beliefs of those who enact them. On the contrary, once reflected upon, they become open to contestation in a way that, when naturalized in bodily action, they are not. Ritual action lies somewhere between pure internalization and explicit articulation; the emphasis and exposure, as it were, that ritual action brings can encourage certain types of dispute and debate, but they tend to stay within the ritual framework, whose organization has already naturalized the most important category differences.

The internalization of categories

What connects the everyday space of ritualization and ritual action is the body that passes between them: the ritual body which has internalized the organizing significance of ritual's category differences. To grasp how this connection works, we can draw on some more terms of Pierre Bourdieu's. For example, when discussing how official language comes to have legitimacy, Bourdieu writes that this recognition is "inscribed in a *practical* state," in "dispositions," as are all forms of symbolic domination (Bourdieu 1991: 50–1, emphasis mine): for "symbolic violence ... can only be exerted on a person predisposed (in his habitus) to feel it" (ibid.: 51). We do not need to go here in any great detail into Bourdieu's difficult concept of "habitus" that underlies this passage; we can simply adopt a working definition of the term as capturing how people's individual actions are shaped, at two removes, by (1) the forces which structure the principles that, in turn, (2) constrain the range of practices in which they can engage. These constraints (the "habitus") work through the body; they are a dimension of the organization of our actions and practices that is *already* in place before we perform, reflect on, or articulate them. This operates "below the level of consciousness, expression and the reflexive distance they presuppose" (Bourdieu 1990: 73). Bourdieu does not refer just to the organization of the individual body in isolation, but to the organization of the spaces such as the home, where bodily experience is orchestrated among its world of objects (ibid.: 76), and the "practical mastery" that every agent has to acquire as she moves through space (Bourdieu 1977: 87–95; discussed by Bell 1992: 107–8).

Catherine Bell has usefully developed these ideas to argue that it is such practical mastery that is the end-point of religious ritualization, "the body invested with a 'sense' of ritual" (Bell 1992: 98). The sense of ritual—of certain forms of action as heightened—is a way in which a broad hierarchy is reinforced through performance. As Bell puts it: "ritualization is a way of acting that is designed and orchestrated to distinguish and privilege what is being done to other, usually more quotidian, activities" (ibid.: 74). In this way ritual performance is able to suggest a "higher" order of things:

> Fundamental to all strategies of ritualization ... is the appeal to a more embracing authoritative order that lies beyond the immediate situation. Ritualization is generally a way of engaging some wide consensus that those acting [in ritual] are doing so as a type of natural response to a world conceived and interpreted as affected by forces that transcend it.
>
> (Bell 1997: 169)

You might object that *media* rituals cannot invoke a transcendent order equivalent to that invoked by religious ritual (which is Bell's subject). Recall, though, that, in so far as media rituals invoke media as a representative of the social center, it is exactly such transcendental claims that follow from a neo-Durkheimian account of the media. My argument, while opposing that claim, takes very seriously the idea that, embedded in certain types of formalized practice we perform in relation to media are category differences that naturalize the *idea* that media are socially central.

What seems difficult, however, is to see how something very large (a claim about the whole social world and media's place in it) can be reinforced, in miniature as it were, through something so small. But this is what is most radical about Bourdieu's concept of "practical mastery": his insight that the most minute details of bodily deportment and language can reproduce larger patterns of social ordering (or at least images of social order). This principle is as relevant to "complex" societies as to "simple" ones. Bourdieu discusses this link in the following passage:

> If all societies ... set such store on the seemingly most insignificant details of *dress*, *bearing*, physical and verbal *manners*, the reason is that, treating the body as a memory, they entrust to it in abbreviated and practical, i.e. mnemonic, form the fundamental principles of the arbitrary content of culture. The principles embodied in this way are placed beyond the grasp of consciousness, and hence cannot be touched by voluntary, deliberate transformation, cannot even be made explicit; nothing seems more ineffable, more incommunicable, more inimitable, and therefore, more precious, than the values given body, *made* body by the transubstantiation achieved by the hidden persuasion of an implicit pedagogy, capable of instilling a whole cosmology, an ethic, a metaphysic, a political philosophy, through injunctions as insignificant as "stand up straight" or "don't hold your knife in your left hand."
>
> (Bourdieu 1977: 94)

But, you might say again, can contemporary *media*—surely, in its details, the most *contested* of institutional sectors—be the focus of injunctions so ideologically saturated as the bodily instructions Bourdieu mentions?

To allay your doubts, here's a thought experiment. As you read this page, imagine that you were told that a well-known television personality had just entered the building: would you go on reading, and in the same way? If you agree with me that almost certainly you would *not*, then we have identified one dimension of contemporary social life to which the term "media rituals" alludes. Media rituals (and ritualization) capture that "extra," largely naturalized, dimension of social life that acknowledges in condensed form the framing power of "the media." We all know this instinctively, but what is hard is to find ways of isolating this dimension with greater precision.

Where are media rituals?

Certainly, unlike with religious rituals, we cannot look for media rituals in a single confined space, such as the church or the mosque. Media processes are too dispersed across space for that. Indeed your action of turning round, and staying turned around, when a media person enters the room, is not yet a media ritual, but it *is* an action organized on a principle (media people are special, therefore worthy of special attention) that can be played out in formalized action, for example in the highly organized spaces of the television studio. Small-scale media rituals can occur even within wider spaces that are not, as such, ritual spaces. So, while much of what goes on at the media theme parks such as Granada Studios Tour in Manchester that I researched for *The Place of Media Power* (Couldry 2000) is not ritual (queuing for food, chatting, looking at exhibits), some things that go on there are media rituals: the occasional meetings with celebrities, the chance to appear "on camera" (or pretend to do so), and so on.

What we are looking for is not just categories at work, but ritualized action. We need to identify those actions where latent media-related categories are put to work in ways that are formalized enough for us to call them media rituals. There are a number of places, still little researched or studied, where we should look for such ritualized actions:

- sites where people cross from the non-media "world" into the media "world," such as studios, or any place where filming or media production goes on;
- sites where non-media people expect to encounter people (or things) in the media (for example celebrities);
- moments where non-media people perform for the media, for example posing for a camera, even if this takes place in the course of action that is otherwise not formalized.

In all these situations, people act out in formalized ways category differences that reproduce in condensed form the idea, or derivatives of the idea, that media are our access point to society's "center." Here are some examples of the type of thing I have in mind:

- people calling out as their presence "on air" is acknowledged (the studio chat show host turns to them and asks them to clap, "show what they feel");
- people either holding back or rushing forward at the sight of a celebrity;
- people holding back before they enter a place connected with the media, so as to emphasize the boundary they cross by entering it (cf. Couldry 2000: 111);
- performances by media people that acknowledge their own specialness before a crowd of non-media people;
- performances by non-media people in certain types of formalized media context, such as a talk show.

Note, finally, that calling something a media ritual (for example a talk show performance) does not prevent it from also having intense *personal* significance. The ritual of televised confession is one contemporary media setting where Bourdieu's theory of practical mastery meets Foucault's theory of power as productive of new regimes of the self. Foucault (1981) analyzed how the ritual of confession (before the priest, the doctor, the psychoanalyst) is structured by the power differential between confessor and interlocutor. In spite of the greater complexity of its audience, the television confession too is a ritual form, structured around certain category differences (host versus confessor, ordinary space versus studio space, ordinary stories versus stories that have passed through television) that only make sense because of the power differential which they both disguise and naturalize. Given this, it is a form open to any number of individual and temporary negotiations, as part of the contests over any socially marked difference (whether gender, class, ethnicity, or sexuality). My main emphasis will be on the questions of form, rather than such individual contestations, but my argument is quite consistent with the importance of the latter as well.

Media ritualization spans, then, intense personal performance (a person revealing private truths before unknown millions) and the seeming banality of everyone turning round because a media celebrity has entered the room. Both—and everything that lies between them—are part of how we live out as "truth" the myth of the mediated center.

Notes

1 This is one place where, quite directly, Bourdieu strives to merge a Marxist and a Durkheimian perspective. For an interesting, but ultimately unconvincing, argument that this merger is impossible, see Garnham (1994).

19 Remembering news about violence

Jolyon Mitchell

Remembering news images

Which violent news images do viewers remember? In order to provide at least a provisional answer to this question I carried out a series of informal interviews and group discussions, primarily, though not exclusively, in different British locations between 2002 and 2005, investigating which violent news images diverse audiences remembered.[1] Most of this questioning took place before the July 7, 2005 London bombings, though in the weeks afterwards several respondents I spoke with recalled the image of a tangled red bus in Tavistock Square, and a women holding a white burns mask to her face as a man helps her away from Edgware Road tube station. Prior to these attacks the most commonly recalled violent images included many from Iraq: vehicles ablaze after car bomb explosions in Baghdad; naked masked prisoners paraded in Abu Ghraib jail; a marine shooting an injured man in a mosque in Fallujah; and videos of pleading hostages. Alongside these images many recollected pictures of children running out of School No. 1 in Beslan, South Russia; a shattered train in Madrid; and, most consistently, a number of images related to the events in Manhattan on September 11, 2001. Many people were able to describe exactly where they were, what they were doing, and how they felt when they heard about or saw this news. This kind of remembering, where individuals are able to remember many precise details, is often described as an example of a "flashbulb memory" (Conway 1995). Understanding how this kind of remembering works is complicated by the fact that images from "spectacular" news events, such as an airliner flying into a skyscraper, were initially repeated again and again.

Other violent images mentioned by some respondents included a crouching boy and father in Gaza, a teenage suicide bomber with his arms raised at a checkpoint, a young man helped out of a devastated Bali nightclub, and bombs being dropped over Afghanistan. Less commonly recalled were the pictures of bullet-riddled tenements in Sarajevo (Bosnia), devastated buildings in Grozny (Chechnya), bodies being pulled out of mass graves in Bosnia, piles of corpses strewn about a church in Rwanda, and a man showing severe scars from machete wounds inflicted by the local Janjaweed militia in Darfur. Significantly, images from Rwanda and Sudan were the only African countries mentioned. Even taking into account these limits, there remains an extensive geographical spread. The space which separates viewers from these violent events is partly collapsed through electronic communication technologies. In our "global village" (see McLuhan 1962; McLuhan and Powers 1992), many of its residents have become increasingly aware of the violence experienced by their "electronic" neighbors. While this process shrinks the world, it also further highlights the divide between those who watch and those who go through the actual trauma.

Viewers who lived close to conflict or who had experienced violence first-hand found that this proximity colored their memories of violent news. For example, a Serbian woman from Belgrade recalled pictures of the state television station damaged by NATO bombing in April 1999, admitting her memory was reinforced by having seen the devastation with her own eyes. Others found the recycling of graphic news images led to more immediate recall. [...] The recycling of news images can accentuate the immediacy of the violence, collapsing the barriers not only of space but also of time. For example, consider how old newsreels from the Second World War were recycled to further ethnic hatred in both Serbia and Croatia in the early 1990s.

Alongside the proximity and the recycling of news images I discovered another reason for viewers remembering what they had seen: identification. The actual religious affiliation of viewers appears to contribute to what is remembered. For instance, some of the older respondents from Northern Ireland recalled pictures of "Bloody Friday" in Belfast in 1972,[2] and others recalled the Remembrance Sunday bombing at Enniskillen in 1987,[3] while both young and old mentioned images of the aftermath of the Omagh Bombing in 1998.[4] Out of thirty Protestants, aged between 39 and 69 years old, not one recalled images from "Bloody Sunday," where thirteen Catholics had been killed.[5] Lack of recall, of course, does not mean that this group had no knowledge of what had happened over thirty years before, it simply suggests that they were more swiftly drawn to recollect images of violence which provoked a stronger emotional reaction: in this case against their own community. Part of the reason for this is that memories which make a significant emotional impact tend to ensure greater retention in what is often described by cognitive psychologists and neuroscientists as the episodic or autobiographical memory (Tulving 1983; Rubin 1999).

Many Muslims found the depiction of violence against fellow Muslims in both Iraq and Afghanistan particularly distressing; others were enraged. Given the generally sanitized and patriotic coverage frequently found on most of the major US networks (Friend 2003), it is not unreasonable to claim, with Rampton and Stauber, that many American viewers were initially more likely to remember positive images from the second Gulf War such as the toppling of Saddam Hussein's statue in *al-Firdos* (Paradise) Square, or the rescue of American POWs, while in the Arab world the "images that come to mind" will be humiliated Iraqi prisoners of war or the 12-year-old boy, Ali Ismail Abbas, who lost both his arms and legs, along with most of his family, in a bombing raid on Baghdad (Rampton and Stauber 2003: 201). The toppled statue is widely regarded now as a "media event" or "pseudo event," with as many journalists watching as crowds celebrating. It took on iconic status, being used symbolically to represent the fall of Saddam Hussein's regime. The long shot revealing what was left outside the frame was seen by journalists but was rarely if ever used in the US or the UK (see Lewis *et al.* 2006). If it had been, audiences would have seen how small the crowd actually was. Rampton and Stauber's hypothesis is believable especially when contrasting the reporting of the war by American channels such as Fox with that by Arab channels such as Al Jazeera. The picture of Ali was less commonly seen in the US. Nevertheless, I found several British viewers, who already had profound misgivings about the war, described the image of Ali as more "significant" than seeing the statue being pulled down.

According to a report by Reuters, many Muslim viewers said that the images repeatedly shown on Arab stations of a Marine shooting a severely injured Iraqi in a Mosque fueled "growing hatred against America and helped create more 'terrorists.'" This claim is hard to demonstrate, but the power of such images should not be underestimated. For instance, a Dubai-based engineer admitted that "I am not a jihadist, I am just a normal Muslim but such scenes are pushing me to Jihad." For him this appears to be only the tip of the iceberg: "This is one of the things we saw on TV. God knows how many crimes they have committed which we have not seen" (Nakhoul 2004). In extreme cases violent images may actually be used to motivate terrorists. According to *The Sunday Times* and several other newspaper reports, one of the failed London bombers claimed: "Religion had nothing to do with this. We watched films. We were shown videos with images of the war in Iraq" (quoted by Leppard and Follain 2005). In these and other cases, religious or cultural propinquity appears to have heightened the perceived significance of specific news images.

Viewers who lived in comparatively peaceful situations, when reflecting upon violent news found that it was more often distant dramatic images, such as the pictures emerging from the denouement of the Moscow theater siege (October 2002) or from suicide attacks in Riyadh or Casablanca (May 2003), rather than local black-eyes and inanimate melting icebergs, that jostled to the front of their consciousnesses. Unsurprisingly, given the focus of my questioning, no one among these different groups of viewers described pictures relating to more chronic, hidden or structural forms of violence, such as environmental degradation, economic injustice, and domestic abuse; though one 50-year-old North American male did speak about images of hurricane-force winds peeling off the roof of a factory in Florida, and, of those asked after the event, many spoke of the "violence" of the Boxing Day Tsunami in 2004 and Hurricane Katrina in August 2005.

Apart from the London 2005 bomb attacks and their aftermath, only a few of the mainland British respondents recalled pictures from the news connected with local violence. Three exceptions stand out. One middle-aged woman, from a small rural village in Yorkshire, vividly remembered seeing on television news a line of policemen using truncheons to beat back hunt protestors outside the House of Commons in London in 2004. Another woman who lived close to Hungerford recalled, "as if it was yesterday," images of the empty streets of the small Berkshire market town following the shootings by Michael Ryan which left sixteen dead in 1987. A third woman from North East England recalled a photograph of a badly battered old-age pensioner in Newcastle, who had been beaten up for a bag of fish and chips.[6] On the basis of conversations with these respondents either physical proximity or local knowledge appears to have influenced how these particular news images were appropriated.

What observations emerge from these discussions of visual memories of news violence? First, and unsurprisingly, pictures more recently seen were more commonly remembered. Recent pictures that were frequently named by one group were often not even mentioned several months later. There were a few exceptions, such as images related to the terrorist attacks on New York, but it appears that while many pictures were not entirely forgotten, they were over-laid by a new layer of news images. The ubiquity of violent images combined with the continuous flow of news ensures that many pictures are lost or at least pushed into the recesses of the episodic memory as new images are broadcast. Second, and closely related to the first point, a good number of these viewers recognized that they were engaged in viewing a never-ending cycle of violent images. Some psychologists describe this as a threefold process: in the first few moments an event is first received by the "iconic memory," where it is processed through a "recognition buffer"; it can then become absorbed by the "short term visual memory." This processing by the working memory can last up to thirty seconds, as the visual imprint is then transformed and in some cases becomes part of the "long term visual memory," where an image is invested with greater meaning or significance (Baddeley [1976] 1985: esp. 188–234). While there are other theories describing how the visual memory works, it is clear that viewers develop varied unconscious and conscious practices for remembering and then interacting with such depictions of violence.

Third, as suggested earlier, geographical, cultural, and communal proximity had a bearing upon which images were remembered. It is not surprising that some members of the Protestant communities in Northern Ireland remembered attacks on their own community more vividly than the hurts inflicted upon Catholics. Nor is it unexpected to find that some people living close to Hungerford found the news reports about the shootings particularly disturbing. Proximity, however, is not a determining factor, judging by the massive response to the shooting of fifteen 5- and 6-year-olds and their teacher in Dunblane, on March 13, 1996, by people from all over the world. For example, consider how one viewer was affected by what he saw and heard:

> That evening I casually switched on the BBC news via British Forces TV as usual. The horror of the report just made me cry instantaneously—something that had never happened to me before. For some while thereafter I

was unable to look at our first son, who was also five years old, because he reminded me of the innocence of the victims.[7]

Similarly, news about the shootings at a Port Arthur tourist site in Tasmania (1996) and a Columbine high school in Colorado, USA (1999), were remembered by many respondents in Scotland even though they were many thousands of miles away from the event. Prior to the advent of the telegraph, similar stories would take several weeks or months to travel the globe. In the age of instantaneous connection, geographical distance is no barrier to rapid sharing of such tragic stories. Resonating with the Dunblane story, these distant tragedies were brought close by immediate news images and reports. Fourth, many of the respondents did not make a distinction between seeing spectacular acts of terrorism and seeing images from recent wars when watching the news. It was usually much easier to remember the spectacular event rather than the context in which it was set. Leading on from that point, consider the absences in the responses. Unsurprisingly given the comparative paucity of images and coverage, self-inflicted and structural violence were rarely remembered. Domestic violence, which as I have suggested elsewhere is usually left outside the news frame, was never recalled.

Fifth, and finally, while the sources of news images remembered were primarily from television channels, other sources, such as the internet and newspapers, played an important role for informing some viewers [...] Television news is not produced and received in a communicative vacuum. Younger viewers in particular are turning to web-based news reports to supplement and even replace their television viewing. In the USA, for example, the heaviest users of the internet as a source of news are those under the age of 30 (Potter 2005: 412) Dramatic news images are now regularly reused, recycled, and discussed in many different media locations. This circulation and discussion of specific news images, on the web, in newspapers, and on the radio, contributes to some images being remembered more than others.

Since the early 1980s memory researchers have explored in ever greater detail how recollections go beyond the temporary short-term memory to longer-term storage. Why do some painful or traumatic memories persist (see Herman 1992: esp. 175–95)? Why do some violent news reports, or violent films, stick so firmly in the memory? Some researchers have suggested that the traces of specific images move from the "working memory" (which processes what has been seen) to the "autobiographical memory" (part of what is sometimes also described as episodic or long-term memory) partly because of the emotional resonance of a particular event (see Baddeley 1986; Andrade 2001: 3–30). In fact viewers of news may remember even more clearly than participants or eyewitnesses. For instance, while many viewers of 9/11 have clear memories of the attacks, many of those actually involved were so traumatized that their memories are far more blurred (see Kirshenblatt-Gimblett 2003).

Admittedly news images rarely have the power to traumatize in the way that participating in an actual experience has; nevertheless, watching certain news reports can be a troubling experience. Images such as a church full of corpses in Rwanda or a bloodied body in the streets of Baghdad can persist as a memory, even when it is desirable to wipe them out of consciousness. There is an element of truth in Montaigne's aphorism "Memory tells us not what we choose, but what it pleases" (quoted in Grayling 2001: 182). There is an untamable quality to memories, which makes it hard to control or to predict which ones will persist or recur: "In the short term, persistence is a virtually inevitable consequence of difficult experiences. But for the long term, confronting, disclosing, and integrating those experiences we would most like to forget is the most effective counter to persistence" (Schacter 2003: 178). Some memory researchers have found that viewers who attempt to suppress violent images are more likely to remember what they have seen (ibid.: 176–7). [...]

Responding to violent news

In "peaceful" countries, what are the common responses to the kaleidoscopic range of violent images? Typically, many viewers switch off or switch over, such is the regularity of these violent narratives. As Stanley Cohen suggests, there are many *States of Denial* or ways to block out what is seen (Cohen 2001). Changing channels comes in numerous forms, from turning the page to crossing over to the other side with the help of the remote control. "In a world that moves steadily from massacres to genocide, from images of chaos, destruction, death and madness, from the gassing of Kurds ... to the streets and fields of slaughter of Rwandans, the public," according to Susan Moeller, "resorts to compassion fatigue as defence mechanism against the knowledge of horror" (Moeller 1999: 226).[8] Compassion fatigue may be a journalistic cliché to some scholars, but for others it is a reality that finds its roots in the apparently never-ending repetition of images of suffering and violence. This can lead to a sense of powerlessness, where viewers feel they can do nothing to counter the violence that confronts them even if at second hand. Or it can provoke strong feelings of anger and even violent reactions, as witnessed by the attacks on Asians, assumed to be Muslims, in Britain and the USA following recent terrorist attacks.

The repetitive litany of violence is hard to avoid. If it is not suicide bombings or executions in Iraq, then it may be violent demonstrations against cartoons mocking the Prophet Mohammed in Beirut or Kabul, or stories of a small boy murdered on a housing estate. In a discussion about the reporting of violence, the Papal pastoral instruction *Communio et Progressio* (May 23, 1971, p. 43) worries specifically that if "bloody events are too realistically described or too frequently dwelt upon, there is a danger of perverting the image of human life." This may be detrimental to audiences' perception of the world and "may leave violence and savagery as the accepted way of resolving conflict." These claims are not tested out and are hard to prove conclusively, but nevertheless are almost as common a refrain as the criticism of violent films. [...]

News may only provide selected memories and framings, but it still serves an important role in confronting us with vivid reminders of our violent world. Journalists can intentionally and unintentionally bear false witness, but many risk their lives to bear witness to the reality of suffering caused through different forms of violence. Through the craft of journalists, audiences can themselves become witnesses to distant violence. In order to develop the discussion further I now want to turn to how some news stories are subject to amnesia.

Forgotten news

The rampages of the so-called "Lord's Resistance Army" (LRA) in Northern Uganda, the recurring border conflicts between Eritrea and Ethiopia, and the strafing by helicopters of villagers in central or Southern Sudan to clear the way for oil exploration (Stewart and Sankey 2001) rarely make it into the frames of Western news channels. There are notable exceptions to this practice of exclusion.[9] For example, coverage of refugees fleeing the apparent ethnic cleansing carried out by the Janjaweed militia in Darfur, Western Sudan, found its way to the top of some British news bulletins or front pages of newspapers for a time.[10] Nevertheless, often celebrity stories take priority, allowing television channels to ignore the destruction of over 2,000 villages and what the UN has described as "war crimes and crimes against humanity." For instance, in June 2005, CNN, Fox News, NBC, ABC, and CBS "collectively ran 55 times as many stories about Michael Jackson as they ran about the genocide in Darfur," leading one writer for the *New York Times* to muse: "If only Michael Jackson's trial had been held in Darfur" (Kristof 2005).[11] Likewise, the war in the Democratic Republic of the Congo (D.R. Congo) is estimated to have claimed over three million lives in the first decade of the twenty-first century, but has received limited coverage in the majority of the Western media.[12] Some reports put the figure higher: over four million deaths in the D.R. Congo in five years (Keane 2003). If this number of casualties had occurred in Europe or North America the conflict would have received far more global media attention. These hostilities in Central Africa have led to much more loss of life and injury than any other fighting since the Second World War, and yet they often remain largely hidden from public view.[13] If such violence is covered in the West it is often towards the end of news bulletins in abbreviated reports.

Journalists repeatedly use the phrase "Africa's Forgotten War" to describe these and similar conflicts.[14] This journalistic stock phrase contains a kernel of truth, though it is more accurate to speak in the plural of Africa's forgotten wars. Many journalists recognize that wars in Africa are frequently left outside the news frame. Aid workers sometimes describe the country where they work as suffering from a "forgotten war" as a way of attempting to wrench the West's attention onto potential humanitarian disasters. For example, in 2003 the British development charity Action Aid's chief executive Salil Shetty claimed: "Liberia is Africa's forgotten war. If the international community does not intervene, it could become another Rwanda."[15] Such descriptions and predictions are then used by journalists to frame particular conflicts, as they attempt to awaken Western public opinion.

Religious leaders also make use of the "forgotten war" motif as a way of pleading for aid, dialogue, and peace-making. Under the headline "John Paul II Recalls 'Forgotten Wars,'" the Vatican's international news agency Zenit described how the Pope, during one of his general audiences in Rome, reminded his audience of around 25,000 that while the media may have forgotten them there are conflicts "lacerating Africa," which are sowing death, hatred, and poverty:

> From Angola to the Great Lakes, from Congo-Brazzaville to Sierra Leone, from Guinea Bissau to the Democratic Republic of the Congo, from the Horn of Africa to Sudan, there is a long and bitter series of internal conflicts, as well as inter-Nation conflicts which, above all, strike innocent peoples and affect the lives of the Catholic communities.
>
> (John Paul II, quoted in Zenit 1999)

There are many forgotten wars in Africa, and forgetfulness is heightened by what is left outside the news frame. For a girl orphaned in the 1999 rebel attacks on Freetown, Sierra Leone, or for a boy too poor to go to his mother's funeral in warn-torn Liberia, or for a young mother who lost her leg from a land mine left over from the Angolan Civil Wars, it is impossible to erase the consequences of war. In their lives these wars are unforgettable. [...]

Why does this matter? News reports may entertain, but they can also inform voters and policy-makers of the realities of forgotten or hidden forms of violence. Africa is the only continent in the world, according to the World Bank, to become poorer in the last twenty-five years. Nearly 50 percent of the population of Sub-Saharan Africa is trying to survive on less than $1 a day.[16] The world's twenty-five least developed countries, according to the United Nations Development Programme (UNDP), are all in Africa (UNDP 2003). Life expectancy is lower in Sub-Saharan Africa than on any other continent. Preventable diseases account for many deaths, which are the result of malnutrition, vitamin deficiency, and poor hygiene, accentuated by the fact that half the population lacks access to safe water. Two-thirds of the world's AIDS cases are to be found in Sub-Saharan Africa (UNAIDS 2004). The expensive drugs needed to assist those living with HIV have until recently been unavailable to most people living in this region. In blunt terms, "twice a week" a "Hiroshima bomb strikes the toddlers of the Third World. Every month, more than a million of them die unnecessarily" (Van Ginneken 1998: 25). The majority of these children live in parts of Africa, and their deaths normally go unnoticed. "The major media do not paint this as an acute disaster which warrants immediate attention" (ibid.). A further difficulty is that in the comparatively rare instances when these issues are covered, African countries are often caricatured as isolated places of little hope whose troubles are homegrown, ignoring how inextricably connected the continent is with the rest of the global and political economy.[17] In a brief news report it is hard to investigate whether civil wars and other less obvious forms of violence find their roots in the colonial divisions of the nineteenth century and the cold war hostilities of the twentieth. There are undoubtedly notable exceptions, to be found in documentaries, weekend newspaper supplements, or alternative news websites, but news, which primarily focuses on the spectacular or proximate, can further contribute to certain kinds of forgetfulness. [...]

The *New Internationalist*, in the November 2001 issue entitled "Twin Terrors," highlighted how on September 11, 2001, as well as several thousand victims of terrorism roughly 24,000 people died from hunger, 6,020 children were killed by diarrhea, and 2,700 were killed by measles.[18] The weekly magazine *West Africa* produced a cartoon a few days after the September 11 attacks entitled "The Day the World Stopped," by the artist Bisi Ogunbadejo. It was made up of four scenes. The first has a picture of a city being bombed, with bystanders saying, "Here they come again." The caption with this image is: "The latest of many attacks on our part of the world." The second picture has a devastated city, with a picture of a globe on wheels driving by in the foreground. The caption is: "The world went by as usual." A double line separates these two images from the bottom two. The third picture has a plane going over a skyline reminiscent of New York towards two skyscrapers, with a bystander pointing and saying, "Oh my God." The caption was: "The first attack on their patch of the world ... " The final picture is of a devastated city, but this time the globe on wheels has stopped, with a door opening like the back of an ambulance. People dressed in white carry the injured on stretchers, loading them into the back of the globe. The caption, following on from the previous one, reads: " ... the world stopped and did something."[19]

This cartoon, along with the observations from the *New Internationalist*, leads us towards an important set of questions: why is it that when about 3,000 people died on September 11 most news broadcasters and newspapers around the world provided saturation coverage for days and sometimes weeks afterwards, while when over three million die in the D.R. Congo it is largely ignored by the media? Why is it that while it only took minutes for the world to know of the unfolding tragedy in New York, it would take months before the full horror of the 100 days of killing came to light in Rwanda? To widen the scope of the questions for a moment, why is it that 9/11, or 7/7 (the London bombings), or 9/3 (the Madrid bombings) become dates to remember, while the dates of the first bombing of Afghanistan or Baghdad, or the start of the Rwandan Genocide, are far less widely known (see Sobrino 2004; Morris 2005)? Restating these questions is in no way meant to belittle the trauma, the heartbreak, and the lasting pain caused by the terrorist attacks on America in September 2001,[20] Madrid in 2004, and London in 2005. Nor is it intended to ignore the significance or evil nature of these events. It is, rather, an attempt to explore critically why news is framed in the way that it is. Behind this investigation is the belief, well expressed by Rowan Williams, that the trauma can offer a breathing space; and in that space there is the possibility of recognising that we had an experience that is not just a nightmarish insult to *us* but a door into the suffering of countless other innocents, a suffering that is more or less routine for them in their less regularly protected environments.

(Williams 2002: 63)

News seldom provides a breathing space, sometimes sliding towards breathless reportage of tragedy piled upon tragedy. Occasionally, however, the trauma depicted on the news can take the viewers' breath away.

Notes

1 I carried out these surveys in a range of contexts, which included asking mixed groups which images of violent news could be remembered; recorded (on tape or on paper) based on questions and discussions in Cambridge (2002), Northampton (2002), Isle of Man (2003), Edinburgh (2002–5), Durham (2004), London (2004), and Belfast (2004). There were over 400 respondents, who were from different age groups and a variety of social, religious, and educational backgrounds.

2 Bloody Friday refers to the events in Belfast on Friday July 21, 1972, where the IRA (Irish Republican Army) detonated 22 bombs which, in just over one hour, killed nine people and seriously injured approximately 130 others, of whom at least 40 were Catholic: "Many watching the television news reports were reduced to tears by horrifying pictures of firemen and rescue workers ... scraping up the remains of human beings into plastic bags ... " (Bardon 1992). On the thirtieth anniversary memories were brought to the fore by a statement in the republican newspaper *An Phoblacht* (*Republican News*), which offered "sincere apologies" to the families of those killed on Bloody Friday.

3 On Sunday, November 8, 1987, just before 11:00 a.m., an IRA bomb exploded without warning, bringing down a wall upon the assembling crowd near the war memorial in Enniskillen; 11 people were killed and 63 injured.

4 On Saturday, August 15, 1998, at 3:10 p.m., a 500 lb bomb planted by a dissident republican group, the Real IRA, exploded in a crowded shopping street in Omagh, killing 29 people and injuring another 220.

5 On Sunday, January 30, 1972, 13 demonstrators were shot dead by British paratroopers during a civil rights march in Londonderry.

6 The 77-year-old Marie Watson died of her injuries eleven days after the attack (April 2002).

7 Colin Basham, "On This Day." Online. Available HTTP: http://news.bbc.co.uk/onthisday/hi/witness/march/13/newsid_2840000/2840773.stm (accessed December 9, 2010).

8 Some of her criticisms are now dated following 9/11 and the resulting increased interest and investment in covering foreign news.

9 See, for instance, Adam Mynott's report for the BBC's *10 O'Clock News*, November 26, 2004, on the fighting between the LRA and the Ugandan government troops. Over pictures of soldiers in the bush, Mynott explained that this is a long-running war with no front line: "It's been described as Africa's forgotten conflict."

10 See, for example, front-page headlines in *The Scotsman*: "Sudan: The Forgotten Genocide," May 21, 2004; "Crisis in Sudan: Every Refugee Child under Five Faces Death Unless UN Acts," June 10, 2004; "Sudan: No Escape from Bloodlust," June 17, 2004; "New Atrocities in Sudan as UN Deadline Looms," August 24, 2004; and

"UN's Shame over Sudan," September 18, 2004. See also "The Tragedy of Sudan," in *Time*, October 4, 2004, pp. 44–58, including the photographic essay by James Nachtwey; and "The New Killing Fields," a BBC 1 *Panorama* report by Hilary Anderson, November 21, 2004.

11 See also the *Tyndall Report* for detailed monitoring statistics. Online. Available http://www.tyndallreport.com/yearinreview.php3.

12 See "Africa's Great War," *Economist*, July 6, 2002, pp. 55–8.

13 There are exceptions, such as Clayton (2006).

14 See, for example, PBS *Online Newshour*, "Africa's Forgotten War: The Deadly Border Conflict between Ethiopia and Eritrea," April 19, 2000; *Online BBC News*, "Africa's Forgotten War," Mark Doyle reports from the West African state of Congo-Brazzaville, November 14, 1999; UN Office for the Coordination of Humanitarian Affairs, *Irin News.Org* (Integrated Regional Information Networks) "Liberia Is Africa's forgotten war," June 12, 2003. See also reference to Adam Mynott's LRA in Northern Uganda in note 9 above.

15 See UN Office for the Coordination of Humanitarian Affairs, *Irin News.Org*, "LIBERIA: 30,000 Displaced People Living in a Stadium," June 12, 2003.

16 See World Bank data and statistics, http://www.worldbank.org/data/ (accessed December 13, 2010).

17 For an effective demonstration of these connections, see Northcott (1999: chs 1, 4 and 5). For a discussion of the vast inequalities between rich individuals and poor nations, see Hicks (2000: esp. Parts One and Three). See also Hollenbach, S.J. (2002: esp. ch. 7, "Poverty, Justice and the Good of the City").

18 *New Internationalist*, 340, November 2001, p. 19. They were assuming annual deaths were evenly spread.

19 Bisi Ogunbadejo, 'Watching Developments', *West Africa*, September 24–30, 2001, p. 10.

20 See, for example, the moving tributes to the six broadcast-maintenance engineers who were working for New York area television stations on the top floors of Tower One of the World Trade Center, in Gilbert *et al.* (2002: 253–62).

20 Religious literacy and public service broadcasting

Introducing a research agenda

Elaine Graham

The "post-secular" condition

Despite the predictions of secularization theorists, a distinguishing feature of Western societies such as the UK in the twenty-first century is that religion has not disappeared from the public sphere. Yet this is a paradoxical situation. On the one hand, many faith-based organizations are experiencing a heightened public prominence as partners with government in the delivery of welfare and other public services (Dinham *et al.* 2009), and interest in personal spirituality beyond creedal and institutional expressions of religion continues to be strong. On the other hand, however, levels of formal institutional affiliation and membership in mainstream denominations continue to decline; and public skepticism towards religion is increasing (Voas and Ling 2010). This seemingly paradoxical co-existence of the religious and the secular takes us into unprecedented territory, sociologically and theologically, and is giving rise to talk of the emergence of a "post-secular" society (Keenan 2002; Bretherton 2010: 10–16).

Post-secular society represents a challenge to the conventions of modern Western liberalism, which grants access to religious actors in the public realm only on the most conditional of terms (Habermas 2006). Yet the new prominence of religion means that public discourse and public space become more differentiated but potentially more polarized, with a small but increasingly well-mobilized religious minority operating alongside a majority of disaffiliated non-believers who may have little or no first-hand understanding of religious belief or practice. This raises the question of how far public authorities, indeed the population at large, should be expected to be familiar with the concepts, knowledge, and vocabulary by which to talk about religion or to empathize with those of faith. Whilst some sections of that majority may hold a strongly secularist position, arguing that religion should claim no legitimate place in public discourse, others may argue that pragmatically speaking it is necessary to reach a degree of accommodation with faith-based perspectives. The terminology of "religious literacy" has been adopted as one response.

Talk of "religious literacy" originates in state or public education, where it is considered one of the objectives of religious education in schools (Carr 2007). In the UK, a daily act of collective worship and some form of religious instruction have been required by law since 1944; but as British society has become more diverse religiously and culturally, such provision is less about the observance of a shared Christian heritage and more about negotiating the pluralism of religious beliefs and practices in a multi-cultural society. More broadly, however, the new public visibility of religion has extended the use of the term "religious" or "faith" literacy to apply to the training of government and public services personnel. Recent changes to equal opportunities legislation in the United Kingdom have proved something of a catalyst. The Employment Equality (Religion or Belief) Regulations of 2003 and the Equality Act of 2006 represent the extension of basic protection against discrimination to questions of "religion and belief." Since employers and service providers are now required to be more aware of religious factors affecting employees and clients, there has naturally been a greater sensitivity towards matters of faith in relation to everyday practice and the law.

The body responsible under equal opportunities legislation, the Equality and Human Rights Commission (EHRC), has identified that the addition of "religion" to its other equality streams—gender, race, disability, and sexual orientation—is potentially problematic in terms of definition and impact. As its recent report argues, "religion" cannot be reduced to one single marker of identity, such as "belief," and may (or may not) map on to other variables such as ethnicity. Religion, it concludes, "is not a 'thing' with uniform characteristics, but a collective term for a diverse range of beliefs, practices and institutions" (Woodhead and Catto 2009), which could make identification of grounds for discrimination quite complex.

The implicit question within the report, however, is whether discrimination might derive as much from sins of omission as of commission—in other words, by ignorance of another's religious beliefs or practices. The Report recorded that the EHRC had indeed received complaints from religious organizations "of 'cultural' discrimination, including prejudice, misunderstanding, indifference or ignorance about religion" (ibid.: 15). Whilst incidents of religious beliefs and believers "being misunderstood, denigrated, ignored, trivialised, distorted or ridiculed, including by the media, in education, and in public discourse" (ibid.), do not amount to direct discrimination in terms of the tangible withholding or misdirection of physical goods and services, they do expose the tension between liberal principles of freedom of expression—including the right to challenge the beliefs and actions of others—and respect for cultural difference, including religious practices and identities. It is perhaps not surprising, therefore, that the Report goes on to identify religious literacy training as one component of a strategy to improve relations between those of different faiths and none. It therefore suggests that curricula in Religious Education (RE) might be revised, to emphasize "belief" as a generic quality inherent in everyone, and that RE might be directed towards learning skills of critical exploration into a range of beliefs and values rather than "about" religious "others."[1] It concludes:

> The issue of how religious–religious and religious–secular learning takes place was recognised to be key, but multi-faceted. It involves not only

schooling but further and higher education, the media, cultural representation, local initiatives, research on religion and religious representation.

(Woodhead and Catto 2009: 28)

But what is religious or "faith" literacy? And how is it communicated, learned, or taught? What are its essential features, and its potential benefits—and for whom? Is it perceived as favoring the Religious Studies graduate, seeking a competitive edge in the job market as religious literacy consultant (Burke 2005)? Or government, in terms of enhanced information-gathering and intelligence, in pursuit of "preventing violent extremism" (Department of Communities and Local Government 2007)? Or welfare service-users from black and ethnic minority groups, in terms of improved and targeted provision? Or society at large, pursuing greater "social cohesion" rather than the fragmentation into parallel communities divided by ethnic, cultural, and religious barriers (Cantle 2001)?

Religious literacy and the media

As the EHRC Report suggests, however, if the promotion of religious literacy is entering the consciousness of public institutions and service providers, it may be that media and popular culture are as influential as more formal sectors such as education. Such a suggestion is reinforced by trends in contemporary scholarship in religion, media, and culture which argue that popular culture and media perform an increasingly influential role in articulating and constructing people's perceptions and orientations to the sacred.

Stig Hjarvard argues that as formal religious affiliation declines, the media assume greater prominence as conduits of religious ideas (Hjarvard 2008a). This he terms the "mediatization" of religion, meaning that media become increasingly more powerful sources of representations, understandings, and experiences of faith for many consumers of media. This has its post-secular manifestations as well:

> Studying the ways religion interconnects with the media provides evidence of tendencies of secularization and of re-sacralization, and it may be possible that both tendencies are at work at the same time—although in different areas and aspects of the interface between religion and media.
>
> (Hjarvard 2008a: 10)

So a core research question emerges: if consumption of various forms of electronic media constitutes an increasingly influential source of experiences, attitudes, and understandings of religion, what role might the media play in relation to debates about "religious literacy" in the West? I would argue that such research would have a currency in terms of addressing the complexities of "post-secular" social policy as well as connecting powerfully with existing scholarship in media, culture, and religion. It does this in a number of respects:

first, it locates the media not just as powerful sources of information but as increasingly influential in constructing and defining the very categories of "religion" and "the religious." Second, it focuses not only on producers but also on consumers of media as environments we inhabit in everyday life. Third, it attends both to formal, institutional religious beliefs and practices and also to other forms of ritualized and sacred spaces and environments—physical, imagined, or virtual—in which people's exploration of religious and spiritual dimensions of identity, meaning, and action may take place.

Parallels and organizing categories

To begin, such a research proposal would need a critical hermeneutics of suspicion towards the very terminology of "religious literacy" itself. What are the underlying values beneath its promotion? Here, a range of research examining the wider political implications of the co-option of faith-based organizations across a range of public policy might offer insightful parallels. In their redeployment as partners with government, religious groups are regarded as rich sources of social capital, exemplars of exactly the kind of localism and accessibility beloved of policy-makers. The first decade of the twenty-first century has seen a proliferation of initiatives and agencies in the UK which cast faith-based organizations as central to the formation of healthy civil society (Dinham *et al.* 2009). Yet much of this is critical of what it sees as the political co-option of faith-based organizations into being implicated in government-led agendas of social cohesion or the market without any possibility for independence (Commission on Urban Life and Faith 2006; Furbey 2009). Others, speaking from a more theological position, maintain that the Church colludes with the false logic of secularism if it allows itself to be reduced simply to just another arm of local civil society (Bretherton 2010).

So, in many respects, the same questions have already been and continue to be asked of the role of "faith" in relation to wider social and governmental objectives as might be asked of religious literacy: how is "religion" constructed in relation to wider social goods? Who is perceived to benefit; is the ultimate end one of improving the quality of life of local citizens, or of pursuing a government-driven agenda of social cohesion and social control? Of co-opting "good" religion as a means of inoculating marginalized communities against imagined threats of "bad" religion? Just as faith-based actors have learned to identify such critical questions in relation to programs of partnership in service delivery, urban regeneration, community development, and so on, therefore, so too might we ask questions about the nature of religious literacy, and the kinds of social and political ends it is construed as serving.

Additionally, it might also help to construct some kind of organizing typology around the promotion of religious literacy, reflecting its multi-dimensional and contested nature, the better to understand the various aims and ends to which it is directed. I shall experiment here with three tentative paradigms of "religious literacy." First, in some contexts it is understood as a project defined by a paradigm of individual choice, in which the imparting of *information* is privileged and in which knowledge of religious and cultural diversity is directed towards compliance with equal opportunities legislation. It is informed by a "general liberal agnosticism concerning any and all broad normative perspectives" (Carr 2007: 660), which precludes any assertion of value-judgments concerning truth-claims. The danger is that religion is reduced to a series of facts— dates of religious holidays for public institutions, for example—that are devoid of any attempt to find shared grounds for dialogue or mutual critique. Religion is objectified as exotic—something other people engage in—leaving the impression that "religious beliefs and experiences are mostly separate from other aspects of human life and conduct" (ibid.: 662).

Second, there is a strand of religious literacy which operates more within a confessional environment, such as a faith school. Such a paradigm is oriented towards the building of religious *character* and identity: a process of *formation*, enabling an individual member of a faith-community to understand and inhabit their own tradition more fluently. We may see at work here the influence of the "linguistic turn" in which truth-claims of religious, moral, or philosophical propositions can only be judged as "shorthand affirmations of local culture-sustaining customs and practices" (ibid.: 663). Religious literacy, according to this model, is as much performative or experiential as it is cognitive. The difference between a culture of information—of individual learning *about*—and a culture of formation—of learning *within* a collective community of character— reflects a conviction

> that our moral and spiritual values are matters less of personal choice than cultural inheritance. On this view, we enter the world not as existentially free choosers of our individual and social destinies, but as members or citizens of pre-existing associations or institutions.
>
> (Carr 2007: 665)

Religious teachings and traditions are regarded as "action-guiding world-views" in the pursuit of character formation and the elaboration of narratives of truth and obligation as forms of practical reason. Such claims are best acquired, however, by means of immersion in the very practices and traditions of the community in question, and assume that all participants are located in a particular world-view, religious or otherwise.

A third paradigm reflects the impact of Stephen Prothero's call for programs of religious literacy in public schools as a tool of "empowered citizenship" (Prothero 2007). Given the historic separation of Church and State in the US, Prothero's intervention in the debate is a controversial one, but he is concerned with the promotion of empathy towards the "lived experience" of many kinds of faith, within an overall context of the *cultivation* of the skills of civic responsibility. Yet arguably it offers a better fit with the contemporary combination of a liberal sensibility towards freedom of speech and expression alongside a post-secular resistance to the logic of modernity that simply brackets out religion and spirituality from public reason. It argues instead that an informed acknowledgment of the religious dimensions to culture—in all their diversity and ambivalence—is a necessary and desirable part of citizenship.

It represents a commitment that "some broad acquaintance with the great religious narratives of humankind ... is an educational *sine qua non*" (Carr 2007: 668), although there will be differences of opinion regarding the normative and binding nature of any religious narrative or tradition. This kind of model of religious literacy seeks to move beyond information, beyond even the community of character formation, into a more dialogical and risky space. Religious literacy in the context of citizenship requires a willingness to move from description to evaluation, and to acknowledge our own subjectivity within the process of acquiring or sharpening our own religious literacy. It may also require a greater imagination towards the "otherness" of religion—that it cannot be reduced to moral axioms, or to history, or that religious truth-claims are not best judged according to propositional or scientific criteria.[2] Yet, paradoxically, it seeks to reclaim some of the very normality of religion: its everyday embeddedness in the practices of everyday life, as well as in the broader currents of history and society.

Religious literacy and the media

I have already pointed to the importance of work which emphasizes the prominence of media and media consumption in constructing people's everyday worlds, including their religious and spiritual beliefs, identities and practices (Graham 2007; Hjarvard 2008a; Lynch 2006). Such scholarship argues convincingly, however, that media serve not so much to report or depict religion as *a priori* but to construct our very understandings of the nature of "religion" itself. Hjarvard argues that the media are now in the service of audiences and commercial interests:

> the media increasingly organize public and private communication in ways that are adjusted to the individual medium's logic and market considerations. Other institutions are still represented in the media, but their function becomes progressively more that of providers of raw material, which the media then use and transform for the purpose of the media themselves. The liturgy and iconography of the institutionalized religions become a stockpile of props for the staging of media narratives.
>
> (Hjarvard 2008a: 17–18)

This has serious consequences for religious bodies. As secularization detaches them from first-hand exposure to the general public, they are required to engage with the media as a surrogate or vicarious agent to ensure the maintenance of a public profile. Yet the very same logic of secularization that makes them dependent on the media requires them to conform to the logic of the media:

> Presence in the sphere of public discourse is a socio-political currency now controlled by the contemporary guarantors of the public sphere: the media ... Public religion finds itself desperately needing presence in the public sphere, yet it must surrender control over its own construction, its own subjectivity, in order to have access here.
>
> (Hoover and Venturelli 1996: 261)

Does this imply that media can no longer be harnessed to the ends of other social institutions; that they now drown out other alternative providers of "information, tradition and moral orientation" (Hjarvard 2008a: 13) such as religion, family, or education? Part of Hjarvard's thesis is that media are now detached from roots in wider social contexts and construct their own systems of meaning, identity, and practice rather than contributing to an autonomous life-world of politics, religion, or culture. Such an analysis challenges any conception of the role of media in promoting religious literacy as that of mere neutral service provider.

So, what kind of research project might this be? I would envisage it to contain both theoretical and empirical components. For example, we might want to explore further how, historically, various parts of the media industry have understood their role in relation to religion. If Hjarvard is correct, and the "mediatization" of religion has become more acute and problematic as commercial and deregulated media have displaced traditional institutions of broadcasting, then it may be particularly instructive to trace the history of a public service broadcasting organization such as the British Broadcasting Corporation to ascertain how it understood its mission to "inform, educate and entertain" the nation (Briggs 1993; Wolfe 1984; Crisell 2006).

Public service broadcasting has traditionally taken such a broader, non-commercial task as one of its priorities, not least in relation to religious broadcasting, supported by protocols regarding advisory bodies and so on (Leigh 1992).[3] We might therefore ask how such a tradition ought to be extended to embrace some sort of religious literacy, and whether it could be compatible with other pressures—economic, political, and commercial—on contemporary media industries?

But if that asks questions of the producers of media, then clearly such a project would have much to do with the consumers of various forms of factual and entertainment media. This is consistent with contemporary moves in the study of religion, media, and culture towards emphasizing the "vernacular" as well as official dimensions of religion, not to mention the shift from "broadcast" to "interactive" forms of new media in everyday life.

There is much about "religious literacy" as a social program that is easily instrumentalized. We may warm to the sentiment that more information about a subject can never do us harm; or, as Miroslav Volf puts it, writing in the shadow of 9/11—and responding, in part, to that very liberal secularist call for a continued separation of the religious from the public—we need more religion, not less, since education in our own value-stance and those of others will breed tolerance rather than division (Volf 2002). This may be too simplistic (and over-rationalistic), however, since, as my first model of religious literacy indicated, knowledge may engender facts but little understanding. Furthermore, we are still left with the procedural dilemma of how to construct the rules of engagement around faith and public reason, secular or post-secular (Dinham *et al.* 2009).

Current debates about religious literacy may place too much emphasis on the formal sectors of religious education or equal opportunities training, at the expense of considerations of our everyday exposure to a range of different media—albeit with their own commercial, political, or ideological agendas. For that reason, any further research into the promotion of religious literacy needs to consider how the everyday life-world of electronic media may serve to shape us as actors, consumers, and citizens in a world where the tensions and interactions between sacred and secular are more lively and potent than ever.

Notes

1 A recent report on Religious Education in state (community) schools in England and Wales, similarly, concludes that pupils of faith are often precluded from owning their own commitments because teaching about religion in schools frequently stresses facts and moral principles at the expense of lived experience (OFSTED 2010).

2 Cf. Karen Armstrong's discussion of the failure of contemporary debates in science and religion to differentiate between "mythos" and "logos" as distinct types of discourse (Armstrong 2009: 2–4).

3 The shift from an exclusively Christian emphasis to an understanding of religious broadcasting in a more pluralistic society is reflected in the changes in the self-understanding of the Central Religious Advisory Committee for the BBC (now the Standing Conference on Religion and Belief) during the 1960s and 1970s—see Leigh 1992: 290.

21 Everyday faith in and beyond scandalized religion

Tom Beaudoin

Catholic scandal, changing practice

I write about the significance of religion in everyday life from the vantage of having participated in Roman Catholicism, which, it must be frankly admitted, has made itself a secretive and abusive church,[1] built on "homosocial" (Sedgwick 1985) power: men governing men and excluding women; men in a culture of homoerotic images too often and too loudly denying genuine life beyond heterosexuality; and willing to go to great lengths to protect male narcissism (cf. Jordan 2000). How, then, could one study everyday life in relation to such religion without accounting for the everyday ethical habitat of the tradition and institution that is ingredient to speaking in the first place?

The physical-spiritual violence toward thousands and thousands of young souls in the past several decades calls fundamentally into question the content and purpose of thinking for and with Catholicism. As theologian Stephen Pattison has argued, the "long-overdue 'discovery' of child abuse must be to Western theologians what the challenge of the poor has been to colleagues in South America—an imperative to a fundamental re-visioning of theology" (Pattison 2007b: 166). Sexual abuse of minors is the awful lodestar for all future North American Catholic theology. My professional "right" to speak theologically of lived religion is bound up with this responsibility because it goes to the potential decadence and inbuilt violence in my theological subjectivity (cf. Butler 2005). It should bear on what one thinks religion research is for. There is an ethical habitation of the researcher of everyday sacrality that has to do with accounting for the practices of self and sacred that make up the subjectivity and knowledge landscape of the researcher (Beaudoin 2007).

In the case of the theologian, that subjectivity is typically explicitly linked to the faith and practice of the religious community. Given that constitutive relationship to the community, no North American theologian can fail to notice Catholics in the context of scandal continuing to redefine their Catholic practice away from normative Catholicism.

While there may be some disagreement on exact figures, the major trends of research[2] are increasingly established: a long-term decline in "vocations" to the ordained priesthood and to religious life; a steady decrease in official sacramental life (meaning fewer marriages, baptisms, confessions, funerals); increasingly common marriage of Catholics to non-Catholics; diminished recourse to annulments when Catholics divorce; a falling off of mass attendance; rising numbers of Catholics, even majorities, who report views counter to official teaching, saying women can be ordained (to the diaconate and to the priesthood), that homosexuality is acceptable, that conscience is the most important arbiter in moral decision-making, and that people from other Christian traditions and even other religions—or none at all—may be saved; an erosion of trust and investment of personal resources in the institutional church and its future; a decline in felt "Catholic guilt" and a "sense of sin"; and that students who go through Catholic schools are likely to disagree with what is taken to be normative Catholicism today.

Theologically informed accounts of practice

How do studies of religion in everyday life treat this shifting "secular" space? In the United States, at least three overlapping scholarly discourses speak authoritatively on everyday Christian practice: practical and pastoral theologies, sociology of religion, and works that occupy a middle ground of theologically informed social science or social-scientifically informed theology. All these are in principle close to everyday life in church and society, wanting to interpret and direct it.[3]

This is a fairly diverse set of texts. What joins them are two qualities: first, their research focus—religion, faith, and spirituality as ordinary, everyday, and lived; second, their effectiveness. All of these texts and authors are having a substantial impact on the North American religious practice scene, especially through religious and academic institutions (influencing new catechisms, ministry handbooks, grant awards, publishing decisions, and pastoral plans and programs at the national, regional, and local levels). To be sure, there are limits to this influence, and it is easy to imagine that a strong majority of spiritual practitioners in North America know nothing of this literature. But even those practitioners have to live in a society, and in relation to religious and academic institutions, that propagate these research orientations. But my argument for theological salience is not only from influence; it is from use of resources: is this what we as researchers really want to be doing with our finite resources and influence? It is thus a question of ethics, about what we are doing to ourselves and each other when we denominate the everyday religiously, and is thus a spiritual-political question of responsibility for the scholar of lived religion. Research effectiveness is of interest to practical theology because practical theologians have a self-conscious commitment to informing, forming, and at the limit transforming practice,[4] and therefore have an interest in theories and practices of change in theologically significant situations. The study of lived religion in contemporary culture matters ethically because studies of ordinary practice end up with spiritual-political effects in the United States.

Yet practical and pastoral theologians who are charged with a concern for the ordinary continue to struggle to render it sufficiently, if their under-attention to critical-historical and cultural studies of religion in general and Christianity in particular is any indication. Ecclesially interested social-scientific studies, by contrast, have typically under-theorized the theological presuppositions and character of the categories that drive their research. This discursive situation sets the stage for a hidden normativity that in the United States context is frequently concerned with the maintenance or recuperation of religious identity. One fundamental theological challenge, then, is to find a way of registering the ordinary between the pastoral/practical and social-scientific in a way that is theologically incisive for our time. In the United States, social scientists, religion scholars, and theologians need a completely new working relationship.

What Christianity contributes normatively

What might theologians find if they spoke from such an intersection of social science, religion, and theological study, while being challenged by the deep redefinition of Catholic practice, catalyzed by the reality of abuse and cover-up? Theologians can highlight Christianity's inventive power for both making and domesticating persons out of cultural materials. The theologian may focus on how Christianity orchestrates identities in an historical way, in its capacities for both courage and decadence opening space for our awareness of new habitations.

This requires treating Christianity not as pure discourse directly representing untainted revelation, but an ever-new site for historically mongrel, but always contested, forms of experience, an assemblage of cultural materials out of which come innumerable pathways offering to be taken up as "traditions" of Christianity, depending on the needs of the present of the rhetors for whom the appeal to a tradition is necessitated. Christianity in its origins is an unruly cultural assemblage of ancient philosophical schools, religions (especially Judaisms), and cultures, constantly rehearsed and refigured by ever-new placement in and as cultural practice. This is particularly important for making critical and contemporary sense of the classic sources of faith in the Bible and early Christianity. On this reading, it is not necessary in principle to choose between Christianity and another spiritual or religious way of life. To be a Christian, or for Christianity to have happened in one's life, is to also find oneself with possibilities outside Christianity, to be a person of other faiths, other cultures, other times, other practices. It is to be hypercontextual in the sense of doing and saying things that are twenty centuries' residue for the present moment, not all equal and never merely "available," of course.

Practical theology has often thought that its task is to defend a continuity of practice (of faith) as distinct from (but usually complementary to) a continuity of doctrine, to look at lived life (including ministerial life) as a contrast to a systematic presentation of the faith, or sometimes as an instantiation of such systematicity. But the more practical theology fights this rearguard action, the more its vision narrows and its analytical richness atrophies. It shares with systematic theology a resistance to mourning the lack of ownership over faith and an anxiety about the genuinely new, which is also an anxiety about the ordinary (often enough expressed by theologians as the vacuity or epiphenomenality of ordinary life). Instead, practical theology as a Christian theology from the North American present should privilege the ethics of theological work: practical theology should be that which studies the constitution of the praxis of faith, orchestrations of identity with respect to claiming power, praxes of significance for Christian faith and life, found in patterned actions that bear on relation to what Christians may name God. This study occurs through a critical account of theological knowledge, testing how theology can make critical and reflexive sense of practice in faith and culture. The practical theologian faces the contingency and vulnerability of historical practices, accounting for the ways that registering them as theologically significant (typically as "religious" or "spiritual," but also occasionally as "secular") makes the world into a particular kind of place to inhabit with creative responsiveness to life's given character.

The style of practical theology suggested here, then, is a pre-Christian practical theology. In its genealogical orientation it experiences theological thought's ethical exertion not primarily in justifying, warranting, applying, or interpreting theological claims, but on an interdisciplinary-historical suspension of theological claims to attention, in the interest of understanding how these claims on Christian attention have emerged, a therapy for allowing theology a more critical, self-aware, and freeing role in our lives; second, in its particular commitment to perforating the presumed essences of Christianity, it roots them especially in what is thought of as "secular," "pagan," or the "non-theological." Correlative to these points is a third: the priority of research on "indigenous" religions, philosophies, and cultures, from Greek and Roman antiquity to contemporary media culture—the focus remaining on the importance of situating Christianity's antecedent beliefs and practices, with reference to what we may be within the world now.

Theological conduct today

We ought to make our Christian and Christian-influenced surveys of everyday life, which are common and well funded in the United States, seem increasingly impossible to maintain. I urge North American scholars to ask: Is it ethical to analyze whether people are Christian in the ways that we have? I do not mean, is it ethical to get into people's "personal" lives, are the questions too invasive, or is there something improper about asking people questions about their faith or belief? I mean, is it ethical to give people the impression that this is what counts as Christianity? That this is what it is to be religious? In a media culture, by asking people about their religious beliefs and religious practices, scholars propagate not only data about religion, but a way of handling religion, a way of thinking about it, that is picked up by other scholars, students, journalists, government officials, the educated public. Scholars of practice in theology are still learning how to register two complex phenomena, the ordinary (as quotidian, everyday) and the spiritual (as sacred, religious), with the awareness to let them turn up outside the terms congenial to religious institutions, capitalist economies, and modern governments. Outside the terms of expected subjectivities. Why? From the viewpoint of Christian theology—a limited vantage point, no doubt, but also one that can help make and unmake the tangents of freedom and coordinates of constriction bound up with Christian power—it is no longer clear why we need to look to ahistorical, systematic, conscious, verbal, and proper specifications of Christian revelation as a way of talking about faith in everyday life.

How can theology manage this? Three recent developments in theology, namely deconversion, ordinary theology, and plural habitation, are promising interlocutors for the ethical task specified in this chapter.

The emerging *deconversion* literature has meant to register the varieties of faith practice in the secularizing contexts of Europe and the United States. By stressing the study of deconversion, the research of these scholars (including practical theologian Heinz Streib) makes two theological moves. First, it highlights the traditional "bias" of theological study of faith praxis toward conversion to Christianity and adherence to the religious tradition in question (Streib *et al.* 2009: 18–31). This bias has had the effect of making progress in faith toward an institutionally (sometimes rendered as "biblically") defined goal of orthodoxy or orthopraxis the theologian's own mission and criterion for evaluating situations from a Christian perspective. Of equal importance, the deconversion perspective emphasizes, is the process by which a particular faith praxis is left behind or transcended, so the theological topic becomes not only the complex dynamics of entering and joining, but that of leaving and disassociating, with every "conversion-to" also a "deconversion-from." Second, this focus for practical theology is a way of appreciating the decisions people make in contemporary culture to disaffiliate from traditions, to remain "partially" in traditions, or even to inhabit multiple traditions multiply. Deconversion as a concept makes room for multiple "trajectories" in dispensing with a faith identity or praxis. It has room for those who move from one religion, denomination, or praxis of faith to another as an expression of what they take to be a deeper faith (which is more traditionally the realm of conversion discourse), although it retains its interest in the practices involved in people "moving out" as much as in how they "move in." It is able to appreciate a palette of forms of leaving a faith (ibid.: 93–112). In this way, it tries to calibrate what Charles Taylor names the proliferation of ways of finding "fullness" in our secular age (Taylor 2007: 5ff.). This research on "deconversion" is relatively new, and has yet to make an impact on the U.S. practical theology scene, but would be a welcome intervention that could assist Catholic practical theologians in thinking about the dynamics of secular Catholicism. The deconversion literature, by taking seriously the emplacement of faith practices in contemporary social practices, holds much more lightly than most practical theology a need to understand transformation as a liberation for a kind of already-comprehended ecclesial existence. The theological rhetoric of promoting Christianity, which one finds in most North American practical theology (Moore 2004: 169–95), seems muted or even absent from this research, a characteristic of strategic significance for this era of Catholicism.

In a complementary way, a proposal for the existence and study of *ordinary theology* has been made by practical theologian Jeff Astley. He ties his study to the renaissance of practical theology in the last generation, and argues that there are grounds for finding substantial theology not only among the credentialed in academic and ecclesial life, but also among the overwhelming majority who are the uncredentialed in pastoral life, those "ordinary Christians" who have a way of expressing themselves that so often seems to provoke evaluation and correction by the cultured theological educator (whether pastoral worker or academic). Astley (2002: 1) argues that this ordinary theology can be found in how people talk and act regarding matters both ordinary and extraordinary, insofar as that talk or action goes to what he calls "living theologically in response to our learning of Christ." Astley has chosen an evocative phrase in which to anchor his study, but this phrase is not unpacked. It seems to contain many meanings: "learning of Christ" as the catechetical or instructional study of Christ (that is, the power of learning "about" or studying Christ); "learning of Christ" as a first encounter, initiation, or introduction to Christ (that is, the power of initial exposure to Christ); Christ's education as known by us (that is, the learning that Christ himself underwent and how that positions how we experience him); or our learning "as such" that is "of Christ" (that is, the education Christians get that is in some sense christic, whether or not it is explicitly about christology). I highlight the many possibilities of this evocative phrase because for Astley ordinary theology is just such a rambunctious (but not random) collection of attitudes toward Christ that are carried by lay Christians. Ordinary theology is a kind of theology that expresses "how faith comes and goes" and should sensitize practical theologians to its existence and contours. This requires two substantial changes of theological perception on the part of academic theologians: first, academic theology must learn to value ordinary Christian faith as relativistic, tied to personal, emotional events and stories, and expressing the ways people have learned of holding life together; second, he suggests that academic theologians do not stop being "ordinary" theologians as academics (ibid.: 45–95, 123–62). The qualities he finds in ordinary theology, he finds as well in academic theologizing, suggesting that academic theology is a way of doing ordinary theology in a more professionally appropriate register, but in which the "ordinariness" of the life of the theologian still structures their discourse.

A third model for rethinking ordinary sacred/spiritual identities comes from the theology of religions and interreligious dialogue. One development in the first decade of the twenty-first century there has been the notion of plural habitation, whether known as "multiple religious belonging," "double belonging," or by similar titles. Multiple belonging is a way of describing how ordinary religious practice works in various contemporary societies such as India,

Sri Lanka, or Japan, and is also a position advocated for Westerners by some scholars (Cornille 2002; Knitter 2009). This literature has not yet been crossed substantially with research on what have been called secular spiritualities, like sports, new age, Alcoholics Anonymous, popular music, and much more (Van Ness 1996; Lynch 2007a). Consistent with the ethical position developed in this chapter would be the effort to bring together cultural studies of secular spiritualities with theologies of religions, and to search after how many contemporary people are already multiply religious in ordinary practice insofar as they engage in cultural practice with reference to claiming power in heterogeneous sites: temple and club, music fan culture and church, sport and mosque. Multiple belonging may prove a gateway to secularity being a legitimate belonging place. This discourse of multiple belonging may be the way theology slowly opens to reality while holding on to its recent past. Continued research into ordinary sacrality will open up these categories as to what sorts of multiplicity count as spiritual belonging.

In all three of these approaches, the theologian risks decadence without their work bearing the weight[5] of the scandalous abuse of persons and power, and concomitant redefinitions of religious practice referenced earlier in this chapter. Insofar as deconversion, ordinary theology, and multiple belonging open theological subjectivity (and contemporary "spirituality") to the contingency and responsibility of the making–unmaking of identity to which religious tradition bears witness, theology can live in the present with sufficient hope and criticality.

In the study of lived religion, the ethical task of a theologian working from a spiritually and politically influential tradition like Catholicism, in a land of religious faith and scandal such as the United States, will be increasingly clear: to be the agent of dispossession. By dispossession, I mean what theology and the life it encourages must hand over to retain its hope, to aid legitimate, beautiful, and courageous strangeness. The theologian brings together cultural, social-scientific, and historical studies of religion with practical theologies, for the sake of showing how there are new spaces for lived religion allowed by how people are already living, and by how the tradition itself has gotten put together, in aid of the strengths toward which persons and communities already tend in their operative spiritualities, religious or secular.

Notes

1 The psychologist Mary Gail Frawley-O'Dea, in her study of the psychological causes of the Catholic sex abuse scandal, argues, based on the limits of church reporting about abuse, and various kinds of underreporting on the part of victims, that the approximately 11,000 victims reported by the John Jay College of Criminal Justice study represent only a portion of probable victims between 1950 and 2002, and that it is "reasonable to estimate that over fifty thousand young people were abused by priests over the fifty years encompassed by the [John Jay] study" (Frawley-O'Dea 2007: 6). Among many other works on this topic, see also Frawley-O'Dea and Goldner (2007), Hidalgo (2007), Bruni and Burkett (2002), France (2004), Sipe (1995), and Berry (2000).

2 Such studies include Froehle and Gautier (2000), Dinges *et al.* (2001), Smith with Denton (2005), D'Antonio *et al.* (2007), Baggett (2009), and Pew Forum on Religion and Public Life (2008).

3 Practical theologians typically study theology in ordinary life, whether as livable doctrines (Charry 1997), as distinctive and traditional ordinary practices that realize Christian goods today (Bass 2010), as transformative inventions of a gendered habitus in relation to the other (Graham 2002), or as practical reasoning in faith (Browning 1991), to name a few approaches. The labor of practical theology, in the words of Ruard Ganzevoort, is "tracing the sacred" in contemporary life (Ganzevoort 2009). Recent works, too, in sociology of religion that are theologically informed provide a counterpart for practical theology. I am thinking here of the many works on generational differences in Catholic identity (for example Dinges *et al.* 2001), or of the influential output of the recent National Study of Youth and Religion in the United States, which has produced already several books (www.youthandreligion.org, accessed December 9, 2010). There are also a number of recent works somewhere between practical theology and sociology of ordinary life, extending from studies like Freitas (2008), a quantitative and qualitative study of the "hookup culture" on American college campuses, to handbooks for youth ministers in academic and pastoral contexts like Dean (2010), with contributions by several practical theologians aligning theological with sociological findings on young people.

4 Many practical theologians argue this position, most influentially Don Browning, Elaine Graham, and Richard Osmer.

5 Cf. the theology of Ignacio Ellacuria in Michael Lee's (2008) excellent study.

22 Public media and the sacred

A critical perspective

Gordon Lynch

One of the major projects for sociologists of religion in the West in recent decades has been the attempt to study forms of meaning and value beyond traditional forms of institutional religion (see, e.g., Luckmann 1967). As increasing numbers of people in many Western societies no longer identify with or participate in traditional religious beliefs and activities, so sources of meaning and value beyond traditional forms of religion have begun to attract greater scholarly attention.

This chapter forms part of an on-going attempt to contribute to this broader project of thinking about sources of meaning and value in contemporary culture through a renewed focus on the concept of the sacred. The concept of the "sacred" has gone through difficult times recently in the study of religion, with many scholars cautious about using it because of its association with a tradition of religious studies influenced by the work of Mircea Eliade. Eliade (1959) understood the sacred as an ontological reality which finds expression through different kinds of religious structure across human cultures (e.g. myth, ritual, sacred time and space). This notion has, however, been criticized particularly by scholars influenced by post-structuralism, who are skeptical about any claims to be able to identify ahistorical, universal essences in social life (e.g. McCutcheon 2003). Eliade's understanding of the sacred looks to many contemporary scholars more like an attempt to interpret different cultures through a particular theological lens than a genuinely useful tool for social and cultural analysis.

The approach to the sacred taken in this chapter represents a different intellectual tradition to the ontological theories of the sacred offered by scholars such as Eliade. Rather than seeing the sacred as an ontological reality in the structure of the cosmos or the essence of human being, the approach taken here adopts a *cultural sociological* perspective. Here, the sacred is seen as a particular kind of cultural structure whose precise form and content vary significantly across different historical contents. This cultural sociological approach emerged initially from Emile Durkheim's (1912) theory of the sacred in his seminal book *The Elementary Forms of the Religious Life*, but has been subsequently developed by sociologists such as Edward Shils (1975), Robert Bellah (1967) and, most recently and most extensively, Jeffrey Alexander (1988a, 1988b, 2003).

Drawing on this cultural sociological tradition, I will begin here by defining the sacred as a *communicative structure, common across human societies, which orientates people towards absolute realities that have a normative claim upon the conduct of social life, around which collective forms of thought, feeling, action, and identity are formed.* Through this discussion I will also use the more specific term "sacred forms" to refer to *specific, contingent forms of the sacred made up of a constellation of particular symbols, a shared moral community, and forms of thinking, feeling, and acting specific to that sacred form.* I have provided a more detailed explanation of the conceptual roots of these definitions elsewhere (see Lynch forthcoming). But a couple of brief explanatory comments are necessary here.

First, when I refer to the sacred as a communicative structure that directs people towards absolute realities, I am not intending to take the same kind of ontological position as Eliade. Rather, I am suggesting that the sacred is a relatively universal phenomenon across human cultures because the very possibility of social life rests on the ability of people to engage in meaningful collective communication about fundamental normative realities in relation to which social life is structured (Rothenbuhler 1998). The absolute realities which sacred forms mediate are not necessarily realities in any profoundly ontological sense, but are rather taken to be realities by the individuals and groups for whom they are sacred. Furthermore, these are not realities in the sense of laws of nature, or physical facts of material existence, but moral realities that provide the framework in which people assume their lives should be lived. To illustrate this, we could observe, for example, the number of groups and movements since the eighteenth century for whom the idea of the "nation" has had a sacred significance. As Benedict Anderson (1991) has observed, however, the very idea of the "nation" is an imagined community, originally made possible in modern societies by new forms of print media such as the novel and the newspaper. Nations are not ultimate, ontological realities. But for those deeply moved by nationalist or patriotic sentiment, the nation is experienced as an absolute reality, for which it may be legitimate in particular circumstances to kill others and meaningful to sacrifice one's own life.

Second, whilst some pre-modern societies may have been organized more in relation to a single sacred form, modern societies tend to be characterized by the simultaneous presence of multiple forms of the sacred. By this I am not only referring to the different sacred forms associated with the plurality of religious traditions in modern society, but also thinking about the ways in which specific aspects of social and cultural life have acquired sacred significance, including the autonomous, expressive, and authentic self, democracy, gender, nature, human rights, the care of children, private property, and the free market. Each of these has come to be seen, in different contexts, as an absolute reality which lays moral claims on contemporary life. By referring to multiple forms of the sacred, I am not suggesting that society consists of a loose confederation of small tribes, each gathered around its own unique form of the sacred. The reality of modern social life is more complex than this. Instead individuals and groups live their lives under the simultaneous influence of multiple sacred forms which exert different fields of gravitational pull over their lives.

Having made these introductory observations by way of defining a cultural sociological approach to the sacred, we can turn to the central claim of this chapter: *public media are the primary institutional structure in modern societies through which people reproduce and contest sacred forms.*[1]

This claim requires some unpacking before we can begin to consider some of its ethical implications. First, as a communicative structure and process about absolute, normative realities, the sacred is always dependent on particular media through which people can draw together around common sacred symbols. In pre-modern Western societies, these media often, although not exclusively, took a religious form: icons, the body and blood of Christ on the altar, relics, or the working of a religious symbol into the flags behind which armies marched. This meant that conflict over the meaning and implications of particular sacred forms also took the form of conflicts over the content of religious media such as the use of space and objects on the altar or the decorative qualities of church interiors. In modern times, however, popular disengagement with traditional religious spaces and the rise of new forms of mass media have created a new set of cultural conditions for engaging with sacred forms. Rather than fighting over the stripping of the altars, contemporary conflicts over sacred forms are more likely to be fought over and through public media, including newspapers, books, television programs, interactive websites, and digital video and audio downloads, aided and abetted by the use of new social media.

Second, it is reasonable to claim that public media are the primary institutional structure through which people engage and contest sacred forms in contemporary society because of the extent to which these media are available across society, as well as the amount of time and resource people put into their use. As Nick Couldry (2002) has argued, public media have become one of the primary means through which society tells stories about itself, and at times this necessarily involves the representation of particular sacred forms. Furthermore, public media are the framework through which people encounter sacred forms that are enacted through other social institutions. The legal system, for example, plays an important role in the symbolic maintenance of particular sacred forms (e.g. human rights or the sacrality of the care of children). But most people will only encounter the restitution of the breach of these sacred forms in the legal system, for example in a trial concerning the abuse of a child, through the media coverage of that case. Public media are therefore the structure and space through which people in contemporary society most commonly encounter the representation of sacred forms. This is not to suggest that these representations necessarily inspire deep identification in their audiences. Indeed, Jeffrey Alexander and Jason Mast (2006) have argued that one of the marks of pluralist, modern society is that it becomes ever harder for performances of the sacred through public media not to be regarded with cynicism, if not outright opposition, by sections of the audience.

Third, as we noted above, emotions play an important part in people's engagement with sacred forms, in the sense both of the emotions evoked by deep identification with a sacred form as well as the emotions evoked by its pollution. This suggests that it is important to attend to the ways in which public media go beyond conveying factual information to encouraging particular forms of feeling in their audiences. As Mervi Pantti and Johanna Sumiala (2009) have argued, for example, media coverage of widely mourned deaths goes beyond conveying information to cueing particular kinds of shared emotional response in the audience. In such contexts, it may be as important for public figures to demonstrate their own emotion through the media—for example with a politician breaking down in tears at a press conference about the death of school-children—as it is for them simply to fulfill their official responsibilities. News media are arguably of particular importance in this regard. By offering stories about "real" events, news media have the potential to draw their audiences into direct experiences of the celebration or pollution of particular sacred forms. The fact that such stories are "real"—told in relation to people who are shown to be hopeful, brave, or suffering—gives their narrative representation of sacred forms particular emotional power.

Finally, by referring to sacred forms, public media draw the boundaries of acceptable moral community. In doing so, they give substance to our understanding of "society," establishing who can be considered a full or responsible citizen, or who indeed can be considered "humane" or "inhuman." On the day on which I am writing this chapter, newspapers in London are giving prominent coverage to the story of a young woman from a privileged background who participated in a group's homophobic assault on a gay man who was walking with his partner in Trafalgar Square, which later led to that man's death. Coverage of this story has emphasized the decency of the deceased man, as well as his grieving friends and family, and implies that it is particularly shocking that a well-educated young woman should have participated in such a bigoted attack. In this story, the boundaries of acceptable moral community are drawn firmly in ways that include the deceased and exclude his assailant. One of the things that is striking about this case is that these lines might not have been drawn so clearly in British media less than a century ago, in a social context in which to be openly gay was to court social exclusion. Although the sacred act of defining the boundaries of acceptable moral community appears to be a common feature of most human societies, the ways in which these boundaries are drawn are open to continual change and challenge (Alexander 2006; Eyerman 2008). Public media become a key structure through which these symbolic boundaries are drawn and contested (Alexander and Jacobs 1998; Jacobs 2000).

If public media are, then, a primary structure through which people reproduce and contest sacred forms, what are the ethical implications of this? Nick Couldry is right to critique the "myth of the mediated center," the assumption that public media provide direct access to the center of social reality (see Couldry, Chapter 18). Indeed the ability of public media successfully to frame stories about social life in terms of particular sacred forms rests largely on the assumption that such media provide direct and unadulterated access to important realities that have a moral claim on people's lives. But whilst we should be critically aware of the assumptions about public media that make these processes possible, it is difficult to imagine another social structure that could perform the role of making widely shared communication about sacred forms possible across modern societies. For now, public media are set to remain the most commonly used reference point for people's engagement with sacred forms. The question, then, is not so much what structure might replace public media in this role, but what kind of media practice is required if this role is to be performed in ways that encourage healthy democratic societies.

First, it is important that public media are not organized around a monolithic form of the sacred which is taken to be the authoritative reference point for the whole of social life. The history of the twentieth century demonstrates that sacred forms can be most damaging when a single sacred form is closely associated with social and political elites who use their power to impose identification with that form, or suppress anything that might challenge its dominance. This is seen most obviously in totalitarian political movements such as Nazism and Stalinism, where the sacred symbolism of these movements provided the grounds on which vast numbers of civilians were killed as threats or pollutants to that sacred order (Burleigh 2006). But even in democratic societies, particular sacred forms can become culturally dominant in highly damaging ways. In the Irish Republic, for example, the dominance of a sacred vision of the Irish Catholic nation, supported by religious and political elites, contributed to a cultural context in which Irish media kept stories of the widespread abuse and neglect of children in Catholic institutions out of public view for many decades. Instead of replicating a dominant, sacred form, public media should function as spaces in which a critical interplay between different sacred forms is possible. Through this process there is a better chance that different kinds of contemporary sacred commitment can be made accountable for their effects. This is a challenging aim, though, in a context in which contemporary media economies and technologies have encouraged the segmentation of public media along increasingly ideological lines (think, for example, of TV channels such as Fox News or MSNBC in the United States). In such a segmented context, it becomes easier for audiences to congregate around particular media outlets which uncritically circulate their particular sacred commitments, encouraging greater polarization between different sacred forms (or even competing interpretations of the same sacred form). Both media producers and audiences have an ethical responsibility to play in supporting more critical and nuanced media content.

Second, media producers have a responsibility in terms of the ways in which their stories draw strongly emotive, moral boundaries. As with the case of polarized media content appealing to particular sacred commitments, so there can be a strong commercial motivation for such emotive content. The attempt to hold large, popular audiences in the context of an increasingly competitive media market-place has encouraged the "tabloidization" of media (Conboy 2005), in which media content is increasingly focused on human interest stories with sensationalized content. The media construction of moral outrage in the context of stories about the breach or pollution of sacred forms therefore not only plays a symbolic role, but can have an underlying commercial imperative of attempting to engage and hold audience attention through highly emotive content. Strongly felt emotion—whether about someone's treasonable behavior towards one's country or their abuse of a child—is an inevitable part of the communicative structure of sacred forms. But the sustained evoking of such emotion to support commercial interests is problematic, encouraging the repeated performance of such emotion rather than critical reflection about the effects of such emotion or the symbolic boundaries on which such emotions rest. One case in point is the way in which Western Muslims have increasingly found themselves positioned in sensationalized tabloid content as being beyond the acceptable moral boundaries of society. A recent example of this was the controversy over the so-called "Ground Zero Mosque" encouraged by media outlets such as Fox News and the *New York Post*, who represented and circulated moral outrage in response to the suggestion that an Islamic religious center be allowed "within" the sacred space of Ground Zero. Such media content—which suggests that Muslims do not have a proper place within the moral and symbolic boundaries of society—clearly finds an audience that identifies with its powerful sentiments. But it also rests on simplistic characterizations of Islam, constructing symbolic boundaries in ways that are more likely to encourage prejudice and conflict, than the kind of understanding advocated by Elaine Graham (see Chapter 20).

Finally, media producers also face particular ethical challenges in balancing their notions of professional practice with the fact that this practice is deeply implicated with the sympathetic reproduction of sacred forms. This was recently demonstrated in Britain when the BBC decided in January 2009 not to broadcast a humanitarian appeal for those suffering during the intense conflict of Israel's military operation in Gaza. The rationale for this decision by the BBC's senior managers was that to broadcast such an appeal would undermine the BBC's claims to impartiality, which they regarded as a defining feature of its professional ethos. The decision drew a strong public response from a wide range of people who objected to the inhumanity of failing to support humanitarian efforts for the suffering civilian population of Gaza. This case demonstrated the bind in which media producers can find themselves, in relation to the mediation of sacred forms. On the one hand, BBC coverage of the Gaza conflict had given considerable attention to civilian suffering, including the traumatizing and killing of Gazan children, and in doing so evoked strong moral sentiments associated with the sacralization of the care of children. Yet, at the same time, senior managers in the BBC believed that to support the symbolic restitution of this sacred form by broadcasting a humanitarian appeal risked alienating part of its audience who sympathized with Israel's actions. As they were to discover, however, pulling back from the appeal did little to help the BBC's profile as a morally responsible, impartial broadcaster for another significant part of its audience, who objected strongly to this decision. The case of the BBC and the appeal for Gaza thus demonstrates the complexities of the representation of sacred forms in the work of public broadcasters who are trying to serve a broad social remit. Sacred forms provide the moral terrain onto which these broadcasters map their news coverage and social commentary. But at the same time, identification with sacred forms, and competing inter-pretations of sacred forms, can prove highly divisive (Lukes 1975). Given the importance of the communicative structures of the sacred it seems implausible to imagine that it would be possible, or even desirable, for such public broad-casters to pull back from the representation of any sacred forms at all. But what is needed is a greater reflexivity of the sacred role of public media amongst those working within the media industries, in which the complexities of the mediation of sacred forms can be openly discussed.

These ethical pleas for more nuanced and thoughtful media practice in relation to sacred forms may seem idealistic in the context of a media market-place that appears to reward those who offer their audiences the emotional satisfactions of uncritical identification with sacred stories. But they are already being addressed through public media itself. One of the striking features of the contemporary media landscape is that, as public media play an increasingly important role in shaping the ways in which people engage with many different aspects of social life (Hjarvard 2008a), so new media products which reflect critically on the content and role of public media are becoming more popular. In the United States, television shows such as *The Daily Show* and *The Colbert Report* (see Clark, Chapter 10) provide a critical analysis of the ways in which other media outlets construct the reality of social life in emotive and polarized terms. In Britain, there has also been a longer tradition of critical attention to the work-ings of media industries through the satirical current affairs magazine *Private Eye*. If public media provide many challenges in terms of how we live with sacred forms in modern societies, it may also provide us with resources for how we continue to think these through.

Notes

1 When using the term 'institution' in the context of this claim, I have in mind the definition used by Anthony Giddens (1984: 17) in his theory of structuration: "The most deeply embedded structural properties, implicated in the reproduction of soci-etal totalities, I call *structural principles*. Those practices which have the greatest time–space extension within such totalities can be referred to as *institutions*."

Bibliography

Adorno, T.W. (1976) *Introduction to the Sociology of Music*, trans. E.B. Ashby, New York: Seabury.

—— (1990) "On Popular Music," in S. Frith and A. Goodwin (eds.) *On Record: Rock, Pop, and the Written Word*, New York: Pantheon Books, pp. 301–14.

—— (1991) *The Culture Industry: Selected Essays on Mass Culture*, London: Routledge.

Ajami, F. (2001) "What the Muslim World Is Watching," *New York Times Magazine*, November 18, p. 48.

Akhtar, R.S. (2000) *Media, Religion and Politics in Pakistan*, Oxford: Oxford University Press.

AlArabiya (2009) "'Islamic MTV' Blends Muslim Art with Western Culture," AlArabiya, March 10. Online. Available http://www.alarabiya.net/articles/2009/03/10/68148.html (accessed June 7, 2010).

Al-Ghabban, A. (2007) "Global Viewing in East London: Multi-ethnic Youth Responses to Television News in a New Century," *Journal of European Cultural Studies*, 10: 311–26.

Alexander, J.C. (1988a) "Introduction: Durkheimian Sociology and Cultural Studies Today," in J.C. Alexander (ed.) *Durkheimian Sociology: Cultural Studies*, Cambridge: Cambridge University Press, pp. 1–22.

—— (1988b) "Culture and Political Crisis: 'Watergate' and Durkheimian Sociology," in J.C. Alexander (ed.) *Durkheimian Sociology: Cultural Studies*, Cambridge: Cambridge University Press, pp. 187–224.

—— (2003) *The Meanings of Social Life: A Cultural Sociology*, New York: Oxford University Press.

—— (2006) *The Civil Sphere*, Oxford: Oxford University Press.

Alexander, J.C. and Jacobs, R.N. (1998) "Mass Communication, Ritual and Civil Society," in T. Liebes and J. Curran (eds.) *Media, Ritual and Identity*, London: Routledge, pp. 23–41.

Alexander, J.C. and Mast, J. (2006) "Introduction: Symbolic Action in Theory and Practice: The Cultural Pragmatics of Cultural Action," in J.C. Alexander, B. Giesen and J. Mast (eds.) *Social Performance: Symbolic Action, Cultural Pragmatics and Ritual*, Cambridge: Cambridge University Press, pp. 1–28.

Ammerman, N. (ed.) (2007) *Everyday Religion: Observing Modern Religious Lives*, Oxford: Oxford University Press.

Amos, J. (2003) "Organ Music 'Instills Religious Feelings,'" BBC News, September 8, 2003. Online. Available http://news.bbc.co.uk/1/hi/sci/tech/3087674.stm (accessed November 12, 2005).

Anderson, B. (1991) *Imagined Communities: Reflections on the Origins and Spread of Nationalism*, London: Verso.

Andrade, J. (2001) *Working Memory in Perspective*, Hove, East Sussex: Taylor and Francis.

Appadurai, A. (ed.) (1986) *The Social Life of Things: Commodities in Cultural Perspective*, Cambridge: Cambridge University Press.

—— (1990) "Disjuncture and Difference in the Global Cultural Economy," in M. Featherstone (ed.) *Global Culture: Nationalism, Globalisation, Modernity*, London: Sage, pp. 295–311.

Appadurai, A. and Breckenridge, C.A. (1992) "Museums are Good to Think: Heritage on View in India," in I. Karp and S.D. Lavine (eds.) *Museums and Communities: The Politics of Public Culture*, Washington, DC: Smithsonian Institute, pp. 34–55.

Armstrong, K. (2009) *The Case for God: What Religion Really Means*, London: Bodley Head.

Arweck, E. (2006) *Researching New Religious Movements: Responses and Redefinitions*, London: Routledge.

Asad, T. (1993) *Genealogies of Religion*, Baltimore and London: The Johns Hopkins University Press.

Ashworth, P. (2009) "Humanist Joins BBC Faith Panel," *Church Times*, April 24.

Assmann, J. and Baumgarten, A. (eds.) (2001) *Representation in Religion*, Leiden: Brill.

Associated Press (2003) "Barbie Deemed Threat to Saudi Morality," *USA Today*, September 10, 2003. Online. Available http://www.usatoday.com/news/offbeat/2003-09-10-barbie_x.htm (accessed June 8, 2010).

Astley, J. (2002) *Ordinary Theology: Looking, Listening, and Learning in Theology*, Burlington, VA: Ashgate.

Augustine (1961) *Confessions*, trans. R.S. Pine-Coffin, Harmondsworth: Penguin.

Awan, A. (2007) "Virtual Jihadist Media: Function, Legitimacy and Radicalizing Efficacy," *Journal of European Cultural Studies*, 10: 389–408.

Ayubi, N. (1991) *Political Islam*, London: Routledge.

Babb, L.A. and Wadley, S.S. (eds.) (1995) *Media and the Transformation of Religion in South Asia*, Philadelphia: University of Pennsylvania Press.

Baddeley, A.D. [1976] (1985) *The Psychology of Memory*, London: Harper & Row.

—— (1986) *Working Memory*, Oxford: Oxford University Press.

Baggett, J.P. (2009) *Sense of the Faithful: How American Catholics Live Their Faith*, New York: Oxford University Press.

Barasch, M. (1992) *Icon: Studies in the History of an Idea*, New York: New York University Press.

Bardon, J. (1992) *A History of Ulster*, Belfast: Blackstaff Press.

Barker, E., Beckford, J.A. and Dobbelaere, K. (eds.) (1993) *Secularization, Rationalism, and Sectarianism: Essays in Honour of Bryan R. Wilson*, New York: Oxford University Press.

Bass, D. (ed.) (2010) *Practicing Our Faith: A Way of Life for a Searching People*, 2nd edn., San Francisco, CA: Jossey-Bass.

Baudrillard, J. (1988) *America*, London: Verso.

Bauman, Z. (1990) "Modernity and Ambivalence," in M. Featherstone (ed.) *Global Culture: Nationalism, Globalisation, Modernity*, London: Sage, pp. 160–8.

Beaudoin, T. (1998) *Virtual Faith: The Irreverent Spiritual Quest of Generation X*, San Francisco, CA: Jossey-Bass.

—— (2003) *Consuming Faith: Integrating Who We Are with What We Buy*, Lanham, MD: Sheed & Ward.

—— (2007) "Popular Culture Scholarship as a Spiritual Exercise: Thinking Ethically with(out) Christianity," in G. Lynch (ed.) *Between Sacred and Profane: Researching Religion and Popular Culture*, London: I.B. Tauris.

Beck, U. and Lau, C. (2005) "Second Modernity as Research Agenda: Theoretical and Empirical Explorations in the 'Meta-Change' of Modern Societies," *British Journal of Sociology*, 56 (4): 525–57.

Becker, J. (2004) *Deep Listeners: Music, Emotion and Trancing*, Bloomington: Indiana University Press.

Bell, C. (1992) *Ritual Theory, Ritual Practice*, New York: Oxford University Press.

—— (1997) *Ritual: Perspectives and Dimensions*, New York: Oxford University Press.

Bell, M. (1996) *In Harm's Way: Reflections of a War-Zone Thug*, Harmondsworth: Penguin.

Bellah, R.N. (1967) "Civil Religion in America," *Daedalus*, 96(1): 1–21.

—— (1970) *Beyond Belief: Essays on Religion in a Post-Traditional World*, New York: Harper & Row.

—— (1974) "Civil Religion in America," in R.E. Richey and D.G. Jones (eds.) *American Civil Religion*, New York: Harper Forum Books.

Belting, H. (1994) *Likeness and Presence: A History of the Image before the Era of Art*, trans. E. Jephcott, Chicago: University of Chicago Press.

Benham, P. (1993) *The Avalonians*, Glastonbury: Gothic Image Publications.

Beniger, J. (1986) *The Control Revolution: Technological and Economic Origins of the Information Society*, Cambridge, MA: Harvard University Press.

Benjamin, W. (1977) "Das Kunstwerk im Zeitalter seiner technischen Reproduzierbarkeit," in *Illuminationen: ausgewählte Schriften*, Frankfurt am Main: Suhrkamp, pp. 136–69.

Bennett, A. (2005) *Untold Stories*, London: Faber & Faber and Profile Books.

Bennett, J. (2001) *The Enchantment of Modern Life: Attachments, Crossings, and Ethics*, Princeton, NJ: Princeton University Press.

Berger, P. (1967) *The Sacred Canopy*, Garden City, NY: Doubleday.

Berger, P. and Luckmann, T. (1967) "Aspects sociologiques du pluralisme," *Archives de sociologie des religions*, 23: 117–27.

—— (1999) *The Desecularisation of the World*, Washington, DC: Ethics and Public Policy Center.

Bernstein, L. (1976) *The Unanswered Question: Six Talks at Harvard*, Cambridge, MA: Harvard University Press.

Berry, J. (2000) *Lead Us Not into Temptation: Catholic Priests and the Sexual Abuse of Children*, Urbana: University of Illinois Press.

Bhabha, H. (ed.) (1990) *Nation and Narration*, London: Routledge.

Bigsby, C.W.E. (ed.) (1976) *Approaches to Popular Culture*, London: Edward Arnold.

Birman, P. (2006) "Future in the Mirror: Media, Evangelicals, and Politics in Rio de Janeiro," in B. Meyer and A. Moors (eds.) *Religion, Media, and the Public Sphere*, Bloomington and Indianapolis: Indiana University Press, pp. 52–72.

Bland, K. (2000) *The Artless Jew: Medieval and Modern Affirmations and Denials of the Visual*, Princeton, NJ: Princeton University Press.

Bloch, M. (1989) *Ritual History and Power*, London: The Athlone Press.

Borowik, I. and Jablonski, P. (1995) *The Future of Religion: East and West*, Kraków: Nomos.

Boucher, D. (1996) "Sūtra on the Merit of Bathing the Buddha," in D.S. Lopez, Jr. (ed.) *Religions of China in Practice*, Princeton, NJ: Princeton University Press, pp. 59–68.

Bourdieu, P. (1977) *Outline of a Theory of Practice*, Cambridge: Cambridge University Press.

—— (1984) *Distinction: A Social Critique of the Judgement of Taste*, trans. R. Nice, Cambridge, MA: Harvard University Press.

—— (1990) *The Logic of Practice*, Cambridge: Polity.

—— (1991) *Language and Symbolic Power*, Cambridge: Polity.

—— (2000) *Pascalian Meditations*, Stanford, CA: Stanford University Press.

Bowman, M. (1993) "Drawn to Glastonbury," in I. Reader and T. Walter (eds.) *Pilgrimage in Popular Culture*, Basingstoke and London: Macmillan, pp. 29–62.

—— (2003–4) "Taking Stories Seriously: Vernacular Religion, Contemporary Spirituality and the Myth of Jesus in Glastonbury," *Temenos*, 39–40: 125–42.

—— (2005) "Ancient Avalon, New Jerusalem, Heart Chakra of Planet Earth: Localisation and Globalisation in Glastonbury," *Numen*, 52(2): 157–90.

—— (2008) "Going with the Flow: Contemporary Pilgrimage in Glastonbury," in P.J. Margy (ed.) *Shrines and Pilgrimage in the Modern World: New Itineraries into the Sacred*, Amsterdam: Amsterdam University Press, pp. 241–80.

Bradley, M.Z. (1986) *Mists of Avalon*, London: Sphere Books.

Brantlinger, P. (1983) *Bread and Circuses: Theories of Mass Culture as Social Decay*, Ithaca, NY: Cornell University Press.

—— (1990) *Crusoe's Footprints: Cultural Studies in Britain and America*, New York: Routledge.

Brehm, S. (2009) "Jon Stewart and Stephen Colbert: Exposing Religious Incongruity," unpublished M.A. thesis, Florida State University.

Brennan, G.T. (1939) *Angel Food: Little Talks to Little Folks*, Milwaukee, WI: Bruce Publishing.

—— (1941) *Angel City: A Book for Children from Six to Sixty*, Milwaukee, WI: Bruce Publishing.

Bretherton, L. (2010) *Christianity and Contemporary Politics*, Oxford: Wiley-Blackwell.

Brewer, J. and Porter, R. (eds.) (1993) *Consumption and the World of Goods*, London: Routledge.

Briggs, A. (1993) "Christ and the Media: Secularization, Rationalism, and Sectarianism in the History of British Broadcasting, 1922–76," in E. Barker, J. Beckford and K. Dobbelaere (eds.) *Secularization, Rationalism, and Sectarianism: Essays in Honour of Bryan R. Wilson*, Oxford: Clarendon Press, pp. 267–86.

Brown, P. (1969) *Augustine of Hippo*, Berkeley: University of California Press.

Browne, R. (ed.) (1982) *Objects of Special Devotion: Fetishism in Popular Culture*, Bowling Green, OH: Popular Press.

Browne, R.B. and Fishwick, M. (eds.) (1978) *Icons of America*, Bowling Green, OH: Popular Press.

Browning, D. (1991) *A Fundamental Practical Theology: Descriptive and Strategic Proposals*, Minneapolis: Fortress Press.

Bruce, S. and Wallis, R. (1992) "Secularization: The Orthodox Model," in S. Bruce and R. Wallis (eds.) *Religion and Modernization: Sociologists and Historians Debate the Secularization Thesis*, Oxford: Clarendon Press, pp. 8–30.

Brueggemann, W. (2007) "What Would Jesus Buy?," *Sojourners*, November 2007. Online. Available HTTP: http://www.sojo.net/index.cfm?action=magazine.article&issue =soj0711& article = 071110 (accessed January 5, 2009).

Bruni, F. and Burkett, E. (2002) *A Gospel of Shame: Children, Sexual Abuse, and the Catholic Church*, New York: Perennial.

Buck-Morss, S. (1992) "Aesthetics and Anaesthetics: Walter Benjamin's Artwork Essay Reconsidered," *October*, 62 (Autumn): 3–41.

Bunt, R.G. (2010) "Surfing the App Souq: Islamic Applications for Mobile Devices," *CyberOrient*, 4(1). Online. Available http://www.cyberorient.net/article.do?articleId=3817 (accessed October 2, 2010).

Burke, D. (2005) "Entrepreneurial Consultancies in Religious Studies," paper presented at the Ninth Quality in Higher Education International Seminar, Birmingham, January 27–28. Online. Available http://qualityresearchiinternational.com/ese/burkefv.doc (accessed June 20, 2010).

Burleigh, M. (2006) *Sacred Causes: Religion and Politics from the European Dictators to Al-Qaeda*, London: Harper Perennial.

Butler, J. (1990) *Awash in a Sea of Faith: Christianizing the American People*, Cambridge, MA: Harvard University Press.

—— (1991) "Historiographical Heresy: Catholicism as a Model for American Religious History," in T. Kselman (ed.) *Belief in History: Innovative Approaches to European and American Religion*, Notre Dame, IN: University of Notre Dame Press, pp. 286–309.

Butler, J. (2005) *Giving an Account of Oneself*, New York: Fordham University Press.

Byrd, D. (2010) "World Halal Travel Industry Grows," *Voice of America*, November 10, 2010. Online. Available http://www.voanews.com/english/news/middle-east/World-Halal-Travel-Industry-Grows-107062228.html (accessed November 10, 2010).

Callon, M. and Latour, B. (1981) "Unscrewing the Big Leviathan," in K. Knorr-Cetina and A. Cicourel (eds.) *Advances in Social Theory and Methodology*, London: Routledge & Kegan Paul.

Calvert, K. (1992) *Children in the House: The Material Culture of Early Childhood, 1600–1900*, Boston: Northeastern University Press.

Campbell, C. (1987) *The Romantic Ethic and the Spirit of a Modern Consumerism*, Oxford: Basil Blackwell.

Campbell, H. (2004) "Challenges Created by Online Religious Networks," *Journal of Media and Religion*, 3(2): 81–99.

—— (2007) "Who's Got the Power? The Question of Religious Authority and the Internet," *Journal of Computer-Mediated Communication*, 12(3). Online. Available http://jcmc.indiana.edu/vol12/issue3/ (accessed December 29, 2010).

—— (2010) *When Religion Meets New Media*, London: Routledge.

Canclini, N.G. (2001) *Consumers and Citizens: Globalization and Multicultural Conflicts*, Minneapolis: University of Minnesota Press.

Cantle, T. (2001) *Community Cohesion: A Report of the Independent Review Team*, London: Home Office.

Carey, J. (1989) *Communication as Culture*, Boston: Unwin Hyman.

Carley, J.P. (1996) *Glastonbury Abbey: The Holy House at the Head of the Moors Adventurous*, Glastonbury: Gothic Image Publications.

Carr, D. (2007) "Religious Education, Religious Literacy and Common Schooling: A Philosophy and History of Skewed Reflection," *Journal of Philosophy of Education*, 41(4): 659–73.

Carrette, J. (2000) *Foucault and Religion*, London: Routledge.

—— (2007) *Religion and Critical Psychology: Religious Experience in the Knowledge Economy*, London: Routledge.

Carrette, J. and King, R. (2005) *Selling Spirituality: The Silent Takeover of Religion*, London: Routledge.

Casanova, J. (1996) "Global Catholicism and the Politics of Civil Society," *Sociological Inquiry*, 66: 356–73.

Castelli, E. (2004) Presentation to the Conference Media, Religion and Culture, New York University, May 8.

Castells, M. (1996) *The Rise of the Network Society*, Oxford: Blackwell.

Cesari, J. (2004) *When Islam and Democracy Meet: Muslims in Europe and in the United States*, Basingstoke: Palgrave Macmillan.

Charry, E.T. (1997) *By the Renewing of Your Minds: The Pastoral Function of Christian Doctrine*, New York: Oxford University Press.

Chatterji, A.P. (1989) "The *Ramayana* and Indian Secularism," *Intermedia*, 17/5.

Chaves, M (1994) "Secularization as Declining Religious Authority," *Social Forces*, 72(3): 749–74.

Chidester, D. (2000) "The Church of Baseball, the Fetish of Coca-Cola and the Potlatch of Rock'n'roll," in B. Forbes and J. Mahan (eds.) *Religion and Popular Culture in America*, Berkeley: University of California Press.

—— (2005) *Authentic Fakes*, Berkeley: University of California Press.

Chidester, D. and Linenthal, E. (eds.) (1995) *American Sacred Space*, Bloomington: Indiana University Press.

Christian, W. (1992) *Moving Crucifixes in Modern Spain*, Princeton, NJ: Princeton University Press.

Clark, L.S. (2003) *From Angels to Aliens: Teenagers, the Media and the Supernatural*, Oxford: Oxford University Press.

—— (2007a) "Why Study Popular Culture? Or How to Build a Case for Your Thesis in a Religious Studies or Theology Department," in G. Lynch (ed.) *Between Sacred and Profane: Researching Religion and Popular Culture*, London: I.B. Tauris, pp. 5–20.

—— (ed.) (2007b) *Religion, Media and the Marketplace*, New Brunswick, NJ: Rutgers University Press.

—— (2008) "When the University Went 'Pop': Exploring Cultural Studies, Sociology of Culture, and the Rising Interest in the Study of Culture," *Sociology Compass*, 2(1): 16–23.

—— (forthcoming) "Considering Religion and Mediatization through a Case Study of *J + K's Big Day* (The J K Wedding Entrance Dance): A Response to Stig Hjarvard," *Culture and Religion*.

Clayton, J. (2006) "In a Disease-Ridden and Stinking Swamp, Thousands Hide from War," *The Times*, April 3, 2006, p. 29.

Cohen, S. (2001) *States of Denial: Knowing about Atrocity and Suffering*, Cambridge: Polity.

Coleman, S. and Elsner, J. (1995) *Pilgrimage Past and Present in the World Religions*, Cambridge, MA: Harvard University Press.

Colin, C. (2004) "Just Be," *Yoga Journal*, Winter, p. 74.

Commission on Urban Life and Faith (2006) *Faithful Cities: A Call for Celebration, Vision and Justice*, London: Methodist Publishing House.

Conboy, M. (2005) *Tabloid Britain: Constructing a Community through Language*, London: Routledge.

Conway, M. (1995) *Flashbulb Memory*, Hove: Lawrence Erlbaum Associates.

Cornille, C. (ed.) (2002) *Many Mansions? Multiple Religious Belonging and Christian Identity*, Maryknoll, NY: Orbis.

Corrigan, J. (ed.) (2004) *Religion and Emotion: Approaches and Interpretations*, Oxford: Oxford University Press.

Cortese, A. (2003) "They Care about the World (and They Shop, Too)," *New York Times*, July 20, 2003, Sections 3, 4.

Couldry, N. (2000) *The Place of Media Power*, London: Routledge.

—— (2002) *Media Rituals: A Critical Approach*, London: Routledge.

Cranz, G. (2000) *The Chair: Rethinking Culture, Body, and Design*, New York: W.W. Norton.

Crary, J. (2001) *Attention, Spectacle, and Modern Culture*, Boston: MIT Press.

Crawford, L. (2005) "To Live Simply Is to Live Well," *Natural Solutions: Vibrant Health, Balanced Living*, February 1, 2005. Online. Available http://www.naturalsolutionsmag.com (accessed September 28, 2009).

Crisell, A. (2006) *An Introductory History of British Broadcasting*, 2nd edn., London: Routledge.

Csikszentmihalyi, M. and Rochberg Halton, E. (1981) *The Meaning of Things: Domestic Symbols and the Self*, Cambridge: Cambridge University Press.

Csordas, T. (2004) "Asymptote of the Ineffable: Embodiment, Alterity, and the Theory of Religion," *Current Anthropology*, 45(2): 163–84.

Cummings, T. (1984) "Your Church and Copyright," *Buzz*, March, p. 33.

—— (1992) "Marching to a Different Drum," *Cross Rhythms*, July/August, p. 52.

—— (1995) "5 Years: British CCM's Past, Present and Future," *Cross Rhythms*, April/May, p. 24.

Cutting, T. (2004) *Beneath the Silent Tor: The Life and Work of Alice Buckton*, Glastonbury: Appleseed Press.

Czubkowska, S. and Raczkowski, G. (2006) "15-lecie Radia Maryja" [15 Years of Radio Maryja], *Przekrój*, November, 30: 12–16.

Damian, T. (2010) "The Romanian Orthodox Church: Post Communist Transformation," *Religion in Eastern Europe*, 30(1): 18–25.

Dant, T. (1999) *Material Culture in the Social World*, Buckingham: Open University Press.

—— (2005) *Materiality and Society*, Maidenhead: Open University Press.

D'Antonio, W.V., Davidson, J.D., Hoge, D.R. and Gautier, M.L. (2007) *American Catholics Today: New Realities of Their Faith and Their Church*, New York: Rowman & Littlefield.

Dawson, Lorne L. and Cowan, Douglas E. (eds.) (2004) *Religion Online: Finding Faith on the Internet*, New York and London: Routledge.

Dayan, D. and Katz, E. (1992) *Media Events: The Live Broadcasting of History*, Cambridge, MA: Harvard University Press.

De Abreu, M.J.A. (2002) "On Charisma, Mediation, and Broken Screens," *Etnofoor*, 15(1/2): 240–59.

—— (2005) "Breathing into the Heart of the Matter: Why Padre Marcelo Needs No Wings," *Postscripts*, 1(2/3): 325–49.

De Certeau, M. (1984) *The Practice of Everyday Life*, Berkeley: University of California Press.

De Vries, H. (2001) "In Media Res," in H. De Vries and S. Weber (eds.) *Religion and Media*, Stanford, CA: Stanford University Press, pp. 3–42.

De Vries, H. and Weber, S. (eds.) (2001) *Religion and Media*, Stanford, CA: Stanford University Press.

De Witte, M. (2003) "Altar Media's *Living Word*: Televised Christianity in Ghana," *Journal of Religion in Africa*, 33(2): 172–202.

—— (2005a) "The Spectacular and the Spirits: Charismatics and Neo-Traditionalists on Ghanaian Television," *Material Religion*, 1(3): 314–35.

—— (2005b) "'Insight,' Secrecy, Beasts, and Beauty: Struggles over the Making of a Ghanaian Documentary on Audiovisual Spirits? Styles and Strategies of Representing 'African Traditional Religion' in Ghana," *Postscripts*, 1(2/3): 277–300.

Deacy, C. and Arweck, E. (eds.) (2009) *Exploring Religion and the Sacred in a Media Age*, Farnham, Surrey: Ashgate.

Dean, K.C. (ed.) (2010) *OMG: A Youth Ministry Handbook*, Nashville: Abingdon Press.

Deming Andrews, E. and Andrews, F. (1937 [1964]) *Shaker Furniture*, New York: Dover.

—— (1966) *Religion in Wood*, Bloomington: Indiana University Press.

DeNora, T. (2000) *Music in Everyday Life*, Cambridge: Cambridge University Press.

—— (2001) "Aesthetic Agency and Musical Practice: New Directions in the Sociology of Music," in P.N. Juslin and J.A. Sloboda (eds.) *Music and Emotion: Theory and Research*, Oxford: Oxford University Press, pp. 161–80.

Department of Communities and Local Government (2007) *Preventing Violent Extremism Pathfinder Guidance*, London: Home Office.

Dinges, W.D., Johnson, M., Gonzales, Jr., J.L. and Hoge, D.R. (2001) *Young Adult Catholics: Religion in the Culture of Choice*, Notre Dame, IN: University of Notre Dame Press.

Dinham, A., Furbey, R. and Lowndes, V. (eds.) (2009) *Faith in the Public Realm: Controversies, Policies and Practices*, Bristol: Policy Press.

Dobbelaere, K. (1987) "Some Trends in European Sociology of Religion: The Secularization Debate," *Sociological Analysis*, 48: 107–37.

Douglas, M. (1984) *Purity and Danger*, London: Routledge.

Douglas, M. and Isherwood, B. (1979) *The World of Goods*, New York: Basic Books.

Dryzek, J. (2006) "Transnational Democracy in an Insecure World," *International Political Science Review*, 27: 101–19.

Du Bois, W.E.B. (1986) *The Souls of Black Folk*, New York: Bantam Books.

Dufrenne, M. (1973) *The Phenomenology of Aesthetic Experience*, Evanston, IL: Northwestern University Press.

Durand, J. and Massey, D.S. (1995) *Miracles on the Border: Retablos of Mexican Migrants to the United States*, Tucson: University of Arizona Press.

Durkheim, E. (1912) *The Elementary Forms of Religious Life*, Oxford: Oxford University Press.

—— (1915) *The Elementary Forms of the Religious Life*, trans. J. Ward Swain, New York: Free Press.

—— (1965) *The Elementary Forms of the Religious Life*, trans. J. Ward Swain, New York: Free Press.

—— (1995) *The Elementary Forms of Religious Life*, trans. K. Fields, Glencoe, IL: Free Press.

Echchaibi, N. (2011) "Transnational Masculinities in Muslim Televangelist Cultures," in R. Hedge (ed.) *Circuits of Visibility: Gender and Transnational Media Cultures*, New York: New York University Press.

Eck, D. (1998) *Darshan: Seeing the Divine Image in India*, New York: Columbia University Press.

Edelman, D. (1996) *The Triumph of the Elohim: From Yahwisms to Judaisms*, Grand Rapids, MI: Eerdmans.

Ehrlich, L. (1983) "X-Ray Music: The Volatile History of Dub," in S. Davis and P. Simon (eds.) *Reggae International*, London: Thames & Hudson, pp. 105–9.

Einstein, M. (2008) *Brands of Faith: Marketing Religion in a Commercial Age*, New York: Routledge.

Eisenstadt, S. (2000) "Multiple Modernities," *Daedalus*, 129 (1): 1–29.

Eliade, M. (1959) *The Sacred and the Profane*, New York: Harcourt.

Elkins, J. (2001) *Pictures and Tears*, London: Routledge.

Emerich, M. (2006) "The Spirituality of Sustainability: Healing the Self to Heal the World through Healthy Living Media," unpublished dissertation, University of Colorado.

Enyedi, Z. (2003) "The Contested Politics of Positive Neutrality in Hungary," *West European Politics* 26(1): 157–76.

Epstein, E.J. (1972) *News from Nowhere: Television and the News*, New York: Random House.

Erney, D. (2004) "The Eco-Conscience," *Organic Style*, December, p. 88.

Eyerman, R. (2008) *The Assassination of Theo van Gogh: From Social Drama to Cultural Trauma*, Durham, NC: Duke University Press.

Ezzy, D. (2001) "The Commodification of Witchcraft," *Australian Religious Studies Review*, 14(1): 31–44.

Farmer, H.H. (1954) *Revelation and Religion: Studies in the Theological Interpretation of Religious Types*, London: Nisbet.

Fass, P.S. and Mason, M.A. (eds.) (2000) *Childhood in America*, New York: New York University Press.

Finke, R. and Stark, R. (1992) *The Churching of America, 1776–1990: Winners and Losers in our Religious Economy*, New Brunswick, NJ: Rutgers University Press.

Fitzgerald, T. (2007) *Discourse on Civility and Barbarity*, Oxford: Oxford University Press.

Foote, K. (1997) *Shadowed Ground: America's Landscapes of Violence and Tragedy*, Austin: University of Texas Press.

Forbes, B.D. and Mahan, J. (2000) *Religion and Popular Culture in America*, Berkeley: University of California Press.

Foucault, M. (1981) *The History of Sexuality*, vol. 1, Harmondsworth: Penguin.

France, D. (2004) *Our Fathers: The Secret Life of the Catholic Church in an Age of Scandal*, New York: Broadway Books.

Francis of Assisi (1963) *The Little Flowers of St Francis*, London: Dent.

Fras, M. (2011) "Religion and Politics in Poland after 1989," unpublished Ph.D. thesis, Open University.

Frawley-O'Dea, M.G. (2007) *Perversion of Power: Sexual Abuse in the Catholic Church*, Nashville: Vanderbilt University Press.

Frawley-O'Dea, M.G. and Goldner, V. (eds.) (2007) *Predatory Priests, Silenced Victims: The Sexual Abuse Crisis and the Catholic Church*, Mahwah: Analytic Press.

Freedberg, D. (1989) *The Power of Images: Studies in the History and Theory of Response*, Chicago: University of Chicago Press.

Freitas, D. (2008) *Sex and the Soul: Juggling Sexuality, Spirituality, Romance, and Religion on America's College Campuses*, New York: Oxford University Press.

Friend, D. (2003) "A War Waged in Images," *American Photo* magazine, September/ October 2003. Online. Available http://www.digitaljournalist.org/issue0309/dfriend.html (accessed December 9, 2010).

Frith, S. (1981) *Sound Effects: Youth, Leisure, and the Politics of Rock "n' Roll*, New York: Pantheon.

—— (1996) *Performing Rites: Evaluating Popular Music*, Oxford: Oxford University Press.

—— (2007) *Taking Popular Music Seriously: Selected Essays*, Aldershot: Ashgate.

Froehle, B.T. and Gautier, M.L. (2000) *Catholicism USA: A Portrait of the Catholic Church in the United States*, Maryknoll, NY: Orbis.

Froese, P. (2001) "Hungary for Religion: A Supply-Side Interpretation of the Hungarian Religious Revival," *Journal for the Scientific Study of Religion*, 40(2): 251–68.

Furbey, R. (2009) "Controversies of 'Public Faith,'" in A. Dinham, R. Furbey and V. Lowndes (eds.) *Faith in the Public Realm: Controversies, Policies and Practices*, Bristol: Policy Press.

Furedi, F. (2010) "Celebrity Culture," Symposium: Celebrity around the World, *Society*, 47(6): 493–97.

Gabler, N. (2000) *Life: The Movie*, New York: Vintage.

Gans, H. (1979) *Deciding What's News*, New York: Pantheon.

Ganzevoort, R. (2009) "Forks in the Road When Tracing the Sacred," presidential address at the biennial meeting of the International Academy of Practical Theology, Chicago, Illinois, August 3.

Gaonkar, D.P. (2001) *Alternative Modernities*, Durham, NC: Duke University Press.

Garnham, N. (1994) "Bourdieu, the Cultural Arbitrary and Television," in C. Calhoun, E. Lipuma and M. Postone (eds.) *Bourdieu: Critical Perspectives*, Cambridge: Polity, pp. 178–92.

Geaves, R. (2005) *Aspects of Islam*, London: Darton, Longman and Todd.

Geertz, C. (1973) "Religion as a Cultural System," in *The Interpretation of Cultures*, New York: Basic Books, pp. 87–125.

Gell, A. (1998) *Art and Agency*, Oxford: Oxford University Press.

Gerasimo, P. (2009) "The Better Good Life: An Essay on Personal Sustainability," *Experience Life*, April, pp. 49–54.

Gibson, J. (1986) *The Ecological Approach to Visual Perception*, Hilldale, NJ: Lawrence Erlbaum Associates.

Giddens, A. (1984) *The Constitution of Society*, Cambridge: Polity.

—— (1990) *The Consequences of Modernity*, Cambridge: Polity.

—— (1991) *Modernity and Self-Identity: Self and Society in the Late Modern Age*, Stanford, CA: Stanford University Press.

Gifford, P. (2004) *Ghana's New Christianity: Pentecostalism in a Globalising African Economy*, London: Hurst.

Gilbert, A., Hirschkorn, P., Murphy, M., Walensky, R. and Stephens, M. (eds.) (2002) *Covering Catastrophe: Broadcast Journalists Report September 11*, Chicago: Bonus Books.

Gillespie, M. (1993) "Soap Opera, Gossip and Rumour in a Punjabi Town in West London," in *National Identity and the Europe: The TV Revolution*, London: British Film Institute, pp. 25–43.

—— (1994) "Sacred Serials, Devotional Viewing and Domestic Worship," in R. Allen (ed.) *To Be Continued: Soap Operas around the World*, New York and London: Routledge, pp. 354–80.

—— (1995) *Television, Ethnicity, and Cultural Change*, London and New York: Routledge.

Gillis, J.R. (1994) "Memory and Identity: The History of a Relationship," in J.R. Gillis (ed.) *Commemorations: The Politics of National Identity*, Princeton, NJ: Princeton University Press, pp. 3–24.

Gilman, E.B. (1986) *Iconoclasm and Poetry in the English Reformation*, Chicago: University of Chicago Press.

Gilmore, L. (2010) *Theater in a Crowded Fire: Ritual and Spirituality at Burning Man*, Berkeley: University of California Press.

Gilroy, P. (1993) *The Black Atlantic: Modernity and Double Consciousness*, London and New York: Verso.

—— (2003) "Between the Blues and the Blues Dance: Some Soundscapes of the Black Atlantic," in M. Bull and L. Back (eds.) *The Auditory Culture Reader*, Oxford: Berg, pp. 381–95.

Ginsburg, F. (2006) "Rethinking the 'Voice of God' in Indigenous Australia: Secrecy, Exposure, and the Efficacy of Media," in B. Meyer and A. Moors (eds.) *Religion, Media, and the Public Sphere*, Bloomington and Indianapolis: Indianapolis University Press, pp. 188–204.

Ginsburg, F., Abu-Lughod, L. and Larkin, B. (eds.) (2002) *Media Worlds: Anthropology on New Terrain*, Berkeley: University of California Press.

Glaston Group (2005) *Glastonbury: A Pilgrim's Perspective*, Glastonbury: Glaston Group.

Goin, P. and Starrs, P.F. (2005) *Black Rock*, Reno and Las Vegas: University of Nevada Press.

Göle, N. (1996) *The Forbidden Modern: Civilization and Veiling*, Ann Arbor: University of Michigan Press.

Gracyk, T. (2007) *Listening to Popular Music: Or, How I Learned to Stop Worrying and Love Led Zeppelin*, Ann Arbor: University of Michigan Press.

Graham, E.L. (2002) *Transforming Practice: Pastoral Theology in an Age of Uncertainty*, Eugene: Wipf and Stock.

—— (2007) "What We Make of the World: The Turn to Culture in Theology and the Study of Religion," in G. Lynch (ed.) *Researching Religion and Popular Culture*, London: I.B. Tauris, pp. 63–81.

Grayling, A.C. (2001) *The Meaning of Things: Applying Philosophy to Life*, London: Weidenfeld and Nicolson.

Grier, P. (2010a) "Stephen Colbert on Capitol Hill: Did He Endorse Pledge for America?" *Christian Science Monitor*, September 24, 2010. Online. Available http://www.csmonitor.com/USA/Election-2010/Vox-News/2010/0924/Stephen-Colbert-on-Capitol-Hill-Did-he-endorse-Pledge-for-America (accessed December 29, 2010).

—— (2010b) "Stephen Colbert Congressional Testimony: Why Was He Invited?" *The Christian Science Monitor*, September 27, 2010. Online. Available http://www.csmonitor.com/USA/Election-2010/Vox-News/2010/0927/Stephen-Colbert-congressional-testimony-Why-was-he-invited (accessed November 10, 2010).

Guadeloupe, F. (2006) "Chanting Down the New Jerusalem: The Politics of Belonging on Sint Maarten and Saint Martin," Ph.D. dissertation, University of Amsterdam.

Guha-Thakurta, T. (1986) "Artisans, Artists and Mass Picture Production in Late 19th and Early 20th Century in Calcutta," paper presented at the South Asia Research Conference, School of Oriental and African Studies, University of London, May.

Gunter, B. and Viney, R. (1994) *Seeing Is Believing: Religion and Television in the 1990s* (Independent Television Commission Research Monographs Series), London: John Libbey & Co.

Habermas, J. (1987) *The Theory of Communicative Action: A Critique of Functionalist Reason*, vol. 2, trans. T. McCarthy, London: Polity.

—— (2006) "Religion in the Public Sphere," *European Journal of Philosophy*, 14(1): 1–25.

—— (2008) "Notes on a Post-Secular Society," *New Perspectives Quarterly*, 25(4): 17–29.

Hackett, R.I.J. (1998) "Charismatic/Pentecostal Appropriation of Media Technologies in Nigeria and Ghana," *Journal of Religion in Africa*, 28(3): 1–19.

Halal World Forum (2010) Promotional Video. Online. Available http://www.youtube. com/watch?v=QuhmTfI_XYE&feature=related (accessed September 2, 2010).

Hall, D.D. (1990) *Worlds of Wonder, Days of Judgment: Popular Religious Belief in Early New England*, Cambridge, MA: Harvard University Press.

—— (ed.) (1997) *Lived Religion in America: Toward a History of Practice*, Princeton, NJ: Princeton University Press.

Hall, S. (1980) "Recent Developments in Theories of Language and Ideology: A Critical Note," in S. Hall, D. Hobson, A. Lowe and P. Willis (eds.) *Culture, Media, Language: Working Papers in Cultural Studies 1972–1979*, London: Hutchinson, pp. 157–62.

—— (1992) "The Question of Cultural Identity," in S. Hall, D. Held and T. McGrew (eds.) *Modernity and Its Futures*, Cambridge: Polity, pp. 273–326.

Hall, S. and Jefferson, T. (1976) *Resistance through Rituals: Youth Subcultures in Post-war Britain*, London: Hutchinson.

Hambrick-Stowe, C.E. (1982) *The Practice of Piety: Puritan Devotional Discipline in Seventeenth-Century New England*, Chapel Hill: University of North Carolina Press.

Hamelink, C. (1999) *The Ethics of Cyberspace*, London: Sage.

Hammer, O. (2004) *Claiming Knowledge: Strategies of Epistemology from Theosophy to the New Age*, Leiden and Boston: Brill.

Handelman, D. (1998) *Models and Mirrors: Towards an Anthropology of Public Events*, 2nd edn., Oxford: Berg.

Hanegraaff, W. (1999) "New Age Spiritualities as Secular Religion: A Historian's Perspective," *Social Compass*, 46(2): 145–60.

—— (2007) "The New Age Movement and Western Esotericism," in Daren Kemp and James R. Lewis (eds.) *Handbook of New Age*, Leiden and Boston: Brill, pp. 25–50.

Hangen, T. (2002) *Redeeming the Dial: Radio, Religion and Popular Culture in America*, Chapel Hill: University of North Carolina Press.

Hannerz, U. (1990) "Cosmopolitans and Locals in World Culture," in M. Featherstone (ed.) *Global Culture: Nationalism, Globalisation, Modernity*, London: Sage, pp. 237–53.

Harding, S.F. (1994) "The Born-Again Telescandals," in N.B. Dirks, G. Eley and S.B. Ortner (eds.) *Culture/Power/History*, Princeton, NJ: Princeton University Press, pp. 539–56.

—— (2000) *The Book of Jerry Falwell, Fundamentalist Language and Politics*, Princeton, NJ: Princeton University Press.

Hargreaves, D.J., Miell, D. and MacDonald, R.A.R. (2002) "What Are Musical Identities, and Why Are They Important?" in R.A.R. MacDonald, D.J. Hargreaves and D. Miell (eds.) *Musical Identities*, Oxford: Oxford University Press, pp. 1–20.

Hart, J. (2009) "When Less Is Enough," *Experience Life*, April, pp. 82–4.

Harvey, G. (2005) *Animism: Respecting the Living World*, London: Hurst and Company.

Harvey, J. (1995) *Visual Piety: The Visual Culture of Welsh Nonconformity*, Cardiff: University of Wales Press.

—— (1999) *Image of the Invisible: The Visualization of Religion in the Welsh Nonconformist Tradition*, Cardiff: University of Wales Press.

Hayes-Conroy, A. and Martin, D.G. (2010) "Mobilising Bodies: Visceral Identification in the Slow Food Movement," *Transactions of the Institute of British Geographers*, 35(2): 269–81.

Heatley, C. (2007) "Faith in Fashion," BBC Online, March 29, 2007. Online. Available http://www.bbc.co.uk/leicester/content/articles/2007/03/28/islamic_fashion_show_feature. shtml (accessed August 7, 2010).

Hebdige, D. (1979) *Subculture: The Meaning of Style*, London: Methuen.

Heelas, P. (1996) *The New Age Movement*, Oxford: Blackwell.

Hefner, R.W. (1998) "Multiple Modernities: Christianity, Islam and Hinduism in a Globalizing Age," *Annual Review of Anthropology*, 27: 83–104.

Helland, C. (2007) "Diaspora on the Electronic Frontier: Developing Virtual Connections with Sacred Homelands," *Journal of Computer Mediated Communication*, 12(3). Online. Available http://jcmc.indiana.edu/vol12/issue3/ (accessed December 21, 2010).

Henriques, J. (2003) "Sonic Dominance and the Reggae Sound System Session," in M. Bull and L. Back (eds.) *The Auditory Culture Reader*, Oxford: Berg, pp. 451–80.

Herbert, D. (2003) *Religion and Civil Society: Rethinking Public Religion in the Contemporary World*, Aldershot: Ashgate.

Herbert, D. and Fras, M. (2009) "European Enlargement, Secularisation and Religious Re-publicisation in Central and Eastern Europe," *Religion, State and Society*, 37(1–2): 81–97.

Herman, J.L. (1992) *Trauma and Recovery: From Domestic Abuse to Political Terror*, London: Pandora.

Herrin, J. (1982) "Women and the Faith in Icons in Early Christianity," in R. Samuel and G. Stedman Jones (eds.) *Culture, Ideology and Politics*, London: Routledge & Kegan Paul, pp. 56–83.

Hexham, I. (1983) "The 'Freaks' of Glastonbury: Conversion and Consolidation in an English Country Town," *Update*, 7(1): 3–12.

Hicks, D. (2000) *Inequality and Christian Ethics*, Cambridge: Cambridge University Press.

Hidalgo, M.L. (2007) *Sexual Abuse and the Culture of Catholicism: How Priests and Nuns Become Perpetrators*, New York: Haworth.

Higonnet, A. (1998) *Pictures of Innocence: The History and Crisis of Ideal Childhood*, London: Thames & Hudson.

Hills, M. (2002) *Fan Cultures*, London: Routledge.

Hirsch, M. (2004) "Bernard Lewis Revisited," *Washington Monthly*, November 2004. Online. Available http://www.washingtonmonthly.com/features/2004/0411.hirsch.html (accessed February 5, 2006).

Hirschkind, C. (2001) "The Ethics of Listening: Cassette-Sermon Audition in Contemporary Egypt," *American Ethnologist*, 28(3): 623–49.

—— (2006) "Cassette Ethics: Public Piety and Popular Media in Egypt," in B. Meyer and A. Moors (eds.) *Religion, Media, and the Public Sphere*, Bloomington and Indianapolis: Indiana University Press, pp. 29–51.

Hjarvard, S. (2008a) "The Mediatization of Religion: A Theory of the Media as Agents of Social Change," *Northern Lights*, 6: 9–26.

—— (2008b) "The Mediatization of Society: A Theory of the Media as Agents of Social and Cultural Change," *Nordicom Review*, 29(2): 105–34.

—— (forthcoming) "The Mediatization of Religion: Theorising Religion, Media, and Social Change," *Religion and Culture*.

Hobsbawm, E. and Ranger, T. (eds.) (1983) *The Invention of Tradition*, Cambridge: Cambridge University Press.

Hoggart, R. (2009) *The Uses of Literacy*, Harmondsworth: Penguin.

Hollenbach, S.J., D. (2002) *The Common Good and Christian Ethics*, Cambridge: Cambridge University Press.

Hoover, S. (2006) *Religion in the Media Age*, New York: Routledge.

—— (2009) "Complexities: The Case of Religious Cultures," in K. Lundby (ed.) *Mediatization*, New York: Peter Lang Publishing, pp. 123–38.

Hoover, S. and Clark, L.S. (eds.) (2002) *Practicing Religion in the Age of the Media: Explorations in Media, Religion, and Culture*, New York: Columbia University Press.

Hoover, S. and Lundby, K. (eds.) (1997) *Rethinking Media, Religion and Culture*, Thousand Oaks, CA: Sage.

Hoover, S. and Venturelli, S.S. (1996) "The Category of the Religious: The Blindspot of Contemporary Media Theory?" *Critical Studies in Media Communication*, 13(3): 251–65.

Hopkinson-Ball, T. (2007) *The Rediscovery of Glastonbury: Frederick Bligh Bond Architect of the New Age*, London: Sutton Publishing.

Horsfield, P., Hess, M.E. and Medrano, A.M. (eds.) (2004) *Belief in Media: Cultural Perspectives on Media and Christianity*, Aldershot: Ashgate.

Hoskins, J. (1998) *Biographical Objects: How Things Tell the Stories of People's Lives*, London: Routledge.

Huron, D. (2006) *Sweet Anticipation: Music and the Psychology of Expectation*, Cambridge, MA: MIT Press.

Huyler, S.P. (1999) *Meeting God: Elements of Hindu Devotion*, New Haven, CT: Yale University Press.

Ismail, F. (2001) "Showing the True Face of Islam," *New Straits Times (Malaysia)*, November 18, p. 1.

Ivakhiv, A.J. (2001) *Claiming Sacred Ground: Pilgrims and Politics at Glastonbury and Sedona*, Bloomington and Indianapolis: Indiana University Press.

Jackson, T. (2010) "Stephen Colbert for the Least of These," *God's Politics Blog*, September 27, 2010. Online. Available http://blog.sojo.net/2010/09/27/stephen-colbert-for-the-least-of-these/ (accessed November 15, 2010).

Jacobs, R. (2000) *Race, Media and the Crisis of Civil Society: From Watts to Rodney King*, Cambridge: Cambridge University Press.

James, W. (1982) *The Varieties of Religious Experience*, Harmondsworth: Penguin.

Jansson, A. (2002) "The Mediatization of Consumption: Toward an Analytical Framework of Image Culture," *Journal of Consumer Culture*, 2(5): 5–31.

Jenkins, H. (ed.) (1998) *The Children's Culture Reader*, New York: New York University Press.

—— (2006) *Convergence Culture*, New York: New York University Press.

Jenks, C. (1996) *Childhood*, New York: Routledge.

Jensen, R. (2000) *Understanding Early Christian Art*, London: Routledge.

Jerome (2009) "Letter 55, To Amandus," trans. W.H. Fremantle, G. Lewis and W.G. Martley. Online. Available http://www.newadvent.org/fathers/3001055.htm (accessed August 16, 2010).

Jhally, S. (1989) "Advertising as Religion: The Dialectic of Technology and Magic," in I. Angus and S. Jhally (eds.) *Cultural Politics in Contemporary America*, New York: Routledge, pp. 217–29.

Johnson, L.K. (2002) *Mi Revalueshanary Fren: Selected Poems*, London: Penguin.

Johnston, R. (ed.) (2007) *Reframing Theology and Film: New Focus for an Emerging Discipline*, Grand Rapids, MI: Baker Academic.

Jones, S. (1988) *Black Culture, White Youth: The Reggae Tradition from JA to UK*, London: Macmillan Education.

—— (1998) "Information, Internet and Community," in S. Jones (ed.) *Cybersociety 2.0*, London: Routledge.

Jordan, M.D. (2000) *The Silence of Sodom: Homosexuality in Modern Catholicism*, Chicago: University of Chicago Press.

Juergensmeyer, M. (2001) Remarks to the annual meeting of the Society for the Scientific Study of Religion, Columbus, OH, November.

Junior Catholic Messenger (1937) "She Saw Her Angel," *Junior Catholic Messenger*, September 29, 4: 20.

—— (1940) "Dick the Dreamer," *Junior Catholic Messenger*, September 25, 7(3): 20.

—— (1941) "Your Guardian Angel," *Junior Catholic Messenger*, October 1, 8.

—— (1942a) "Father Brown Says," *Junior Catholic Messenger*, September 9, 9(1): 36.

—— (1942b) "Windmill Willie," *Junior Catholic Messenger*, September 9, 9(1): 4.

—— (1942c) "Things Needed for Mass," *Junior Catholic Messenger*, November 18, 9: 63.

Kandra, G. (2010) "Stephen Colbert Cites Matthew 25," *The Deacon's Bench*, September 20, 2010. Online. Available http://blog.beliefnet.com/deaconsbench/2010/09/stephen-colbert-cites-matthew-25.html (accessed October 5, 2010).

Kane, P.M. (1994) *Separatism and Subculture: Boston, Catholicism, 1900–1920*, Chapel Hill: University of North Carolina Press.

Kant, I. (1951) *Critique of Judgment*, trans. J.H. Bernard, New York: Hafner Publishing Company.

Keane, F. (2003) "Africa's Forgotten and Ignored War," *BBCi News UK Edition*, October 18, 2003. Online. Available http://news.bbc.co.uk/1/hi/programmes/from_our_own_correspondent/3201770.stm (accessed December 29, 2010).

Keenan, W. (2002) "Post-Secular Sociology: Effusions of Religion in Late Modern Settings," *European Journal of Social Theory*, 5: 279–90.

Kellner, D. (1992) *The Persian Gulf TV War*, Boulder, CO: Westview Press.

Kelly, K. and Cooke, L. with Funcke, B. (eds.) (2008) *Francis Alÿs: Fabiola; An Investigation*, New York: Dia Art Foundation.

Kennedy, J.W. (2010) "Stephen Colbert Crossed a Line by Bringing His Comedy Central Routine to Congress," *Beliefnet.com: Catholics, Media, & Culture*, September 29, 2010. Online. Available http://blog.beliefnet.com/catholicsmediaandculture/2010/09/stephen-colbert-crossed-a-line-by-bringing-his-comedy-central-act-to-congress.html (accessed December 29, 2010).

Kincaid, J.R. (1992) *Child-Loving: The Erotic Child and Victorian Culture*, New York: Routledge.

—— (1998) *Erotic Innocence: The Culture of Child Molesting*, Durham, NC: Duke University Press.

King, R. (1999) *Orientalism and Religion: Postcolonial Theory, India and "the Mystic East,"* London: Routledge.

Kirshenblatt-Gimblett, B. (2003) "Kodak Moments, Flashbulb Memories: Reflections on 9/11," *TDR: The Drama Review*, Spring (T177), 47(1): 11–48.

Klarreich, E. (2001) "Feel the Music," *Nature Science Update*, November 27. Online. Available http://www.nature.com/news/2001/011129/pf/011129–10_pf.html (accessed October 30, 2005).

Klein, N. (2000) *No Logo*, London: Flamingo.

Knightley, P. (2004) *The First Casualty: The War Correspondent as Hero and Myth-Maker from Crimea to Iraq*, Baltimore and London: Johns Hopkins University Press.

Knitter, P.F. (2009) *Without Buddha I Could Not Be a Christian*, Boston: Oneworld.

Kopf, B. (1995) "Unnatural Highs," *The Wire*, 140 (October): 26–30.

Kopytoff, I. (1986) "The Cultural Biography of Things: Commoditization as Process," in A. Appadurai (ed.) *The Social Life of Things: Commodities in Cultural Perspective*, Cambridge: Cambridge University Press, pp. 64–91.

Kraidy, M. (2009) *Reality Television and Arab Politics: Contention in Public Life*, Cambridge: Cambridge University Press.

Kristof, N.D. (2005) "All Ears for Tom Cruise, All Eyes on Brad Pitt," *New York Times*, July 26, 2005.

Kuhnel, B. (2001) "Jewish Art and Iconoclasm: The Case of Sepphoris," in J. Assmann and A. Baumgarten (eds.) *Representation in Religion*, Leiden: Brill, pp. 161–80.

Kuryluk, E. (1991) *Veronica and Her Cloth*, Oxford: Basil Blackwell.

Kwabena Asamoah-Gyadu, J. (2004) "Pentecostal Media Images and Religious Globalization in Sub-Saharan Africa," in P. Horsfield, M.E. Hess and A.M. Medrana (eds.) *Belief in Media: Cultural Perspectives on Media and Christianity*, Aldershot: Ashgate, pp. 65–80.

Laclau, E. (1990) *New Reflections on the Revolution of Our Time*, London: Verso.

Lakoff, G. and Johnson, M. (1980) *Metaphors We Live By*, Chicago: University of Chicago Press.

Lambek, M. (2004) "Comment on Thomas Csordas, 'Asymptote of the Ineffable,'" *Current Anthropology*, 45(2): 179.

Lamont, G. (2002) *The Spirited Business*, London: Hodder & Stoughton.

Latour, B. (1993) *We Have Never Been Modern*, Cambridge, MA: Harvard University Press.

—— (2005) *Reassembling the Social: An Introduction to Actor-Network Theory*, Oxford: Oxford University Press.

Lau, K.J. (2000) *New Age Capitalism: Making Money East of Eden*, Philadelphia: University of Pennsylvania Press.

Law, S. and Lives, E. (1982) *Keep Music Legal: From the Manuscript to Mass Production*, London: Sea Dream Music.

Leberecht, T. (2004) "How Far Are We From Circus Maximus?" Online. Available http://iplot.typepad.com/iplot/2004/12/index.html (accessed December 4, 2010).

Lee, M. (2008) *Bearing the Weight of Salvation: The Soteriology of Ignacio Ellacuria*, New York: Crossroad.

Leigh, I. (1992) "Regulating Religious Broadcasting," *Ecclesiastical Law Journal*, 2: 287–304.

Leppard, D. and Follain, J. (2005) "Third Terror Cell on Loose," *The Sunday Times*, July 31, p. 1.

Lessig, L. (2008) *Remix*, London: Penguin.

Levitin, D. (2007) *This Is Your Brain on Music: Understanding a Human Obsession*, London: Atlantic Books.

Levitt, T. (1983) *The Marketing Imagination*, London: Macmillan.

Lewis, J., Brookes, R., Mosdell, N. and Threadgold, T. (2006) *Shoot First and Ask Questions Later: Media Coverage of the 2003 Iraq War*, New York: Peter Lang.

Liebes, T. and Katz, E. (1990) *The Export of Meaning: Cross-Cultural Readings of "Dallas,"* New York: Oxford University Press.

Linenthal, E. (2001) *The Unfinished Bombing: Oklahoma City in American Memory*, New York: Oxford University Press.

Lopez, D.S. (ed.) (1996) *Religions of China in Practice*, Princeton, NJ: Princeton University Press.

Lord, D.A. (1948) *Stories of the Angels*, New York: Devotional Publishing.

Luckmann, T. (1967) *The Invisible Religion*, London: MacMillan.

Lukes, S. (1975) "Political Ritual and Social Integration," *Sociology*, 9(2): 289–308.

Lull, J. (1988) *World Families Watch Television*, Beverly Hills: Sage.

Lunn, E. (1990) "The Frankfurt School in the Development of the Mass Culture Debate," in R. Roblin (ed.) *The Aesthetics of the Critical Theorists: Studies on Benjamin, Adorno, Marcuse and Habermas*, Lewiston, NY: E. Mellen Press, pp. 26–84.

Lurie, R.D. (2009) *No Certainty Attached: Steve Kilbey and the Church*, Portland: Verse Chorus Press.

Lyden, J. (ed.) (2010) *The Routledge Companion to Religion and Film*, London: Routledge.

Lynch, G. (2005) *Understanding Theology and Popular Culture*, Oxford: Blackwell.

—— (2006) "The Role of Popular Music in the Construction of Alternative Spiritual Identities and Ideologies," *Journal for the Scientific Study of Religion*, 45(4): 481–8.

—— (2007a) *The New Spirituality*, London: I.B. Tauris.

—— (ed.) (2007b) *Between Sacred and Profane: Researching Religion and Popular Culture*, London: I.B. Tauris.

—— (2010) "Religion, Media and Cultures of Everyday Life," in J. Hinnells (ed.) *The Routledge Companion to the Study of Religion*, 2nd edn., London: Routledge, pp. 543–57.

—— (forthcoming) *The Sacred in the Modern World: A Cultural Sociological Approach*, Oxford: Oxford University Press.

McAllester Jones, M. (1991) *Gaston Bachelard Subversive Humanist*, Madison: University of Wisconsin Press.

McChesney, R.W. (1999) "Introduction," in N. Chomsky, *Profit Over People: Neoliberalism and Global Order*, New York: Seven Stories Press.

McCloud, S. (2003) *Making the American Religious Fringe: Exotics, Subversives, and Journalists, 1955–1993*, Duke: University of North Carolina Press.

McCutcheon, R. (2003) *The Discipline of Religion: Structure, Meaning, Rhetoric*, London: Routledge.

McDannell, C. (1991) "Interpreting Things: Material Culture Studies and American Religion," *Religion*, 21: 371–87.

—— (1995) *Material Christianity: Religion and Popular Culture in America*, New Haven, CT: Yale University Press.

—— (2011) *Spirit of Vatican II: A History of Catholic Reform in America*, New York: Basic Books.

Macdonald, D. (1944) "A Theory of Popular Culture," *Politics*, 1(1): 20–3.

MacGregor, N. (2010) *A History of the World in 100 Objects*, London: Allen Lane.

McGuire, M. (2008) *Lived Religion: Faith and Practice in Everyday Life*, New York: Oxford University Press.

McKendrick, N., Brewer, J. and Plumb, J.J.H. (eds.) (1982) *The Birth of a Consumer Society: The Commercialization of Eighteenth-Century England*, Bloomington: Indiana University Press.

McKinley, E.H. (1995) *Marching to Glory: The History of the Salvation Army in the United States, 1880–1992*, Grand Rapids, MI: W.B. Erdmans Publishing.

McLuhan, M. (1962) *The Gutenberg Galaxy*, Toronto: University of Toronto Press.

—— (1964) *Understanding Media: the Extensions of Man*, London: Routledge.

McLuhan, M. and Powers, B. (1992) *The Global Village: Transformations in World Life in the Twenty First Century*, Oxford: Oxford University Press.

Maffesoli, M. (1996) *The Contemplation of the World: Figures of Community Style*, Minneapolis: University of Minnesota Press.

Mahmood, S. (2001) "Rehearsed Spontaneity and the Conventionality of Ritual: Disciplines of Salāt," *American Ethnologist*, 28(4): 827–53.

Mandaville, P. (2001) *Transnational Muslim Politics: Reimagining the Umma*, London: Routledge.

Mandel, R. (2002) "A Marshall Plan of the Mind: The Political Economy of a Kazakh Soap Opera," in F. Ginsburg, L. Abu-Lughod and B. Larkin (eds.) *Media Worlds: Anthropology on New Terrain*, Berkeley: University of California Press, pp. 211–28.

Manovitch, L. (2001) *The Language of New Media*, Boston: MIT Press.

Marks, L. (1999) *The Skin of the Film: Intercultural Cinema, Embodiment and the Senses*, Durham, NC: Duke University Press.

Marshall, P., Gilbert, L. and Ahmanson, R.G. (eds.) (2009) *Blind Spot: When Journalists Don't Get Religion*, Oxford: Oxford University Press.

Marx, K. (1976) *Capital*, vol. 1, trans. B. Fowkes, Harmondsworth: Penguin.

Mattelart, A., Delcourt, X. and Mattelart, M. (1984) *International Image Markets: In Search of an Alternative Perspective*, London: Comedia.

Mattelart, A., Emmanuel, S. and Cohen, J. (1994) *Mapping World Communication: War, Progress, Culture*, Minneapolis: University of Minnesota Press.

Mazzarella, W. (2004) "Culture, Globalization, Mediation," *Annual Review of Anthropology*, 33: 345–67.

Melucci, A. (1989) *Nomads of the Present*, London: Hutchinson Radius.

—— (1996) *Challenging Codes*, Cambridge: Cambridge University Press.

Merici, M.A. (1931) "Devotion to the Holy Guardian Angels," *Catholic School Journal*, 31: 349–54.

Merleau-Ponty, M. (2002) *Phenomenology of Perception*, trans. C. Smith, London: Routledge.

Mettinger, T. (1995) *No Graven Image? Israelite Aniconism in Its Ancient Near Eastern Context*, Stockholm: Almqvist and Wiksell International.

Meyer, B. (1992) "If You Are a Devil You Are a Witch and, If You Are a Witch You Are a Devil: The Integration of 'Pagan' Ideas into the Conceptual Universe of Ewe Christians in Southeastern Ghana," *Journal of Religion in Africa*, 22(2): 98–132.

—— (1995) "Delivered from the Powers of Darkness: Confessions about Satanic Riches in Christian Ghana," *Africa*, 65(2): 236–55.

—— (1998a) "Commodities and the Power of Prayer: Pentecostalist Attitudes Towards Consumption in Contemporary Ghana," in B. Meyer and P. Geschiere (eds.) *Globalization and Identity: Dialectics of Flow and Closure, Development and Change*, 29(4): 751–77.

—— (1998b) "Make a Complete Break with the Past: Memory and Post-Colonial Modernity in Ghanaian Pentecostalist Discourse," *Journal of Religion in Africa*, 27(3): 316–49.

—— (1999) *Translating the Devil: Religion and Modernity among the Ewe in Ghana*, Trenton, NJ: Africa World Press.

—— (2004a) "Christianity in Africa: From African Independent to Pentecostal-Charismatic Churches," *Annual Review of Anthropology*, 33: 447–74.

—— (2004b) "'Praise the Lord … ': Popular Cinema and Pentecostalite Style in Ghana's New Public Sphere," *American Ethnologist*, 31(1): 92–110.

—— (2005a) "Mediating Tradition: Pentecostal Pastors, African Priests, and Chiefs in Ghanaian Popular Films," in T. Falola (ed.) *Christianity and Social Change in Africa: Essays in Honor of J. D. Y. Peel*, Durham, NC: Carolina Academic Press, pp. 275–306.

—— (2005b) "Religious Remediations: Pentecostal Views in Ghanaian Video-Movies," *Postscripts*, 1(2/3): 155–81.

—— (2006a) "Impossible Representations: Pentecostalism, Vision, and Video Technology in Ghana," in B. Meyer and A. Moors (eds.) *Religion, Media, and the Public Sphere*, Bloomington and Indianapolis: Indiana University Press, pp. 290–312.

—— (2006) "Religious Revelation, Secrecy and the Limits of Visual Representation," *Anthropological Theory*, 6(3): 431–53.

—— (2006c) "Modern Mass Media, Religion, and the Dynamics of Distraction and Concentration," concluding lecture to the conference Modern Mass Media, Religion, and the Question of Community, University of Amsterdam, June 30.

—— (ed.) (2010) *Aesthetic Formations: Media, Religion and the Senses*, Basingstoke: Palgrave Macmillan.

Meyer, B. and Geschiere, P. (eds.) (1998) *Globalization and Identity: Dialectics of Flow and Closure, Development and Change*, 29(4).

Meyer, B. and Moors, A (eds.) (2006) *Religion, Media, and the Public Sphere*, Bloomington and Indianapolis: Indiana University Press.

Meyer, B., Morgan, D., Paine, C. and Plate, B. (2010) "The Origin and Mission of Material Religion," *Religion*, 40(3): 207–11.

Meyer, L.B. (1956) *Emotion and Meaning in Music*, Chicago: University of Chicago Press.

Meyrowitz, J. (1986) *No Sense of Place: The Impact of Electronic Media on Social Behaviour*, New York: Oxford University Press.

Michalski, S. (1993) *The Reformation and the Visual Arts*, London: Routledge.

Miller, D. (1987) *Material Culture and Mass Consumption*, Oxford: Blackwell.

—— (1992) *"The Young and Restless* in Trinidad: A Case of Local and Global in Mass Consumption," in R. Silverstone and E. Hirsch (eds.) *Consuming Technologies*, London: Routledge, pp. 162–82.

—— (2008) *The Comfort of Things*, Cambridge: Polity.

Miller, P. (1939) *The Seventeenth Century*, Boston: Beacon.

—— (1953) *From Colony to Province*, Boston: Beacon.

Mitchell, J. (2007) *Media Violence and Christian Ethics*, Cambridge: Cambridge University Press

—— (forthcoming), *Promoting Peace, Inciting Violence: The Role of Religion and Media*, London: Routledge.

Mitchell, J. and Marriage, S. (2003) *Mediating Religion: Conversations in Media, Religion and Culture*, London and New York: T & T Clark, Continuum.

Mitchell, J. and Plate, B. (eds.) (2007) *The Religion and Film Reader*, London: Routledge.

Mitchell, W.J.T. (1994) *Picture Theory*, Chicago: University of Chicago Press.

Moeller, S.D. (1999) *Compassion Fatigue: How the Media Sell Disease, Famine, War and Death*, New York and London: Routledge.

Molotch, H. (2003) *Where Stuff Comes From: How Toasters, Toilets, Cars, Computers, and Many Other Things Come to Be as They Are*, New York: Routledge.

Moore, L.R. (1994) *Selling God: American Religion in the Marketplace of Culture*, Oxford: Oxford University Press.

Moore, M.E. (2004) "Purposes of Practical Theology: A Comparative Analysis Between United States Practical Theologians and Johannes Van der Ven," in C.A.M. Hermans and M.E. Moore (eds.) *Hermeneutics and Empirical Research in Practical Theology*, Boston: Brill.

Morgan, D. (1998) *Visual Piety: A History and Theory of Popular Religious Images*, Berkeley: University of California Press.

—— (2005) *The Sacred Gaze: Religious Visual Culture in Theory and Practice*, Berkeley: University of California Press.

—— (2008a) "Introduction: Religion, Media Culture – the Shape of the Field," in D. Morgan (ed.) *Key Words in Religion, Media and Culture*, London: Routledge, pp. 1–19.

—— (2008b) "The Materiality of Cultural Construction," *Material Religion*, 4(2): 228–9.

—— (ed.) (2009) *Religion and Material Culture: The Matter of Belief*, London: Routledge.

—— (ed.) (2010) *Key Words in Religion, Media and Culture*, London: Routledge

—— (forthcoming) *The Embodied Eye: Religious Visual Culture and the Social Life of Feeling*, Berkeley: University of California Press.

Morgan, D. and Promey, S. (eds.) (2001) *The Visual Culture of American Religions*, Berkeley: University of California Press.

Morley, D. and Robins, K. (1989) "Space of Identity," *Screen*, 20(4): 3–15.

Morris, B. (2000) *In the Place of Origins: Modernity and Its Mediums in Northern Thailand*, Durham, NC: Duke University Press.

Morris, C. (2005) *Things Shaken, Things Unshaken: Reflections on Faith and Terror*, London: Epworth Press.

Mukerji, C. (1983) *From Graven Images: Patterns of Modern Materialism*, New York: Colombia University Press.

Nakhoul, S. (2004) "Arabs Enraged at U.S. Soldier Shooting Wounded in Iraq," Reuters, November 17, 2004. Online. Available http://www.commondreams.org/headlines04/1117–22.htm (accessed December 9, 2010).

Nandy, A. (1983) *The Intimate Enemy: Loss and Recovery of Self under Colonialism*, New York: Oxford University Press.

Nasr, V. (2009) *Forces of Fortune: The Rise of the New Muslim Middle Class and What It Will Mean for Our World*, New York: Free Press.

Niderost, E. (2010) "Silent Cinema as Historical Mythmaker," in S. Mintz and R. Roberts (eds.) *Hollywood's America: Twentieth-Century American through Films*, Oxford: Wiley-Blackwell, pp. 43–53.

Nobel, S. (2006) *The Prosperity Game*, Findhorn: The Findhorn Press.

Norman, D. (2004) *Emotional Design: Why We Love (or Hate) Everyday Things*, New York: Basic Books.

Norris, P. and Inglehart, R. (2006) *Sacred and Secular: Religion and Politics Worldwide*, Cambridge: Cambridge University Press.

Northcott, M. (1999) *Life After Debt: Christianity and Global Justice*, London: SPCK.

Office for Standards in Education, Children's Services and Skills (OFSTED) (2010) *Transforming Religious Education: Religious Education in Schools 2006–09*, Manchester: OFSTED.

Ohm, Britta (forthcoming) "The Secularism of the State and the Secularism of Consumption: 'Honesty', 'Treason' and the Dynamics of Religious Television in India and Turkey," *European Journal of Cultural Studies*, 14(5).

Önçü, A. (2006) "Becoming 'Secular Muslims': Yasar Nuri Öztürk as a Super-subject on Turkish Television," in B. Meyer and A. Moors (eds.) *Religion, Media, and the Public Sphere*, Bloomington and Indianapolis: Indiana University Press, pp. 227–50.

Oosterbaan, M. (2006) "Divine Mediations: Pentecostalism, Politics, and Mass Media in a Favela in Rio de Janeiro," Ph.D. dissertation, University of Amsterdam, 2006.

Orsi, R.A. (1985) *The Madonna of 115th Street: Faith and Community in Italian Harlem, 1880–1950*, New Haven, CT and London: Yale University Press.

—— (1988) *The Madonna of 115th Street*, New Haven, CT: Yale University Press.

—— (1996) *Thank You, Saint Jude: Women's Devotion to the Patron Saint of Lost Causes*, New Haven, CT: Yale University Press.

—— (1997) "Everyday Miracles: The Study of Lived Religion," in D. Hall (ed.) *Lived Religion in America: Toward a History of Practice*, Princeton, NJ: Princeton University Press, pp. 3–21.

—— (2005) *Between Heaven and Earth: The Religious Worlds People Make and the Scholars Who Study Them*, Princeton, NJ: Princeton University Press.

Ortega y Gasset, J. (1950) *The Revolt of the Masses*, New York: New American Library.

Ouspensky, L. (1992) *Theology of the Icon*, Crestwood, NY: St. Vladimir's Seminary Press.

Pantti, M. and Sumiala, J. (2009) "Till Death Do Us Join: Media, Mourning Rituals and the Sacred Centre of the Society," *Media Culture and Society*, 31(1): 119–35.

Parkins, W. (2004) "Out of Time: Fast Subjects and Slow Living," *Time Society*, 13: 363–82.

Parkins, W. and Craig, G. (2006) *Slow Living*, New York: Berg.

Partridge, C. (2005) *The Re-Enchantment of the West: Alternative Spiritualities, Sacralization, Popular Culture and Occulture*, vol. 1, London: T & T Clark International.

—— (2006) *The Re-Enchantment of the West: Alternative Spiritualities, Sacralization, Popular Culture and Occulture*, vol. 2, London: T & T Clark International.

—— (2009) "Religion and Popular Culture," in L. Woodhead, H. Kawanami and C. Partridge (eds.) *Religions in the Modern World: Traditions and Transformations*, 2nd edn., London: Routledge, pp. 489–522.

—— (2010) *Dub in Babylon: Understanding the Evolution and Significance of Dub Reggae in Jamaica and Britain from King Tubby to Post-Punk*, London: Equinox.

Patel, A.D. (2008) *Music, Language and the Brain*, New York: Oxford University Press.

Patel, E. (2010) "An iPhone App for the Modern Muslim," *Muslim Voices*, February 2, 2010. Online. Available http://muslimvoices.org/iphone-app-modern-muslim/ (accessed June 9, 2010).

Pattison, S. (2007a) *Seeing Things: Deepening Relationships with Visual Artefacts*, London: SCM Press.

—— (2007b) "'Suffer Little Children': The Challenge of Child Abuse and Neglect to Theology," in *The Challenge of Practical Theology: Selected Essays*, Philadelphia: Kingsley.

Penley, C. (ed.) (1988) *Feminism and Film Theory*, London: Routledge.

Pew Forum on Religion and Public Life (2008) "U.S. Religious Landscape Survey." Online. Available http://religions.pewforum.org (accessed August 11, 2010).

Phillips, H. (1998) "Hearing the Vibrations," *Nature Science Update*, August 13, 1998. Online. Available http://www.nature.com/news/1998/980813/pf/980813-3_pf.html (accessed October 30, 2005).

Pike, S. (2001) "After Columbine: Demonic Teens on the Internet, God's Martyrs in the Headlines," presentation to the Religion and Popular Culture Division, American Academy of Religion, Denver, November 18.

—— (2005) "No Novenas for the Dead," in L. Gilmore and M. Van Proyen (eds.) *AfterBurn: Reflections on Burning Man*, Albuquerque: University of New Mexico Press.

Pinney, C. (2002) "The Indian Work of Art in the Age of Mechanical Reproduction: Or, What Happens When Peasants 'Get Hold' of Images," in F. Ginsburg, L. Abu-Lughod and B. Larkin (eds.) *Media Worlds: Anthropology on New Terrain*, Berkeley: University of California Press.

—— (2004) *Photos of the Gods: The Printed Image and Political Struggle in India*, London: Reaktion Books.

—— (2006) "Four Types of Material Culture," in C. Tilley, W. Keane, S. Küchler, P. Spyer and M. Rowlands (eds.) *Handbook of Material Culture*, London: Sage, pp. 131–44.

Plate, S.B. (2003) "Introduction: Filmmaking, Mythmaking, Culture Making," in S.B. Plate (ed.) *Representing Religion in World Cinema: Filmmaking, Mythmaking, Culture Making*, New York: Palgrave, pp. 1–15.

Pollman, J. (1978) "CB Radio as Icon," in R.B. Browne and M. Fishwick (eds.) *Icons of America*, Bowling Green, OH: Popular Press, pp. 161–76.

Possamai, A. (2002) "Cultural Consumption of History and Popular Culture in Alternative Spiritualities," *Journal of Consumer Culture*, 2: 197–218.

—— (2003) "Alternative Spiritualities and the Cultural Logic of Late Capitalism," *Culture and Religion*, 4(1): 31–45.

Postman, N. (1982) *The Disappearance of Childhood*, New York: Delacorte Press.

Potter, W.J. (2005) *Media Literacy*, 2nd edn., Thousand Oaks, CA: Sage.

Primiano, L. (1995) "Vernacular Religion and the Search for Method in Religious Folklife," *Western Folklore*, 54: 37–56.

Prince, R. and Riches, D. (2000) *The New Age in Glastonbury: The Construction of Religious Movements*, New York and Oxford: Berghahn Books.

Promey, S.M. (1993) *Spiritual Spectacles: Vision and Image in Mid-Nineteenth Century Shakerism*, Bloomington: Indiana University Press.

Prothero, S. (2007) *Religious Literacy: What Every American Needs to Know – and Doesn't*, New York: Harper One.

Rajagopal, A. (1999) "Thinking through Emerging Markets: Brand Logics and the Cultural Logic of Political Society in India," *Social Text*, 17(3): 131–50.

—— (2001) *Politics After Television: Hindu Nationalism and the Reshaping of the Public in India*, Cambridge: Cambridge University Press.

Ramet, S. (2009) "Reconfiguring the Polis, Reconceptualizing Rights: Individual Rights and the Irony of History in Central and Southeastern Europe," *Perspectives on European Politics and Society*, 10(1): 87–100.

Rampton, S. and Stauber, J. (2003) *Weapons of Mass Deception: The Uses of Propaganda in Bush's War on Iraq*, London: Robinson.

Rappaport, R. (1999) *Ritual and Religion in the Making of Humanity*, Cambridge: Cambridge University Press.

Ray, M.L. (1973) "A Reappraisal of Shaker Furniture and Society," *Winterthur Portfolio*, 8: 107–32.

Ray, P.H. and Anderson, S.R. (2000) *The Cultural Creatives: How 50 Million People are Changing the World*, New York: Three Rivers Press.

Real, M. (1989) *Super Media*, Thousand Oaks, CA: Sage.

Reckford, V. (1977) "Rastafarian Music: An Introductory Study," *Jamaica Journal*, 11: 1–13.

Redden, G. (2005) "The New Age: Towards a Market Model," *Journal of Contemporary Religion*, 20(2): 231–46.

Riis, O. and Woodhead, L. (2010) *A Sociology of Religious Emotion*, Oxford: Oxford University Press.

Ritzer, G. (1999) *Sociological Theory*, 3rd edn., New York: McGraw-Hill.

—— (2004) *The Globalization of Nothing*, London: Sage.

Roberts, A. and Roberts, P. (2003) *A Saint in the City: Sufi Arts of Modern Senegal*, Seattle: University of Washington Press.

Robins, K. (1991) "Tradition and Translation: National Culture in Its Global Context," in J. Corner and S. Harvey (eds.) *Enterprise and Heritage: Crosscurrents of National Culture*, London: Routledge, pp. 28–41.

—— (1995) *Into the Image*, London: Routledge.

Roodenburg, H. (2004) "Pierre Bourdieu: Issues of Embodiment and Authenticity," *Etnofoor*, 16(1/2): 215–26.

Roof, W.C. and McKinney, W. (1987) *American Mainline Religion: Its Changing Shape and Future*, New Brunswick, NJ: Rutgers University Press.

Rose, N. (1996) "Governing 'Advanced' Liberal Democracies," in A. Barry, T. Osborne and N. Rose (eds.) *Foucault and Political Reason*, London: UCL Press, pp. 37–64.

Rosenthal, M. (2007) *American Protestants and TV in the 1950s*, Basingstoke: Palgrave Macmillan.

Rothenbuhler, E. (1998) *Ritual Communication: From Everyday Conversation to Mediated Ceremony*, London: Sage.

Roy, O. (2004) *Globalised Islam: The Search for a New Ummah*, London: Hurst.

Rubin, D. (ed.) (1999) *Remembering our Past: Studies in Autobiographical Memory*, Cambridge: Cambridge University Press.

Rushdie, S. (1991) *Imaginary Homelands*, London: Granta Books.

Russell, A. (2011) *Networked: A Contemporary History of News in Transmission*, Cambridge: Polity.

Said, E. (1979) *Orientalism*, New York: Vintage.

—— (1988) "Identity, Negation and Violence," *New Left Review*, 171: 46–62.

—— (1990) "Narrative and Geography," *New Left Review*, 180: 81–100.

—— (1997) *Covering Islam: How the Media and the Experts Determine How We See the Rest of the World*, New York: Vintage.

Sánchez, R. (2001) "Channel-Surfing: Media, Mediumship, and State Authority in the María Lionza Possession Cult (Venezuela)," in H. De Vries and S. Weber (eds.) *Religion and Media*, Stanford, CA: Stanford University Press, pp. 388–434.

Sarkissian, A. (2009) "Religious Establishment in Post-Communist Polities," *Journal of Church and State*, 51(3): 472–501.

Scarry, E. (1985) *The Body in Pain: The Making and Unmaking of the World*, New York: Oxford University Press.

Schacter, D.L. (2003) *How the Mind Forgets and Remembers: The Seven Sins of Memory*, London: Souvenir Press.

Scharf, R.H. (1996) "The Scripture on the Production of Buddha Images," in D.S. Lopez, Jr. (ed.) *Religions of China in Practice*, Princeton, NJ: Princeton University Press, pp. 261–7.

Schiller, H.I. (1969) *Mass Communications and American Empire*, New York: A.M. Kelly.

—— (1973) *The Mind Managers*, Boston: Beacon.

Schmidt, L.E. (2000) *Hearing Things: Religion, Illusion and the American Enlightenment*, Cambridge, MA: Harvard University Press.

Schopen, G. (1998) "Relic," in M.C. Taylor (ed.) *Critical Terms for Religious Studies*, Chicago: University of Chicago Press, pp. 256–68.

Schulz, D. (2003) "'Charisma and Brotherhood' Revisited: Mass-Mediated Forms of Spirituality in Urban Mali," *Journal of Religion in Africa*, 33(2): 146–71.

—— (2006) "Morality, Community, Publicness: Shifting Terms of Public Debate in Mali," in B. Meyer and A. Moors (eds.) *Religion, Media, and the Public Sphere*, Bloomington and Indianapolis: Indiana University Press, pp. 132–51.

—— (2008) "Soundscape," in D. Morgan (ed.) *Key Words in Religion, Media and Culture*, London: Routledge, pp. 172–86.

Sconce, J. (2010) "Rally to Restore Visibility," *Ludic Despair*, November 1, 2010. Online. Available http://ludicdespair.blogspot.com/2010/11/rally-to-restore-visibility.html (accessed November 10, 2010).

Scott, J. (2001) *Power*, Cambridge: Polity.

Sedgwick, E.K. (1985) *Between Men: English Literature and Male Homosocial Desire*, New York: Columbia University Press.

Seligman, A. (1990) "Moral Authority and Reformation Religion: On Charisma and the Origins of Modernity," *International Journal of Politics, Culture, and Society*, 4(2): 159–79.

—— (2000) *Modernity's Wager: Authority, the Self, and Transcendence*, Princeton, NJ: Princeton University Press.

Shapiro, P. (1995) "Bass Invader: Jah Wobble," *The Wire*, 140 (October): 32–35.

Shils, E. (1975) *Center and Periphery: Essays in Macrosociology*, Chicago: University of Chicago Press.

Shirky, C. (2009) "A Speculative Post on the Idea of Algorithmic Authority," November 15, 2009. Online. Available http://www.shirky.com/weblog/2009/11/a-speculative-post-on-the-idea-of-algorithmic-authority/ (accessed December 29, 2010).

Singer, S. (2001) "Unbelieving West," *Jerusalem Post*, November 30, p. 9A.

Sinha, V. (2011) *Religion and Commodification: "Merchandizing" Diasporic Hinduism*, New York: Routledge.

Sipe, A.W.R. (1995) *Sex, Priests, and Power: Anatomy of a Crisis*, New York: Brunner/Mazel.

Sister Mary I.H.M. (1937) "Preparing the Little Child for Christmas," *Journal of Religious Instruction*, 8: 303–6.

Sloboda, J. (2005) *Exploring the Musical Mind: Cognition, Emotion, Ability, Function*, Oxford: Oxford University Press.

Smith, C. (1998) *Evangelicalism: Embattled and Thriving*, Chicago: Chicago University Press.

—— (ed.) (2003) *Power, Interests and Conflict in the Secularization of American Public Life*, Berkeley: University of California Press.

Smith, C. with Denton, M.L. (2005) *Soul Searching: The Religious and Spiritual Lives of American Teenagers*, New York: Oxford University Press.

Smith, C.S. (2005) "The Market McDonald's Missed: The Muslim Burger," *New York Times*, September 16, 2005. Online. Available http://www.nytimes.com/2005/09/16/international/europe/16halal.html (accessed August 7, 2010).

Smith, P. and Alexander, J.C. (2005) "Introduction: The New Durkheim," in J.C. Alexander and P. Smith (eds.) *The Cambridge Companion to Durkheim*, Cambridge: Cambridge University Press, pp. 1–40.

Sobchack, V. (2004) *Carnal Thoughts: Embodiment and Moving Image Culture*, Berkeley: University of California Press.

Sobrino, J. (2004) *Where Is God? Earthquake, Terrorism, Barbarity and Hope*, trans. M. Wilde, Maryknoll, NY: Orbis Books.

Spyer, P. (2001) "The Cassowary Will Not Be Photographed," in H. de Vries and S. Weber (eds.) *Religion and Media*, Stanford, CA: Stanford University Press, pp. 304–20.

—— (2005) "The Body, Materiality, and the Senses," in C. Tilley, W. Keane, S. Küchler, P. Spyer and M. Rowlands (eds.) *Handbook of Material Culture*, London: Sage, pp. 125–9.

Sreberny-Mohammedi, A. (1991) "The Global and the Local in International Communications," in J. Curran and M. Gurevitch (eds.) *Mass Media and Society*, London, New York and Melbourne: Edward Arnold.

Stark, R. and Bainbridge, W.S. (1985) *The Future of Religion: Secularization, Revival and Cult Formation*, Berkeley: University of California Press.

Starrett, G (1998) *Putting Islam to Work: Education, Politics and Religious Transformation in Egypt*, Berkeley: University of California Press.

Stein, S. (1987) unpublished paper presented at American Studies Association meeting, New York City, 1987.

Stein, S.J. (1992) *The Shaker Experience in America: A History of the United Society of Believers*, New Haven, CT and London: Yale University Press.

Steiner, G. (1988) *Real Presences: Is There Anything in What We Say?*, London: Faber & Faber.

Stengs, I. (2007) *Worshipping the Great Modernizer: The Cult of King Chulalongkorn, Patron Saint of the Thai Middle Class*, Singapore: Singapore University Press.

Stewart, S. and Sankey, C. (eds.) (2001) *The Scorched Earth: Oil and War in Sudan*, London: Christian Aid.

Stolow, J. (2005) "Religion and/as Media," *Theory, Culture and Society*, 22(2): 137–63.

Stout, D.A. and Buddenbaum, J.M. (eds) (2001) *Religion and Popular Culture: Studies on the Interaction of Worldviews*, Ames: Iowa State University Press.

Streib, H., Hood, Jr., R.W., Keller, B., Csöff, R.-M. and Silver, C. (2009) *Deconversion: Qualitative and Quantitative Results from Cross-Cultural Research in Germany and the United States of America*, Göttingen: Vandenhoeck and Ruprecht.

Sturken, M. and Cartwright, L. (2001) *Practices of Looking: An Introduction to Visual Culture*, Oxford: Oxford University Press.

Sullivan, D. and Abed-Kotob, S. (1999) *Islam in Contemporary Egypt: Civil Society versus the State*, Boulder, CO: Lynne Rienner.

Sullivan, H.P. (1937) "Instructing Little Children: Some Notes on 'Morning and Night Prayers' and 'Prayers before and after Meals,'" *Journal of Religious Instruction*, 7: 739.

Sumiala-Seppänen, J., Lundby K. and Salokangas, R. (eds) (2006) *Implications of The Sacred in (Post) Modern Media*, Göteborg, Sweden: Nordicum.

Sutcliffe, S.J. (2003) *Children of the New Age*, London: Routledge.

Sweet, L.I. (ed.) (1993) *Communication and Change in American Religious History*, Grand Rapids, MI: Eerdmans.

Tahboub, D. (2010) "Donald Trump and Amr Khaled: Is Religion Coming to the Market?" *Elaph*, January 15, 2010. Online. Available http://www.elaph.com/Web/NewsPapers/2010/1/524223.html (accessed June 6, 2010).

Tamen, M. (2001) *Friends of Interpretable Objects*, Cambridge, MA: Harvard University Press.

Taylor, B. (2010) *A Pilgrim in Glastonbury*, Glastonbury: Abbey Press.

Taylor, C. (2002) *Varieties of Religion Today: William James Revisited*, Cambridge, MA: Harvard University Press.

—— (2007) *A Secular Age*, Cambridge, MA: Harvard University Press.

Thirsk, J. (1978) *Economic Policy and Projects: The Development of a Consumer Society in Early Modern England*, Oxford: Oxford University Press.

Thomas, K. (1971) *Religion and the Decline of Magic*, New York: Scribner.

Thompson, J.B. (1995) *The Media and Modernity*, Stanford, CA: Stanford University Press.

Thompson, W.F. (2009) *Music, Thought and Feeling: Understanding the Psychology of Music*, New York: Oxford University Press.

Thornham, S. (ed.) (1999) *Feminist Film Theory: A Reader*, New York: New York University Press.

Tillich, P. (1932 [1956]) *The Religious Situation*, trans. H.R. Niebuhr, New York: Meridian.

—— (1953) *Systematic Theology: Volume 1*, London: James Nisbet.

—— (1989) *On Art and Architecture*, New York: Crossroad.

Toop, D. (1995) *Ocean of Sound: Aether Talk, Ambient Sound and Imaginary Worlds*, London: Serpent's Tail.

Tuchman, G. (1980) *Making News*, New York: Free Press.

Tulving, E. (1983) *Elements of Episodic Memory*, Oxford: Oxford University Press.

Turner, V. (1966) "Colour Classification in Ndembu Ritual," in M. Banton (ed.) *Anthropological Approaches to the Study of Religion*, London: Tavistock, pp. 47–83.

UNAIDS (2004) *UNAIDS 2004 Report on the Global AIDS Epidemic*, Geneva, Switzerland: UNAIDS.

UNDP (2003) *Human Development Report 2003: Millennium Development Goals: A Compact Among Nations to End Human Poverty*, New York and Oxford: Oxford University Press.

Van de Port, M. (2005) "Circling Around the *Really Real*: Spirit Possession Ceremonies and the Search for Authenticity in Bahian Candomblé," *Ethos*, 33(2): 149–79.

—— (2006) "Visualizing the Sacred: Video Technology, 'Televisual' Style, and the Religious Imagination in Bahian Candomblé," *American Ethnologist*, 33(3): 444–62.

Van der Toorn, K. (ed.) (1997) *The Image and the Book: Iconic Cults, Aniconism, and the Rise of Book Religion in Israel and the Ancient Near East*, Leuven: Peeters.

Van der Veer, P. (2008) "Religion, Secularism and the Nation," *India Review*, 7(4): 378–96.

Van Dijk, R. (2005) "Silence of the Camp: Modernity and the Pentecostal Negotiation of an Auditory Identity in Ghana," paper presented to the Research Team Pentecostalism, VU University Amsterdam, September 7.

Van Ginneken, J. (1998) *Understanding Global News: A Critical Introduction*, London: Sage.

Van Ness, P. (ed.) (1996) *Spirituality and the Secular Quest*, New York: Crossroad.

Van Rooden, P. (1996) "Friedrich Schleiermacher's *Reden über die Religion*," *Theoretische Geschiedenis*, 23: 419–38.

Veal, M.E. (2007) *Dub: Soundscapes and Shattered Songs in Jamaican Reggae*, Middletown, CT: Wesleyan University Press.

Verrips, J. (2006a) "Aisthesis and An-aesthesia," *Ethnologia Europea*, 35(1/2): 27–33.

—— (2006b) "Ottolandse onderzoekservaringen bekeken in het licht van het ludieke," *In de Marge*, 15(3): 20–5.

Voas, D. and Ling, R. (2010) "Religion in Britain and the United States," in A. Park, J. Curtice, K. Thomson, M. Phillips and E. Clery (eds) *British Social Attitudes 26th Report*, London: Sage, pp. 65–87.

Volf, M. (2002) "More Religion, Less Violence," *Christian Century*, April 10–17: 32.

Walker, P. (2001) *Pulling the Devil's Kingdom Down: The Salvation Army in Victorian Britain*, Berkeley: University of California Press.

Wallace, A.F.C. (1966) *Religion: An Anthropological View*, New York: Random House.

Wallis, R. (1984) *The Elementary Forms of the New Religious Life*, London: Routledge.

Warner, S. (1993) "Work in Progress toward a New Paradigm for the Sociological Study of Religion in the United States," *American Journal of Sociology*, 98: 1044–93.

Watt, T. (1991) *Cheap Print and Popular Piety, 1550–1640*, Cambridge: Cambridge University Press.

Welsh, G.F. and Howard, D.M. (2002) "Gendered Voice in the Cathedral Choir," *Psychology of Music*, 30: 102–20.

Werbner, P. (2002) "The Place which Is Diaspora: Citizenship, Religion and Gender in the Making of Chaordic Transnationalism," *Journal of Ethnic and Migration Studies*, 28(1): 119–33.

Wesch, M. (2007a) "Information RE/volution," video essay, October 12, 2007. Online. Available http://www.youtube.com/watch?v=-4CV05HyAbM (accessed December 29, 2010).

—— (2007b) "The Machine Is Us/ing Us," video essay, January 31, 2007. Online. Available http://www.youtube.com/watch?v=6gmP4nk0EOE&feature=channel (accessed December 29, 2010).

West, E. and Petrik, P. (eds) (1992) *Small Worlds: Children and Adolescents in America, 1850–1950*, Lawrence: University of Kansas Press.

Whitfield, G.M. (2002) "Bass Cultural Vibrations: Visionaries, Outlaws, Mystics, and Chanters," *3 a.m. Magazine*. Online. Available http://www.3ammagazine.com/musicarchives/2002_oct/bass_cultural_vibrations.html (accessed October 25, 2005).

Wickham, C. (2004) "The Path to Moderation: Strategy and Learning in the Formation of Egypt's Wasat Party," *Comparative Politics*, 36(2): 205–28.

Williams, R. (2002) *Writing in the Dust: Reflections on 11th September and Its Aftermath*, London: Hodder & Stoughton.

Willis, P. (1978) *Profane Culture*, London: Routledge.

Wilson, B. (1966) *Religion in Secular Society*, London: C.A. Watts.

—— (1982) *Religion in Sociological Perspective*, Oxford: Oxford University Press.

Wilson, C. and Gutierrez, F. (1985) *Minorities and Media: Diversity and the End of Mass Communication*, Newbury Park, CA: Sage.

Winkelman, M. (2009) "Shamanism and the Origins of Spirituality and Ritual Healing," *Journal for the Study of Religion, Nature and Culture*, 3–4: 458–89.

Winston, D. (1999) *Red Hot and Righteous: The Urban Religion of the Salvation Army*, Cambridge, MA: Harvard University Press.

—— (forthcoming) "Religion and the News," in *Cambridge Handbook of American Religious History*, Cambridge: Cambridge University Press.

Winston, K. (2010) "Behind Colbert's Right-Wing Funny Man, a Quiet Catholic Faith," *Religion News Service*, October 12, 2010. Online. Available http://www.religionnews.com/index.php?/rnspremiumtext/singlewnet/behind_colberts_right_wing_funny_man_a_quiet_faith1/ (accessed December 29, 2010).

Witkin, R.W. (1998) *Adorno on Music*, London: Routledge.

Wobble, J. (2010) "Welcome to My World." Online. Available http://www.30hertzrecords.com/ (accessed June 26, 2010).

Wolfe, K. (1984) *The Churches and the British Broadcasting Corporation 1922–1956*, London: SCM Press.

Wollaston, I. (1994) "Sharing Sacred Space? The Carmelite Controversy and the Politics of Commemoration," *Patterns of Prejudice*, 28(3–4): 19–27.

Woodhead, L. with Catto, R. (2009) *"Religion or Belief": Identifying Issues and Priorities*, AHRC/ESRC Religion and Society Programme, Manchester: Equality and Human Rights Commission.

Woodhead, L. and Heelas, P. (eds) (2000) *Religion in Modern Times: An Interpretive Anthology*, Oxford: Blackwell.

World Values Survey (2010) Online. Available http://www.wvsevsdb.com/wvs/WVSAnalizeQuestion.jsp (accessed December 7, 2010).

Wullschläger, J. (1995) *Inventing Wonderland: The Lives and Fantasies of Lewis Carroll, Edward Lear, J.M. Barrie, Kenneth Grahame, and A.A. Milne*, New York: Free Press.

York, M. (2004) "New Age Commodification and Appropriation of Spirituality," in J.R. Lewis (ed.) *The Encyclopedic Sourcebook of New Age Religions*, Amherst, NY: Prometheus Books.

Zelizer, B. (1992) *Covering the Body*, Chicago and London: University of Chicago Press.
—— (2005) "Finding Aids to the Past: Bearing Personal Witness to Traumatic Public Events," in E. Rothenbuhler and M. Coman (eds) *Media Anthropology*, Thousand Oaks, CA: Sage.
Zenit (1999) *The Daily Dispatch: The World Seen from Rome, April 21*, Rome: Zenit.
Zoepf, K. (2005) "Bestseller in Mideast: Barbie with a Prayer Mat," *New York Times*, September 22. Online. Available http://www.nytimes.com/2005/09/22/international/middleeast/22doll.html (accessed June 3, 2010).

Index